10549459

AF

The Critical Spirit

Photograph by Haskell A. Kaitz

HERBERT MARCUSE

The Critical Spirit

ESSAYS IN HONOR OF
HERBERT MARCUSE

EDITED BY
KURT H. WOLFF AND
BARRINGTON MOORE, JR.

*With the Assistance
of Heinz Lubasz
Maurice R. Stein
and E. V. Walter*

BEACON PRESS
Boston

The editors wish to express their warm thanks to Elizabeth Carol Moore for her editorial assistance in preparing this volume for publication.

Copyright © 1967 by Beacon Press

Library of Congress catalog card number: 67 – 24890

Published simultaneously in Canada by Saunders of Toronto, Ltd.

Beacon Press books are published under the auspices of
the Unitarian Universalist Association

All rights reserved

Printed in the United States of America

B
29
C7
c.2

Contents

What Is The Critical Spirit?

To ANSWER THE QUESTION in a straightforward factual manner first: *The Critical Spirit* is of course a collection of essays in honor of Herbert Marcuse, or, as the Germans say, a *Festschrift*. The French, who may be less discreet about these and other intellectual problems, generally call such collections *Mélanges*. "Miscellanies" they have indeed frequently come to be, reflecting the technical specialization and general fragmentation of contemporary thought. As editors, we do not believe that this volume has altogether escaped this and other blights of our century. Nevertheless, just as the human personality, for all its quirks and individual peculiarities, usually displays some unifying pattern, so may *The Critical Spirit* take on form because it reflects from many different angles the interests and attractions, the antipathies and aversions, of one provocative thinker. At this point one might go on with a solemn and measured assessment of Herbert Marcuse's intellectual outlook and achievements, but that is a notion that would provoke from him a deprecatory snort, partly because he is very much alive and thinking.

In no sense is *The Critical Spirit* an agreed upon elaboration of themes in Marcuse's writings. Nor is it a manifesto from those sharing a credo. Intellectual and temperamental differences among editors and contributors render such a prospect rather odd. Indeed at one point, as scraps of news about the preparation of the *Festschrift* filtered back to Professor Marcuse, he suggested jokingly that printing the correspondence instead of the book might attract more readers. Underneath these disagreements and crosscurrents, on the other hand, we are all grappling with a coherent set of problems. There is a strong undertow of agreement about *what issues matter* — if not how to solve them. Those who have found delight in the company of Herbert Marcuse share concerns that are political, in a sense that goes far beyond the mechanics of government. They are also inclined to be skeptical about presently respectable ways of denying the relevance of such concerns to serious intellectual work. This note of doubt and concern gives to *The Critical Spirit* a certain unity of tone and content. From time to time Herbert Marcuse expresses this note very well in his own way by a favorite remark: For a rational human being, the right to be frightened is the most important one left today.

Before commenting further on the intellectual pattern into which these essays fall, it might be well to say a few words about its more personal aspects, the human magnet that attracted them. The *Festschrift* owes its inception to a group of Marcuse's colleagues at Brandeis University who wished to honor him as one of their most distinguished intellectuals. Pooling their knowledge of Marcuse's career and interests and with help from others, they asked for contributions of essays from many scholars in Europe and the United States. Once word of the undertaking got about, there was the interesting result that several scholars whose personal connection with Professor Marcuse was limited asked for an opportunity to pay their respects in this fashion. From this harvest the editors did their best to prune and select, without regard to station.

Many essays show that they derive from the life and interests of a distinguished refugee from the Nazi holocaust. They express in current form some of the continental influences that many years ago helped to shape a significant intellectual milieu, that of the Institute of Social Research of Frankfurt am Main (and of New York during World War II). Here was a scholarly group where Marxism was taken seriously but not as holy writ and where, especially in the case of Herbert Marcuse himself, the influence of Hegel was more powerful than that of Marx. Further, the *Festschrift* makes clear the effect of these intellectual currents upon others whose life has been passed elsewhere. To choose one example arbitrarily, the opening essay by M. I. Finley displays both technical mastery of a recondite topic and an informed concern with related wider issues. The same applies to many of the other essays.

Upon turning to the Table of Contents, anyone familiar with Marcuse's writings will recognize a certain appropriateness in the fact that the first section, The Political Concerns of Philosophy, is the largest. Here the contributors explore two related themes. Several of the essays examine the social background, intellectual significance, and wider influence of conceptions of the world ranging from past heresies to what is presently somewhat disreputable. Through these essays there is an undercurrent of argument on behalf of the legitimacy of ideas that have at some point been the object of severe attack. A second and closely related theme takes the form of a plea for committed curiosity in the study of human affairs. Throughout both types of explorations there is no consistent line of orthodoxy, and indeed there is considerable variety. By implication, and even directly, the authors of some essays reverse the polarity of Marcuse's thinking by their refusal to take for granted that political philosophy constitutes an appropriate manner of thinking today, or that there really *is* such a thing as political philosophy. Similarly, if one recalls Professor Marcuse's respect for Hegel (and for Max Horkheimer), a reader may find a touch of amiable piquancy, as well as matter for serious reflection, in Professor Horkheimer's advocacy of the relevance today of Schopenhauer over Hegel. In this section, and in *The Critical Spirit* as a whole, it is possible to distinguish continental modes of thought and expression from English and American ones. At times, nevertheless, they may blend, as in the essay on historical method by Howard Zinn. His critique of what passes for objectivity and his plea for commitment as the basis of a sense for the historically significant are rarities mainly among American historians. The more unusual note occurs in his thesis that the acceptance of specific values can and must accompany the most scrupulous respect for canons of intellectual honesty and for evidence opposed to an author's most cherished hopes.

The mere suppression of hope in the name of a narrow version of scientific realism is of course anathema to Marcuse. Naturally his outlook does not imply any denial of the importance of prevailing realities, especially political and social ones, but rather the use of critical intelligence to transcend and overcome these realities. Art and imagination have a crucial part to play in this process. Hence it is fitting that the first section of *The Critical Spirit*

closes with Hans Meyerhoff's critical reflections on the search for
eternal Platonic truths and that the next section begins with Sir
Herbert Read's reaction to some of Marcuse's reflections on the
place of art in society, today and in the future. There is some discussion, in subsequent essays, of the critical response aroused by
the triumphal advance of bourgeois culture. That theme, however, is a secondary one. The problem of cultural decay in our
own time receives rather more attention. The variety of methods
brought to bear here is particularly striking: the reflective essay
spanning the centuries of Western experience; the comparative
biography of two figures facing somewhat similar problems in
different countries and cultural traditions; the careful analysis of
a single literary text; and the quantitative analysis of several best
sellers. Each author uses the method congenial to him, in order
to shed light on some aspect of the blocking of bourgeois ideals
and of the decay of these ideals, along with their partial achievement in real life. By suggesting how the fragments of an outlook that once nerved men to topple thrones have been strewn
over culture's bargain counter in the twentieth century, Leo
Lowenthal's discussion introduces the reader directly to the plight
of industrial society.

The third section of *The Critical Spirit* discusses this plight.
The spirit of these essays is indeed critical: several established
views about the origins and workings of both capitalism and socialism come under severe scrutiny. Here too critical rationality
demonstrates a willingness to examine its own tenets, including
those of the thinker in whose honor this collection exists. In "The
Limits of Integration" Paul Mattick uses Marxist analysis to suggest that Marcuse's thesis about the capacity of modern industrial
society to prevent change by absorbing and deflecting critical
opposition could turn out to be an example of confusing the
ephemeral present with more permanent trends. It would be an
ironical turn of fate if one of Herbert Marcuse's central ideas
were shown within twenty years to be another form of the illusion he had always attacked. Even if the question is presently unanswerable, the fact that it is raised disproves charges of sectarian
dogmatism that are levelled from time to time against those with
an intellectual position to the left of semi-official optimistic lib-

eralism. The more specific essays tend to undermine further this comforting view of modern society by casting doubts on the viability of the rule of law, on the role of the independent entrepreneur and social critic during an important stage in the development of capitalism, and on the importance of Marxist doctrine as opposed to concrete circumstances in what was perhaps the most crucial decision so far taken by a socialist regime. The third section closes with a study of intellectual attempts to break through that cake of intellectual custom which has in very different ways throughout human history played no small part in preventing the emergence of a happier world.

The final section illustrates how some of Professor Marcuse's main ideas appear to some of his thoughtful students and the reasons for his powerful impact upon them. It is clear here, and elsewhere in these essays, that much of his appeal to young and old stems from the delicious mixture he is — of a rare human warmth, joined to a sparkling and sparking intellect, the whole bubbling up in "buoyant pessimism" (as one old friend aptly declared).

From the rich inspiration of Herbert Marcuse we have then in *The Critical Spirit* a considerable range in philosophical outlook and subject matters. Not all of these studies are equally persuasive. Nevertheless each writer confronts, either explicitly or by very clear implication, a major intellectual and political issue, and does so from an unconventional standpoint. Ranging widely in time and space for their choice of themes, the contributors converge in their efforts to uphold conceptions of liberation that the past has condemned and the present denies. All of them, and the scholar to whom we present this collection, have been struck by sparks from the same fire. If the light that comes thereby often flickers, if some of us are not quite sure of the strange shapes that we see with it, these shortcomings may be the fault of our own eyes, not those of Herbert Marcuse's vision.

THE EDITORS

PART ONE

The Political Concerns of Philosophy

Utopianism Ancient and Modern

M. I. FINLEY

I

EVER SINCE Thomas More gave the world the word Utopia early in the sixteenth century, a semantic cluster has grown round it, or perhaps I should say a spectrum of meanings, of great range and complexity, and of no little confusion. I shall not attempt a formal definition, but a certain amount of narrowing of the field of discourse is an unavoidable preliminary. To begin with, there is an inherent pun in the word itself, which is normally and mistakenly overlooked. The initial letter "u" stands for the Greek "ou" ("no," "not") and hence Utopia is Nowhere. But by the exercise of a little imagination the "u" can also stand for the Greek prefix "eu" ("good," "well") and then we get "good place," "ideal place." That this alternative is not wholly fanciful is proved by two lines of the "Meter of IV Verses in the Utopian Tongue" appended to More's work, which read, in the sixteenth-century English translation: "Wherfore not Utopie, but rather rightely / My name is Eutopie: a place of felicitie."

All Utopian thinking has an element of fantasy, of dreaming, or at least of yearning, for a better life and a better world. And all men dream in this way, about themselves and their families if not about society in general or the world at large. A poem by Cercidas of Megalopolis, at the end of the third century B.C., be-

---

This is a much enlarged and revised version of a paper originally presented to the Congressus Internationalis Antiquitas Graeco-Romana ac Tempora Nostra in Brno on April 14, 1966. My thanks are due to friends with whom I have been able to discuss the subject, Dr. Jan Pečírka of the University of Prague and MM. J.-P. Vernant and Pierre Vidal-Naquet of the Ecole des Hautes Etudes.

3

gins, "I blame Zeus because he did not turn that fellow Xenon, who is packed with malice and a mass of incontinence, into a child of poverty, thereby giving *us* a flood of silver that now runs to waste." Then he goes on to a generalized lamentation, "To what sort of sovereign, then, or to which of the sons of Heaven, can one turn in order to discover how to get one's desert — when the Son of Cronus, who begat us all and gave us all birth, shows himself a mere stepfather to some and a real father to others?"[1]

Cercidas was a Cynic philosopher, but that fact is not relevant in the present context. Such sentiments decrying one aspect of the human condition could have been expressed, and have been, by millions of despairing individuals in many different societies. They are only one step removed from the imprecatory lead tablets (*tabellae defixionum*) buried in the ground by Athenian peasants in the fourth century B.C., calling upon various demons and evil spirits to destroy a neighbor's crops and render his flocks sterile, and his wife, too. One further step carries us to the fantasies and projects characteristic of the opium or hashish addict or of the victim of schizophrenia or paranoia. Professor Frank Manuel has pointed out that the *Description of a New World, Called the Blazing World,* by Margaret Cavendish, Duchess of Newcastle, published in 1666, "has much in common with the delusions of Dr. Schreber which Sigmund Freud analyzed in a famous paper."[2] We must not be too quick to rule all this out as irrelevant. Let us remember that Fourier also had schemes for heating the North Pole and sweetening the ocean which are not really distinguishable from the projects of a paranoiac — and Fourier was an influential "Utopian socialist."[3] Let us also remember that in ordinary speech "utopian" has not only a positive connotation but even more commonly a negative, pejorative one: "impractical," therefore useless and even dangerous because it diverts attention and effort from the realizable.

Yet, for purposes of the present analysis, we must divide the

[1] Translated by Ernest Barker, *From Alexander to Constantine* (Oxford 1959), 58 – 9.

[2] F. E. Manuel, "Toward a Psychological History of Utopias," *Daedalus,* 94 (1965), 293 – 322, at p. 293.

[3] See Ernst Bloch, *Das Prinzip Hoffnung* (Frankfurt 1959), 549.

spectrum at some point and the obvious step is to draw the distinction formulated by Professor Northrop Frye: ". . . we should expect to find that the more penetrating the utopian writer's mind is, the more clearly he understands that he is communicating a vision to his readers, not sharing a power or fantasy dream with them," a vision that derives "from an analysis of the writer's present society."[4] That element of analysis, of criticism, is what brings the important Utopias back from Nowhere to reality in a way that the purely private, not to mention the lunatic, fantasies do not. That is what makes them a worthy subject of historical analysis, as distinct from a purely Freudian or other analysis proper to individual psychology. Much as the two kinds of analysis may overlap, the distinction remains valid and fundamental.

We are largely restricted to literary formulations, and we run a risk thereby. Ancient writers, virtually without exception, reflect the views and sentiments and prejudices of the educated classes, which means the upper classes. So do most writers throughout modern history. An awareness of that familiar bias does not get us very far in trying to reconstruct what the submerged classes thought, but it should warn us against the common intellectualist fallacy of seeking some particular book behind every popular idea or popular action. The way in which scholars persistently took it for granted that a book by Iambulus provided the inspiration for the Sun-State of the followers of Aristonicus in Asia Minor towards the end of the second century B.C. is perhaps the best example of this fallacy at work in the study of ancient history, as we shall soon see.

By "Utopian writer" I do not wish to restrict myself to the formal constructors of Utopias (although the emergence of that particular kind of writing in different historical periods is itself an important aspect of the whole question). We must look at the Phaeacian section of the *Odyssey* as well as at Plato's *Republic* or at Iambulus. There is an unfortunate convention among historians of Graeco-Roman antiquity to throw much of this writing into the loose category of the "novel" (*der griechische Roman*), and by implication (or sometimes explicitly) to denigrate it as some-

[4] "Varieties of Literary Utopias," *Daedalus*, 94 (1965), 323–47, at pp. 330, 339.

thing second-rate, not really deserving the same serious attention as something else called "philosophy."[5] Of course there is a valid distinction, and of course Iambulus was no Plato, but just as a modern novelist may be a better analyst and a more profound critic of his society, so the possibility cannot be rejected *a priori* that even an Iambulus may in some respects teach us as much about ancient society as a Plato.

Utopian ideas and fantasies, like all ideas and fantasies, grow out of the society to which they are a response. Neither the ancient world nor the modern world is an unchanging entity, and any analysis of Utopian thinking which neglects social changes in the course of the history of either antiquity or modern times is likely at some point to go badly wrong. Nevertheless, a conceptual analysis which treats all western Utopian thought *en bloc* to begin with, may be useful. This is what I shall do in much of my paper, moving freely in time and in both directions, accepting the risk for the moment of being over-schematic and unhistorical. Before I have finished, I hope to bring the analysis back to a proper historical one.

II

The very word Utopia suggests that the ideal society is not actually or wholly attainable. Nevertheless, every significant Utopia is conceived as a goal towards which one may legitimately and hopefully strive, a goal not in some shadowy state of perfection but with specific institutional criticisms and proposals. Utopia transcends the given social reality; it is not transcendental in a metaphysical sense. All this sets the social Utopias apart from the Garden of Eden, under which I subsume the various primitivistic images, whether the perfect, simple, innocent society is located in the distant past, in a Golden Age, or in a far-off place.

There is a sense in which a Garden of Eden shares a quality of criticism with Utopia, specifically in the idea, explicit or implicit, that a world without evil is not even conceivable, let alone possible, so long as the two chief roots of evil are present, namely,

[5] This is not said in criticism of the fundamental work of Erwin Rohde, *Der griechische Roman und seine Vorläufer* (reprint, Darmstadt 1960), pt. II.

strife over wealth and property and strife arising from sexual drives. But such primitivistic dreams immediately depart from social Utopias in their fabulous, magical quality. "The golden race," says Hesiod in his *Works and Days* (lines 116–8), "had all good things; for the fruitful earth unforced bare them fruit abundantly and without toil." In the Garden-of-Eden fantasies, animals are well-behaved and kindly, men live far beyond the mortal span, disease is unknown, so that wealth and sexual rivalry and strife of every kind automatically disappear because they are utterly meaningless and pointless. Innocence becomes the only quality of life. Nature takes care of everything.

Understandably human as all this is, it cannot serve either as a goal or as a paradigm. Nor was it meant to. One need only compare Hesiod's account of the Golden Age with his prescriptions for the Iron Age. There is no escape from the latter; the sole hope is to toil and to be honest and thus, with the help of the gods, one may ease one's burdens. No more. There is not a whisper in Hesiod of a way by which to change or transcend the present state, to re-approach the Golden Age. The Golden Age is firmly located in myth and in mythical time. It serves to define the Iron Age by its opposite, to define and in a sense to explain the evil that man is eternally doomed to live with, above all, to die. The question posed at the very beginning of the *Works and Days* is just that, Why is the world so full of evil? The first answer is traditional, the myths of Prometheus and Pandora. Hesiod tells them very briefly and then continues, without a pause, "I will sum up to you another tale," the tale of the ages ("races," strictly) of man.[6]

In one important respect, of course, I should not have used "Garden of Eden" as the generic term. In Judaeo-Christian religious thinking the myth of the Golden Age was tied to life on earth in a new way; myth and history, mythical time and historical time met together. The notion became central that some men can look forward to a return to the Golden Age, to the Last Judgment and the Resurrection. That will come about by act of grace and not by social action, and it will be a Golden Age only for the elect. One may prepare for it, but only ritually or by mar-

[6] See J.-P. Vernant, *Mythe et pensée chez les Grecs* (Paris 1965), ch. 1.

tyrdom and not by changing society. Hence not even within this
conceptual framework is the Golden Age a Utopia. The history
of Christianity has produced examples enough of men and movements who insisted that social reform and Utopianism are irrelevant and even misleading. It has also produced impatient men and
movements, unwilling to wait forever for the final triumph, and
to these I shall return shortly.

The Graeco-Roman world never achieved a successful image
of the Kingdom of Heaven, and therefore the Greeks and Romans were not faced with either the prospects or the alternatives
available to the Christian. Some of the philosophical schools provide a thin analogy: when the early Cynics, for example, argued
that everything external to man's inner virtue is irrelevant, they rejected social reform, and *a fortiori* Utopianism, in a way that is
reminiscent of certain Christian thinkers. Crates of Thebes, in the
late fourth century B.C., wrote a poem to the "city Pera" which is
"fair, fruitful, squalid, owning nought" and over which men do
not go to war.[7] (*Pera* is the Greek word for a leather food-pouch.)
But for the bulk of the population there was little consolation
in doctrines which demanded unrelenting austerity, self-restraint
and self-discipline without the reward of eternal salvation. Private
fantasies and magical practices flourished; at least on earth one
could both dream and try to help oneself privately in mundane
matters. Examples could already be found in Homer which they
all knew by heart. In the *Odyssey* Phaeacia has Utopian overtones
— it exists in isolation, it is luxuriously rich, it offers boundless
hospitality — but it is also fabulous: the Phaeacians are the ideal
seafarers, for they "have no pilots and no rudders . . . ; but (the
ships) themselves understand the thoughts and intents of men"
(8.557 – 9). Not even the later Utopian writers could all escape
these pulls. Both Euhemerus slightly and Iambulus rather mas-
sively mixed the fabulous with the critical. Euhemerus, writing
about 300 B.C., described a Sacred Isle in which spices grew virtually without human effort and in which a single plant, the
poliuros, sufficed for food, drink and medicine. Iambulus, whose
date is unknown though it must fall somewhere between Alexander and Augustus, visited an island in the Indian Ocean where

[7] Quoted in Diogenes Laertius, 6.85.

men had rubbery bones as well as forked tongues which permitted them to carry on two conversations simultaneously, and where they lived to the age of 150 without illness, when they lay down and slept eternally. At the end, Iambulus concedes that it is all a fable: after a stay of seven years, he says, he and his companions were expelled as "evildoers."[8]

For all the criticism implicit in the social and political arrangements, we are nevertheless in Cloudcuckooland, as the satirists were quick to point out. We are back to personal fantasies dressed in community form. They were common fantasies in antiquity, judging from the proverbial contexts in which the phrase "life under Cronus" (or "under Saturn" in the Roman equivalent) recurs in the literature. Even the educated enjoyed them. Herodotus is a quarry of relevant tales, intermixed with his Scythians and Amazons and Hyperboreans. Alexander's campaign in India produced a new outcropping (as did the great explorations at the beginning of the modern era). Euhemerus even borrowed the idea of a priestly caste from India and introduced it into his social structure, a very strange idea indeed for a *Greek* Utopia. But the only expression of these dreams in action known to me was in the Saturnalian type of festival, widely spread in Greece as well as in Rome, under various names including the Cronia, when the slaves sat at table and their masters waited on them. Nothing, I suggest, could more perfectly symbolize the fantasy aspect, the reduction of the element of genuine criticism to an Aristophanic joke. The joke became a cruel one when late Roman emperors proclaimed their reigns as a Golden Age, when the court poet Claudian in A.D. 400 celebrated the new century in language consciously reminiscent of the Sibyl, who had written: "For the all-bearing earth will give her best fruit without end to mortals, bread, wine and wild olive. . . . And streams will flow with sweet white milk, and cities will be full of goods and the fields will be fat; nor will there be swords nor the din of battle on the face of the earth. . . ."[9] Claudian and his imperial patrons, like Virgil before him,

[8] On Euhemerus, see especially Diodorus, 5.41.4–46.7; on Iambulus, Diodorus, 2.55.1–60.1.

[9] *Oracula sibyllina* 3.743–50, translated in A. O. Lovejoy and G. Boas, *Primitivism and Related Ideas in Antiquity* (Baltimore 1935), 86.

were trading on — I should even say mocking — the traditional dream-fantasies of the oppressed.[10]

One specific situation within the Graeco-Roman orbit seems to have been exceptional and it is interesting enough to warrant a digression. I refer to the Heliopolis, the Sun-State to which a certain Aristonicus summoned the slaves and oppressed poor of Asia Minor in 132 or 131 B.C. The background is as follows. In 133, King Attalus III of Pergamum bequeathed his kingdom to Rome in his will. Aristonicus, a bastard member of the royal family, challenged the bequest, laid claim to the throne, and started a civil war. When the normal methods of usurpation proved unsuccessful, he turned as a last resort to the slaves and half-free peasants, promising them the Sun-State. The movement was crushed, with no little difficulty, by the Romans, the kings of Bithynia and Cappadocia, and the Greek cities of Asia Minor acting in concert against a common threat. Our sources, which are very brief anyway, concentrate on the military side of the uprising. They tell us absolutely nothing about Aristonicus's promises, apart from emancipation from bondage, and only once is there a mention of the Sun-State. "Going into the interior," writes the geographer Strabo (14.1.38), "he quickly assembled a multitude of poor men and slaves, whom he won over by a promise of freedom and whom he called Heliopolitans." That statement, which I have quoted in full, is not exactly informative. Yet that, together with the additional fact that Aristonicus was joined by the Stoic philosopher, Blossius of Cumae, the former mentor of the Gracchi, is the sole basis for the once common assumption that Aristonicus proposed to introduce in real life in Asia Minor the social and political regime projected by the Utopian writer Iambulus, who said of his islanders that above all other gods they honour the sun, "after whom they name both the islands and themselves."[11]

It has in recent years been demonstrated that the supposed connection between Aristonicus and Iambulus, a modern idea not

[10] See I. Hahn, "Die soziale Utopie der Spätantike," *Wiss. Z. Univ. Halle, ges.-sprachwiss. Kl.,* 11 (1962), 1357 – 61.

[11] Diodorus, 2.59.7.

mentioned in any existing ancient source, is without foundation.[12] Nevertheless, Strabo's reference to the Sun-State, for all its emptiness, is unlikely to be something he invented and therefore some explanation is required. It is just possible that both Iambulus and Aristonicus shared a common tradition in one respect, and that is my reason for this digression. There was nothing in the inherited Greek myths or rituals to warrant the patronage of the very insignificant sun-god Helios. But there is evidence of a long-standing link in Near Eastern religions between the divine sun and justice, and in Asia Minor in the second century B.C. there was a very strong infusion of Near Eastern religions, especially among the slaves and lower classes. I am therefore tempted to wonder whether there is not a parallel here, in the link between a kind of Messianism and social revolution, in particular with the millenarian or chiliastic movements that emerged in Europe during the later Middle Ages and again in the nineteenth century.[13] These were movements which took seriously the Christian promise that one day the two streams, the mythical and the earthly, would come together in the final triumph of justice. Salvation, the return to the Garden of Eden, was declared by prophetic voices to be at hand.

If my guess about the Sun-State of Aristonicus should prove to have merit — and I know of no evidence from which to test it — it would take us outside the Graeco-Roman orbit for all meaningful purposes. The other slave and peasant revolts of antiquity were neither salvationist nor Utopian. Their aims were to obtain freedom for themselves at the minimum, to turn the social relations upside down at the maximum; to turn themselves into masters and their former masters into slaves, but not to alter the fundamental structure of society. Insofar as religion played a role it

[12] See most recently J. C. Dumont, "A propos d'Aristonicos," *Eirene*, 5 (1966), 189–96; F. Bömer, *Untersuchungen über die Religion der Sklaven in Griechenland und Rom*, III [Akad. d. Wiss. u. Lit., Mainz, *Abh. d. geistes-u. sozialwiss. Kl.* (1961), no. 4], 154–73; V. Vavřínek, *La révolte d'Aristonicos* [Rozpravy Československé Akad. Věd (1957), no. 2].

[13] See Norman Cohn, *The Pursuit of the Millennium* (reprint, Harper Torchbooks, 1961); E. J. Hobsbawm, *Primitive Rebels* (Manchester 1959), ch. 4–6.

was purely ancillary, for example, to give the leader a charisma, which has nothing to do with bringing about a return to Paradise or a Golden Age.[14] Millenarian movements, by contrast, are not only salvationist in the religious sense; they are also wholly vague about their social aims, about the structure of the society to be achieved or even about how it is to be brought about. "The movement," Professor Howard Kaminsky has pointed out, "always subscribes to an ideology that empties the existing social order of all value; it also invariably takes the form of a physical movement — a withdrawal from the existing order. Thus on the one hand its ideology is arbitrary, extravagant, and fantastic; on the other hand its social structure is all but nonexistent: it is a perfectly plastic mass, without the solidity that comes from a practical, working relationship with reality."[15] These are the responses of "pre-political people," in Eric Hobsbawm's phrase. Like all Garden-of-Eden conceptions, millenarian visions must in a strict analysis be distinguished from Utopia. Utopia may be Nowhere, it may be extravagant and unattainable, but its protagonists are decidedly neither pre-political nor without "a practical, working relationship with reality."

III

As a framework for the analysis of Utopia, I suggest two antithetical pairs of elements, which may also serve as a kind of definition by specification. The first antithesis is between a static and a dynamic Utopia, or, phrased differently, between an ascetic and a want-satisfying Utopia. The second antithesis is between an egalitarian and a hierarchical Utopia.

Since Utopia belongs to the realm of the real world, not of myth, it can never, strictly speaking, start from the natural sufficiency of goods which characterizes the Garden of Eden. There

[14] See J. Vogt, "Zur Struktur der antiken Sklavenkriege," in his *Sklaverei und Humanität* [*Historia*, Einzelschr. 8 (1965)], 20–60; P. Green, "The First Sicilian Slave War," *Past & Present*, 20 (1961), 10–29; E. A. Thompson, "Peasant Revolts in Late Roman Gaul and Spain," *Past & Present*, 2 (1952), 11–23.

[15] In *Millennial Dreams in Action*, ed. Sylvia L. Thrupp [*Comparative Studies in Society and History*, Supp. 2 (1962)], 215.

the sheer abundance, always renewed and never exhausted, eliminates greed, gluttony, licentiousness, and the conflicts they generate. The real world, in contrast, had long been faced not by abundance but by an absolute insufficiency of resources. My first antithesis then divides neatly into two chronological periods separated by the Industrial Revolution. Ancient or early modern Utopias had perforce to accept scarcity of goods as a datum, and therefore to stress simplicity, the curbing of wants, asceticism, and a static society. Then came the release of new sources of energy and with it a flood of technological Utopian imagination, from Condorcet and Fourier through Jules Verne to H. G. Wells. They grasped that for the first time in history the technical possibilities had been created for a new kind of Utopia, one in which abundance replaced scarcity, in which human and social possibilities had taken a leap forward to something previously unthinkable outside the world of myth.

The new possibilities also created new doubts. Not all nineteenth century Utopians shared the new dynamic, want-satisfying vision. There was concurrently an ascetic trend, to be seen in the Owenite and Fourierist colonies in the United States, in Thoreau and in William Morris. There were now, in other words, alternative and conflicting proposals growing out of the examination and critique of industrial society. Earlier these choices simply did not exist. As has been well said by Professor J. H. Hexter of More's *Utopia*, "The Utopian economy does not justify itself as modern economies do by claiming to give men in the fullest measure the things they want. . . . The justification for the Utopian system in all its aspects, economic and other, is that it provides all men with what they need in the measure that they need it; and while men ought to have what they need, they certainly do not need and ought not to have in full, or any other measure, whatever they happen to want."[16] Modern critics of excessive materialism may say that, too, but Thomas More and his predecessors *had* to say it, unless they wished to flee to Cloudcuckooland. Even some of the fabulous Utopians, such as Iambulus, writing in a more sophisticated climate than that of Hesiod and with some-

16 J. H. Hexter, *More's Utopia* (reprint, Harper Torchbooks, 1965), 70–71.

thing of a background of philosophical inquiry in the intellectual atmosphere, introduced a very considerable ascetic element. His case is especially interesting because he admitted that in his island material conditions did not require this. The restrictions on, and controls of, the diet which he proposed, for example, constituted a consciously disciplinary device; they performed a moral function, not an economic or hygienic one.

The matter of moral discipline and reform is implicit in the phrase I have just quoted about Thomas More — men "certainly do not need and ought not to have . . . whatever they happen to want." All social Utopias base themselves on some more-or-less radical social changes — in the property regime, with respect to trade, and so on — but then even the static, ascetic ones begin to diverge on the extent to which these social changes would be sufficient in themselves to produce moral behavior (and not merely necessary conditions). The so-called "communist colonies" of the nineteenth century tended to the rather Arcadian view that on the whole the quiet, non-competitive life would bring about the desired moral transformation. The model of the monastery comes to mind. At the other extreme there is of course Plato, for whom even his very radical social reorganization would accomplish little or nothing without the elaborate educational program and who believed that the whole molding process would have to be repeated in every generation in order to hold the Republic intact. In his own way, Thomas More was on Plato's side on this question, but they then broke sharply on my second antithesis: the one constructed an almost completely egalitarian Utopia, the other a strictly hierarchical one.

IV

In antiquity it is hard to find any Utopian thinking which is not hierarchical. As Lewis Mumford has said, "It was easier for these Greek utopians to conceive of abolishing marriage or private property than of ridding utopia of slavery, class domination and war."[17] This is sharply underscored by the ancient satirists of

[17] Lewis Mumford, "Utopia, The City and The Machine," *Daedalus*, 94 (1965), 271–92, at p. 277.

Utopia: witness Aristophanes in the *Ecclesiazusae*. That play ends in a comic riot ridiculing the sexual ideas of the Utopians (which, it should be stressed, does not deprive the criticism of its seriousness), but the heart of the attack lies in nine words in the Greek (lines 651–2): Question — Who then will till the soil? Answer — The slaves.[18] The interchange goes on to develop a number of half-serious and half-ridiculous corollaries but we need not pursue it further.

It is a pity that we are so ill-informed about the men and ideas who were the butt of Aristophanes and the other comic writers of his day,[19] or about their successors. Hippodamus of Miletus and Phaleas of Chalcedon are known only from Aristotle's criticisms of them in the *Politics*, and that reveals little more than that Hippodamus proposed a three-class social structure and that Phaleas, who may have been only marginally a Utopian anyway, wished to retain private property in land and to control it and that he proposed to turn all manufacture over to state-slaves. No egalitarianism there, clearly. What is left of the work of Euhemerus is abridged and garbled, but Diodorus leaves no doubt that his Sacred Isle was divided into castes; whether three or five castes remains an open question, but that is not of any importance in the present context.[20] Diodorus also has a brief story about the tiny Lipari Islands off Sicily where for a time land was held in common in the sixth century B.C. However, this was an emergency measure — half the small community cultivated the land while the other half waged a piratical conflict with the Etruscans — and gives no insights into ancient Utopian thinking.[21] Of Aristonicus's Heliopolis, as I have already said, we know absolutely nothing. Nearly two centuries earlier, Alexarchus, younger brother of the Cassander who ruled Macedonia for a time after the death of Alexander the Great, founded an Ouranopolis, a City of Heaven,

[18] Cf. his *Plutus*, 510 ff.

[19] See the quotations preserved in Athenaeus, 6.94–98 (267E–270B).

[20] Attempts to put right the confusions in Diodorus do not in the least alter my point; see e.g. H. Braunert, "Die Heilige Insel des Euhemeros in der Diodor-Ueberlieferung," *Rheinisches Museum f. Philologie*, n.F. 108 (1965), 255–68.

[21] Diodorus, 5.9; see R. J. Buck, "Communalism in the Lipari Islands," *Classical Philology*, 54 (1959), 33–39.

on Mt. Athos, called himself the Sun and invented a secret language. And Alexarchus carries us all the way back to lunacy and its personal fantasies.

We are therefore left only with the Republic as a subject for detailed analysis. Plato's attitude to class and labor is a heavily nuanced one. His Guardians may live off the involuntary labor of others but they do not exploit anyone for their own enrichment or even, strictly speaking, for their own benefit, and they, of all men, live a life of asceticism and strict discipline. Nor is labor merely dismissed as an activity fit only for slaves (nor as a punishment for sin). Labor is a necessity; more than that, it has positive qualities: there is legitimate pride in skill and craftsmanship, there is the moral discipline it induces, there is even a sense in which one may speak of a vocation of labor. But there is also an immutable hierarchy of values, in which labor occupies the lowest rank of acceptable and necessary activities, and this is matched by a hierarchy of social classes and backed by a metaphysical doctrine of the nature of the soul.

For all his radicalism, in sum, Plato, like the other ancient Utopians, could never depart from the notion of the natural inequality of men. Nor could Zeno: he simply cut the Gordian knot in his Republic by excluding all men who were not virtuous, not morally good.[22] The real world was a chaos. The function of the Utopians was to remedy it through order, regularity and virtue. They differed in their remedies and their explanations, in the depth and breadth of their thinking, but they agreed that inequality had to remain, re-structured, so to speak, but not abolished. And on that absolutely fundamental nexus of ideas the modern world broke dramatically with Thomas More. It must be remembered that *Utopia* was first published in Latin as early as 1516, in a posthumous English translation in 1551, and in transla-

[22] The key passage is Diogenes Laertius, 7.32 – 33. Although Zeno's *Politeia*, an early and perhaps his earliest work, has been taken as a Utopia, that is an illusion in my opinion. Its form can be explained by its explicit purpose, an attack on Plato's *Republic*. Zeno proposed to cure the ills of society by ignoring all but the good men and by abolishing social institutions, not by changing them, just as the later Stoics preached the equality and universal brotherhood of all men as an ideological justification for the preservation in real life of the grossest inequalities, ending with absolute monarchy.

tions into all the major European languages by the end of the sixteenth century. I shall quote just one sentence: "Husbandry is a science common to them all in general, both men and women, wherein they be all expert and cunning." One can almost match that in Iambulus, but he was at least half in the world of myth and Thomas More decidedly was not.[23] More's egalitarianism did not win the day by any means. The authoritarians, those whose Utopia was to be imposed from above and maintained by domination, were perhaps in the majority, from Campanella to Wells. But More was nonetheless explosive in his conception: a new possibility was opened up, though at first only for Utopia, and no opposition could again remove that possibility from men's consciousness.

From the sixteenth century on, the history of the role and psychology of labor is a corollary and equally complex part of the complex history of modern society, with its class structure and its value systems. I cannot even begin on that subject, but I cannot resist one pathetic quotation from Nathaniel Hawthorne's *Blithedale Romance*, published in 1852 and based on the experiences of the Utopian colony called Brook Farm, a few miles outside Boston, which existed from 1841 to 1846. Hawthorne wrote as follows:

"The peril of our new way of life was not lest we should fail in becoming practical agriculturalists but that we should probably cease to be anything else. While our enterprise lay all in theory, we had pleased ourselves with delectable visions of the spiritualization of labor. It was to be one form of prayer and ceremonial of worship. Each stroke of the hoe was to uncover some aromatic root of wisdom heretofore hidden from the sun. Pausing in the field, to let the wind exhale the moisture from our foreheads, we were to look upward and catch glimpses into the far-off soul of truth. In this point of view, matters did not turn out quite so well as we had anticipated. . . . The clods of earth, which we so constantly belabored and turned over and over, were never etherealized into thought. Our Thoughts, on the contrary, were fast

[23] More's egalitarianism was not quite complete, it should be noted. There were, for example, the Siphograuntes with their "perpetual licence from laboure to learninge."

becoming cloddish. Our labor symbolized nothing. Intellectual activity is incompatible with any large amount of bodily exercise. The yeoman and the scholar — the yeoman and the man of finesse and moral culture . . . — are two distinct individuals, and can never be melted or wedded into one substance."

V

Ancient writers would have agreed with Hawthorne's conclusion, despite their Arcadian glorification of the rustic life, and they would have been completely puzzled why he had to suffer his Arcadian failure before he discovered so obvious a truth. Neither Xenophon nor Virgil went to his villa to labor. Brook Farm was no doubt a pathetic and melancholy experience, yet the very attempt reveals the unbridgeable gap that exists between us and antiquity. I have already indicated two reasons for saying that: first, the fact that it was not possible by any means to bring about an equitable society in antiquity, given the poor resources, the low level of technology, and the absence of any growth possibilities (other than conquest) in the economy and the absence of the very idea of progress; second, the acceptance of human inequality, and therefore of the necessity of domination, as natural and immutable. I must now add a third element, and that is the smallness of scale on which men operated and in which they thought. For ancient Utopians it was axiomatic that Utopia was possible only in a small, face-to-face community. Contrariwise, those who looked to mankind in general, to the universe — the Cynics with their *cosmopolis,* the Stoics with their brotherhood of all men — were precisely the thinkers who, insofar as they remained consistent and rigorous in their thinking, turned their backs on society altogether.

In the present day, and for the first time in history, all problems are technically soluble; there is widespread acceptance, no matter how superficially or with whatever reservations, of the idea that equality and freedom (however defined) are necessary elements in justice and a just society; and everything is on a gigantic, even terrifying, scale. This last is a fairly new element in the situation, and one of the highest importance. By scale I refer not only to geography or technology or national territory but to the scale of organization which modern life requires. Even if we and the ancients did not differ on the other two issues, this matter of scale would of itself be sufficient to render their social Utopias irrelevant today.

What, then, is the present position with regard to Utopian writing and thinking? The answer is that we seem to have turned the whole tradition upside down. In western literature today, at least outside the socialist sphere, satires on Utopia have become very prominent, as Northrop Frye noted, while there is a paralysis of genuine Utopian thought.[24] Another commentator said this more brutally when he entitled a course of lectures *From Utopia to Nightmare.*[25] "If alert readers once sat down with Bellamy's *Looking Backward* or Wells's *A Modern Utopia*," today they "seem more likely to meditate upon Huxley's *Brave New World* or Orwell's *Nineteen Eighty-Four.*"[26] (I take no responsibility for the word "alert.") This newer kind of satire is radically different from the ancient, that of Aristophanes, for example, in the *Birds* or the *Ecclesiazusae.* For the latter the joke about Utopianism was its absurdity, its impracticality, its impossibility. For our own satirists, however, there is no joke at all; on the contrary, they attack Utopia because it is in fact possible and achievable, and because it then turns out to be Dystopia for them, the opposite of Utopia. Huxley prefaced *Brave New World* with a quotation from Berdyaev: "Les utopies apparaissent comme bien plus réalisables qu'on ne le croyait autrefois. Et nous nous trouvons actuellement devant une question bien autrement angoissante: Comment éviter leur réalisation définitive?"

All major movements for social reform and of course all revolutions (and not a few wars) have been animated by a spirit of Utopianism (though not necessarily by a specific blueprint for Utopia). They then turn out not to have attained Utopia, even at their best, and there is an inevitable let-down. Voices are raised against both the social changes and the underlying Utopianism, against the possibility of human progress, against man's potenti-

---

[24] "Varieties of Literary Utopias," *Daedalus,* 94 (1965), 324 – 347, at p. 327.
[25] Chad Walsh, *From Utopia to Nightmare* (London 1962).
[26] *Ibid.,* 11.

ality for good. Contemporary Dystopias seem but another example. But they are a special kind of example. The fact that in principle the technological, economic and political problems are now soluble has had a powerful impact for at least two reasons. First, it has concentrated the attention so completely on practical and immediately available solutions that it has narrowed the field in which the traditional kind of Utopian imagination can play, when it has not barred the door to it altogether. Second, the solutions require constant enlargement of the already enormous scale of operations. That element of scale takes us further and further from traditional Utopianism, ancient or modern. It generates its own tensions and fears; in traditional terms, the fear that the age-old struggle to achieve a balance between freedom and order has finally been lost forever. "The capabilities (intellectual and material) of contemporary society," Herbert Marcuse has phrased it, "are immeasurably greater than ever before — which means that the scope of society's domination over the individual is immeasurably greater than ever before."[27]

If Utopian thinking is to recover from its present state of paralysis, it will have to break with its past. "The available resources make for a *qualitative* change in the human needs."[28] Social and political engineering have been given over to the practical imagination. Utopia must therefore take the next transcending step. After the elimination of the burdens of want and struggle and war there would still remain the burdens of fear and guilt, of domination. What Oscar Wilde said in *The Soul of Man under Socialism* has lost none of its force: "A map of the world that does not include Utopia is not worth even glancing at."

[27] *One-Dimensional Man* (Boston and London 1964), x.
[28] H. Marcuse, *Eros and Civilization* (Boston 1955, 1966), 93.

Primitive Society in Its Many Dimensions

STANLEY DIAMOND

HERBERT MARCUSE is a radical, root and branch. That is to say, he does not believe that the pathology inherent in our society can be cured by applied sociologists, Christian Scientists, or the rote indulgence in an even more sophisticated technology. Always we find Marcuse in opposition, a radical fundamentalist, in the trajectory of Marx and Freud. He deals always with the whole society, and rejects the epaulets of any particular discipline. He represents, in the quite technical sense, Man as antithesis to a uni-dimensional social mechanism, in a time of false synthesis, mechanical compromise, consensus; and he is, of course, a man of flesh and blood in opposition. Marcuse's fusion of analysis and vision exposes the interlocking vertical strata of culture, from the economic to the aesthetic. He has pressed a formidable academic intelligence into the service of his view, an intelligence that probes the possibilities of a more humane and passionate society by creating images of what we are and what we must do to become what we wish to be. To that end, I submit to him this image of multi-dimensional primitive society, a necessary starting point for the debate about the nature and growth of civilization, a beginning which neither Plato nor Marx nor Freud found it possible to evade.

The word "primitive" connotes a series of related sociological, political, economic, psychological and psychiatric meanings. The problem for contemporary anthropology, a problem that will not down, despite a semantic barrage, is more precisely to define the attributes of primitive society. That is, "primitive" implies a certain level of history and a certain mode of cultural being. This requires, *first*, that we distinguish primitive institutions from those of archaic civilizations; and correlatively, that we distinguish

21

primitive from peasant usages, while keeping alert to the subtle problem of continuities, both real and apparent. We are led, in turn, to focus concretely on the internal and external processes through which primitive communitarian societies are restructured into civilized, class organized polities.

Second, we must focus empirically on the great variety of forms and usages encountered among primitives.

Third, we must then attempt to develop a model of primitive society by translating the diverse formal modes actually encountered into a series of generalized, typical attributes.

Finally, as anthropologists, it behooves us to exercise our critical social sense by contrasting archaic and contemporary civilizations with the primitive model and specifying the attenuation or absence of the functional equivalents of primitive forms and usages in civilized societies, and the probable consequences thereof.

Previous theorists (among them, Marx, Morgan, Redfield, Radin) who attempted to define. primitive societies, that is, to give concrete, historical content to a level of organization called primitive, were, in the most general sense, correct; but more sophisticated, subtle, and detailed definitions are essential if we are to use our knowledge of primitives as a means of furthering our critical understanding and, hopefully, our humane shaping of the processes of civilization. This undertaking, which we have inherited from the European Enlightenment, is explicit in the work of Morgan, who wrote of the next phase of human society as reconstituting, on a higher level, the principles of the ancient *gentes;* it is the source from which Marx derived his sense of the possibility of non-alienated labor; it was the basis for Redfield's sense of the moral society; it is central to Radin's assessment of the role of the ritual drama; indeed one can hardly find an anthropologist of note from Tylor to Lévi-Strauss, who does not critically evaluate aspects of civilization as comparatively revealed in studies of primitive communities.

However, lineal, secular, one-dimensional notions of progress, which are disrespectful of human personality, that is, of the full spectrum of man's behaviour as a social being, have become current ontological and epistemological pre-suppositions. But we cannot afford to break our dialogue with history; "History teaches us everything, even the future," said Lamartine. Should we not, then, ceaselessly put questions to the primitive past, in the spirit of our great predecessors, which will help us to understand our contemporary dilemmas, by revealing necessary aspects of man's existence for which modern equivalents may be created? Students of man are often apt to become manipulators of men, or their merely academic teachers, but it is as students, as critics, as hunters on the track of the human potential and the human necessity, that we are, I believe, most appropriately engaged.

There are, perhaps, ten major, interrelated, typical attributes (I have not yet refined them to the abstract point of functions), realizing themselves in a diversity of specific forms, which comprise any historically justifiable, inductive model of primitive society. They are as follows:[1]

1. *Economic communalism.* That is, economic exploitation of man by man, as we know it in modern and archaic civilizations, is absent. Correlatively, there are no economic classes, in the sense that any paramount group may be said to own the means of production, although a chief may, in his person, symbolize the property rights of a particular unit. Primitive economies are natural economies; they lack true money. The three related attributes of civilized money — that is, money as an abstract, intrinsically valueless medium for appropriating surplus, storing value, and deferring payment or delaying exchange — do not adhere to primitive money. The latter serves as a counter or symbol of value, as in native Dahomey (which was an archaic civilization, not a primitive society), where cowries were used to represent tribute that was actually collected in kind from the local communities by the king's agents. But exchange among primitives is usually effected by barter or gift. These converge toward being, literally, donations, akin to sacrifices, that is, not merely a giving of goods, but a giving of oneself. While civilized money tends to alienate man from his labor by transforming that essential function of his humanity into an abstract commodity, by detaching it from him, by transferring considerations of "worth" and "value" from a human

[1] The following ten points have been condensed from the author's "The Search for the Primitive" in *Man's Image in Medicine and Anthropology*, Iago Galdston, ed., International Universities Press, 1963.

to a marketing context, primitive exchange has the contrary effect: social value and social effort are directly expressed and understood; they strengthen the sense of community. Indeed, the major emphasis in most forms of primitive exchange seems to be on *giving*, and this may be accompanied by attitudes ranging from the hostile to the generous. The primitive gift may serve an "economic" purpose, within a reciprocal system, but, like most significant activities in primitive society, it is multi-functional, a focus for the expression of a wide range of emotions and purposes.

2. *Leadership is communal and traditional*, not political or secular. The chief of a clan or the patriarch of a family is respected as the embodiment of clan, family, or tribal heritage. In many societies, a clan chief is simply the oldest member of the group. Obeisance toward these figures is symbolic, a sign of respect towards one's tradition, and thus of self-respect.

Leadership may also be situational and/or based on skill. Primitive societies abound in "chiefs." In any one tribe, e.g., the Anaguta of the high Nigerian Plateau, there may be hunting, work, dance, women's age grade, and fishing chiefs. These leaders function only in specific contexts and for limited periods of time; usually, their primacy is based on capacity in the particular activity. Almost everyone in the society, at one time or another, is in a "chiefly" position.

Leadership may be, further, a function of generalized rank and status, which automatically accrues to every normal member of the group through the mere fact of his having attained a certain age or undergone certain experiences. The association of traditional leadership with shifting, situational, and "automatic" types of status leadership reduces the occasions for what can be termed "broad spectrum" social hostility, while diminishing the alienation that develops in response to arbitrary, remotely exercised, and impersonal authority. Primitive societies are democratic (as Kroeber pointed out), though they are not reductively "equalitarian." Equality is not construed as identity in primitive life. Leadership is reasonably distributed and exercised.

3. *Laws, as we know them, do not exist.* Society operates through custom and by well understood informal sanctions, not

by a legal apparatus, administered from above in the interests of this or that group, i.e., not by codified laws. There are no special legal functionaries; there is no specific and exclusively legal apparatus. The multitudinous occasions for law that we are familiar with in civilization, e.g., commercial rights, governmental levy, and bureaucratic function, simply do not occur in primitive society. As Tylor put it, "one of the most essential things that we can learn from the life of rude tribes is how society can function without the policemen to keep order."

4. *Primitive societies tend to be systems in equilibrium; they are not disrupted by institutional conflicts, although they contain well-structured, often cyclical, conflicts among institutions; and, of course, personal conflicts do exist.* The former is exemplified in the limited struggles among sodalities, and in certain types of institutionalized deviancy; the latter in the ordinary play of personalities, which may intensify to witchcraft. Indeed, the built-in social mechanisms for the expression of hostility, which these structured conflicts partly are, help strengthen the social fabric; the society, so to speak, recognizes and provides for a wide range of human expression.

The primitive, then, is a conservative; his society changes its essential form only under the impact of external circumstances, or in response to drastic changes in the natural environment. Institutional disharmonies never reach the point of social destruction, or, correlatively, of chronic, widespread individual disorganization.

5. *There is a very high degree of integration among the various major modalities of culture.* Between religion and social structure, social structure and economic organization, economic organization and technology, the magical and the pragmatic, there are intricate and harmonious correlations. These correlations have two major effects: (a) they tend toward the optimal practical efficiency of the system; and (b) they integrate a whole series of emotions and attitudes around a given activity, rather than isolating or abstracting the activity from its human context. An obvious example of the first effect is the maximal use of technology by primitive economic systems; so far as I know, no primitive economic system is dysfunctional with the available technology.

Neither does it utilize technology in a wasteful or inefficient way, no matter what "bizarre" means are brought into play to dispose of surplus beyond the point where the subsistence needs of the group are met, or to stimulate exchange. The second effect is exemplified in the validation of practical activities by magico-religious means, as in the classic case of the expert Trobriand canoe maker, who confirms the step-by-step construction of his craft with spell and incantation.

6. *The ordinary member of primitive society participates in a much greater segment of his social economy than do individuals in archaic and in technically sophisticated, modern civilizations.* The average primitive, relative to his social environment and the level of science and technology achieved, is more accomplished, in the literal sense of that term, than are most civilized individuals. A major reason for this functional integrity is in his control of the processes of production; that is, the primitive, in creating a tool, creates it from beginning to end, uses it with skill, and controls it. He has no schizoid sense of it controlling him, and he has direct access to the fruits of his labor, subject to the reciprocal claims of his kinsmen.

7. *Society is holistic and moral (not moralistic); it is organized on a kin or tribal, not a political, basis.* All significant economic, social and ideological activities are discharged within and among kin or quasi-kin groupings whether these are nuclear families, joint families, clans, clusters of clans, or the various types of sodalities. Society thus functions on a personal, corporate and traditional, rather than on an impersonal, civil and individualized basis. This *personalism*, splendidly illustrated by Hallowell, is the most historically significant feature of primitive life and extends from the family outward, to the society at large and ultimately to nature itself. It seems to underlie all other distinctive qualities of primitive thought and behavior. Primitive people live in a personal, corporate world, a world that tends to be a "thou" to the subject "I," rather than an "it" impinging upon an objectively separate, and divided, self. Consciousness for the primitive is the most common condition in the universe, a perception that is also found, in more civilized and abstract forms, in the work of Whitehead, Haldane, and Teilhard de Chardin.

8. *Primitive modes of thinking are substantially concrete, existential and nominalistic, within a personalistic context.* This does not suggest a lack of abstract capacity (all language, all culture and convention flow from this phylogenetic human endowment), but it does indicate an emphasis functional with the kinship structure of primitive society and a lack of concern with the specific types of abstraction that may be called, in the Western civilized world, Platonic. Context and existence, rather than essence, constitute the established aspects of thought.

9. *The ritual drama is a culturally comprehensive vehicle for group and individual expression at critical junctures in the social round or personal life cycle, as these crises are enjoined by the natural environment or defined by culture.* In such ceremonies, art, religion and daily life fuse, and cultural meanings are renewed and re-created on a stage as wide as society itself. In a sequence from archaic to modern civilization, we can trace the process through which religion, drama and daily life split apart. The drama, the primary form of art, retreats to the theater, and religion escapes into the church. The sacraments, those formalized remnants of the primitive crisis rites, and the "theater," the "play," develop into carefully cultivated and narrowly bounded conventions. Civilized participation in culture becomes increasingly passive, as culture becomes increasingly secularized. Among primitives, rituals are cathartic and creative. They are cathartic in that they serve as occasions for open, if culturally molded, expressions of ambivalent feelings about sacred tradition, constituted authority, animal and human nature, and nature at large. These rituals are also creative in the dramatic revelation of symbols and the anticipation and elaboration of new roles for individuals; they make meanings explicit and renew the vitality of the group. Such rituals are, I believe, primarily *expressive*, as opposed to the predominantly binding, compulsive, "ritualistic" behavior encountered as neurotic phenomena among civilized individuals.

The primitive ritual also differs from ritualized *group* occasions in civilized society; the latter strive toward repression of ambivalence rather than recognition and consequent cultural use. One can hardly imagine a "burlesque of the sacred," taking place at, let us say, a patriotic ceremony; in this sense all state structures tend toward the totalitarian. But, among primitives, sacred events are, as noted, frequently and publicly caricatured, even as they occur. In primitive rituals, the fundamental paradoxes of human life — *love and hate, the comic and the tragic, dedication and denial*, and their derivatives — are given free, sometimes uninhibited, even murderous, "play." Yet the sanguine and terrifying aspects of primitive life, which civilized individuals could hardly sustain, precisely because of the immediate personal contexts in which they occur, do not begin to compete with the mass, impersonal, rationalized slaughter that increases in scope as civilization spreads and deepens. The contrast is not merely in the exponential factor of technology; in primitive society, taking a life was an *occasion;* in our phase of civilization it has become an abstract, ideological compulsion. Certain ritual dramas or aspects of them acknowledge, express and symbolize the most destructive, ambivalent, and demoniacal aspects of human nature; in so doing, they are left limited and finite; that is, they become self-limiting. For this, as yet, we have no civilized parallel, no functional equivalent.

10. *Clear delineation of the human person within a social, natural and supernatural (that is, self-transcendent) setting.* The primitive realization of the person, the "sense of self," if you will, is achieved through the affective elaboration of critical events in the life cycle, and by the ramifying personal relationships that are the very definition of primitive society. This process of *individuation* is the antithesis of ideological "individualism." Ideological individualism is a reflection of what Redfield calls *individualization;* the latter is a symptom of civilization — and denotes the increasingly mechanical separation of persons from each other, as a result of the shrinkage and replacement of primitive, organic ties by civil, collective connections. These prominent features of primitive society should lead us to anticipate an exceedingly low incidence of the chronic characterological, or psychoneurotic, phenomena that seem to be growing with civilization, as Meyer Fortes, among others, has indicated. This reflects my own experience; I would add only that the disciplined expressiveness of primitive societies, together with traditional social and economic supports, results, also, in a greater structural tolerance of psychotic manifestations, no matter how we define them or what

their actual incidence may be, relative to civilized cultures. The foregoing attributes of primitive society may be summarized in this simple statement; the primitive society is a *community*, springing from common origins, composed of reciprocating persons, and growing from within. Here we have the basis for a multi-form critique of contemporary civilization.

That is to say, from studying primitive peoples through the screen of our civilization, from plunging into history, we learn that, although human nature as a system of interlocking potentials remains constant, specific, perhaps mutually exclusive types of realization along with what we are obliged to consider distortions, do indeed occur. The model of Man that resolves out of close study of primitive society is clearly complementary to man in maximally politicized civilizations, such as our own. I do not deny the existence of continuities, but share with Lévi-Strauss the view that they are non-specific, insubstantial. The points of complementarity have been implied above. We are essentialist, abstract-analytical, secular, impersonal, collective, mechanical, specialized, acquisitive, exploitative, progressive, in our social and intellectual character. *They* are existentialist, nominalistic, communal, personal, organic, sacred, individuated, multi-dimensional, conservative. These qualities (and their precise naming is, to some degree, arbitrary) are generated through the contrasting primitive and civilized social structures. We may put the matter as follows — differential social consciousness actualizes certain potentials of being and nullifies others. Moreover, each quality has its negative. Where we, for example, no longer ritualize our cultural existence, except through the residual, passive-defensive and compulsive means metaphorically documented by Freud, they, the primitives, symbolize their personal perception and mastery of their environment through rituals that renew human, social, and natural existence. But the potential negative in the primitive experience is the denial of nature as a paradigm of processes of which Man is a manifestation, but by no means the center. The negative of our notions of science is in Man splitting himself into object and observer, and the concomitant loss of the person as an integrated subject, as a partner in a universe of persons.

In examining such complementarities, we are struck by the possibility of synthesis; but for complementarities, in the areas that interest us, to develop beyond the condition of paired opposites and to confront each other as antitheses to theses, foreshadowing synthesis, requires, as it did for Socrates, a concretely political transformation of intellectual insight. Social reconstruction based upon historical considerations of human nature, and the thus far segregated expressions that have dominated the successive eras of man can be programmatic only to a limited degree. It is not, and cannot be, a question of grafting primitive forms on civilized structures or, need it be said again, of "retreating" into the primitive past. It is not a question of regaining lost paradises or savage nobility, neither of which ever existed in the manner imputed to their authors; they were merely straw constructions to be blown down by the kind of easy and baseless irony which Voltaire addressed to Rousseau. The problem, and it remains the central problem of anthropology, is to conceptualize contemporary forms that will reunite man with his past, reconcile the primitive with the civilized, making progress without distortion theoretically possible, or, at least, enabling us to experience the qualities that primitive peoples routinely display. This, in turn, demands innovation of the highest order, even if nourished on despair, innovation equivalent to the genius that Lévi-Strauss detects, for example, behind the kinship paradigms of primitive people. What better place is there to begin than with the rational devolution of bureaucracy, the common ownership and decentralization of the basic means of production, for which we have the techniques at hand and for which we must develop the apposite social imagination. Human beings have lived in analogous circumstances before, we learn from anthropology, and it seems essential that we learn to do so again, albeit on a higher level and in different forms. Reflexive, merely determined behavior, *signalled* behavior, condemns us to the destructive course of our civilization, to the irresponsibility of our fate.

Manicheanism in the Enlightenment

RICHARD H. POPKIN

IT IS AN HISTORICAL ODDITY that at a time when Manicheanism was hardly a living theological issue, when practically no adherents of this creed were alive, it became a major issue of intellectual concern for Pierre Bayle, Voltaire, Hume, and Gibbon. In this paper I shall examine what led to this brief revival of interest in Manicheanism, and what role it played in Enlightenment thought.

Manicheanism in its various forms was a vital force in Christendom up to the twelfth century. The attacks by the Church Fathers indicate that Manicheanism had a tremendous appeal in ancient times, and was practically a rival religion to Christianity for several centuries. The successes of the Paulicians, Bogomils, West, and the incorporation of the Bogomils into the Ottoman dom to its foundations. The brutal crushing of the Cathari in the West, and the incorporation of the Bogomils into the Ottoman Empire in the East ended the Manichean threat to Christianity. The victory was so complete that in most 17th-century writings on the problem of evil, Manicheanism is hardly ever mentioned. Although the Reformation and Counter-Reformation brought St. Augustine's views to the center of the theological stage, it was his theory of Grace and his answer to Pelagianism that attracted the greatest interest. Various sects hurled, as the vilest accusation against their opponents, the charge that they were Pelagians or semi-Pelagians, not that they were Manicheans. The latter were remembered as now fortunately defunct heretics who held to an odious theory and had abominable sexual-religious practices, while the Pelagians (as well as the Socinians and Spinozists) were a living threat to be found behind the explanations of the source of evil and the nature of Grace of the Jesuits and the Arminians.

Suddenly, when Pierre Bayle's great *Dictionnaire historique et critique* appeared in 1697, Manicheanism became a major intellectual issue. In his articles "Manichées," "Marcionites," "Origen," and "Pauliciens," Bayle set forth the shocking claim that Manicheanism is difficult, if not impossible, to refute by reason, and that it is only really answered by faith, not by argument. Bayle's "defense" of Manicheanism, and his contention that no satisfactory orthodox explanation of the occurrence of evil is possible, startled the intellectuals of his time, and made the consideration of Manicheanism the order of the day. Bayle's clarification, added to the second edition of the *Dictionnaire* of 1702, made his charges even more forceful, and led to many attempted refutations, such as Leibniz's *Theodicée*, and Bishop William King's *De Origine Mali*. Isaac de Beausobre's two-volume *Histoire critique de Manichée et du Manichéisme* (1734 – 36) provided a sober historical "defense" for the Manichean position, challenging many of the then accepted facts and charges about the movement. Though Beausobre's study hardly had the impact of Bayle's, it added to the interest and concern with Manicheanism during the Enlightenment.

Why should the learned world suddenly have rediscovered this ancient heresy, and have worried about its explanation of the occurrence of evil? Could Bayle's perverse interest in outlandish movements and ideas suffice to account both for his taking the time and trouble to figure out arguments in favor of Manicheanism, and for his audience's taking this as most exciting and challenging? I submit that there is much more to the phenomenon of concern with Manicheanism in the Enlightenment. When one looks into one of Bayle's main sources for his information on the Paulicians, the Arminian Manicheans, one finds that he draws heavily from Bishop Bossuet's *Histoire des variations des églises protestantes*. Bossuet had devoted a section to the history of the New Manicheans, the heretics of Toulouse and Albi. While constantly insulting Manicheanism for its doctrines and its practices, Bossuet also, and more importantly, charged that the Albigensian Manicheans were the actual and the doctrinal ancestors of the Protestants. And, in his picture, since he claimed that the beliefs and practices of the medieval Manicheans were so dreadful, this constituted a condemnation of the Reformation. If the Reformers are the lineal descendants of the abominable Manicheans, then their views (and perhaps their practices) are equally horrendous.[1] Pascal, in his *Écrits sur la Grâce*, had made the charge on doctrinal grounds, and had said of the ancient heretics, "les Manichéens étaient les Luthériens de leur temps, commes les Luthériens sont les Manichéens du nôtre."[2]

Both Bayle and Beausobre apparently entered the fray because of the Catholic attacks on the Reformers. Beausobre, a Calvinist minister in Berlin, was led to his study from his concern with Reformation controversies and with Catholic charges.[3] Bayle seems to have been concerned either because of the attack on Protestantism or that on Manicheanism. He may have been a genuine Manichean himself. He came from the area south of Toulouse that was Albigensian territory. His concern might possibly have resulted from his being a genuine underground survivor, and from his being one of the very, very few actual living adherents of secret Manicheanism.[4] (One of Bossuet's complaints was that the nasty Albigensians so disguised their views that they were able to pass themselves off as regular members of the Christian communities, that they behaved like Marranos, leading a double-life.[5]) It is more likely that it was his Protestant background that accounted for Bayle's interest in the matter. Bayle was the son of a Calvinist pastor. His family had been severely persecuted, his older brother dying in prison for the cause. Bayle himself had to flee from his native France, after his reconversion to Calvinism. He returned only in disguise, and had to flee once again because of the events preceding the Revocation of the Edict of Nantes.

1 Jacques Bénigne Bossuet, *Histoire des variations des églises protestantes* (Paris 1688), Tome II, Livre xi, pp. 162 – 63.

2 Blaise Pascal, *Écrits sur la Grâce*, Quatrième Écrit, in *Oeuvres complètes*, ed. Louis Lafuma (New York 1963), p. 340.

3 On Beausobre's career see the article "Beausobre, Isaac," in Alexander Chambers, *The General Biographical Dictionary* (London 1812), IV, pp. 290 – 94.

4 On Bayle's life see Elisabeth Labrousse, *Pierre Bayle*, Tome I (The Hague 1963). At the end Madame Labrousse states, "Plutôt que sur la dépouille d'un des premiers déistes du XVIIe siècle, il se pourrait bien que la fosse commune de l'Eglise wallonne de Rotterdam se soit refermée le 31 décembre 1706 sur celle d'un des derniers manichéens de l'histoire" (pp. 270 – 71).

5 Bossuet, *op. cit.* (note 1), p. 138.

His first works published from his exile in Rotterdam, the *Pensées diverses sur la comète, Critique générale de l'histoire du calvinisme du M. Maimbourg,* and the *Commentaire philosophique,* all were answers to Catholic attacks and Catholic arguments. So, when Bossuet and others charged that the Protestants were really believers in the most abominable heresy in the history of Christianity, it seems reasonable that an able and maybe ardent Protestant polemicist would have risen to the bait.

Beausobre answered the Catholic charges by showing historically both that the Manichean view was relatively reasonable at the time offered, and that the Manicheans probably did not actually engage in abominable sexual-religious practices. Bayle was not concerned to argue the history of the matter (though, as Beausobre pointed out, he should have, especially since he usually was interested in getting at the facts in the case[6]), and was willing to take Bossuet's data at face value.[7] Instead Bayle concentrated on showing the plausibility of Manicheanism, and the implausibility of the orthodox Christian account of the reasons for the occurrence of evil. Since there was so little of the Manichean side of the argument, Bayle devoted his ingenuity to constructing that side of the story. And he insisted that he was just trying to show, for the *n*th time, that Christianity could not be supported by reason but could only be accepted by faith.[8] The force of Manicheanism as a

---

[6] Isaac de Beausobre, *Histoire critique de Manichée et du Manichéisme,* (Amsterdam 1734), I, p. 3. "Feu M. Bayle nous a donné, dans son Dictionnaire, un Article de *Manichée* & des Manichéens: mais il me semble, qu'il auroit mieux fait, ou de l'omettre, ou de le composer autrement. Il devoit traiter cette matière en Critique. . . . Je crois donc, que feu M. Bayle auroit dû nous donner une Histoire aussi exacte, qu'on peut l'avoir de l'Hérésiarque *Manichée,* & nous marquer précisément ses opinions, plûtot que de s'amuser à pousser & à orner, comme il l'a fait, les arguments des Manichéens. Un DICTIONNAIRE HISTORIQUE ET CRITIQUE demandoit qu'il fît le premier, & le dispensoit certainement du second."

[7] See Bayle, art. "Paulicians," and remarks B, C, and D of the complete article.

[8] Bayle, *Dictionnaire,* art. "Manicheans," Rem. D, p. 150; "Paulicians," Rem. F, p. 186; and "Second Clarification," pp. 409–420. All pages, references and citations, unless otherwise indicated are to my translation, Pierre Bayle, *Historical and Critical Dictionary, Selections* (Indianapolis and New York 1965).

rational theory would be one way of answering Bossuet. However, I believe that what Bayle actually accomplished, whether intentional or not, was to present his age with the force and plausibility of the counter-theory to Christianity. And, in an era when many were beginning to have doubts about the merits of the Christian world-view, a forceful presentation of the dialectical strength of Manicheanism over Christianity could have had far-reaching effects on the intellectuals of the time.

The case Bayle set forth was that the strength of Manicheanism lay in its explanation of the *fact* of evil, not in its metaphysical or theological arguments. Bayle insisted, and Hume and Voltaire were to echo his view, that everybody's clearest conception of the nature of the universe, whether seen in naturalistic or supernaturalistic terms, was that it was based upon, and governed by, a unitary principle of order. Nobody, Bayle observed, believed on philosophical grounds, that the world is constituted of, or results from, two or more substances or forces. Neither the Judeo-Christian theologians nor the Spinozists conceive of the world in Manichean terms. They were all looking for a unitary explanation of what was going on. And, anyone who accepted the Scriptural account of the world, even partially, saw the world as *all* ultimately resulting from one source or principle. But, all of this notwithstanding, Bayle maintained that in accounting for the facts of human experience the Manichean theory was far superior to any unitary view, and that the unitary view as an explanation could only be accepted irrationally or fideistically.[9]

Anyone who is already five or six years old, Bayle asserted, knows of the occurrence of pain and evil. Anyone who studies human affairs knows that, "Properly speaking, history is nothing but the crimes and misfortunes of the human race."[10] But, also, as any observer can tell, there is also some virtue and some good in the world. (Otherwise another kind of unitary theory would be obvious, namely that everything is bad and that everything is caused by some evil principle.) Then, given the mixture of happiness and misery, of virtue and vice, in the world, the most plau-

---

[9] Bayle, art. "Manicheans," Rem. D, pp. 145 – 47.
[10] Bayle, art. "Manicheans," Rem. D, p. 147.

sible explanation of it all, according to Bayle, was the Manichean one.[11]

The attempts to account for the facts of human experience on a unitary theory, Bayle contended, are all intellectually hopeless. Bayle employed his great dialectical skill in making utterly ridiculous the explanations of the occurrence of evil in a world created and ruled by a good God. The stock pious views are turned into hilarious farce. Bayle challenged all of the theological and metaphysical explanations from ancient times down to the seventeenth century with Manichean criticisms that he refurbished or invented for the occasion. And after leaving the intellectual attempts to account for the occurrence of evil without admitting a Manichean theory in shambles[12] (and Bayle went so far as to suggest that the orthodox Christian satanic theory of evil bordered on becoming a Manichean view, except that God was still the author of the Devil[13]), Bayle set forth what he thought was the sole remaining intellectual response for a Christian believing in a unitary explanation. First, the believer should recognize that the strength of Manicheanism as a way of accounting for the facts in the case, and that the hopelessness of orthodox theology to do so, only show the weakness of human reason. "It [reason] is a principle of destruction and not of edification. It is only proper for raising doubts, and for turning things on all sides in order to make the dispute endless. . . . It is only fit to make man aware of his own blindness and weakness, and the necessity for another revelation. That is the one of Scripture. It is there that we find the means to refute invincibly the hypothesis of the two principles. . . ."[14]

These invincible means turn out to be that if the message of Scripture is accepted on faith, and on faith alone, then the believer knows (as part of the revealed message) that an infinitely good and holy principle is the cause of the occurrence of evil. It is no longer a question of whether it is plausible or consistent to

[11] *Ibid.*, p. 147, "For if all mankind were wicked and miserable, there would be no need to have recourse to the hypothesis of two principles. It is the mixture of happiness and virtue with misery and vice that requires this hypothesis."

[12] Bayle, art. "Manicheans," Rem. D, pp. 147–52; "Paulicians," Rem. E, esp. pp. 169–79, Rem. F, pp. 180–86, and Rem. M, pp. 187–93.

[13] Bayle, art. "Paulicians," Rem. H.

[14] Bayle, art. "Manicheans," Rem. D, p. 151.

explain the evil in the world in terms of the actions of a good and all-powerful God. For the believer, it is just an indisputable fact (since it is revealed) that God is the only causal principle. If the Manichean objector invented by Bayle asks how this can be possible, he is simply answered with the news, "this however is in fact the case, and therefore this is very possible." And, Bayle insisted, arguing from the maxim that "From the act to the potency is a valid inference" is the *only* serious rebuttal to Manicheanism.[15] Since, according to Scripture, it has happened that a good God has produced or permitted evil, it is therefore possible that He can do so. We may not be able to explain how He can do it, and any and all attempts to explain this may (in Bayle's hands) turn out to be contradictory or silly, but the orthodox believer can just insist on the fact that it has happened, since the Bible says so. Then, the fact that the Manicheans possess a better explanation of what goes on makes no difference, since it has ceased to be a question of what is the most reasonable way to explain experience. The orthodox view is *the* explanation, whether intelligible or not.

Bayle's "answer" to Manicheanism by abandoning reason for blind faith became more pronounced in his official reply to the charge of the Consistory of the French Reformed Church that he had favored Manicheanism in his articles in the *Dictionnaire*. In "Pauliciens," Bayle had said, "Who will not admire and deplore the fate of our reason? Behold that here the Manicheans, with a completely absurd and contradictory hypothesis, explain experiences a hundred times better than do the orthodox. . . ."[16] In his second clarification, appended to the second edition of the *Dictionnaire* of 1702, dealing with Manicheanism, Bayle made the irrationality and the fideistic side of his "defense" even sharper. At the conclusion of this essay, he said that his views about Manicheanism would not give offense if one remembered that the religious mysteries are liable to objections that natural reason cannot answer, that the explanation of evil in religious terms is "one of the most incomprehensible mysteries of Christianity," and that Manicheanism, considered in itself, is contrary to the ideas of or-

[15] Bayle, art. "Manicheans," Rem. D, p. 152, and art. "Paulicians," Rem. E, esp. pp. 168 and 175–76.
[16] Bayle, art. "Paulicians," Rem. E, p. 173.

der, has all sorts of difficulties as an explanation, and that Bayle's view is actually what the most orthodox theologians say. He ended this "defense" with,

> There will perhaps be some people who will find my ref-
> utation of Manicheanism imperfect because I do not answer
> the objections set forth by me as made by the Manicheans. I
> beg those who are bothered about this to remember that as
> for evident answers drawn from the natural light, I do not
> know of any, and as for answers that Scripture can furnish,
> they are found in innumerable controversial books.[17]

Bayle's contention that, regardless of how it might appear, what he was saying was the same as what was put forth by the most orthodox theologians is borne out by a look at the *Jugement sur les méthodes rigides et relâchées, d'expliquer la providence et la grâce* by Bayle's arch-enemy, Pierre Jurieu. Bayle keeps re-ferring to this work as the source of his theology, and, no matter how perverse or scandalous Bayle's views on theological matters became, he always insists that he is just saying what that most orthodox theologian, Pierre Jurieu, asserts.[18] In the *Jugement sur les méthodes*, Jurieu attacks all sorts of liberal, moderate or ra-tional theories of Providence and Grace, charging them with Pelagianism. (Manicheanism is not discussed at all as a possible ex-planation of what is going on.) Every theory that tries to avoid making God the author of evil gets into insoluble problems, "Car tout aussi-tôt qu'on reconnoît une Providence générale & qui s'étend à tout, de quelque manière qu'on la conçoive la difficulté renaît, & quand on croit avoir fermé une porte, elle rentre par une autre."[19] We have to accept that God is a perfect and all-good

[17] Bayle, Second Clarification, "How what I have said about the objec-tions of the Manicheans should be considered," p. 420.

[18] Jurieu, in his final answer to Bayle, *Le Philosophe de Roterdam accusé, atteint et convaincu* (Amsterdam 1706), desperately tried to show how his views are not the same as Bayle's irrationalistic fideism. Cf. esp. pp. 110–18. Nonetheless, Jurieu's theology, as Bayle was always glad to show, was, at least partially, irrationalistic and fideistic, and could be used to defend Bayle's contentions.

[19] Pierre Jurieu, *Jugement sur les méthodes rigides et relâchées, d'ex-pliquer la providence et la grâce* (Rotterdam 1686), p. 105. This work is a most interesting critique of late 17th-century theodicies. Both it and its author deserve more scholarly attention.

being, and that He is the cause of everything, including evil. How this is possible is a mystery. But since we cannot understand anything about God, there is no reason for not accepting the mystery.[20]

Bayle follows Jurieu's view that it is not possible to give an adequate or consistent account of the occurrence of evil on orthodox Christian terms. This orthodox view recognizes the unintelligibility of the events, given the revealed premises the believer accepts. Bayle just adds to this picture two features which he contends are related to the orthodox thesis; one, that Manicheanism is more consistent and satisfying as a rational and natural explanation of the occurrence of evil;[21] the other, that the believer should just announce that God is the only cause, that He is all-good and is the cause of evil, on the basis of faith in Scripture, and nothing more. By making the ridiculousness of the announcement most apparent through his brilliant dissection of various religious explanations of the problem of evil, Bayle succeeded in making the Manichean theory more appealing for those eighteenth-century thinkers who were losing or who had lost their faith. If the counter-case to Christianity was more satisfying as an account of what was going on for enlightened and rational man, why then fly to a blind faith in an unintelligible view presented in Scripture rather than accept the rational conclusion? If the counter-case to Christianity is more consistent and reasonable, what does this show about the merits of Christianity for those imbued with the Newtonian spirit of enquiry? Bayle's alleged fideism, always put in the most absurd and jocular vein, ceased to have any serious appeal as a way of dealing with intellectual problems. Then the "orthodox" presentation put forth by Bayle no longer was a way of defending Calvinist predestination theory, but a way of showing the intellectual force and appeal of anti-Christianity. If it could be the case that the heretical Manichean theory, which no serious philosopher had held to since Saint Augustine, was actually a more satisfactory explanation of the world we live in, then

[20] Jurieu, *ibid.*, p. 116.

[21] Jurieu held that the view that beliefs should be based on evidence, was, among other things, Manichean, in that the Manicheans want to base faith on reason. Cf. Jurieu, *La Religion du Latitudinaire avec l'apologie pour la Sainte Trinité, appellée l'heresie des trois Dieux* (Rotterdam 1696), pp. 332 – 32.

the intellectual force and appeal of the Christian world-view would be seriously, if not fatally, weakened for an age which put considerations of natural reason first, and which regarded a retreat to faith as part of the dark, unenlightened superstitious ages of the infancy of mankind. And so, Bayle's bombshell, taken out of its fideistic setting in his works, supplied the Enlightenment with a major anti-Christian, anti-Jewish perspective, a major way of showing the inadequacy and the intellectual silliness of the Biblical view of the world. Theologians and philosophers like Isaac Jacquelot,[22] Bishop King and G. W. Leibniz could devote their intellectual energies to trying to show that the problem of evil could be explained rationally and within the theistic assumptions of Judeo-Christianity (and offering arguments that Bayle had already pretty well disposed of[23]), but the damage had already been done. Practically no one may have become a Manichean as the result of Bayle, but many were reinforced in their anti-Christian tendencies by seeing that the theory long regarded as abominable, absurd, etc., by Christendom could be shown to be much more plausible and consistent than Christianity if judged apart from the Revelation. Manicheanism after Bayle, if not really a live option, was at least a living way of seeing the inadequacy of Christianity as *the* way of explaining the known world in rational-scientific terms. Bayle, in reviving and reinforcing the arguments for Manicheanism vis-à-vis the orthodox account of the occurrence of evil, had offered the following generations of intellectuals a way of exposing the theoretical weakness of Christianity once they no longer had much faith. And so, as David Hume summed up the intellectual situation towards the end of the eighteenth century, if one had antecedent knowledge that a good God caused everything, it might be possible à la Leibniz and Dr. Pangloss to figure out an account for the miserable events that take place. But if one started with the facts of human and natural history, then one would have to admit that, "Here the MANI-CHAEAN system occurs as a proper hypothesis to solve this diffi-

22 See Isaac Jacquelot's *Examen de la Théologie de Mr. Bayle* (Amsterdam 1706), esp. part II.

23 For instance, see David Norton's "Leibniz and Bayle: Manicheism and Dialectic," *Journal of the History of Philosophy*, II (1964), pp. 23 – 36.

culty [the occurrence of evil]: And no doubt, in some respects, it is very specious, and has more probability than the common hypothesis, by giving a plausible account of the strange mixture of good and ill which appears in life."[24] Hume, as we shall see, like almost everyone else, did *not* adopt Manicheanism as an explanation for what is going on. But he did see it, and use it, as a counterfoil to the previous prevailing orthodoxy to show how intellectually weak the Christian theodicy was.

Bayle's presentation of the theoretical merits of Manicheanism was the major way that this heretical view came alive, and played a vital role in eighteenth-century thought. Another quite different and much less significant factor in the revival of Manicheanism was that of Isaac de Beausobre, who had been a French Reformed minister in Saumur, Holland and Germany. Beausobre claimed that he was doing what Bayle should have done, that is, setting forth a precise and careful account of the history of Manicheanism, rather than amusing himself by inventing arguments for it, and pushing them forward. In the course of his elaborate two-volume "objective" study of the matter, Beausobre not only made clear what the Manichean views and practices were, but he also tried to show how plausible and how innocuous they were, and to excuse what had usually been taken as the dangerous heretical element. First of all, Beausobre insisted, there is nothing more evident than the existence of God, and nothing more obscure than His Nature. The Manicheans, along with everyone else, have just been trying to comprehend the incomprehensible, with some good and some bad results, in many ways resembling various ancient Jewish and Greek theories.[25] The Manichean theory, he maintained, developed from a denial of creation *ex nihilo*, and from the belief in the pre-existence and eternity of matter, the cause of evil. These views were held almost universally before the origin of Christianity and, he argued, were plausible on the then state of knowledge and understanding.[26] And, if matter

[24] David Hume, *Dialogues Concerning Natural Religion*, ed. N. Kemp Smith, 2nd ed. (Edinburgh 1947), Part XI, p. 211.

[25] Beausobre, *Histoire critique de Manichée et du Manicheisme* (Amsterdam 1734), Livre III, Chaps. 1 and 2, I, pp. 465 – 487.

[26] *Ibid.*, Livre V, Chaps. 1 – 6, II, pp. 144 – 254.

were the cause of all evil, then "Manichée étoit forcé de dire, ou que Dieu n'a point crée la Matière, ou que Dieu est la Cause des Maux, extrémité qu'il vouloit éviter à quelque prix que ce fût."[27] So, the reasonable Manichean motive, to avoid making God the author of evil, led to the two-principle theory. And, Beausobre insisted, all of the ancient thinkers were trapped in the same dialectical net until and unless they became capable of denying the basic assumption that matter is the necessary cause of evil, and of accepting the doctrine of creation *ex nihilo*. The long philosophical and theological tradition of antiquity made it historically intelligible that many people would become Manicheans. The initial inconceivability of the creation-*ex-nihilo* thesis, and the fact that this thesis is only known by history and tradition (presumably the Bible and the Oral Tradition) made it difficult for many to accept the new point of view. By now, since different assumptions are made, the belief in the eternity of matter would be an important metaphysical error. But Beausobre insisted that Manicheanism, as a theory, though wrong on Christian and modern metaphysical standards, only constituted a philosophical error, and not a religious one, unless certain irreligious conclusions were drawn from it.[28]

The charge that Manicheanism was so awful because of the abominable practices that followed from it is rebutted by Beausobre by arguing that these purported practices did not actually occur, and that the nasty Catholics have invented the slanderous accusations. Bayle had been willing to accept Bossuet's innuendo at face value, but Beausobre insisted on going back into the written records to see if there was any basis for claiming that the Manicheans engaged in "hideous" sexual-religious practices (so "hideous" that he was afraid to describe them except in a Latin footnote). After examining the charges, and the sources for them, Beausobre concluded, "Il me semble que j'ai suffisament démontré que les abominations Manichéennes sont de pures calomnies."[29]

Beausobre's "defense" of Manicheanism is hardly like Bayle's. He does not argue that Manicheanism is now a superior or more

27 *Ibid.*, II, p. 269.
28 *Ibid.*, II, pp. 239–240 and 245.
29 *Ibid.*, II, p. 744.

plausible explanation of the occurrence of evil, but only that it once was, and that its development and popularity can be accounted for. In also contending that Manicheanism, as a theory, is not so bad, as long as it is kept from reaching certain irreligious conclusions, and as a practice, it was not hideous or abominable, Beausobre really was minimizing it as a negative force to Christianity. His long erudite work, though "scandalous" in saying so many good things about the notorious Manichean heretics, and in defending their honor, hardly caused the stir that Bayle's treatment of the subject did. The Jesuits attacked Beausobre in the *Mémoires de Trévoux*. Frederick the Great seems to have been impressed, and both Gibbon and Voltaire were influenced by Beausobre's presentation,[30] but were it not for Bayle's breathing new force and new life into Manicheanism, all Beausobre's learning would have amounted to little but pedantic information. Coupled with Bayle's effect on the Republic of Letters, Beausobre's "objective" picture of how Manicheanism arose, and to what degree it was plausible, moral and even religious, helped reinforce the renewed interest in and concern with the ancient heresy.

Three Enlightenment figures who exhibit this interest and concern are Gibbon, Hume, and Voltaire. For Gibbon, the Paulicians and the Cathari represent not the villains of the Middle Ages, as they did for Bossuet, but a heroic liberating anti-Christian force. Their Manicheanism led them to challenge fundamental religious and institutional tenets of Christianity. The medieval persecutions of these heretics brought "the seeds of reformation" to the West; "the invincible spirit which they had kindled still lived and breathed in the Western world." The Paulicians and their heirs "protested against the tyranny of Rome, embraced the Bible as the rule of faith, and purified their creed from all the visions of the Gnostic theology."[31] Rather than seeing Manicheanism as part of the dark side of man's early history, Gibbon portrayed it as

[30] See the article on Beausobre in Alexander Chambers, *The General Biographical Dictionary*, IV, pp. 293 – 94.

[31] Edward Gibbon, *The Decline and Fall of the Roman Empire* (London 1957), Vol. V, Chap. LIV, p. 501. The whole chapter is a very laudatory picture of the role of the medieval Manicheans.

one of the best things that ever happened. He happily embraced
Bossuet's claim that the Reformation is due to medieval Manicheanism, and made it the force that supplied the vital energy
needed for the Reformation, which, in turn, in spite of its aberra-
tions, destroyed the forces of superstition and authority. Gibbon
was not really concerned with the merits of Manicheanism as a
doctrine *per se*, but with the effects of it as a movement. As such, its
effects were most salutary, and the medieval Manicheans deserved
to be considered among the nobler ancestors of modern enlightened man. It was, of course, to be expected that in Gibbon's
overturning of the traditional evaluation of the contribution of
Christianity to world civilization, the contributions of the anti-
Christians, such as the Manicheans, would rise in esteem and interest. The destructive effects of the Manicheans on organized
Christianity were their real achievements. Their doctrines were
mainly meritorious for justifying their attacks on Christian superstition and authority. Thus, for Gibbon, Manicheanism is of interest and concern mainly for its role in enabling us to reach the
Age of Enlightenment, rather than as a theory to guide us today.

It is Voltaire and Hume who took it most seriously as a doctrine, as *the* explanation for what is going on, and who finally
gave it up, on much the grounds that Bayle condemned it, as the
philosophy of the Enlightenment. Voltaire derived his interest
and concern with Manicheanism from both Beausobre and Bayle.
All his life he was concerned with the problem of evil, and like
many of his contemporaries, such as Alexander Pope, he was trying to explain it. Apparently it was only late in his career that
Voltaire gave serious consideration to the material and arguments
in Bayle and Beausobre. The evidence from his discussions of the
problem of evil indicates that it was Beausobre's learned tomes
which had the first impact on Voltaire. He had read Bayle's views
on Manicheanism by the 1730's, but was not particularly impressed. Neither was he excited when Frederick the Great wrote
him about Beausobre in 1736, or eulogized him in 1738.[32] But in
1752, when Voltaire suddenly became completely concerned with

[32] Haydn T. Mason, "Voltaire and Manichean dualism," *Studies on
Voltaire and the Eighteenth Century* (ed. T. Besterman), XXVI (Geneva
1963), pp. 1144 – 46; and *Pierre Bayle and Voltaire* (Oxford 1963), pp. 68 – 9.

the Manichean theory, it was apparently Beausobre who aroused his interest, and then he began to realize the force of Bayle's discussions.[33] For Voltaire the problem of explaining the occurrence of evil became more and more vexing in terms of the data of history and present-day human experience. Accounting for the Lisbon Earthquake posed the problem more forcefully. The "optimism" of Leibniz, Shaftesbury, and Pope that, in spite of what was or is happening, ultimately all is good, became not only unacceptable, but also a travesty. Voltaire was able to see Manicheanism as a genuine counter-explanation that would make much more sense of the actual events. In *Candide*, Voltaire introduced a main character, Martin, who could say "mais la vérité du fait est que je suis manichéen."[34] When Candide said that he must be kidding, since there are no Manicheans left in the world, Martin replied that he really was one, and that he was unable to think in any other way. Martin's Manicheanism goes well beyond Bayle's version. Not only is the positive independent existence of evil a more plausible way of accounting for what goes on, it also provides a most pessimistic means for social criticism. Bayle had offered the history of wars, disasters, etc., and man's injustice to man as *a posteriori* evidence of the plausibility of Manicheanism. Martin portrays everything that he and Candide see outside of El Dorado as a vast panorama of evil. Everything occurring in human affairs is bad — "je vous avoue qu'en jetant la vue sur ce globe, ou plutôt sur ce globule, je pense que Dieu l'a abandonné à quelque être malfaisant. . . ."[35] It is not just that there are two fundamental causal principles, one good and one evil, but Martin's grim vision is much worse, that only the evil principle is operative in the human world. The pessimistic note in Bayle's presentation has been transformed or extended into one of utter hopelessness. All human existence is seen as the result of the operation of the bad force, and nothing can be done about it. As an interpretation of the human scene, Voltaire makes Martin's picture *the* answer to

[33] Voltaire, letter to Formey, 2 Jan. 1752, in *Correspondence*, Besterman ed., #4158. See Mason, "Voltaire and Manichean Dualism," pp. 1147–48, and *Bayle and Voltaire*, p. 69.

[34] Voltaire, *Candide*, Bilingual edition ed. by Peter Gay (New York 1963), p. 180.

[35] *Ibid.*, p. 180.

optimism. Not only is it as consistent as the Leibniz-Shaftesbury-Pope view, it becomes overwhelmingly convincing as the way to construe all events. Martin's Manicheanism becomes not just a dialectical way of showing how unreasonable Judeo-Christianity or optimism is, but a horrible nightmarish possibility that might actually characterize the events of human history. The overpowering force of this negative picture of the world becomes so great and so tempting that at the end Martin says: "Travaillons sans raisonner, . . . c'est le seul moyen de rendre la vie supportable."[36] Apparently any attempt to understand the world would lead to seeing the real strength of Martin's version of Manicheanism, and along with this, the utter hopeless pessimism of this view. The effect of such a realization would be completely demoralizing, and would make living in such a doomed world unbearable.

Voltaire probably was not a Manichean, but he was very strongly tempted by the version he introduced as both an explanation of why the world is as bad as it is, and a pessimistic reaction to the eighteenth-century scene. One of Voltaire's enemies, the Abbé C. M. Guyon, had said of *Candide* that "la fureur de M. de V. & de ses Confrères est de vouloir rétablir le Manichéisme,"[37] and Voltaire had written Frederick II in 1759, "Je suis Manichéen comme Martin."[38] Events like the Seven Years' War and the Lisbon Earthquake had sorely shaken Voltaire's faith in the ultimate goodness of events and in hopeful developments to come. At the period when this gloomy outlook was growing on him, Voltaire enthusiastically read Beausobre, and probably reconsidered the Manichean materials in Bayle. In these circumstances, Martin's Manicheanism (which bears only a very slight resemblance to the original or medieval variety) became a living option for him. Rather than just as a theoretical possibility, as it was for Bayle, or as an appealing past historical phenomenon, as it was for Beausobre and Gibbon, Martin's Manicheanism seems to have been a frightening vision of the world that its author, Voltaire, actually

[36] *Ibid.*, p. 296.

[37] Abbé Claude Marie Guyon, *Suite de l'Oracle des nouveaux philosophes* (Berne 1760), p. 410.

[38] Voltaire, letter to Frederick II, c. 5 June 1759, in *Correspondence*, ed. Besterman, #7617.

saw as a genuine possible picture of what was going on. In this respect Voltaire may well have been the only man of modern times who actually envisioned what a Manichean world might be like. He saw that just taking the theory seriously destroyed the plausibility of either the traditional Judeo-Christian picture of the world, or that of the modern optimists.

But Martin's Manicheanism was so negative and so hopeless that not even its author could fully accept it, especially when living in such an enthusiastic age. The problem of why there is evil in the world may not be soluble, and Manicheanism may be both the sole theory that relieves God of the responsibility for the occurrence of evil, as well as the most plausible account. But, at the same time some factors led Voltaire both in *Candide* and afterwards to refuse to assent completely to Martin's gloomy theory about the world.

If all events were caused by the evil principle, then everything should be bad. But even the glummest social criticism only reveals that sometimes bad events occur, and that their occurrence is intermittent. Wars, murders, etc., are exceptional and unusual events, not the regular ones, as should be the case if mankind were entirely ruled by the evil principle. If there are then two or more causal principles that govern all events, and, in classical Manichean terms, are warring with each other, there should be just a chaotic confusion of events, instead of the regular lawful cosmic order discovered in Nature by Newtonian science. The order in Nature for Voltaire, as well as for Bayle and Hume, became a final bulwark against the adoption of Manicheanism as *the* theory of nature of the universe. The overwhelming force of the evidence of lawful patterns and of design indicated that ultimately one force caused or ruled all events. The fact that all events are not bad further indicated that this force could not be the one of Martin's Manicheanism.[39]

Although Voltaire may not have shared the optimism of Pope, or the enthusiasm of doctrine-of-progress advocates like Condorcet and Condillac, he was unwilling to come to the conclusion that ultimately all is hopeless. He construed the version of Mani-

[39] Mason, *Bayle and Voltaire*, p. 75, and Voltaire, *Dictionnaire philosophique*, ed. J. Benda et R. Naves (Paris 1954), art. "Méchant," pp. 301 – 4.

cheanism set forth in Bayle's articles as making evil completely ineradicable. When he first contemplated the destruction unleashed by the Lisbon Earthquake, and the explanations that could be offered to account for this, he could only conclude that all that man could do was "souffrir, se soumettre en silence, adorer, et mourir." After exploring the depths of the Manichean vision and concluding, as he did in *Micromégas* and elsewhere, that man is unable to comprehend what is ultimately going on in the universe, Voltaire added, "Mais il pouvait encore ajouter l'*espérance.*"[40] And there was enough reformist optimism in his soul, so that *Candide* ended not with Martin's pessimism, and his rejection of theorizing as the only way to make life bearable, but with Candide's statement, "il faut cultiver notre jardin."[41] At least there was some limited, not entirely futile, way of dealing with the universe. For Voltaire, and perhaps only for him in the Enlightenment, there had been a genuine struggle with the possibility that Manicheanism might be true. As one recent commentator has said, "To Bayle, the problem of evil is a polemical controversy; for Voltaire it is a personal torment."[42] The totally negative and totally hopeless picture of the world offered by Martin apparently for a period seemed to Voltaire the explanation of why there is evil in the world. Manicheanism, so construed, was hardly the liberating force that Gibbon had made of it, nor the great revolutionary reform movement it had been in the Middle Ages (as the rationale for struggling against existent evil). It was the counsel of ultimate despair. In order to reject it, and to leave some most minimal room for hope, Voltaire was willing to pay the price of a fundamental ultimate scepticism. Attempts at theoretical explanation had to be set aside in order to avoid coming to Martin's Manichean view. The few straws had to be held most firmly that indicated that there can be any way of finding a good

[40] Voltaire, "Poème sur le désastre de Lisbonne," in *The Age of Enlightenment*, ed. O. E. Fellows and N. L. Torrey (New York 1942), p. 436. N. 43 gives Voltaire's original ending. In n. 45 it is pointed out that one manuscript reads, "Mais pouvait-il encore ajouter l'*espérance?*" See George R. Havens, "The Conclusion of Voltaire's *Poème sur le désastre de Lisbonne,*" *Modern Language Notes*, LVI (1941).

[41] Voltaire, *Candide*, p. 298.

[42] Mason, *Bayle and Voltaire*, p. 77.

rather than a bad universe, a glimmer of hope rather than complete gloom. Working without theorizing, and adoring the world rather than despising or cursing it, allowed for a kind of rejection of Martin's Manicheanism. Bayle's arguments for the plausibility of Manicheanism had gone too far to allow for the theoretical rejection of the view, or for the theoretical adoption of the Judeo-Christian or optimistic alternatives. But Voltaire's transformation of the pessimistic element in Bayle's version into a totally negative view had made Manicheanism too gloomy even for a pretty pessimistic eighteenth-century figure. And so, Voltaire, rather than give in to complete despair, personally opted for an ultimate doubt about the nature of the universe, a non-theoretical life of limited action and a somewhat optimistic adoration of the cosmos in the hope that it was ultimately good in some sense.

A related but somewhat different Enlightenment reaction to Bayle's revived and reformulated Manicheanism is that offered by David Hume, near the end of his *Dialogues on Natural Religion*. In Part X, Hume pointed out all the evidences of the occurrence of evil at all levels in this world, and then contended, à la Bayle, that it was not possible to infer from the evidence of what happens that the cause must be good. In Part XI (the main discussion of the issue), Hume admitted that if we knew antecedently that the world was created by a supreme intelligence, benevolent and powerful, we might be able to maintain an optimistic view, that all is *really* good, by stressing, again in the style of Bayle, our ignorance as to what is really going on, and why it is. But, if we have to judge what kind of causal principles may be operating from what we experience, and if we consider the kinds of evils that do, in fact, occur, then "Here the MANICHEAN system occurs as a proper hypothesis to solve the difficulty."[43] The Manichean theory, Hume saw, is more plausible than the Judeo-Christian view, if one were at the stage where everything is to be judged from experience rather than in terms of any revelatory information. If one were enlightened enough to reason solely from experience, Manicheanism would be one of the principal hypotheses to be considered.

Having seen its plausibility, its advantage over Christian the-

[43] Hume, *Dialogues*, Part XI, p. 211.

odicy and even a purely Deistic optimism, Hume then proceeded to reject Manicheanism. And, unlike Voltaire, who chose an unintelligible world rather than a Manichean one, Hume chose a valueless one. The basic grounds for rejecting Manicheanism are for Hume what they were for both Bayle and Voltaire, the order in the universe. There are four general possibilities for explaining the occurrence of evil — that the first causes "are endowed with perfect goodness, *that* they have perfect malice, *that* they are opposite and have both goodness and malice, *that* they have neither goodness nor malice."[44] The first two theories are rejected immediately because the experienced mix of phenomena cannot lead to the inference of unmixed causes. Hence only Manicheanism and a valueless universe remain as genuine possibilities. But experience seems to rule out Manicheanism — "the perfect uniformity and agreement of the parts of the universe" do not reveal "any marks of the combat of a malevolent with a benevolent being." Further, "the uniformity and steadiness of general laws seem to oppose" the Manichean hypothesis.[45] Bayle had appealed to our innate ideas of order as to what made Manicheanism ultimately unacceptable, no matter how plausible it might be. Hume appealed to our experience of order. But, unlike Bayle, Hume was not interested in making this rejection of Manicheanism in a Newtonian world the basis for an appeal to faith. Instead, he maintained, "the true conclusion is, that the original source of all things is entirely indifferent to all these principles [of good and evil], and has no more regard to good above ill than to heat above cold, or to drought above moisture, or to light above heavy." This theory of cosmic indifference to values "seems by far the most probable."[46]

Hume, for all of his cynicism about Enlightenment reformist and optimistic views (as expressed, for example in his "Idea of a Perfect Commonwealth"[47]), may have still been sufficiently in-

[44] *Ibid.*, p. 212.

[45] *Ibid.*, pp. 211 and 212.

[46] *Ibid.*, p. 212.

[47] Hume, "Idea of a Perfect Commonwealth," in *Essays and Treatises on Several Subjects* (London 1768), II, p. 563, "Of all mankind there are none so pernicious as political projectors, if they have power; nor so ridiculous, if they want it."

fected with the aspirations of his age to be unwilling to accept what seemed to be the incurable pessimism involved in Bayle's version of Manicheanism. By advancing as an alternative a theory of a valueless universe, of cosmic indifference, and a basically unknowable cause or source of order in the universe, Hume did not preclude the possibility of human endeavor somewhat and in some ways improving man's lot. The theory of cosmic indifference could be compatible with a mild Pelagian attitude, that man could do something to make matters better or worse for man, instead of the envisaged futility involved in Bayle's version of Manicheanism. Both Hume and Voltaire were too much impressed by the Newtonian revolution, even if they failed to be taken in by the argument from design, to accept a Manichean view. They were, however, too impressed by Bayle's dialectical defense of Manicheanism to take seriously the Judeo-Christian or optimistic solution to the problem of evil. Hume opted instead for a valueless universe, rather than one believed to be ultimately good, to be struggled with for whatever good man might produce. This Humean view would lead finally to the "heroic" pessimism of Bertrand Russell's *A Free Man's Worship*, that man should struggle for betterment in the face of a *totally* indifferent cosmos.

The revival of interest and concern with Manicheanism in the late 17th century may have initially been due to an attempt by Catholics like Bossuet to blacken the character of the Reformation, but due primarily to Bayle's counter-attack, and to a lesser degree Beausobre's historical defense, Manicheanism played a vital role in Enlightenment thought. Bayle's contention that Manicheanism was more plausible, according to the natural light, than the Judeo-Christian explanation of the occurrence of evil, fed the Enlightenment disdain for Christian theodicy by showing that the counter-case to Christianity made better sense in terms of the natural, rational, scientific evidence available. This, reinforced with Beausobre's contention that Manicheanism was plausible until the creation-*ex-nihilo* theory was adopted, allowed for a way of opposing Christianity on the level of pure reason alone. If only rational standards were involved, how could one opt for Christianity, or even Deistic optimism, if Manicheanism actually were a more plausible theory?

But, even if Manicheanism could loom large as a counterploy to traditional or renovated theodicies during the Enlightenment, even the best argumentation of Bayle could not make it into an acceptable theory, even to Bayle. Some like Gibbon might see it as the heroic forerunner to Enlightenment, but none, except perhaps for Voltaire during the 1750's, could see it as a real present-day option. The reason for this seems to be that Bayle's version of Manicheanism ran counter both to the ideology of Newtonian science and to the prevailing reformist optimism of the time. Bayle's version would lead to a theory of cosmic disorder, of evil and good in combat and confusion, and to a theory of hopelessness about the eradicability of evil. The overwhelming evidence of universal order seemed to rule out the possibility of cosmic conflict, and the vital conviction that the ills of mankind due to superstition, ignorance, war, etc., could be abolished seemed to rule out cosmic pessimism. In the face of this, Bayle fell back on a kind of blind fideism, Beausobre on a kind of Christian Deism. For Voltaire the problem was much graver, since he could really envisage a Manichean world, all evil. Through Martin he could present a picture of the world as nothing but gloom. But rather than accept this, Voltaire was willing to give up all theorizing, adopt a fundamental scepticism about our ultimate knowledge of the cosmos, and thus retain a hope that the world was nonetheless good, and that our limited efforts could be beneficial. Hume, since he apparently did not suffer from a crisis about the problem of evil, was able to go beyond the mere acceptance or rejection of the Manichean possibility to advancing another that could preclude the whole problem — namely denying any values to the causal principles of the world, and making the question, why is there evil, unanswerable and meaningless unless transformed into a secular problem.

Bayle's version of Manicheanism reinforced one side of Enlightenment thought, its rejection of Christian cosmology, so that it could appeal to the avant-garde. But it ran so counter to its Newtonianism and reformism that even the most sceptical and cynical, like Voltaire and Hume, could not accept it. Bayle's dialectical defense of Manicheanism probably played a major role in undermining intellectual confidence in the Christian world-view, but in those it affected most, it led them to seek either desperately or calmly for more acceptable explanations. Bayle had made Manicheanism into a form of cosmic pessimism, and even the least sanguine of the Enlightenment were not willing to accept that completely. The Enlightenment had too much of a Pelagian tinge to admit defeat on the cosmic level.

In conclusion, it seems odd that although original and medieval forms of Manicheanism were either revolutionary or decidedly reformist movements, the version that made sense in the Enlightenment was neither of these. Perhaps interpreting the Manichean claim in terms of 17th-century substance metaphysics could only lead to the view that if evil genuinely exists, and is caused by an independently existing bad substance, then it cannot be removed from the scene. Such a view would be completely alien to a Pelagian temper of mind, even though earlier Manicheanism could and did provide a rationale for Pelagianism (namely that because the good and evil forces were in combat, human action could aid the good side). The type of theory of metaphysical causality offered by a Descartes, a Spinoza or a Leibniz would lead to the contention that if there were two separate and distinct substances, not in harmony, the resulting events would be chaotic. Manicheanism then, put in the metaphysical frame of the time, would become alien to the prevailing ideology. Its superiority as an explanation of evil could not make up for its basic conflict with the fundamental tenets of the time. And, thus, it would be better to deny, as Hume did, that there was any value causality at all in the universe than to accept the implications of a Manichean metaphysics.

And, if Manicheanism, construed in metaphysical terms, runs counter to Enlightenment ideology, it also seems to run counter to prevailing metaphysical theories from Neo-Platonism onward. Beausobre stressed the point that Manicheanism was plausible before the acceptance of the Christian creation-*ex-nihilo* theory to account for the existence of matter. This and the Plotinian metaphysical monism seem to have sapped the philosophical strength of Manicheanism, since it does not seem to have had any real philosophical defenders, even during its great days in the Middle Ages. Bayle was able to give it forceful, and even insurmountable arguments, but he was unable to make it metaphysically acceptable even to himself. And so, the adjustment to its arguments had to take the form of either complete metaphysical scepticism, or a denial of any metaphysical basis for values. The only form in which anyone seems to have been able to accept Manicheanism is as a form of demonism, as in the case of the Marquis de Sade. But the overtones of the monistic metaphysical tradition, and the rising strength of Pelagianism, especially in its secularized forms from the Enlightenment onward, seem to have precluded Manicheanism from being a live option for modern man. It may have played a strong role in bringing about the Enlightenment, in its Baylean version, but it could not become part of the Enlightenment. Bayle may be right that it is the best known explanation for the occurrence of evil in the world, but the monism of the Judeo-Christian tradition and of Neo-Platonism has left us a legacy that prevents our taking it seriously. Bayle's revival and revivification of Manicheanism may have given it a final moment of glory on the historical stage, and may have tempted the great Voltaire, but, placed in the context of a modern metaphysics and a modern social outlook, it could only appear too alien to be accepted. Perhaps, after the catastrophes of the 20th century have shaken our Pelagian confidence to its roots, and the strength of theological and metaphysical monism has been further eroded, a new Bayle will appear to show how *really* plausible Manicheanism is in the context of recent human history.

Schopenhauer Today

MAX HORKHEIMER

ARTHUR SCHOPENHAUER regarded fame with no less detachment than the majority of thinkers who finally gained it. Public recognition left him so indifferent that when he partook of it at last he did not even have to belittle it, either to himself or to others. He could relish the signs of future veneration and even succumb to the temptation of agreeing with Seneca's optimistic judgment that fame follows merit unfailingly. What great respect for the course of history! Only rarely did the philosopher show so much confidence in the verdict of a humanity, whose cultural decline he prophetically thought more plausible than its progress. As if there could be any certainty that among those forgotten there were no great men: indeed, hardly any age has demonstrated the universality of forgetting as clearly as has the present. In spite of our infinitely refined instruments of perception and its communication — not just because of them — only very few of those are remembered (let alone the thoughts they put on paper) who in Germany gave their lives in a lone attempt to put an end to the national disaster. They are of no lesser stature than their predecessors who were famous. They are gone. For Schopenhauer, however, justice from posterity was guaranteed, as it were, by that same history which in other respects he hated. Posterity was his longing, his utopia. Nietzsche, his successor, was not thus fooled. "I do not want any disciples," he says in *Ecce Homo*. "I

This paper is a translation by Robert Kolben of the author's "Die Aktualität Schopenhauers," in Max Horkheimer and Theodor W. Adorno, *Sociologica II* (Frankfurt a. M., 1962), pp. 124 – 141. The article was a lecture given on the occasion of the hundredth anniversary of Schopenhauer's death, 21 September 1960.

am terribly afraid of being canonized one day. People will understand why I publish this book before: it is to keep them from
playing tricks on me."[1] He was convinced that fame is as despi-
cable as the public opinion which awards it.

In regard to one's contemporaries, in regard to "up-to-dateness,"
Schopenhauer agrees with the author of *Thoughts Out of Season.*
One of the prime conditions of greatness, he writes in the *Parerga*,
is to have no respect at all for one's contemporaries, including
their opinions and views, and the praise and blame resulting from
them.[2] What is "up-to-date" in this sense is what happens to be
considered valid as a result of the interaction between material,
relatively spontaneous, interests and manipulated, secret, and
avowed ones. Truth itself, on the other hand, lies hidden, according to Democritus, deep in a well, and, according to Schopenhauer,
it gets a rap on the knuckles when it tries to come out. In any
case, it has had to hide itself again and again, depending on the
state of events, as Voltaire puts it in his allegory. Up-to-date literature, whether conceived with an eye to the market by instinct
or routine, serves the established order. Even the notion that opposes it is incorporated, assimilated, decontaminated. The controlled consumption of consumer and cultural goods in a
boom period is a match for everything. The late stage of society
is in all cultural matters at once cunning and unassuming, modest
and insatiable — in this respect similar to antiquity in its decline.
It manages to incorporate as its own ornament even criticism,
negative art, resistance. The less of a chance the historical situation gives great works actually to inspire human action, the fewer
the obstacles to their publication; the more diligence scholars
apply to them, the less significant is the effect of their writing.

Schopenhauer's work is not free from such "up-to-dateness."
Still, it has suffered from it less than the work of other great
philosophers, probably because it is so ill-suited to education for
efficiency, even academic efficiency. For that, it rejects too many
pet ideas of employees of Culture and Education; it calls neither

[1] Friedrich Nietzsche, *Gesammelte Werke* (Musarion-Ausgabe), München,
1928, vol. XXI, p. 276.

[2] Arthur Schopenhauer, *Sämtliche Werke*, E. Grisebach, ed., Leipzig, n.d.,
vol. V, par. 57, p. 94.

for Decision, nor for Engagement, nor for the Courage to Be. Schopenhauer does not compensate for the low wages society doles out to the guardians of the spirit by the consciousness of an office that is supposed to be superior to other trades. His work makes no promises. Neither in heaven nor on earth, neither for developed nor for underdeveloped peoples does it hold out that to which leaders of every political or racial hue claim to be guiding their faithful. The apparently comforting title, "On the Indestructibility of Our True Being through Death," announces a chapter that brings despair rather than solace. It is hardly fit to gain friends among the molders of public opinion, except perhaps by the element of denial, for it seems to attribute harshness to existence by showing that existence is necessarily harsh. But Schopenhauer does so little to clothe the negative in a semblance of meaning that he can hardly lead to resignation and conformism.

Yet he saw things too çlearly to exclude the possibility of historical improvement. The ending of almost all manual labor, especially of hard physical labor, is something he foresaw more precisely than most of the economists of his day. But he also suspected what could result from such a change. He took technical, economic, and social improvements into account, but from the very beginning he also perceived their consequences: blind devotion to success and a setback for a peaceful course of events. In sum, I might say, he saw the dialectic of such progress. Not unlike some left-wing Hegelians, who in this respect contradicted their teacher, he decidedly rejected the idea of the State's divinity. To Schopenhauer the good state is nothing else than the quintessence of a reasonable self-interest; its sanctions protect individuals from each other and its own citizens from other states. The state is no moral institution; it rests on force. "At the highest stage," he says, agreeing with the founders of socialism, "mankind would need no state."[3] But he saw no prospect of this ever happening. He deified nothing, neither state nor technology. The development of the intellect rests on that of needs. Hunger, the urge to power, and war have been the greatest promoters of knowledge. The idealistic fable of the ruse of reason, which extenuates the horrors of the past by pointing to the good ends they

[3] Schopenhauer, *Handschriftlicher Nachlass, ibid.*, vol. III, pp. 32 ff.

served, actually babbles out the truth: that blood and misery stick
to the triumphs of society. The rest is ideology.

In the century since Schopenhauer's death, history has had to
admit that he saw straight into its heart. In spite of all the internal
injustice in the various nations around the middle of the last century, there was still something like a European solidarity, a kind
of urbane intercourse among nations, a good deal of discretion
and even respect on the part of great nations towards small ones.
Since his death, history has entered a new phase, progressing
from a balance of power to ruthless competition among nations.
Stiffer competition spurred technology, and the armaments race
began. Rulers and ministers of state were in uniform. The anarchy
of nations and the arms race inevitably led to the age of world
wars, which in turn eventually resulted in the frantic urge for
power in all nations of the world. This was Schopenhauer's prognosis. Struggles among individuals and social groups, domestic
competition and concentration of power are supplemented and
outdistanced by competition and concentration of power abroad.
Schopenhauer shows what it is all about. Material interests, the
struggle for existence, prosperity, and power are the motor; history is the result.

Schopenhauer did not offer philosophic rationalizations for his
experiences of terror and injustice, even in countries with the
most humane administrations. History frightened him. Violent
political change which in recent times is usually brought about
with the aid of nationalistic enthusiasm, he detested. Not having
lived to see the decay of absolutism in its acute phase, with its
torture and witch-hunting, burnings at the stake and other methods of qualified execution, he was not interested in a change of
system. He would rather, as Goethe writes in the *West-Östliche
Diwan,* converse "with clever men, with tyrants" than set out for
the dictatorship of the "unified" people in the company of dema-
gogues and fanaticized masses. His hatred of "patriots" springs
immediately from the threat to his economic independence, resulting from nationalistic rebellions, but indirectly and theoretically,
this hatred is aimed altogether at nationalism and the nationalistic
age, which was then beginning. The fanaticism of unity and the
violence it announced repelled him. He suffered from the same

lack of enthusiasm for the so-called wars of liberation of Prussia as Goethe, and from the same fear of the French revolution of 1830 as Hegel. The great enlighteners of mankind have been very wary of The People as the highest value. Lessing once suggested that men should learn to recognize the stage when patriotism ceases to be a virtue.

"The Nation" — that was the word with which the new forces, opposed to absolutism, stirred up the people. Schopenhauer gave the Germans credit for not indulging, on the whole, in national pride as the English were doing, only one in fifty of whom was prepared to accept criticism of the "stupid and degrading bigotry" of their nation.[4] Of course, later the Germans made up for it all the more, and Schopenhauer was startled to meet in Germany with this kind of demagogy, with "this game of insidious swindlers."[5] For centuries thinkers had denounced mass suggestion and its identical opposite, the inaccessibility of seduced masses, as well as the ferocity of those who have come off badly — all as the result of domination. National pride, like the pride of individuals, is easily injured, even if the wound does not show for a long time. The revenge that follows is blind and devastating. There was a time when fanaticism was a distorted and misunderstood religion. Since St. Just and Robespierre it has taken on the form of exaggerated nationalism, which the strong men in the saddle, when the going is a bit rough, can conveniently call up to rationalize murky instincts. When in an ominous historical moment those in power, no matter how different from one another in other respects, have nothing more to offer to quell the dissatisfaction of the people, they can always let loose on them the peddlers of a nationalistic community, of this mirage of Utopia, and feed them the sugar pill of cruelty. But since historians are not altogether wrong in distrusting generalizations and reflect on differences rather than similarities (as did Schopenhauer) among ruling systems and socio-psychological mechanisms, the reign of terror which broke out in Europe in the first half of the twentieth century, not to speak of Asia and Africa, seemed to be an accident. Anyone who would have dared, in Schopenhauer's day or even at

[4] *Ibid.*, vol. IV, p. 404.
[5] *Ibid.*, vol. V, par. 126, p. 256.

the turn of the century, to predict the course of history up to the present moment would certainly have been decried as a blind pessimist. Schopenhauer was a clairvoyant pessimist.

His fear of the beginning enthusiastic nationalism is a sign of his modernity: to take no bribes from the *Zeitgeist*. He regarded world history sceptically, denouncing it as "the unchanging and permanent," indeed as the unhistorical.[6] Not that he overlooked variations in social injustice, characteristic of various ages and stamping the majority of the people as either slaves or serfs. As to poverty and slavery, he says in *Parerga:* "The fundamental difference is that slaves owe their origin to violence; the poor, to cunning." The reason for this perverted state of society, he continues, for "the general struggle to escape misery, for sea-faring that costs so many lives, for complicated trade interests, and finally for the wars resulting from all this," is at bottom greediness for that superabundance which does not even make men happy.[7] At the same time, such barbarism cannot be abolished, for it is the reverse side of refinement, an element of civilization. Schopenhauer did not remain behind the sociological knowledge of his day — he was faithful to the Enlightenment.[8]

His judgment of the historical situation is based on his theoretical philosophy. Among European philosophers, he pointed to Plato and Kant as his forerunners. What they have in common with him is the gap between the essence of things, that which in itself is, and the world in which men move. What men perceive, what strikes them, how they see everything, depends on their intellectual apparatus and their senses, which in turn depend on the conditions of their biological and social existence. The countryside has a different aspect to the farmer assessing its fertility, to the hunter on the lookout for game, to the fugitive seeking a hiding place, to the pilot trying for a forced landing, to the wanderer, the painter, the strategist, not to mention people of different cultures. And how much more different will it appear to an

[6] *Ibid.*, vol. II, p. 520.

[7] *Ibid.*, vol. V, par. 125, p. 253.

[8] Cf. my "Schopenhauer und die Gesellschaft," "Die Aktualität Schopenhauers," in Horkheimer and Adorno, *Sociologica II*, Frankfurt a. M., 1962, p. 114.

animal, tame or wild, bird or gnat, not only with regard to color, sound, and smell, but also to form and relations. Just as things in space and time are conditioned by the perceiving subject, so are space and time themselves, which are the spectacles, as it were, worn by all who can see, hear, and feel. Pascal once said that to a creature in an infinitesimal, microscopic world which we cannot even perceive, millennia may pass in one of our seconds — thus a human millennium might appear but a moment to some superhuman being. Empirical scientific knowledge, vital to progress, the technical miracles which are the result of observation and which can increase or reduce life's span, are therefore not truth itself but only the semblance of truth. Plato and Kant described the relation between the two spheres, essence and appearance, differently. To Plato, truth was a realm of ordered concepts, and things were their transitory images. Kant taught that the thing-in-itself — that is, being as it exists in eternity, apart from human or animal perspectives — furnishes the subject with the matter necessary for cognition, with the sensible facts, out of which the intellect, with its ordering functions, produces the unitary world, just as a machine processes raw material into the finished product.

This concept of transcendental apperception, with its power and its "file boxes" — the head-office, one might say, of the intellect — was modeled on factory and business management. The intellect manufactures something conceptually solid out of the flux of perceptions, as a factory produces commodities. Over and above the ordering functions, the categories are, so to speak, the goals toward which they work: the ideas of freedom, eternity, and justice, which show the intellect the direction it must take. That these can be found in reason, that they even constitute reason in a certain sense, is Kant's ground for the hope that knowledge, and with it that which is to be known, will attain truth at a point of infinity, and that truth is not merely a means but the fulfillment.

Kant's subtle rescue of utopia was preceded on the European continent by rationalistic systems, which might be regarded as a series of attempts to save, against losing odds, the perfection of eternal being from the onslaught of the new science that was trying to explore appearance. After the end of scholasticism these attempts continued in the seventeenth century with the help of bourgeois reason. The innate ideas from which these systems develop are halfway between Plato's Ideas and Kant's categorical functions. They claim evidence, and evidence is to guarantee the truth, good and sufficient in itself, vis-à-vis the changing, terrifying reality, which since the sixteenth century and the overseas discoveries was marked by social upheavals and religious wars resulting from them. The need for something constructive, something permanent as the meaning behind all change was the motive power of philosophy. In spite of methexis, Plato had left essence and appearance unreconciled: Ideas were everything, transient things nothing. After the coming of Christianity, the world required justification, whether by faith or by concepts.

Rationalism was undermined by scientific thinking, which had been imported from England, where, thanks to the growth of trade and self-government in the towns, the citizens had slowly adapted to reality in a long drawn-out process; where political consciousness took form as a kind of resignation that accorded with religious consciousness; where convention became a religious matter and religion a civic one, and abstract concepts without facts had long lost their prestige. Conceptual realism had made way for nominalism: facts came into their own right, and concepts were mere names. The Magna Charta asserted itself in the theory of knowledge; empiricist philosophy and the mental attitude attendant on it came to be accepted without much friction. But on the Continent this shift took place as a distinct break. The order whose term had come was here realized only much later, and whatever fails to occur at its proper time occurs with violence. Empiricism and the materialism related to it imply criticism, not only of the dominant philosophy and the original perfection of things which it had proclaimed, but also of the conditions of the world, of social and political reality. A new vision of the future world replaced the old: a universal rational society. From St. Augustine to Bossuet history had been understood as progress, as the history of salvation, in which the messianic kingdom was the necessary goal. Translating this into the secular sphere, Holbach and Condorcet saw social history as the path to earthly fulfillment. The dualism had remained: the better, future world was the meaning toward which men oriented themselves. The one thing which the empiricism of the European Enlightenment had in common with the rationalism it superseded was that the image of the future was couched in concepts which were as if innate and could dispense with empirical verification: liberty, equality before the law, protection of the individual, property. The remaining ideas that transcended facts, especially those of positive theology, fell before the empirical-sensualistic critique.

Schopenhauer's revolutionary philosophic achievement rests above all on the fact that in the face of pure empiricism he held to the original dualism that had been the basic theme of European philosophy up to Kant, but that, nevertheless, he did not deify the world-in-itself, the real essence. Since the time of Aristotle, Plato's great disciple, European thinking had held to the principle that the more real, steadfast, and eternal a being was, the greater its goodness and perfection. I know of no philosophic dogma as widely accepted as this one. Men were to orient themselves toward that which was most real: being-in-itself. Philosophy deduced the meaning and laws of transitory life from the eternal, thus expressing or implying satisfaction of all strivings and a reward for all good deeds. Only good could result from being at one with the most real, the best, the most powerful. In a more modern fashion, philosophers tried to base hope on human reason, that hope which formerly rested on the authority of the father and on revelation.

This is the philosophic conviction and at the same time the function of philosophy with which Schopenhauer broke. The highest, the most real, the metaphysical being to which philosophers had directed their view, away from the changing world of existing objects, is *not* at the same time the good. Degrees of reality are not degrees of perfection. Looking at the positively infinite, at the unconditional does not teach man how he should act; it is impossible to refer to the authority of being when one wishes a guide toward a decent course of action. The true essence which is at the bottom of all external things, the thing-in-itself as opposed to appearance, is something that everyone can discover within himself, if only he looks clearly enough and knows how to interpret the experiences of his own nature. It is the insatiable desire for well-being and enjoyment, a desire which wells up every time it has been satisfied, and not the reasons the intellect finds for such strivings, that make up the ineradicable reality of all that is alive, of existence altogether. In the struggle with nature and with men, the intellect serves as a weapon by providing rationalizations with which individuals, interest groups, and nations try to accommodate their demands to the moral precepts in force. The intellect is a function of the struggle for existence in individuals and in the species; it is kindled by resistance and vanishes with resistance.

Schopenhauer's theory of consciousness as a small part of the psyche, by which it is used as a tool — not to mention his many particular observations of normal and pathological psychology — anticipates the basic principle of modern psychoanalysis. The basis for his theory is the ever-flowing source of stimuli: unappeasable will. Each breath is followed by a silence that is already the desire for the next breath, and each moment which passes without satisfying this desire increases the need and its awareness, until they finally fade out. Breathing stands for life. So do eating and drinking: those cut off from them must fight for them, and the higher the stage of development of the living creature, the more subtle and insatiable the struggle becomes. Need and endless striving, kindled again and again, make up the content of history and determine man's relationship to Nature. If the air were not free but the result of work, men would fight for it as they do for land, and they could not do otherwise. Today it already seems as though they might actually have to fight for air. If there ever was an era that could confirm Schopenhauer's views, it is the period since the turn of the twentieth century, when reliance on progress was questioned least. For Schopenhauer the good is far more the ephemeral, thought, and appearance, than that which keeps reproducing itself.

Nevertheless he acknowledged himself a man of the eighteenth century. He was bitter toward the profundity of the "facetious philosophers" (a profundity widely disseminated today, too, in our schools and universities), who slandered "the greatest men of the last century, Voltaire, Rousseau, Locke, Hume . . . those heroes, those ornaments and benefactors of humanity."[9] He com-

9 Schopenhauer, *Sämtliche Werke, ibid.*, vol. III, p. 218.

plained that the venerable word "Enlightenment . . . has become a sort of term of abuse."[10] He identified himself most deeply with the fight against superstition, intolerance, and rationalistic dogmatism. What seemed to him suspect about the Enlightenment, even paradoxical, was the identification of what today or in the future exists in all its power — let alone of gory history — with what ought to be. As the epitome of the good, not even the idea of a future mankind whose members were not trying to exterminate each other, was an adequate compromise for him. He is no good as a reference for the prophets of secular salvation and of even less use to the defenders of the status quo. In the face of theology, metaphysics, and positive philosophy of all kinds, Schopenhauer withdrew philosophic sanction from the solidarity of those who are suffering, from the community of men lost in the universe, but without thereby advocating harshness. As long as there are hunger and misery on earth, he who can see will have no peace. In *Thoughts Out of Season*, Nietzsche quoted with enthusiasm the following passage from Schopenhauer's *Parerga:* "That man leads a heroic life who somehow or other, in spite of overwhelming difficulties and with little or no recompense, fights and eventually wins the battle for what will be of some benefit to all mankind."[11] The more lucid thinking is, the more will it drive towards the abolition of misery; and yet any assurance that this is the ultimate meaning of existence, the end of pre-history, the beginning of reason is nothing but an endearing illusion. The heroic, even the holy life, without ideology, is the consequence of suffering and rejoicing with others, of sharing in the lives of others; perceptive men cannot stop fighting horror until they die. The famous idea that, by devoting themselves completely to transcending egoistic aims, morally great individuals can step out of the cycle of reincarnations has nothing to do with positive bliss. Happiness itself is negative. Even the last utopian escape which his teacher Kant, the greatest German *Aufklärer*, wanted to offer — the idea of the ultimate purpose that human history was to fulfill — was to Schopenhauer, in the face of the horror of this earth, only rationalistic deception; the eudemonistic concept of "the Highest Good"

10 *Ibid.*, p. 216.
11 Nietzsche, *Gesammelte Werke, ibid.*, vol. VII, pp. 76 ff., quoting Schopenhauer, *Sämtliche Werke, ibid.*, vol. V, par. 172 bis, p. 337.

was still more so. Enlightened thought has no need of such illusions.

Basically, the classical idealism of Kant's successors, too, abandoned utopia. In that, they are like Schopenhauer. They regard the discrepancy between the world as it is and as it ought to be as overcome once this discrepancy is canceled in thought. Utopia survives only in rarefied form as the deified subject. The world as it appears is no longer that produced and constituted by men, as in Kant, but instead, as in Fichte, the result of free-floating action or, as in Schelling, the result of self-confirming primordial being. The thing-in-itself is identified with the subject, yet not as the negative but as the unconditioned positive. Hegel saw it as the living concept, the infinite movement, in which an antithesis between thing and thought shows itself as conditioned. But although Schopenhauer hated Hegel, he is not so far from him. The life of the concept, of the Hegelian Absolute, is the contradiction, the negative, the painful. What Hegel calls concept — the system of philosophical determinations that arise out of each other and are in eternal movement — is nothing but the rise and decline of what this system comprehends. The great achievement of Hegel's philosophy lies in the very fact that the concept does not exist outside and independently of what disappears and, as it does, is preserved in the concept. The consolation offered by his "wicked optimism" is in the end the insight into the necessary interweaving of the concepts into the whole, into that brittle unity that is called system. Hegel's recognition of logical structure in the worlds of nature and man, as emphasized in his doctrine of nature and objective mind, is by no means as far removed from Schopenhauer's aesthetic and philosophical reflections as Schopenhauer was inclined to think. Hegel speaks of substantive determination, of the absolute final purpose of world history; ultimately, world history moves towards the absolute mind, the philosophic system, towards mere insight into the whole. On the real course of history, on the other hand, Hegel says: "When we look at this spectacle of the passions and see the consequences of their violence, of the unreason associated not only with them but also, and even primarily, with good intentions and just aims; when we see the attendant wickedness and evil, the ruin of the most flourishing kingdoms which the human mind has produced; then we can only be filled with sorrow over this transitoriness and, insofar as this destruction is not only the work of nature but of the will of men, we must end up in moral grief, in a revolt of the good spirit, if such is in us, against such a spectacle."[12]

Decay and permanence, the dying of the particular and the being of the universal, are one. Hegel is far away from Fichte's positive pathos, even farther from his *Instructions for a Blessed Life* which, to be sure, had lost all eudemonistic attraction even for the author of the *Speeches to the German Nation*. In the destruction of false comfort, Schopenhauer goes a shade beyond Hegel by refusing to recognize, as the ground for deifying existence, the consistency of a system that encompasses the world and thus the development of mankind to the point where philosophic insight becomes possible. The social whole, too, the institutions in which the mind comes into its own, as in art and philosophy, must pass. The absolute mind adheres to the objective and subjective mind of nations, and their fate is to perish, like any group or individual, like anything finite. Reconciliation, the identity of opposites reached through thought, is no real reconciliation, whether it occurs in the present or future state of mankind. The violent stroke of genius by which Hegel, the last great systematizer of philosophy, rescued the positivity of the absolute by including agony and death in it, fails because insight is tied to the living subject and must perish with him.

Hegel's teaching shows that the positivity that distinguishes him from Schopenhauer cannot ultimately stand up. The failure of a logically stringent system in its highest form in Hegel, means the logical end of attempts at a philosophic justification of the world, the end of the claim of philosophy to emulate positive theology. All these attempts rest directly or indirectly on the idea of the world as the work or expression of true mind. But if the world, in its essence and in its actual condition, is *not* necessarily connected with mind, philosophic confidence in the very existence of truth disappears. In that case, truth can be found only in perishable men themselves and is as perishable as they are. Even thinking

[12] Hegel, *Sämtliche Werke*, H. Glockner, ed., Stuttgart, 1949, vol. XI, *Vorlesungen über die Philosophie der Geschichte*, pp. 48 ff.

about transitoriness loses the lustre of the more-than-transitory. Merely faith remains; the attempt to rationalize it was doomed to failure.

Schopenhauer's thinking is infinitely modern, so modern, in fact, that young people have it by instinct. This thinking knows about the contradiction of autonomous truth and is profoundly irritated by it. Philosophy does not move beyond real history. Young people no longer accept thinking that is philosophically out of date. If an attempt is made to pass over or mask the contradictions in which thought inevitably gets entangled, the young lose faith not only in the truthfulness of their elders but in the whole culture in which they participate and whose shares, for many internal reasons, have in any case dropped in value. Technology makes memory superfluous. The young have little reason left to believe the old and their reference to eternal commandments. They try to manage without them. At many universities in America and even in Eastern countries logical positivism has won out, supplanting philosophy. It takes thought itself as mere function, as business. There is no fundamental difference between the production of mathematical formulas and their application in technology and industry. Positivism presents the result implied in the failure of positive philosophy. We need not worry about philosophic truth, as it does not exist anyhow. That is the short-circuit which Schopenhauer's work avoids. He is driven by the passion for truth and, like Spinoza, devoted his life to this passion without making a job of it. But his philosophy gives perfect expression to what young people today feel: that there is no power that can transcend truth — indeed, that truth carries in it the character of powerlessness. According to Schopenhauer, positivism is right against metaphysics because there is nothing unconditional which might guarantee truth or from which it could be deduced. But theological metaphysics is right against positivism because every spoken statement cannot help but make an impossible claim not only concerning an anticipated effect, concerning success, as positivism believes, but also concerning truth in its proper sense, whether or not the speaker intends this. Without thinking about truth and thereby of what it guarantees, there can be no knowledge of its opposite, of the abandonment of mankind, for whose sake true philosophy is critical and pessimistic — there cannot even be sorrow, without which there is no happiness.

According to Schopenhauer, philosophy does not set up any practical aims. It criticizes the absolute claims of programs without itself proposing one. The vision of organizing the earth in justice and liberty, the basis of Kantian thought, has turned into the mobilization of nations and the uprising of peoples. Every revolt following the great French Revolution has reduced the substance of its humanistic content and increased nationalism — or so it appears. The greatest drama of the perversion of faith in humanity into an intransigent cult of the state was offered by socialism itself. The revolutionaries of the International fell victim to nationalistic leaders. A certain state of humanity, venerated as the true one, is an aim among others for which men may justifiably sacrifice themselves. But if it is hypostatized as the absolute aim, then, by definition, there is no authority, neither divine commandment, nor morality, nor even — and I think this is no less important — the personal relation called friendship, which could control it. Every finite being — and humanity is finite — which gives itself airs as the ultimate, the highest, the unique, becomes an idol with a demonic ability to change its identity and take on another meaning. The history of many recent revolutions, in contrast to the theory of Marx, offers frightening examples. Before they seized power, the aim of Lenin and most of his friends was a society of freedom and justice, yet in reality they opened the way to a terroristic totalitarian bureaucracy which certainly does not come closer to freedom than the empire of the Czar. The transition of the new China into sheer barbarism is obvious.

The new idol is the collective *We*. It is not the only one. Insofar as conditional aims or motives for life generally are presented to young people as if they were unconditional, they are met with the scorn of those who have become wise or with mock enthusiasm. They see through the conventionality of arguments for a respectable life that are not founded, as Schopenhauer advocated, on simple common sense and, ultimately, on penal law. Young people can see the unscrupulous practices of moral, adult persons. And just because they accept from their elders only their practical nimbleness but not their pathos, because they understand the

Idea only as a set of rationalizations, they have nothing with which to oppose mass deception. If it is expedient to accept it, it would be merely stupid to resist it. Added to this is an unavowed yearning, a feeling of insufficiency, and defiance, which by repeating evil, unconsciously tries to provoke the good, so that it will show itself even if it is lethal. A skeptical generation is no more immune to participation in misdeeds than is one of believers. Instead, their disillusioned life, despite all pressures toward a career, engenders the pervasive feeling of meaninglessness in which false faith has a fertile soil. In order to resist it, there would have to be a longing for that which is different, a longing that would have passed through culture without, however, having been victimized by any of its hardened forms.

Now I can be clearer about why Schopenhauer is the teacher for modern times. The doctrine of blind will as an eternal force removes from the world the treacherous gold foil which the old metaphysics had given it. In utter contrast to positivism, it enunciates the negative and preserves it in thought, thus exposing the motive for solidarity shared by men and all beings: their abandonment. No need is ever compensated in any Beyond. The urge to mitigate it in *this* world springs from the inability to look at it in full awareness of this curse and to tolerate it when there is a chance to stop it. For such solidarity that stems from hopelessness, knowledge of the *principium individuationis* is secondary. The more sublime and the less rigid a man's character is, the more indifferent will he be about how near to his own ego, or how far from it, a given situation is, and the less will he distinguish between such nearness and distance when his work deals with them; nor can he give up his labors, even if they become those of Sisyphus. To stand up for the temporal against merciless enternity is morality in Schopenhauer's sense. This morality is not influenced either — for if it were, it would remain calculation — by the Buddhist myth of reincarnation, according to which after a man dies, the soul, timeless and spaceless, is supposed to find the body that corresponds to its stage of purification. The merciless structure of eternity could generate a community of the abandoned, just as injustice and terror in society result in the community of those who resist. Persecution and hunger dominate the history of society even today. If young people recognize the contradiction between the possibilities of human powers and the situation on this earth, and if they do not allow their view to be obscured either by nationalistic fanaticism or by theories of transcendental justice, identification and solidarity may be expected to become decisive in their lives. The road leads through knowledge, not only of science and politics, but also of the great works of literature.

What Schopenhauer declared about individuals — that they are an expression of the blind will to existence and well-being — is at present becoming apparent with regard to social, political and racial groups in the whole world. That is one of the reasons why his doctrine appears to me as the philosophic thought that is a match for reality. Its freedom from illusions is something it shares with enlightened politics; the power of conceptual expression, with theological and philosophic tradition. There are few ideas that the world today needs more than Schopenhauer's — ideas which in the face of utter hopelessness, because they confront it, know more than any others of hope.

Beginning: In Hegel and Today

KURT H. WOLFF

Prefatory Note

I MUST APOLOGIZE for the trouble the reader may have with what follows, and I must not. I must, for that part of the difficulty which is due to my not having achieved greater distinctness, and I sincerely do. For the far more important part of the difficulty, however, I cannot apologize, for its source is the very nature of this undertaking. There are actually two kinds of difficulty. One results from the fact that this essay is the event *and* the process of experiencing the time in which we live. The event: here it is, this text. The process: this event as it is coming forth in the presence of fellow men. The time: the horrors, the problems, yet the need to find a "Nevertheless!" that can be as honestly answered for as is at all possible. The need is certainly familiar. Many have tackled it, in various modes — for instance, in the political mode. Such writers have asked: given the unsatisfactoriness if not failure of available political arrangements, say liberalism, totalitarianism, socialism, what more viable arrangement can be devised? In this mode of asking it is taken for granted that the effort to find a "Nevertheless" *is* political, that the horrors and problems of our time are political or are inextricably involved in the political con-

I wish to thank Franco Ferrarotti, Nancy Hahn, Werner Marx, the late Yonina Talmon, and more particularly Walter Kaufmann, Herbert Marcuse, Paul Riesman, and Jay Vogelbaum for responses to earlier drafts, criticisms, questions, and suggestions, although I fear that I have not been able to do right by all of them. Above all, however, I wish to record my profound indebtedness and gratitude to Mildred Bakan for a most attentive reading and an intensive written dialogue which has influenced and, I trust, clarified this paper, enabling me to render it more explicit than it first was.

stellation of this time. My own mode does not deny the political character of the problem, but neither does it take it for granted; it suspends judgment, it "brackets" all predication of the problem. For this mode is so deeply marked by our crisis that it suspends as best it can *all* available received notions, including, precisely, the one according to which the crisis is political (or religious or economic or technological). This mode I have come to call "surrender."[1] (See Paragraphs 41–48, 57–60 below.)

One difficulty, then, is the degree, I think, to which things are not taken for granted, to which assumptions are questioned, to which the questioning is pushed. The second difficulty is that I don't present findings to difficult questions but do the asking with the reader — "in the presence of fellow men." Not that I believe that the discussion of difficult matters must itself be difficult, any more than that the presentation of boredom must be boring. So to assume, however, is to fall into a trap that the artist and the scientist must beware of: the artist must *convey* boredom but not be boring; the scientist must make complex problems clear. Both translate process into event — the artist's or scientist's travail into the final product, the novel, say, or the scientific monograph — this "prefatory note" itself is a product of this nature. By contrast, in what follows I insist on process, in an effort to have the reader participate, which is surely more demanding than reading a novel or even a scientific report, because it questions and asks more of him too. Why do I wish for participation? Because I believe that our crisis is such that it requires being taken more seriously than it would be by reading a translation, and that one mode of so taking it is, precisely, the most immediate possible participation — surrender.

For one of the characteristics of surrender is the greatest im-

[1] "Surrender and Religion," *Journal for the Scientific Study of Religion,* 2 (1962), 36–50; "Surrender as a Response to Our Crisis," *Journal of Humanistic Psychology,* 2 (1962), 16–30; "Surrender and Aesthetic Experience," *Review of Existential Psychology and Psychiatry,* 3 (1963), 209–226; "Surrender and Community Study: The Study of Loma," in Arthur J. Vidich, Joseph Bensman, Maurice R. Stein, eds., *Reflections on Community Studies,* New York: Wiley, 1964, pp. 233–263; "Hinnahme und Rebellion: Eine Interpretation von Camus' *L'homme révolté,*" *Kölner Zeitschrift für Soziologie und Sozialpsychologie,* 17 (1965), 909–936.

mediacy that can be attained. It was Herbert Marcuse who suggested that in my investigation of surrender I ponder what Hegel says on immediacy and who thus gave rise to this essay — its place of publication is as appropriate as it is an honor for me. My study of Hegel, however, has begun with what he writes on "beginning." Thus the question of the "Nevertheless" in the midst of the horrors and the problems of our time has here formulated itself as the question of how I can begin, how one can begin, today.

*   *   *

1. In his search for the ineluctable (*ineluctabilis*, "not-fightable-out-of," "not to be got out of"), a man may be led by the word "the ineluctable" itself. He asks: Where is, what is, that which I cannot get out of? And answers: In myself; the ineluctable is in myself, I myself am ineluctable to myself. He thus cannot help believing: It is *true* that I am. "I am ineluctable to myself" means: "It is true that I am."[2] The true is the ineluctable — but the ineluctable is not necessarily the true, for it may deceive. Hence:

I. *Why is it true that, though true, it is not ineluctable
that the true is the ineluctable?*

2. "True but not ineluctable" means that *the ineluctable is a mode of the true*, thus that there are other modes of the true, that the ineluctable *can* but *must not* be true. It is as if the true beckoned man — beckoned me — to find it in the ineluctable meeting when he is where he is (when I am where I am) and it is where it is, so that there is no getting out of it but being, simple, immediate. "The true is the ineluctable" thus is a sentence which at the same time declares something and claims something, saying both: "It is true that the true is the ineluctable," and: "Be such (or: act in such a way) that what is ineluctable to you is also true."

3. Thus I seek, not the ineluctable, but the true: I seek what I cannot get out of because it is true, not because I cannot get out

---

[2] The proposition is "existentially true" — but see V, 2, 3, and VI, 1. (Roman numerals refer to parts, Arabic numerals following Roman ones, to sections, of this essay. And arabic numerals, not preceded by Roman ones, refer to paragraphs.)

of it: the true in the mode of the ineluctable: being, simple, immediate.

4. This, then, is what "I seek the ineluctable" means. Still, there is this opaqueness of the relation between "the ineluctable," the word, and the ineluctable, that to which the word refers. I seek the ineluctable; yet I am also *not* seeking it, having found it already: being, simple, immediate. But is being, simple, immediate, *the word* "the ineluctable," or is it the ineluctable, *the referent of this word?* The quotation marks seem to vacillate, as if they were now here, now not. I must hope that the word "the ineluctable" *is* the light, the appearance, of the ineluctable, which shines through as this word, and the search for the ineluctable does aim at lifting the ineluctable itself out of its appearance, at understanding, comprehending, it itself, at knowing the truth. For then it would be true that the ineluctable *is* true, namely, *my* mode of the truth; it would be ineluctable that the true *is* the ineluctable.

5. But *is* the search after the ineluctable that is to be lifted out of its appearance, that is to be comprehended? Is the "ineluctable" that behind which lies the ineluctable? To answer Yes is only one way of describing the search; there is another, seemingly opposite one. According to this second way, the search is after the comprehension of the word "ineluctable"; its aim is to lift it, the appearance, out of the ineluctable itself — and the shimmering of the quotation marks may result from my indecision as I am confronted by these two kinds of description. Each of them now sounds inadequate. Clarifying the second promises to clarify the first, too — hence to settle both.

6. "I am ineluctable to myself" means: "It is true that I am." And, now, "It is true that I am" means: "I am ineluctable to myself." Why? Because it is so, because it is true: the question answers itself, is its own answer — we shall have to see (40) whether and in what sense it is an analytic judgment: at any rate, it is a sentence *that merely explicates me:* "I am ineluctable to myself" *means* "It is true that I am": "It is true that I am" *means* "I am ineluctable to myself." But the ineluctable cannot be *more* itself, cannot be *less* appearance that is *not* the light shed by it, than in this certainty of this truth, for, truly, nothing is more certain to me than I myself; and now the task is to let this ineluctability, my

ineluctable certainty of myself as simple, immediate being, *appear*, to let this ineluctable, itself, *as* itself, make its appearance, to comprehend the "ineluctable." This itself that I am I must comprehend, and to comprehend it means to make it appear in such a way as for its *appearance* to be ineluctable, because only its appearance comprehends the ineluctable itself, only as its appearance is it, itself, comprehensible, conceivable: the appearance is the *concept* that mediates the ineluctable itself, that mediates what immediately is *not* comprehensible, *not* conceivable, but can only be lived, experienced.

II. *"Beginning"* and beginning

7. Itself and appearance, however, are thought; my being, I am, precedes my thinking, as well as my certainty (and my doubt) *that* I am. How long has it been true that "I am ineluctable to myself" means "it is true that I am" — how long *before* it got formulated as the proposition that it is so? I no longer know the beginning of this movement between ineluctable and true that I have taken up (or that has taken me up) again and again, but I feel as if *now* its most recent signpost had been erected as this proposition. Perhaps my consciousness of my ignorance of what "beginning" is finds its ground in my no longer knowing that beginning, and this consciousness is possibly as old as that movement — my consciousness that I do not know how one begins; what it means to begin; what one catches how, and by virtue of what (*"prin-ceps," "prin-cipium"*); how something pre-cedes and pro-ceeds; that I do not know either whence I have the faith in tradition, in continuity, the reliance on language, on man speaking on — a reliance that makes me turn to the word "beginning" and some of its relations and at the same time now makes it indifferent to me what "beginning" is in other languages (that is, beyond *principium* and *Anfang*, as well as "commence," from *"cum-initiare,"* to go in together: again the social). At any rate, "beginning" and "'I am ineluctable to myself' means 'It is true that I am,'" *together* mean that I must begin—that I begin — my search for the ineluctable with my experience, myself.

8. This means the existentialization of philosophy, which places being in the self: *I* witness simple, immediate being: who else,

what else could witness it (in this world)? I now must examine this existentialization: by comparing Hegel's analysis of the beginning of philosophy in pure being with an analysis of the beginning of the search for truth (in the mode of the ineluctable) or for the ineluctable (as my mode of the truth) in myself.

9. In such a comparison, I go by Hegel's *Logic*, not, certainly, because he "began" with this work, but because it is there I find that he wrote most explicitly on beginning. There are passages, mainly in the Preface to the *Phenomenology*,[3] in which his thought is more closely related to what follows in this essay, but these passages seem less representative of him in his time. In no way should this paper be regarded as an attempt at a responsible and competent presentation of Hegel's thought on beginning; "beginning in Hegel" refers only to its analysis in the passages from the *Logic* examined in III and IV below. Thus, I merely deal with one of Hegel's discussions of beginning — an important one, if not the most important — in typical reference to him in his time, and to a man, or man, today in *his*. (See the root-question of the inquiry at the end of 10, i.e., the next paragraph.) As to the degree of explicitness to which the procedure of this typification is carried, I can hardly do better than quote Hegel himself: ". . . the thing [subject matter] is not exhausted in its *purpose* but in its *execution*, nor is the *result* the *actual* whole but . . . [only the result] together with its becoming."[4]

10. In demonstrating that the self[5] cannot be the beginning of philosophy, Hegel shows that for him the truth he seeks is *not* truth in the mode of the ineluctable. He doubts that he can arrive at *the* ineluctable through what is ineluctable to *him;* he cannot believe that his self is simple and immediate, which beginning must be. That it must, is ineluctably true for me, too. But for Hegel, only pure or empty being is simple and immediate and hence beginning; for me, it is the I-am, simple, immediate, I-am as simple, immediate being. *How comprehend this difference, and whence does it come?*

11. An answer to this twofold question requires answers to

[3] Cf. esp. Hegel, *Phänomenologie des Geistes*, Johannes Hoffmeister, ed., Hamburg: Felix Meiner, 1952, pp. 22 and 23.
[4] *Ibid.*, p. 11.
[5] A better translation of "*Ich*" than "ego."

four: (1) Why is pure being the beginning of philosophy for Hegel? (2) Why is not the self the beginning of philosophy for Hegel? (3) Why is, for me, I-am as simple, immediate being the beginning of the search for truth as the ineluctable, for the ineluctable as my mode of the truth? (4) Why is not pure being the beginning of this search for me?

III. *Why is pure being the beginning of philosophy for Hegel?*

12. "Pure being," Hegel writes, must "be taken only" as "the pure-immediate," in "pure indeterminateness," for otherwise

> it would be taken as something mediated, as something already continued; [but] something determined contains *other* than the first. It thus is in the *nature of the beginning itself* to be being and nothing else. . . .
> . . . that with which the beginning must be made can be nothing concrete, can be no such thing as contains a relation *within itself*. For, . . . the beginning must not itself be already something first *and* something other; such . . . contains already a having-continued. What makes the beginning, [what is] the beginning itself, must therefore be taken as something non-analyzable, in its simple unfulfilled immediacy, hence *as being*, as the wholly empty.[6]

13. "Why is pure being the beginning of philosophy for Hegel?" In these excerpts, Hegel himself answers the "why," understood in the logical sense, one of its immanent senses, that is, understood in one of the meanings contained in the excerpts and ascertainable without "going outside" them. "Why," however, has another, likewise immanent, sense, the ontological sense; if I inquire into *it*, I ask: What is the starting point of the path (traced in the much longer passage I have excerpted) that leads so ineluctably to beginning in pure being; on which basis is the logically seamless argument erected; where does Hegel begin his discussion of the beginning of philosophy; what is *Hegel's beginning?* It is: " 'beginning' *means* 'pure being'; 'pure being' *means* 'beginning,' " just as for me the beginning is " 'I am ineluctable to

[6] Hegel, *Wissenschaft der Logik*, Georg Lasson, ed., Hamburg: Felix Meiner, 1934, I, 57, 60.

myself' *means* 'It is true that I am'" (and vice versa). Hegel's argument explicates his initial sentence on beginning in pure being, just as "'I am ineluctable to myself' means 'It is true that I am'" (and vice versa) explicates *me* (6). To be sure, Hegel has carried the explication incomparably farther than I have — I am only at the beginning (even though I hope the answers to the third and fourth questions that have come up [11] will move me forward). In both cases, reflection on the ineluctable, no further analyzable sentence leads to the necessary formulation of the beginning of all asking that appears possible-necessary-true at all. The beginning can be no further analyzed because it is, for the asker, the first and last question; beyond it, prior to it, no questions can rise; because it *is* its own answer, the initial question *is* the beginning. If somebody, and thus the original asker himself, wants to go beyond it, inquiring into the beginning of the beginning that it is, then his question must concern the *human being* for whom it is necessary thus to begin. What can be said about the human being who begins with pure being; why is pure being beginning for him?

14. This "why" is no longer immanent — neither in the logical sense (concerning the demonstration of the initial sentence), nor in the ontological sense (concerning the beginning ineluctably held to be true with which the demonstration begins). This "why," instead, comes from outside the demonstration; it is a historical, sociological, psychological why: precisely the question of the human being who undertakes the examination which the answer to the logical and ontological why has made understandable.

15. Hints regarding this human being can be found in Hegel himself, e.g., in the following passage (it, too, from the discussion of beginning, a few pages before the excerpts quoted first):

> The question that appears so important in the culture of the time, whether knowledge of the truth is immediate, simply beginning knowledge, . . . or mediated knowledge, will not be discussed here. . . . it may only be mentioned that there *is* nothing, nothing in heaven or in nature or in the spirit or wherever, that does not contain immediacy as well as mediation, so that these two determinations show themselves as *inseparate* and *inseparable,* and that contrast shows itself as a

nothing. . . . To want to get clear on knowledge already *before* science means to demand that it be discussed *outside* science; *outside* science this cannot be done, at least not in a scientific manner, which alone is in question here.[7]

Here (as elsewhere, including the pages discussed in IV below), Hegel shows that he also thinks of his time and his contemporaries: he counters "the question that appears so important in the culture of the time, whether knowledge of the truth is immediate, simply beginning knowledge," with the claim that nothing exists that is not at once immediate and mediated, and that the distinction between immediacy and mediation makes no sense outside or prior to its scientific discussion. He thus separates — distinguishing, cleaning, purifying — science from life, and declares that the question of the beginning, of "simply beginning knowledge," is not a life question but exclusively a scientific question. He asks: "How does science or philosophy begin?" not: "How can I, how must I begin?" (or "What shall, what must I do?"), and condemns those who so ask as confused and in error. Thus to ask, however, is ineluctable for me, and therefore I am a human being who is condemned by Hegel as confused and in error.[8]

16. Summing up the answer to the first question: Pure being is (for Hegel) the beginning of philosophy because (1) this follows logically, as its analysis or explication, from Hegel's beginning, namely from (2) " 'Beginning' *means* 'pure being,' " and (3) be-

[7] *Ibid.*, I, 52 – 53.

[8] This analysis of Hegel's beginning in pure being leads to a question central to the "sociology of knowledge": whether a socio-historical Why asked of an intellectual position — a Why thus "transcending" this position — can prove it false; whether the ascertainment of its socio-historical origin can diminish if not destroy its validity. Hegel presumably did not think so; at least he insisted that "the refutation [of a philosophical system must] not come from the outside, that is, [must] not take its departure from assumptions that lie outside that system, to which it does not correspond" (*ibid.*, II, 217 [in the context of his "refutation" of Spinoza's system and of his discussion of what is to be understood by such a refutation]. Hegel consequently would probably have considered the third Why as philosophically irrelevant. But he wrote not only a century before the "sociology of knowledge," but also, though not so long, before Marx, even before Feuerbach. Nor, surely, need I insist that I am not trying to "refute" Hegel.

cause this beginning is the not further analyzable sentence for the human being to whom the question of the beginning is an exclusively scientific question, not a question of his life.

IV. *Why is not the self the beginning of philosophy for Hegel?*

17. The answer to this second question is contained in that to the first, but is explicated in a passage in which Hegel himself raises and answers it.[9] The passage is introduced by a reference to an effort made in his time — to locate the beginning of philosophy in the self — and indeed almost reads as if it had been written in order to prove the hopelessness of this effort. The empirical self, Hegel argues, while immediately certain, is not simple but concrete; and trying to make it simple by means of abstraction takes away its immediacy, nor can it eliminate its subjectivity. The "pure self," on the other hand, which by virtue of its universality might be considered as beginning, is not found in "common consciousness." The subjectivity of the self, which cannot be eliminated even in the pure knowledge of it, means that it is "manifold" and hence necessarily "still" caught "in appearance." On the occasion of the present theme, too (of the self as candidate for beginning), Hegel then advances the arguments that we have heard before, according to which only the immediate-simple, that is, pure being, can be beginning.

18. We have already seen in connection with the first question — Why is pure being the beginning of philosophy for Hegel? — that it is answered by his conception of philosophy or science, from which followed, too, that beginning cannot be the self. What is important in the pages referred to for the answer to the second question — Why is not the self the beginning of philosophy for Hegel? — is the conception of the self contained in them. The immediate certainty of the self by no means contradicts Hegel's conception of philosophy which is grounded in beginning as pure being. But it follows from this conception of philosophy that the self is subjective and hence appearance, and that

[9] *Ibid.,* I, 60 – 64.

therefore its relation to truth — the relation of this appearance to truth — cannot be ascertained by analyzing the self. This alone is enough to prove that the self is not the truth and that its candidacy as beginning is illusory.

19. As we did when we came to the analogous point in our attempt to answer the first question (14), we now again leave Hegel's "system." *Then* we asked about the human being for whom beginning is pure being. *Now* we ask about the conception of the self held by this human being. We observed that he affirms the immediate certainty of the self while proving that this certainty is unreliable. *He places all his confidence in "pure knowledge,"* in the light of which the self betrays its invalidity: he *distrusts* the self.[10] To be sure, the self such as we find it cannot be considered unqualifiedly reliable (let alone universal, which it is not by definition); and Hegel distinguishes between it and the pure self. But his distrust of the self as a whole leads him to demonstrate (ontologically) that even the pure self is disqualified as the beginning of pure knowledge (of philosophy, of science).

20. In trying to answer the third question — Why is, for me, I-am as simple, immediate being the beginning of the search for truth as the ineluctable, for the ineluctable as my mode of the truth? (V) — we shall see that, in spite of Hegel's instructive objections to beginning in the self, such a beginning is in need of being considered afresh. In this effort, however (and this anticipates part of the answer), we shall start, as has been suggested already, with a different fundamental attitude, namely, trust in the self; shall let ourselves be guided by different considerations (namely, "everyday," rather than philosophical); and shall work with a different conception of philosophy (the search — likewise mentioned already — for truth as the ineluctable, for the ineluctable as my mode of the truth). But aside from their different fundamental attitudes, different considerations that guide the argument, and different conceptions of their aims, the two enterprises share at least concern with beginning.

[10] Cf. Hegel's criticism of the individual who "invokes feeling, his inner oracle": *Phänomenologie, ed. cit.,* p. 56.

V. *Why is, for me, I-am as simple, immediate being*
the beginning of the search for truth as the ineluctable,
for the ineluctable as my mode of the truth?

21. In approaching the answer to this third question I recall
that "beginning" has been mentioned several times in this exploration, and I find it useful to inspect these occurrences, trying to
clarify what they deal with and to understand the path they
throw light on — up to this point and further.

(1) Occurrences of "beginning" up to this point

22. First: "I no longer know the beginning of this movement
between ineluctable and true"; and I say something about "beginning" in various languages; then:

> At any rate, "beginning" and: " 'I am ineluctable to myself'
> means 'It is true that I am,' " *together* mean that I must begin
> — that I begin — my search for the ineluctable with my ex-
> perience, myself. . . . Hegel's analysis of the beginning of
> philosophy . . . analysis of the beginning of the search for
> truth . . . in myself (7, 8).

The "most recent signpost" (7) of the "movement" is a beginning
recognized *post factum* as spontaneously made. But there also is
mention of the problematics of "beginning" and its various meanings, as well as of the hope that this matter may at least be approached through an analysis of linguistic expressions, and, finally,
of the confidence in the intimate connection between expression
and expressed, hence in the (responsibly) speaking human being
(7). Third, *my* beginning is being formulated, more precisely as
the unification of the "beginning" of any process, of the original
or arch-process, on one hand, and, on the other, of my initial cer-
tainty that I am, whereby each of these two elements, as well as
their unification, is an experience that is not further analyzable
for me, hence is, ineluctably, the I-am, with which I must begin
— for with what else could I begin (cf. 8)? Fourth, the equation
"must begin — begin" shows that the knowledge of the beginning

is the command to follow it, to begin accordingly. Fifth, the immediate meaning of this "accordingly" announces itself, namely, as the existentialization of philosophy (which will be discussed in what still follows in this section and in what will come afterward). I immediately promise the analysis of this existentialization through a comparison of Hegel's analysis of the beginning of philosophy with mine. This formulation raises the question[11] whether I must understand by philosophy the search for truth, whether I must equate philosophy and this search.

23. Second:

> *Hegel's beginning* . . . Hegel's argument explicates his initial sentence on beginning in pure being. . . . Hegel has carried the explication incomparably farther . . . —I am only at the beginning . . . the beginning of all asking that appears possible-necessary-true at all. The beginning can be no further analyzed because it is, for the asker, the first and last question; . . . because it *is* its own answer, the initial question *is* the beginning. If somebody . . . wants to go beyond it, inquiring into the beginning of the beginning that it is, then his question must concern the *human being* for whom it is necessary thus to begin (13).

"Beginning" here means Archimedean point, Eureka, "Here I stand, God help me, amen," initial, not further analyzable sentence, initial question that is its own answer. Insight into this meaning is a first clarification of the "existentialization of philosophy." Although I am "only at the beginning" with my explication, I have indeed begun. And continuing with the "existentialization of philosophy," I say (even though not precisely in these words, which, however, ought to be clearer) that, since the beginning is the beginning, there is nothing that precedes it, but that (in virtue of both history and causality) there is *no* "absolute" beginning. That is, even the beginning in the present sense is not absolute but is precisely such that one can ask about *its* "beginning" only in regard to the human being for which it *is* the ineluctable beginning.

24. Third: Hegel "asks: 'How does science or philosophy begin?' not: 'How can I, how must I begin?' (or 'What shall, what

---

[11] Since touched on: we "work with a different conception of philosophy" (20).

must I do?') . . ." (15). Here the question about the human being that begins as Hegel does is preliminarily answered: the beginning of Hegel's beginning in pure being is a human being that
asks as he does, not one for whom the beginning is his experience,
he himself, I-am as simple, immediate being, and who thus would
ask instead, as we have seen, being condemned for it by Hegel as
in error — but (I now add, anticipating) one whom Hegel would
perhaps not have thus condemned, who he himself would possibly
have been, had he lived at the same time as the other, later one,
that is, had he, too, experienced what has happened between his
time and today.

25. Finally: ". . . we shall see that in spite of Hegel's . . . objections to beginning in the self, such a beginning is in need of being considered afresh" (20). By now the occasions on which
"beginning" has occurred and the respective comments have probably made this assertion more plausible and promising — if only
because it should have become clear that at the juncture reached
at the sentence just recalled, the analysis *had* long since taken its
departure from I-am as simple, immediate being, *had* indeed begun with that beginning, and has not ceased since. This beginning, however, remains to be explicated, to which I now come as
to the more direct answer to our third question.

(2) Beginning and experience of being

26. I-am is, undifferentiatedly, both beginning and begun, thus,
because begun, continuing. That is: *the continuity of the I-am
consists in its beginning-ever-again.* This continuity, however, is
not steady: on the contrary, it is interrupted continually by periods
of non-beginning and is interspersed with elements of non-beginning. For as to time, the periods of non-beginning are incomparably longer than those of beginning, and in the composition of
life, the elements of non-beginning by far outweigh those of beginning: this is a sober characterization of the life of almost all
men, of almost all groups of men, and of mankind. For when do I
begin? In the present investigation I am trying to. But as soon as I
recognize that I, as almost all men, pass most of the time customarily or habitually ("as to time"), and that even most of my

extra-ordinary (serious, difficult, happy, creative — artistic, philosophical, scientific, political, ethical, erotic) activities and states are
interspersed with elements of custom and habit ("in the composition of life"), the extraordinary rareness of what can justifiably
be called beginning becomes evident. And more: the human adult
is *constitutionally* not "initial": in order to meet any situation at
all, he must confront it equipped with what he has learned in the
course of his life (customs, categories, concepts, habits, etc.).
Hence his beginning *cannot* be absolute but only relative (as we
already saw [23]). "Absolute" beginning would require him to
be an impossible *tabula rasa;* nor can we not only not rid ourselves
of all we have learned in order to begin "anew": if we *could*, we
would not begin but perish, probably in a fashion similar to the
new human life, the infant, who would perish if he did not learn
— and furthermore, nothing he learns is purely unique but in large
measure and quality both customary of groups of human beings,
from his family to mankind, and common to these groups.

27. It follows that beginning is neither immediate nor simple,
hence not immediate or simple as pure being or self either: my
manifoldness inevitably *mediates*, and thus also mediates being and
self. Nevertheless, beginning remains immediate and simple for
Hegel (as well as for me). We saw how Hegel proves that only
pure being, but not the self, can be thus characterized, hence
alone be the beginning of philosophy; and I have declared repeatedly that for me I-am, as simple, immediate being, is the beginning of the search for truth as the ineluctable, for the ineluctable
as my mode of the truth. What then, in view of all these contradictions — these at least apparent contradictions — can nevertheless
be established about "beginning"?

28. First: what does it mean that beginning cannot be absolute
(independent of the learned, received, customary), but only relative (to it)? The answer is: *To begin means to find the ineluctable;
to find that which emerges as ineluctable from the most rigorous
questioning of what the person has received, as well as of what he
has observed, thought, felt with the help of the entire apparatus
of the received that is available to him;* it means to find in this
manner that which *relative to* such questioning and examining
appears as *independent* ("set free," "absolute") of all the received,

observed, thought, felt that has been examined; hence, as true and ineluctable — ineluctably true, in truth ineluctable.

29. I cannot conceive of "immediate and simple" other than as of this last: ineluctably true, in truth ineluctable ("[when I am where I am] and it is where it is, so that there is no getting out of it but being, simple, immediate" [2]). "True" or "ineluctable" is *not* a predicate, either of an object or a subject, for as predicate it would mediate, hence not be immediate, and thus not simple either. Instead, "true" or "ineluctable" points to a self-sufficient, undifferentiated *experience*, in which there is no asking or distinguishing (as, e.g., between subject, object, predicate — between, in principle, received the ordinarily quite plausibly distinguished concepts and ideas, in short, among any received elements whatever, as well as between the received and the new); it is the *experience* of "*it is so,*" being, simple, immediate; the experience into which enters the experiencer, too; from which not even he (as, so to speak, received) is distinguished; in which he, too, *is,* and in which undifferentiatedly *the* world and *his* world *is* — but in which, seen from the outside (from before, after, simultaneously from elsewhere), the world is *new,* is *invented, begins.*

30. Second: the definition of beginning as finding what ineluctably emerges from the most rigorous questioning of the received, what sustains the most rigorous examination of the observed, thought, felt, does not sound like the definition of an experience but like the description of an analysis, of a (maximally critical) comprehending. The very distinction between experience and analysis or comprehension, however, is itself received, historical, contingent; it facilitates reference to what *is* but does not attain what *is,* and if one imagines that it does and so insists, one gives a false report that leads knowledge away from what is, instead of toward it. In the experience of "it is so," even *this* distinction (between experience and comprehension) disappears; the distinction is proper only for the *analysis* of the experience, when, indeed, it is not only relevant but requisite. Calling the experience of "it is so" "experience" already falsifies it — just as much as it would be falsified if it were called "analysis": it, itself, is not only unpredicable, as we have seen, but altogether uncategorizable; or, to refer to etymology: "it is so" can be neither proclaimed nor

asserted or contradicted: it is pure being, "empty" (as, we recall, Hegel also calls it [12]), simple; immediate, *not* in any way mediated (though, indeed, *mediable*[12]).

31. If I nevertheless say something about the experience of being — to introduce a shorter expression for "experience of 'it is so'" — distinguishing within it between experience and analysis or comprehsion, or claim that in it undifferentiatedly *the* world and *his* world begins for the experiencer, then I obviously speak from the outside, I analyze it from points of view external to it — approximately from those of the epistemologist, or the experiencer's psychologist or biographer. Recalling now the definition of "beginning" (28) and always speaking epistemologically, analytically, from outside the experience of being, then beginning appears as comprehending what has occurred in the experience of being, what has emerged from it, what has "fought its way out of" it; it appears as translating this into words, as comprehending it as faithfully to the experience as possible; it means *not* to rest content with received notions, *not* to let oneself be persuaded by them, *but to allow the concepts that are required to comprehend the experience to emerge out of the experience itself; not* to compromise with the approximate, probable, plausible, but to strive for the *ineluctably* true, the *truly* ineluctable.

32. Beginning thus is not the experience but its comprehension.[13] It must be understood, however, that comprehension does

---

12 Of which in V, 3.

13 In the *Phänomenologie* (*ed. cit.*, p. 32), Hegel appears to concur: "The immediate existence of the spirit, [i.e.] *consciousness*, has the two moments, of knowledge and of the objectivity that is negative to it [knowledge]. As the spirit develops, and explicates its moments, in this element [consciousness], this contrast [between knowledge and objectivity] accrues to them [these moments], and they [moments] all emerge as phenomena of consciousness. The science of this process is [the] science of the *experience* that consciousness has; the substance comes into view as it and its movement are its object [of consciousness]. Consciousness knows and comprehends nothing but what is in its experience; for what is in the latter is only the spiritual substance, that is, [spiritual substance] as the *object* of its self. The spirit, however, becomes an object, for it is this movement: to become *something other to itself*, that is, to become [an] *object to its self*, and to suspend [*aufzuheben*] this being-other. And [what is] called experience is precisely

not necessarily follow experience in time, for in this case beginning would *follow*, and the question would arise of what *precedes* the beginning. The point is that the temporal dimension is irrelevant. In time, comprehension may follow or coincide with the experience of being; in either case, *it*, comprehension, is the beginning. This means that without it there is no beginning: a mere experience of being — if there *be* such without any comprehending — is no beginning. On the other hand, even from the experiencer's point of view, his very experience of being may be comprehension (comprehension as experience of being): he may *be* in either of these modes, whose temporal disposition, indeed, does not enter. To be sure, one may have an experience of being which is more nearly consummated by the experiencer, who does not turn to the comprehension contained in it, as a state, and which in his memory thus more nearly remains an episode. Not this, but *the experience of being with which comprehension begins*, I call "surrender," and the comprehension, the knowledge coming out of it, "catch" (German "*fangen*," hence "*Anfang*," i.e., "*principium*," from "*capio*," to catch, whence also "con-cept" and "con-ception"): on this, including reasons for the terminology, more below.[14]

33. I said (31) that the continuity of the I-am consists in its beginning-ever-again, but that this continuity is not steady but continually interrupted by periods, and densely interspersed by elements, of non-beginning. This means that beginning, that — we may add now — the experience of being and surrender are rare. For man not only *is* (we have just recalled that ordinarily he is *not*) but — to supplement the logical opposite of being, non-being, by its everyday opposite — he also practices his occupation, devotes himself to his family, eats, sleeps, engages in innumerable

---

this movement in which the immediate, the inexperienced, that is, the abstract, whether of sensible being or only of the simple that is thought, becomes estranged from itself and then returns to itself from this estrangement, and only then is thus presented in its actuality and truth, and becomes the property of consciousness." Note particularly the last sentence.

[14] V, 4. And for anticipations, cf. 7 and 22. The last sentence in the quotation from Hegel in the preceding note is a penetrating analysis of the "catch."

other activities, plays roles, behaves, in short, *leads* a social and historical *life*.[15] These two modes, *being* and *leading a life*, are conceptually distinct; but their empirical relation, not only within the human being, but also among individuals, groups, societies, types of men, types of societies, and historical periods, is highly variable; and the investigation of how this relation characterizes them may serve to ascertain many others of their characteristics — as well as to furnish a basis for advocating and effecting their change, and thus the change of history. The contemporary industrial West, e.g. (as can be understood in an easily available historical perspective), is characterized by a *preponderance of "leading a life" at the cost of "being"* — witness the administered life, bureaucratization, technical reason, alienation, meaninglessness, dissatisfaction, apathy, vicariousness, and much else (VI, 2). "Leading a life," thus, is a concept that refers not only to a systematic circumstance but also, and emphatically, to social-historical circumstances. Because of this intrinsic emphasis on social-historical circumstances, the "beginning" of this concept differs from the "beginnings" of such otherwise significantly related concepts as Heidegger's *"Man"* ("anyone") — or G. H. Mead's "generalized other"; and an analysis of the various relations among all of these would be illuminating. This, at any rate, and what has been said in the present paragraph before, may already suggest the *critical* potential of beginning in the I-am as simple, immediate being that will be pointed out in connection with the answer to the fourth question (VI, 2 and 3).

[15] "The human soul enjoys these rare, classic periods [which may also be read as 'periods of being'], but, apart from them, we are seldom single or unique; we keep company in this world with a hoard of abstractions and reflections and counterfeits of ourselves — the sensual man, the economic man, the man of reason, the beast, the machine and the sleep-walker, and heaven knows what besides, all in our own image, indistinguishable from ourselves to the outward eye. We get borne along, out of sight in the press, unresisting, till we get the chance to drop behind unnoticed, or to dodge down a side street, pause, breathe freely and take our bearings, or to push ahead, outdistance our shadows, lead them a dance, so that when at length they catch up with us, they look at one another askance, knowing we have a secret we shall never share." Evelyn Waugh, *Brideshead Revisited* (1944), Dell Laurel Edition, 1960, pp. 207 – 208.

(3) The possibility of intersubjective existential truth

34. Before we come to the fourth question, however, we must yet state and solve a crucial problem (and, as will result therefrom, more expressly discuss "surrender and catch" [V, 4]). This problem is how the ineluctable truth emerging from the experience of being can be truth beyond its experiencer, can be truth for others too, how it can be not only subjective but also intersubjective truth. The problem, in fact, came up at once: in the recognition that the ineluctable is not the same as the true because what is ineluctable to *me* need not for this reason be true (1). Also alluding to the problem (and hinting at its solution) was the statement that "the true is the ineluctable" is both a declarative and a normative sentence (2), one, that is, which at the same time declares what it says and issues the demand to be such that the ineluctable also be the true. Finally, I claimed that pure being experienced in the experience of being is simple, immediate, in no way mediated but, indeed, *mediable* (30): mediability suggests how the ineluctable truth of the experience of being may also be valid for men other than the experiencer.

35. The first step in pursuing these hints is to distinguish between two kinds of truth: on the one hand, that of common sense and science (disregarding differences between *these*); and on the other hand, precisely that which comes out of the experience of being. The first is what is usually understood by truth: purified and ordered in science, it is indeed the truth of routine behavior, of "leading a life" — let us call it the truth of everyday life, or *everyday or scientific truth;* the second may be called philosophical or *existential truth or the truth of being.*[16] By now it should be clear that the problem at issue concerns only the *possibility of the intersubjective truth of being,* and not of everyday or scientific truth, because in respect to the latter, the present discussion disre-

---

[16] Everyday or scientific truth corresponds to Alfred Weber's truth of civilization and to Max Scheler's positive, scientific truth or truth of domination. Philosophical or existential truth belongs in the domain of Alfred Weber's "culture" and with Scheler's metaphysical and redemptive knowledge.

gards all problems that may be raised by the phenomenon of the experience of being but that are or can be resolved by received philosophies of science.

36. The first step — the distinction between two truths and the realization that only one of them, the truth of being, is at issue — leads to the second: to find the procedure by which the truth of being is verified. For this procedure differs from that which is taken to verify everyday and scientific truth, even though in actuality both procedures are always involved.

37. Unlike the seeker after everyday or scientific truth, the seeker after existential truth compares what he entertains as such with the result of the most rigorous personal (intrasubjective) examination of his most important experiences and truths — to the point where he believes that, as open as he is to subscribing to other than the truth entertained, as widely and as deeply as he knows what everyday and scientific knowledge he has found in any way relevant,[17] and as conscientious as he can be — thus exercising his clearest and fullest consciousness — he cannot help but hold that "it is so." But this means that he compares what he examines in respect to its truth with the results of previous experiences of being he has had — more concisely: with the catch of previous surrenders. And since he himself *is* in his experience of being — since his experience of being also is experience of *his* being — since, therefore, the catch of the surrender is the truth concerning both himself ("subject") and the world ("object"), it follows that the continuity of this truth also is *his* continuity: this truth grows with every surrender and thus increasingly shows him and proves to him the continuity of both this truth and himself. "Himself" is his component of continuity, the component of continuity in his I-am, in which consists his beginning-ever-again, his ever-again-being-in-the-beginning: this sentence supplements the earlier one, "the continuity of the I-am consists in its beginning-ever-again" (26). For if I say *this*, I say that man knows himself, and increasingly comes to know himself, in his experiences of being; that he himself becomes known in them — and not in the long stretches of leading a life that interrupt them, not in the elements of leading a life that permeate them. On the other

[17] Thus the involvement of *both* procedures of verification.

hand, when I say: "The beginning-ever-again of the I-am consists in its component of continuity," I say that only because he *is* can man begin ever again, can he *be again, be anew*. The two sentences explicate the meaning of this: "I-am, as simple, immediate being, is the beginning of the search for truth as the ineluctable, for the ineluctable as my mode of the truth" (27).

38. The two steps taken thus far do not yet get us beyond *intra*-subjective existential truth, whereby the second has shown how this truth may be found. It is a third step, often taken in fact and at any rate possible, which provides us with the analytical tool for the solution of the problem. The solution is hinted at by the *mediability* (just recalled [34]) of the simple immediate being of the experience of being — and even more distinctly by the much earlier claim (6) that the appearance is the concept that mediates the "itself" (the I-am, itself; the ineluctable, being, itself) which immediately is *not* comprehensible or conceivable but can only be lived or experienced. This third step consists in examining the truth entertained *no longer intrasubjectively but in dialogue with another human being*. However, for it to be even theoretically possible that the dialogue fulfill its purpose, that is, yield truth, it must be assumed that the partner is *competent* as an examiner or co-examiner, that is, that he, too, has had or can have experiences of being or at any rate can follow reports on them — that he is such a human being, hence that there are such human beings. And in fact, we hold the relation to one with whom we feel the possibility of such a dialogue, who invites it, or with whom it unexpectedly takes place, to be a particularly personal and important relation: so close is it to the experience of being itself. The reason for this feeling is that the *experience of being is a compo-nent* (even though an exceedingly variable one) *of relations among human beings;* and indeed, these relations approach *being-together* to the degree to which this component determines them. Although the mediability of being is far more often felt than comprehended or conceived or conceptualized, still it probably is an experience of all men, though very variable in degree and kind and variably known and variably entering consciousness. Yet the familiarity with experiences of being and the feeling of importance, reality, truth, essentiality which accompanies such experi-

ences and the relations among men in which they are felt to play a part, suggest the *definition of man* as the being capable of the experience of being and comprehension, as *the being capable of surrender and catch*. With this definition we have found the basis for the possibility of the intersubjective truth of being that we have sought.

39. For just as the sentence, "The true is the ineluctable," is both declarative and normative (2, 34), so also is this definition of man, that is, the sentence, "Man is the being capable of surrender and catch": it, too, both says what it says and issues the demand to make it my own, to act in accord with it, to embody man so defined, to explore in my own life what this definition means for me, what its truth is.

40. This definition of man was alluded to in a passage according to which the answer to the question why it is true that "I am ineluctable to myself" means: "It is true that I am" (and vice versa), is: "Because it is so, because it is true: the question answers itself, . . . it is a sentence *that merely explicates me*" (6) (just as Hegel's " 'beginning' *means* 'pure being' " [and vice versa], as we saw a little later, explicates Hegel [13]) — I added that we would have to see "whether and in what sense" " 'I am ineluctable to myself' means 'It is true that I am' " (and vice versa) is *an analytic judgment* (6). An analytic judgment, I now continue, is (in Kant's sense) one in which the predicate is contained in the subject; the question therefore is whether the sentence "It is true that I am," taken as predicate, is contained in the sentence "I am ineluctable to myself," taken as subject; and the sentence "I am ineluctable to myself," taken as predicate, in the sentence "It is true that I am," taken as subject. In the meantime we have recognized the meaning of I-am as the source of all possible existential truth: it is this concept which makes both these judgments analytic. For on introducing this concept as the explication of "I am," both subject sentences ("I am ineluctable to myself" and "It is true that I am"), as well as both predicate sentences (which read like the subject sentences), read: "It is true that I am, and this is the beginning of all possible existential truth." The feeling that the question recalled at the beginning of this paragraph is its own answer — the element of experience of being that I sensed as the truth of this feeling — has pushed me to comprehend this feel-

ing, to translate it into a concept, namely, to ask whether the above-mentioned sentences are analytic judgments; to answer as I just did; and now to understand that the concept of I-am as source of all possible existential truth, which makes the sentences analytic judgments, does so in the mode of a sentence which, as already indicated by its form, issues a demand, hence is a normative sentence. The demand is: "Be such as to recognize in the *experience of being* the *beginning* of all possible existential truth." Finally, I understand that this last sentence follows as one of the demands issued by the definition of man as the being capable of surrender and catch.

(4) Surrender and catch

41. Meanwhile it may help to clarify the exploration that is going on when I say that I am in the midst of examining an experience of being, my experience of being — in dialogue, I hope, with the reader. Up to this point, analogously to the earlier examination of Hegel's beginning, I have in the present phase, that is, in the examination of the third question,[18] tried to answer it as an ontological question. In Hegel's case, however, it was *I, we,* who did the examining; he did not examine himself. In my own case, I myself am, we ourselves are, doing the examining. In Hegel's case, there is an exact and important sense in which nothing is to be done any more, but *this* case, I hope, is open: the question "How can I, how must I begin?" (or "What shall I, what must I do?" [15, 24]), I hope, remains open as a concern in which I am presently engaged, in which I hope we together are presently engaged. We anticipated that in examining this question we start with a fundamental attitude different from Hegel's, namely, with trust in the self; let ourselves be guided by different considerations, namely "everyday" rather than philosophical ones; and work with a different conception of philosophy, namely, the search for truth in the mode of the ineluctable or for the ineluctable as my mode of the truth (20). Meanwhile, the meaning of this anticipa-

---

[18] "Why is, for me, I-am as simple, immediate being the beginning of the search for truth as the ineluctable, for the ineluctable as my mode of the truth?" (11; all of V thus far).

tion — or at least a sense of it — should have become clearer and more committing so that we feel that something has occurred, is occurring: we are participating in a mediation of being, are in the process of getting hold of an appearance which comprehends a being-itself, an appearance which is its concept; we are in the midst of an examination which concerns us, which, therefore, is "practical," which aims at existential truth (35; VI, 1); we find ourselves "surrendering" and "catching" — as I hope will become more apparent by conceptualization.

42. The essential meaning of the experience of being that I call "surrender" is "cognitive love"; this meaning is essential because whatever other meanings surrender has derive from it; among them: total involvement, suspension of received notions, pertinence of everything, identification, risk of being hurt. To "surrender" means to take as fully, to meet as immediately, as possible: *not* to select, *not* to believe that one can know quickly what is to be understood and acted on, hence what one's experience means, *not* to suppose that one can do justice to the experience with one's received feeling and thinking, even with the received *structure* of that feeling and thinking; to meet it as much as possible in its originality, its itself-ness.

43. "Catch" (32) is the cognitive, intellectual, existential result, yield, harvest, *Fang* (catch) of surrender, the beginning (*Anfang*) made in it (7, 22). Since in surrender the received thinking and feeling are suspended, but surrender is an act or state of cognitive love (like other distinctions of everyday and scientific plausibility, that between act and state, too, is suspended in it), it is followed by a new comprehending, by a new conceiving or conceptualizing. But what is caught (comprehended, conceived), what "catching" (conceiving) means cannot be anticipated (otherwise surrender would not be so unconditional as it is), for its result may not be a concept in the everyday or scientific sense but (for instance) a decision, a poem, a painting, the clarification or urging of an existential question, a change in the person: ontologically it always is a new conceiving, a new concept, a beginning, a new being-in-the-world (32, 37).

And now the other meanings of "surrender" or "cognitive love":

44. Total involvement: in surrender, as in love itself, I am un-

differentiatedly and indistinguishably involved in its occasion and in myself, my act or state, my object or partner: in both cases, distinctions between all of these disappear.

45. Suspension of received notions: in surrender, matters I feel have anything whatever to do with what I want to learn or know, that is, with my exploration, are suspended (these matters include my convictions regarding the credibility of theories, the adequacy of concepts, the validity of assumptions, postulates, generalizations I am familiar with).

46. Pertinence of everything: since ideas select, to say that in surrender "everything is pertinent" is to say, once more, but in a different mode, that received ideas get suspended: "everything" refers to all within the awareness of the surrenderer — as (again) for the lover "everything" about his beloved and about his love is important. In this extreme concentration at the moment and on the moment of surrender, "everything" is important, but "everything else" vanishes. In one process of contraction and expansion, the world becomes experience in its infinity. All that in this experience *disappears* in the surrenderer's concentration is irrelevant both for him and for the person who would understand surrender.

47. Identification: in surrender, man identifies — with it, its occasion, moment, object, himself ("man knows himself, and increasingly comes to know himself, in his experiences of being; . . . he himself [his 'identity'] becomes known in them" [37]). However, identification must be understood (conceptually) as the aim of surrender, not as the aim of its catch. For if it were the aim of the catch, surrender would not be *cognitive* love, the surrenderer would not want to know, but, by definition, would *want* to identify, to assimilate, to "go native," or no more than to change in some other fashion: he would have an experience of being consummated as a state and remembered as an episode (32) (even if as a turning point in his life). But since he wants to *know*, he must move from surrender to catch, must comprehend, conceive, so that he can tell others what has occurred: if identification itself were the catch he could not. And indeed, even the lover must lose himself to find himself, not to lose himself: if he lost himself to lose himself, he would be self-destructive.

48. Risk of being hurt: this last meaning is distinguished from

the preceding ones inasmuch as it characterizes not only surrender but also action on the catch (and, obviously, many other activities and situations). Exclusive of surrender, however, are two kinds of risks of being hurt, both of which may be called "false surrender," because in both surrender is approached but fails, and there is, indeed, *no* surrender. Yet aside from this common characteristic, they differ profoundly from each other. In one kind, an idea — a received notion — abuses, as it were, the promise of surrender, betraying the promise, and thus betraying him who would surrender but does not, because the received notion has too much hold over him for him to let it go, to suspend it: his "cognitive love" is rebuffed, so to speak, and he is left with nothing but what he had but of which he felt that it ought to have been suspended. Let us call this kind of "false surrender," "surrender aborted." In the other kind — which may be termed "surrender betrayed" or "self-betrayal" — the person "suspends" too much: almost cynically, he takes as a received notion that which alone makes surrender possible, namely, the very faith in the possibility of surrender: he suspends his very self which, however, is all he has with which to begin. He thus destroys himself — like the lover who loses himself to lose himself. This kind of risk is the risk of insanity. Both dangers may be avoided by awareness of them and, in case awareness is insufficient and hence fails, by new surrender. Perhaps, however, if awareness fails, the second danger cannot be thus avoided: man's greatness and his death are close neighbors (57).

49. I stressed already (41) that in the section now ending I have understood and answered the question, "Why is, for me, I-am as simple, immediate being the beginning of the search for truth as the ineluctable, for the ineluctable as my mode of the truth?" as before in regard to Hegel's beginning, *ontologically*. The answer has "explicated me" (6, 13, 40); beyond this point, we must proceed in our everyday world, in the everyday world of human beings.[19] (One element of what will become clear thereby — the

---

[19] In my conception, "human being" and "everyday" belong in a mode of discourse distinguished from that of surrender and philosophy (including ontology). A suggestion of the dynamics of the two modes is found in the analysis of Hegel's "beginning" at the points where we moved to Hegel

critical potential of the concept of beginning in the I-am as simple, immediate being — has already been anticipated [33; see VI, 2 and 3].)

VI. *Why is, for me, not pure being the beginning*
of this search (for truth as the ineluctable,
for the ineluctable as my mode of the truth)?

(1) Truth: existential, everyday, scientific

50. Moving on, then, and proceeding as in the beginning of the effort to answer the third question (V), we now recall phases of the ontological beginning which has been occurring so that it may appear more clearly. These phases are passages on the way to the "different conception of philosophy" with which I work (20, n. 11, 41) — perhaps already on the way that this philosophy goes. Most important among them are the statements that for Hegel to begin is "not a question of his life" (16) but (as suggested thereby) that for me it is one of mine; that for me it means Eureka. "Here I stand" (23), and to *have* to begin (22), since "the true is the ineluctable" is both a declarative and normative sentence (2, 34, 39) and I place my confidence in language, in man speaking on (7, 22), and thus in the word "ineluctable" with which I begin again and again or which again and again begins with me (1, 7, 22). All this — beginning as question of life and as Eureka; the demand that what is ineluctable also be true; the ineluctability of language and of responsibly speaking man (and more) — is the "catch" of my (ever again begun) experience of being which, formulated in the definition of man as the being capable of surrender and catch (38), proves the possibility of its intersubjectivity and thus altogether of the intersubjectivity of existential truth. But *what* is ineluctable, *what* — to put it much more specifically — is an analytic (instead of synthetic) judgment

---

"the human being" (13, 14, 16, 19, 24); an assertion of the distinction between the two modes, in contrasting "everyday" and philosophical (20, 41; 50); and a discussion of some aspects of this distinction will be found in VI, 1. The problems of the relation between "everyday" and "leading a life" (33) and between each of these and Husserl's *Lebenswelt* can only be mentioned here.

(6, 40), is a historical question: this shows the distance, both ontological and historical, from Kant's conviction that the difference between analytic and synthetic judgments is *not* historical. On the other hand, however, the conviction that the "itself" experienced in the experience of being is the only human, that is, humanly accessible (relative) absolute (23, 26, 28), wholly corresponds to Kant's idea that the "itself" (even though not the *"thing* in itself" or *as "thing* in itself") is accessible only to "practical," not to "pure" reason — that immediately it can only be experienced, but comprehended, conceived, conceptualized only mediately; that the concept mediates (6, 31, 32). In order to conceive more clearly and comprehensively of the philosophy emerging here, I examine the only time the word "practical" has occurred in this investigation: precisely in reference to this investigation into which we have come and in which we are engaged together, "which concerns us, which, therefore, is 'practical' " (41).

51. "Practical" applies to the philosophy that is the search for truth as the ineluctable, for the ineluctable as my mode of the truth, and the question about whose beginning is not, as in Hegel, how it begins, but "How can I, how must I begin?" or "What shall I, what must I do?" (15, 24) — a *practical* question. The truth of its answer, as we have seen, is existential truth, hence — so we must now add — practical truth. What is the difference between existential and practical truth? In existential truth — the catch or concept of surrender, the response to cognitive love — the distinction, however understood, between "theory" and "practice," appears, if at all, in revised form, for it, too, was suspended in surrender, which assumes nothing, hence no such difference either, but occurs, finds. More precisely: it invents (59) — in it, undifferentiatedly in one event or process, man invents himself and the world, as he comes to understand in the ordering and distinguishing that is the catch, which may include his catching, comprehending, conceiving, conceptualizing what is "practical" for him, even in the original sense of "practical" as that which he must habitually do. "Existential truth" thus is "practical truth" inasmuch as it is comprehensive truth that *includes practical truth.* This points to a further difference between existential and every-

day truth (the truth of routine behavior, of leading a life), as well as, indirectly, to the difference between everyday and scientific truth that is decisive here — whereas thus far these latter two have been contrasted without distinction with existential truth (35), because, unlike existential truth, neither of them presupposes an experience of being. These differences — between existential and everyday truth, as both *practical,* and between everyday and scientific truth — must now be clarified.

52. "The play starts at eight," "the weather is beautiful today," "the city has 100,000 inhabitants," "Miss Smith is pretty," are examples of everyday truth, are everyday truths. They are not only everyday observations (whether true or false) but are also practical, because their intention — expressed or not, conscious or not — is some doing that more or less directly follows from them. "The play starts at eight" may mean, e.g., "So we still have time," or "So we'd better hurry"; "The weather is beautiful today" may mean, e.g., "So I don't need a raincoat," or "So let's take a walk"; "The city has 100,000 inhabitants" may mean, e.g., "So it's probably large enough to have a symphony orchestra" (anticipating future conduct by the speaker, who can look forward to concerts, does not have to go to another city for the purpose, etc.), or "So I'll have to arrange my sales organization according to Plan 5"; "Miss Smith is pretty" may mean, e.g., "So it would be nice to take her to dinner," etc. The practice to which everyday truth leads is everyday practice; if it should be followed — as can, of course, not be predicted — by an experience of being with *its* practice, then *this* is what happens. Everyday truth answers the question, "What should I *do in this kind of situation?*"; existential truth answers the question, "What should I *do at all?*" (15, 24, 51). Everyday truth remains in the domain of customary or habitual practice; existential truth *also* aims at practice, *including* practice that may or should or must be, or become, customary or habitual.

53. Scientific truth, no more than everyday truth, preceded (conceptually [32, 47]) by an experience of being, is, however, in contrast to everyday truth, not practical but theoretical (contemplative). "Scientifically true" applies to sentences dealing with what — including even myself — is *posited* as external to me, as object. Scientific truth is stipulated as potentially valid only in

regard to hypotheses or theories about the world (or part of it) — about the world which is thus posited as objective. It is pragmatic (in contrast to "practical"), namely, in regard to the investigation in which it is sought. As everyday truth is the truth of practical means, scientific truth is that of theoretical means; or, to use Max Weber's terms: while both are "*zweckrational*" (rational relative to a purpose), everyday truth is so practically; scientific truth, theoretically. In contrast to both, existential truth is not *zweckrational* (nor, for that matter, "*wertrational*," rational relative to a "value") but, precisely, in-conceivable in its immediacy *because* immediate, but mediable — mediable by concept, mediately conceivable: here (29–31) as beginning, the catch of surrender, the concept of an experience of being.

(2) Between Hegel and today

54. To inquire empirically into the beginning means to inquire into the human being who begins as he does (13, 14, 16, 19, 24). Hegel emerged as one who "*distrusts* the self" and "*places all his confidence in 'pure knowledge,'* in the light of which the self betrays its invalidity" (19). I, by contrast, am one who trusts the I-am as simple, immediate being, who trusts language, who trusts man speaking on, who trusts "the ineluctable" as road to the ineluctable as my mode of the truth. Hegel condemned a man like me as caught in error (15) but would perhaps not have condemned him, might himself have been such a man, "had he lived at the same time as the other, later one, that is, had he, too, experienced what has happened between his time and today" (24). Of what has happened, only the "sociology of knowledge," Marx, and Feuerbach have thus far been mentioned (n. 8). In what much vaster current does this small movement and do these two men play a part? In what current, that also runs large with beginnings, among them Hegel's, among them mine, and that we must take hold of if we would account for these being different, understandably different beginnings? Thus, finally: "*How comprehend this difference, and whence does it come?*" (10). This is the question which led to the four that we have attempted to answer and on the last of which we are now embarked.

55. Among other elements of the "much vaster current" are the increasing doubt concerning the *power* of "pure knowledge," the "distrust of reason" (Reinhard Bendix), the "eclipse of reason" (Max Horkheimer), man's ever less bearable "one-dimensionality" (Herbert Marcuse) — to mention a few more recent designations. And to recall some only a little older: the increase of functional at the expense of substantive rationality (Karl Mannheim), the "disenchantment of the world" (Max Weber, but already Friedrich Schiller), "anomie" (Emile Durkheim). But more: there is Feuerbach's and, above all, Marx's confronting *human* alienation, the recognition that this element of the Hegelian dialectic (e.g., n. 13) works its destruction among men, *within* man himself; later its appropriation by the sociology of knowledge, which is haunted by it in its epistemological dilemma; the fatally *functional*-rational running amuck of alienation, with its marooning and expending of men, in totalitarianism; the administered life; the bewilderment by the ever denser and more expansive crowd of sensibly more and more awfully different and awfully like people and peoples; the shrinkage of the earth in other ways: its reduction to an available target for the nuclear bomb that nothing survives, to the ever-ready, continuously kept-ready crematorium of mankind; terrestrial claustrophobia and the longing for the moon and other planets; increasing diffusion of Western ideas and institutions with whose help and partly in whose name the West is fought and thus, in its self-confidence and in the confidence in its traditions, also weakened, threatened as it feels itself to be by the rise of "underdeveloped" or "developing" countries that the West would nevertheless "bless" — instead of the whole earth being developed by means of Western technology and its attendant wealth so that (especially with increasing automation) man's history, as struggle for existence and daily bread, could be over and, as pacification in freedom, humanness, and reason, be ushered in: all this, barely sketched, and far more belongs to the "much vaster current" that has been loosened and on the loose since Hegel wrote.

(3) Why is pure being not the beginning of the search for truth as the ineluctable, for the ineluctable as my mode of the truth?

56. Hegel's "pure knowledge" and its beginning in "pure being" presuppose a world that has long since ceased to exist. It was a world in which man felt so as to begin with *it;* in which he conceived of his knowledge of himself as secondary to knowledge of the world — that world; in which he conceived of his own being as a comparatively uncertain addition to "pure being." Since Hegel, the self has indeed not become *more* certain, but the courage to risk the uncertain has grown, wherein Kierkegaard and Nietzsche, Husserl and existentialist philosophers have encouraged us, reminding and convincing us of the courage, helping us to put it into practice. In the world in which *we* live we have nothing but ourselves with which to renew it, reconstitute it, begin. When it was pronounced, "Die and become" still was only the *individual's* experience and fate; today it is mankind's, the world's, and, therefore, is what the individual begins with, which means that he begins with surrender, *today, historically, his experience of being.*

57. In order to emphasize the undifferentiatedness of this experience, I also refer to it as "total." "Total" experience may — and it should — recall "totalitarianism": the word and what it stands for oppose to terror the human being for whom the absolute is not terror but home, whom "extreme situation" remind not only of his death but also of his greatness.

58. The word "surrender" itself, however, is political and polemical or ironical, for again, both the term and its referent oppose the contemporary, official, Western but potentially earthwide consciousness in which the relation to the world is *not* surrender but mastery, control, efficiency, manipulation, outwitting, deception. This relation to the world, moreover, is considered virile, while "surrender" rather has a "female" overtone, woman being thought of as surrendering more than man, who if he did would risk being blamed and blaming himself for losing his virility and becoming "effeminate": "surrender" polemicizes not only politically but sexually, too.

59. The sexual element also figures in two synonyms of "catch," "invention" and "breakthrough." "Invention" is a term justified in view of the catch not being received but new, thus invented "come into" (*in-venire:* "surrender . . . assumes nothing . . . but occurs, finds . . . invents — in it, undifferentiatedly in one

event or process, man invents himself and the world, as he comes to understand in the . . . catch . . ." [51]). If "surrender" has a female ring, "invention," "to come into," suggesting the tabooed "come" that refers to the orgasm of both men and women who "know" each other, is bisexual, that is, *common* to man and woman: human.

60. Thus for the other synonym of "catch," the biblical "breakthrough." As however hopeless, exciting, problematic, or even appealing the world may strike us, we cannot, if we seek the truth, look away either from it or from ourselves but must begin with ourselves, to renew the world. The catch of surrender *is* breakthrough: triumph over what in the world or ourselves would hinder it; victory over barriers; liberation from this or that prohibition or claim; saying Yes where the non-self, the other-than-self says No, No where it says Yes; the feeling or experience of "Lift up your heads, O ye gates, and be ye lift up, ye everlasting doors; and the King of glory shall come in."[20]

[20] Psalm 24, 7.

The Social History of Ideas:
Ernst Cassirer and After

PETER GAY

SEVERAL YEARS AGO, I happened to encounter Herbert Marcuse on the campus of Columbia University. He was carrying a copy of Ernst Cassirer's *Essay on Man*. He hailed me, and pointed to the book in his hand. "I suppose," he said, with that emphasis that is so characteristically his own, "nothing that this man writes is ever *totally* bad."

The remark long haunted me. I was then, and am now, an admirer both of Cassirer the philosopher and Cassirer the historian, and I was inclined to attribute Herbert Marcuse's judgment to his cheerful Mephistophelian spirit — *der Geist der stets verneint* — or, perhaps, to the aversion that a good Hegelian is bound to feel for a good Kantian. For years, then, Marcuse's attitude toward Cassirer and my own attitude were in simple antithesis. Now that I have had further occasion to study Cassirer's work, especially in intellectual history, I am prepared to offer a different view, a synthesis of these two opposing positions. I shall argue that Cassirer's work as a historian was a great achievement, but a flawed one. It is immensely intelligent, immensely suggestive, but not conclusive. Nothing that this man wrote was ever, I suppose, *totally* good.

I

Cassirer's historical method — and it is his method as exemplified in his substantive writings, as much as the writings themselves, that invites our attention — rests on three closely related conceptions and procedures. I propose to call them the objectivity of imagination, the primacy of function, and the rage for coherence.

I take my text for the first of these — the objectivity of imagination — from a story that Cassirer liked to tell: once he was talking with Hilbert, the great mathematician, and in the course of the conversation asked him about one of his students. Hilbert replied: "He is all right. You know, for a mathematician he did not have enough imagination. But he has become a poet and now he is doing fine."[1]

Cassirer himself did not draw the application of this anecdote to history, but its application is apt and liberating. Its lesson serves as a possible escape from an interminable debate that historians have been carrying on at least since Ranke — intellectual historians as much as others. It is the debate between the Positivists and the Idealists; between those who call history a science and those who call it an art; between those who think that history is the study of hard facts which are somewhere out there in the real world, waiting to be collected like so many pebbles on the beach, and those who think that history is an imaginative reconstruction of a chaotic past, a lovely intellectual order imposed upon a mundane mess; between those who think that the historian acquires permanent truths and that his discipline is, in this sense, progressive, and those who argue that each generation must rewrite history, since the history of its predecessors was hemmed in, and spurred on, by perspectives and prejudices, by class loyalties and status anxieties, by religious, ethnic, or national biases.

Cassirer's anecdote suggests that both may be partially right, but right only in relation to a larger, higher, more inclusive conception of history. Cassirer denies that there is an inevitable, radical, fatal disjunction between imagination and discipline. The imagination is not mere fancy; its products are not like Hamlet's clouds, shifting and unpredictable. Nor is the imagination a mere recording instrument. It transforms the actual without violating it: there is a positive connection between the creative function of mind and the discipline of method. This is why Cassirer could appreciatively quote Goethe's remark to Eckermann, praising the

[1] Dimitry Gawronsky, "Ernst Cassirer: His Life and His Work," in Paul Arthur Schilpp, ed., *The Philosophy of Ernst Cassirer* (1949), 35.

Phantasie für die Wahrheit des Realen — "the imagination for the truth of reality."[2]

Cassirer's position — and his epistemological writings show that the anecdote, far from being casual, illustrates that position — liberates the historian from a despairing choice. History is *both* art and science, *both* stable and progressive. Like scientists, historians validly build on the work of their predecessors; unlike scientists, their classics retain permanent validity. The results of history are public; they can be analyzed and verified and modified; its findings, its very methods are open to criticism and hence improvement. By discovering new documents, by creating documents (that is, by transforming into historical clues material that had been disregarded before), by importing new methods from neighboring disciplines, by discovering biases to be biases, a more recent historian has a decisive advantage over an earlier historian. Gibbon's *History of the Decline and Fall of the Roman Empire* is probably the greatest book on Roman history ever written, but the beginning student no longer begins with it: its stature is secure, but it is that of Newton's *Principia Mathematica* — magnificent but dated.

But the student of Roman history, if he does not begin with Gibbon, should end with him. If *The Decline and Fall* does not underlie his apprenticeship, it should crown that apprenticeship. That is only another way of saying that history is an art: a new masterpiece in history, like a new masterpiece in literature, changes the relationship of all to each.[3] Science by definition is a pursuit without classics; history has its classics: its *Peloponnesian War*, its *Kultur der Renaissance in Italien*, its *Société féodale* will never be dated.

Yet — and here lies the remarkable ambivalence of the historian's

[2] See Ernst Cassirer, *An Essay on Man: An Introduction to A Philosophy of Human Culture* (1944, Anchor ed., 1953), 258.

[3] This point has been tellingly made by T. S. Eliot, in his "Tradition and the Individual Talent" (1919): "The existing monuments form an ideal order among themselves, which is modified by the introduction of the new (the really new) work of art among them. The existing order is complete before the new work arrives; for order to persist after the supervention of novelty, the *whole* existing order must be, if ever so slightly, altered. . . ." *Selected Prose*, ed. John Hayward (1953), 23.

craft — the classics of history are of a peculiar character. There is no point in attempting to improve Dante's *Divine Comedy* because we know more astronomy than Dante did, or have a more adequate understanding than Dante had of classical Roman authors. There is no point in arguing with the *Divine Comedy*, even if there is much point in arguing about it. But there is much point in arguing with Gibbon's *Decline and Fall of the Roman Empire*, or Namier's *Structure of Politics at the Accession of George III*. A work of history may be a work of art, calling (like a painting) for iconographical analysis and aesthetic appreciation, but it is also an argument, a structure of propositions, and, unlike its claim to beauty, its claim to truth can be investigated and tested, and its argumentation, its documentation, and its demonstration, confirmed, modified, or rejected.

The contention that history is at once art and science has special relevance to intellectual history. Many of its critics and, I must admit, many of its practitioners, treat intellectual history as an arid exercise in the gathering of quotations; many more of its practitioners, yielding to the allure of dabbling in Nietzsche or Kierkegaard — or Hegel — exploit it as a vehicle for vague, impressionistic constructions, forgetting that intellectual history demands not woolgathering or enthusiasm but rigor and severe, self-restrained intelligence. To write grandly about the *Zeitgeist* is a disease easy to acquire and hard to cure: *Die Zeitgeister die ich rief* (if I may misquote Goethe's *Zauberlehrling* for my own purposes), *werd ich nun nicht los*. Quotations must be illuminated, ordered, given life by synthetic understanding, but intuition must be controlled by method and delicacy.

It follows from all this that while much of the material of intellectual history lends itself to varying interpretations, while the subtle exploration of meanings may lead the historian in several directions, while different perspectives may each claim validity, not all assertions about a thinker or a movement are equally true. Intellectual history, though artistic, strives for the fidelity of a portrait. It follows, further, that the intellectual historian must be precise and concrete before he can be — and in order that he might properly be — sweeping and imaginative. It follows, finally, that while there can be, and often is, progress in the writing of intellectual history — one need only study the literature on Rousseau in its historical order to see that progress is sometimes startling[4] — this progress is uncertain and discontinuous, and the classic insights of a great practitioner who entered the field early may retain permanent value and, more than that, permanent validity. "In my more pessimistic moments," the late Garrett Mattingly wrote not long ago, thinking about the battle over the Renaissance, "I am sometimes inclined to imagine that the historical profession, instead of moving steadily forward through experience and self-criticism to deeper understanding and steadier, more penetrating vision, just swings aimlessly back and forth with the tides of fashion, like the ladies' garment industry." And he concludes with a moderate assertion of which Cassirer would have approved: "I am not saying that the older historians are always better than their revisers. I am just saying that when they have no new, verifiable facts, the newest revisers are not necessarily the soundest."[5] Revisionism is a young man's game; it offers psychological gratification and professional advancement to the reviser, but it is not always, not automatically, of benefit to the craft as a whole.

II

Cassirer's first conception, then, equips the intellectual historian with a general view of the nature of his discipline. His second conception, which I have called "the primacy of function," equips him with his method. "The historian of ideas," Cassirer writes in a discussion of Renaissance historiography, "knows that the water which the river carries with it changes only very slowly. The same ideas are always appearing again and again, and are maintained for centuries. The force and the tenacity of tradition can hardly be over-estimated. From this point of view we must acknowledge over and over again that there is nothing new under the sun. But the historian of ideas is not asking primarily what

[4] See my essay, "Reading about Rousseau," in *The Party of Humanity: Essays in the French Enlightenment* (1964), 211 – 261.

[5] "Some Revisions of the Political History of the Renaissance," in Tinsley Helton, ed., *The Renaissance* (1961), 9, 23.

the *substance* is of particular ideas. He is asking what their *function* is. What he is studying — or should be studying — is less the *content* of ideas than their dynamics. To continue the figure, we could say that he is not trying to analyze the drops of water in the river, but that he is seeking to measure its width and depth and to ascertain the force and velocity of the current."[6]

This precept, as Cassirer was fully aware, is perfectly obvious. But he found it necessary to state it simply because it is rarely observed. Were it observed more often, there would be fewer bootless debates in intellectual history, and less real work for revisionist historians to do. The importance of the principle cannot be overestimated.

Ideas radiate out in two directions: they move horizontally, clashing with other ideas in their time, interacting with the society in which they were born and function. And they move vertically, into the future, to be taken up, used, abused, dissected, by later generations. In turn, ideas receive impulses from two directions: horizontally, from other ideas and from society; vertically, from the past. Each idea therefore, as we seek to understand it fully, presents to us a tightly woven, many-stranded tapestry. This too is obvious, but one favorite manner of dealing with an idea is to state its manifest verbal form, preferably in the guise of a startling pronouncement, and then to search in its past for antecedents or in its future for effects. The hunt for influences — and "influence" is the intellectual historian's favorite word — has become an absorbing pastime.

Now surely the pursuit of an idea into its past or its future, the search for roots or fruits, is a historical enterprise as legitimate as it is important. The search for the origins of Nazism, or modern materialism, need not apologize for itself. But in this search the *function* of ideas is all too often pushed aside in favor of fancied resemblances. Hegel called the state "the march of God through the world"; the Nazis constructed a totalitarian state; Hegel was an ancestor of the Nazis. Everybody knows that; few syllogisms in intellectual history are more familiar. And, until Herbert Marcuse ruined it in his *Reason and Revolution*, there were few to

[6] "Some Remarks on the Question of the Originality of the Renaissance," *Journal of the History of Ideas*, IV (1943), 55.

question it. Yet it is completely misleading.[7] The minor premise
is untrue: the Nazis did not preach the supremacy of the state.
The conclusion is untrue: the Nazis were not Hegelians. But what
is most significant at this point is the status of the major premise,
which, after all, is true. Hegel did speak of the state as the march
of God in the world.[8] The question that must be asked is, What
did the word "state" mean to Hegel, in this paragraph, this book,
his system? Considering the passions that are engaged — and right-
fully engaged — in our analysis of the terrible events of our century, the search for antecedents is of pressing importance, of
supreme relevance, for our self-understanding. But it is precisely
because it is so important and so relevant that the task is so delicate. Everyone who is familiar with the writings of Nietzsche —
with all its glaring faults, all its posturing and absurdities — must
be appalled at the burdens he has been made to carry, the crimes
he is supposed to have inspired. Yet the functionalist analysis of
his writings can make it plain that Nietzsche's blond beast was not
a Nazi, his superman the opposite of a sadistic butcher.

Just as functionalism helps to determine the meaning of words
and ideas in a system, it helps to determine the place of a system in
history. There is widespread skepticism of periodization: to divide the past into meaningful segments by assigning it names is,
we are often told, a mere semantic game. But this is a misjudg-
ment. A name like "Middle Ages" or "Renaissance" or "Enlightenment" carries a great deal of freight: it claims unity within
variety; it claims that some aspects of culture are more significant
than others; it claims that there are discontinuities as well as continuities in the history of the mind. Periods may be conventional
units, but if they are soundly chosen, they are not arbitrary.

Now it is precisely the functional analysis of ideas that makes
meaningful periodization possible. Consider the Renaissance. It is

[7] See Herbert Marcuse, *Reason and Revolution: Hegel and the Rise of
Social Theory* (1941). In its first edition, George H. Sabine's excellent and
influential *A History of Political Theory* (1937) repeated all the current
clichés; in its second edition (1950) as he makes clear in the Preface, Sabine
had changed his mind completely, largely as a result of reading *Reason and
Revolution* (see for this honorable reversal, Sabine, pp. viii, and 620 – 668.)

[8] See Hegel, *Grundlinien der Philosophie des Rechts*, addition to paragraph 258; see also paragraphs 260 and 270.

well known that there has been a vehement, sometimes acrimonious debate over the Renaissance for a century. When did it take place? How long did it last? What were its distinguishing characteristics? And, how many were there — one, several, or none? Some respectable historians claim to see authentic Renaissances in the Carolingian period, others insist that the twelfth century may claim to have experienced a true Renaissance, still others demote what is usually called the Renaissance — the time span between Petrarch and Galileo — into a mere appendix, a simple working out of ideas and tendencies prevalent in the High Middle Ages.

Now — if I may simplify for purposes of this discussion a debate of truly staggering complexity — what the critics of Burckhardt have in common is a failure to see both the function of labels and the function of ideas. The function of the term "Renaissance" is descriptive; it points to a structure of reality different in kind, and therefore deserving a different name, from other structures. To deny the cultural flowering of the twelfth century the title of Renaissance is not to deny that the flowering took place, or to denigrate its achievement. A periodic label is not a decoration to be worn on the chest as a sign of accomplishment.

Besides, to insist on the same name for the work of, say, Roger Bacon and Francis Bacon is to take verbal for functional resemblances. If we study Roger Bacon's programmatic pronouncements, if we ask just what he meant when he asserted that mathematics is the supreme discipline and that experimentation is an essential instrument for the student of nature, it turns out that these pronouncements had no resonance in his culture, little resonance in his own work, and, in any event, a meaning wholly different from similar pronouncements uttered in the seventeenth century by Francis Bacon. It is not an accident that Roger Bacon's writings failed to bring about a scientific revolution, or even a scientific renaissance: precisely like all other educated clerics of his day, he was certain that theology was superior to, and the guide of, philosophy; that what we today call "natural science" was a subordinate part of philosophy; that whatever man might discover by himself about heaven and earth, the best source of information about these matters, as well as all others, was the Holy Word of God; and that in any event, whatever scientific pursuit a good

Christian might engage in, he would engage in it quite literally for the greater glory of God. This is precisely what Cassirer had in mind when he considered Roger Bacon's pronouncements on mathematics as anything but startling: "Mathematics," he writes, "had been an *element* in culture long before the Renaissance; but in the Renaissance, with thinkers like Leonardo or Galileo, it became a new cultural *force*."[9] In the same manner, the so-called "classicism" of the great twelfth century, the devout reading of Cicero, or the so-called "Platonism" of the School of Chartres, was different — and different in kind — from what would be called classicism and Platonism two and three hundred years later in Florence.

Cassirer's functionalism, then, functions as a critical weapon: it exposes what I have elsewhere called "the fallacy of spurious persistence."[10] Medieval Christians piously said, "I trust in God"; modern American coins tell us that "In God We Trust"; but it requires little investigation to understand that this pair of assertions, though identical in logical structure and ostensible meaning, actually refer to different, indeed incompatible, realities. Ideas may pass through centuries unchanged in everything but vocabulary; or, on the contrary, they experience profound changes in meaning hidden behind the continuity of formulation. Beyond this, Cassirer's functionalism has its constructive side; it functions not merely as a warning but as a clue; it points to what in an idea, a philosophy, a movement, a period, is of real historical significance.

III

To advocate the primacy of function is to teach respect for the integrity of the past; to teach acceptance of every idea for its own sake as being equally near to God. And to teach acceptance within the historical context implies the historian's readiness to

[9] Cassirer, "Remarks on the Originality of the Renaissance," *Journal of the History of Ideas*, IV, 51.

[10] See my essay, "Carl Becker's Heavenly City," first published in the *Political Science Quarterly* in 1957, and republished, slightly revised, in my *The Party of Humanity*, 188 – 210.

penetrate beyond surface contradictions to hidden connections. With Cassirer, this readiness took a passionate form, and so I have called his third conception, which defines the goal of intellectual history as its predecessors had defined its nature and its method, a "rage for coherence." No matter how "heterogeneous the objects of human knowledge may be," Cassirer observes, "the forms of knowledge always show an inner unity and a logical homogeneity." The historian "finds his texts not merely in books, in annals or memoirs. He has to read hieroglyphics or cuneiform inscriptions, look at colors on a canvas, at statues in marble or bronze, at cathedrals or temples, at coins or gems. But he does not consider all these things simply with the mind of an antiquary who wishes to collect and preserve the treasures of olden times. What the historian is in search of is rather the materialization of the spirit of a former age. He detects the same spirit in laws and statutes, in charters and bills of rights, in social institutions and political constitutions, in religious rites and ceremonies. To the true historian such material is not petrified fact but living form. History is the attempt to fuse together all these *disjecta membra*, the scattered limbs of the past, and to synthesize them and mold them into new shape."[11]

For Cassirer, who faithfully followed his own prescription, a contradiction in a thinker or a period is not a terminal point but an opportunity. It is the point where research begins, in fact the very inducement to research. In Cassirer's own work, the principle had some remarkably fruitful consequences; in his essays on Greek philosophy or on Goethe's historical sense, on Descartes' Stoicism or on Mendelssohn's religious ideas, Cassirer looks for the *Schwerpunkt*, the *Gesichtspunkt*, the perspective from which the thinker produces his work. Consider Cassirer's essays on Rousseau, a writer notoriously hard to make consistent or coherent. In Rousseau's corpus, book seems to contradict book, life seems to deny philosophy, love of civilization seems to confront, in irreconcilable conflict, hatred of culture, paranoia seems impossible to bring into harmony with philanthropy. Yet Cassirer, by establishing a dynamic relationship between Rousseau's life and Rousseau's

[11] Cassirer, *An Essay on Man*, 224–225.

thought, Rousseau's thought and Rousseau's writings, succeeds in discovering in apparent chaos a vital center, a core at once emotional and intellectual from which Rousseau's total behavior — including his writing — radiates out. Cassirer is constrained to concede that Rousseau changed his mind as he developed, and that he often contradicted himself: any literary man who writes as much as Rousseau, lives as long, as publicly, as frenetically as he, must contradict himself. But Cassirer was undeterred by such contradictions: his Rousseau is a single, a whole man, a believable human being, a reasonable thinker, if with extravagant habits. And it is worth noting that for the most part Cassirer's Rousseau is today the Rousseau of the scholars.[12]

Cassirer's search for coherence in the philosophy of the Renaissance is equally impressive: unlike Lynn Thorndyke, who catalogued elements in past scientific thought he could label "scientific" and others he could label "superstitious," Cassirer looks for the emotional and intellectual dynamic that connected the diverse group of philosophers who together make up what is called "Renaissance philosophy": Pico, the erudite syncretist who takes elements for his thought from all conceivable systems except astrology; Pomponazzi, who reads Aristotle with modern skeptical eyes, but accepts astrology; Nicolas of Cusa, who combines the most varied talents and accomplishments — who was mystic, ecclesiastical politician, early modern philosopher, traditional theologian. The thought of each of these philosophers appears, from a modern perspective, as internally inconsistent, and as incompatible with the others, but Cassirer, as a true historian, avoids the modern perspective, and begins his inquiry into Renaissance philosophy precisely at the point of apparently hopeless contradiction to construct a grand, richly orchestrated harmony.

This search for coherence, as I have said, is a mark of respect for others: it assumes that thinkers of the past were on the whole

---

[12] It was Franz Neumann, Herbert Marcuse's friend and intellectual companion, who first called my attention to Cassirer's articles of 1932 on Rousseau, which I then translated under the title *The Question of Jean-Jacques Rousseau* (1954). The essay remains after thirty-five years in the mainstream of advanced Rousseau scholarship.

intelligent men who would have discarded elements that appeared to them incompatible with the totality of their thought. What later critics, looking back, find to be inconsistent, a thinker in his own time, and for good reason, found perfectly consistent, and his confidence that his thought is a coherent structure when his posterity denies that, is an eminently suitable subject for the intellectual historian's attention: it will shed light on the thinker's character, his culture, his philosophical schools, the live options open to him.

There are, I think, two basic types of intellectual historians: those who, like sadistic teachers, enjoy discovering contradictions and exposing them, to the discomfiture of their victims and their own greater glory; and those who, distressed by disharmony, perform analysis for the sake of synthesis. Cassirer is the supreme example of the second type: he was capable of recognizing and recording the torment of transitional figures like Petrarch, of reporting a philosopher's inability to produce coherence from his discordant desires and conflicting traditions. But he was never comfortable with this kind of disorder, and in consequence he slighted tensions, reduced ambiguities to slightly artificial order. But this, we may conclude, was a venial fault, a flaw which in no way discredits his principle.

IV

The really serious difficulty in Cassirer's conception of intellectual history is not his failure to pay adequate attention to troubling contradictions; the difficulty lies elsewhere, and deeper than this, in his failure to do justice to the social dimensions of ideas. I cannot claim that this is the main reason for Herbert Marcuse's reservations about Cassirer's work, although I think it likely; it is in any event the main reason for my reservations, and it dictated the title of this essay, "The *Social* History of Ideas."

Ernst Cassirer did not view intellectual history as a self-enclosed, narcissistic discipline in which idea confronts idea, and nothing else. He candidly labeled his books to be what they were: his celebrated study of the Enlightenment, for example, plainly calls

itself, *The Philosophy of the Enlightenment;* and he connected
ideas, on many occasions, to their philosophical background. But
there were two directions in which he resolutely refused to go:
inward, to the psychological ground of ideas;[13] and outward, into
society.

In his brilliant analysis of Renaissance philosophy, Ernst Cassirer writes:

> The philosophy of the Quattrocento is divided between
> two tendencies [classical humanism and scholasticism]; but
> the retrograde movement, the attempt at a "restoration" of
> Scholastic forms of thought gradually gains more and more
> breadth and strength. In the last decades of the fifteenth cen-
> tury, in the epoch characterized by the dominance of the
> Platonic Academy in Florence, this movement reached its
> climax. Philosophy is turned into the bulwark against the
> worldly forces that press upon it from all sides. But it cannot
> carry out this assignment without endangering, once again,
> the tentative beginnings of an independent and autonomous
> method which Nicolas of Cusa had made — without trans-
> forming itself once again, and increasingly, into "theology."
> . . . The tension between belief and knowledge has greatly
> increased.[14]

All of this is correct, precisely and movingly observed: it is
true that Florentine Neo-Platonism marks the gradual abandonment of the ideal of the active life, the *vita activa*, that had characterized the civic humanism of earlier humanists like Salutati and
Bruni. But we read Cassirer's book in vain for an account of the
social context in which this retreat took place, and to which this
retreat was a response. Civic humanism declined as political action

---

[13] If I may offer another reminiscence: in my Introduction to Cassirer's
The Question of Jean-Jacques Rousseau I had dared to suggest that Cassirer's
"rationalistic approach to biography is open to criticism . . . a critic who,
like Cassirer, relies on biography cannot afford to neglect completely the
contributions of Freud and of the discipline which he founded" (p. 24). Not
long after these words were published I met Cassirer's widow, and she
referred to them with some rather wry disdain: "My husband," she said,
"had he read these words, would just have smiled."

[14] Ernst Cassirer, *Individuum und Kosmos in der Philosophie der Renaissance* (1927), 65.

became irrelevant in Florence: after the middle of the fifteenth century, the Medici oligarchy tightened its grip and intimidated its intellectuals. As early as 1444, a Humanist was banished from Florence and others went into exile later; the rest saved themselves by internal migration: they increasingly concentrated their attention on art, or pure Latinity, and refurbished the old contemplative ideal.[15]

This instance — there are many others — glaringly illuminates the consequences following upon Cassirer's disregard of the social matrix of ideas; in overlooking significant causes of the Humanists' retreat to contemplation he failed to diagnose its full meaning. Cassirer would surely have agreed in principle that ideas interact with their environment — he was not as unworldly as all that — but his training and his intellectual preferences led him to concentrate, instead, on the relations of ideas to one another, as they struggled for clear definition within a single thinker, a single school, a single culture. And that is why Cassirer stands to the social historian of ideas as Dante's Vergil stands to Dante the pilgrim: as a powerful, knowledgeable, admirable guide who can go only so far and then must surrender his charge to another.

Or, rather, to others. For the social historian of ideas must, I think, abandon one aspect of Cassirer's way of thinking — his rather unpolitical Idealism — in the name, and by the light, of another aspect — his pragmatic functionalism. It would take another essay at least as long as this to justify the tautology that I commend to all historians touching on the products of the intellect: the social historian of ideas must use all the instruments he needs for his particular task, and what instruments he needs will emerge at least in part in the course of his investigations. To say this is not to ask him to be a flabby eclectic; some firm theoretical principles — like Freud's theories of human nature and growth, and

[15] The leading scholar of this aspect of the Renaissance is, of course, Hans Baron. See especially his *The Crisis of the Early Italian Renaissance: Civic Humanism and Republican Liberty in an Age of Classicism and Tyranny*, 2 vols. (1955), and his magnificent earlier essay, *Cicero and the Roman Civic Spirit in the Middle Ages and the Early Renaissance* (1938). The social situation of the Humanists, and the story of their troubles under the Medici, is well analyzed in Lauro Martines, *The Social World of the Florentine Humanists* (1963).

Mannheim's insight into the social character of words — will equip him at the outset to discover historical problems invisible to others, and identify a way toward their solution. But the precise choice of intellectual tools must depend on the character of the idea under investigation, for each idea is different from every other idea.

Yet, for all these differences, all ideas have this much in common: all of them are, in Freud's word, overdetermined; all of them, we might say, have more reasons for existing than they need. And all coexist in several realms at once: all are at least touched by the unconscious, with its crude distortions and insatiable need for gratification; by the stylistic tradition of which it is an expression or against which it is in rebellion; by social, economic, political pressures which lend it its particular urgency and its unique shape. The relative weight of each of these factors will differ from time to time and place to place, but they are all present, and it is to them all that the social historian of ideas must address himself — or leave his assignment uncompleted.

Policies of Violence:
From Montesquieu to the Terrorists

E. V. WALTER

ALTHOUGH THE REIGN OF TERROR in the French Revolution is ordinarily and correctly identified with the epoch of September
1793 to July 1794, when the Robespierrist group controlled the
state, the systematic use of violence was not restricted to that period. Terrorism in varying degrees and of one kind or another
ranged throughout the revolutionary decade, beginning with the
Great Fear of 1789, extending to the White Terror of 1795, to
the Second Directory, and to the Jacobin revival of 1799. Nevertheless, the reactionary terrors were silent as far as the history of
theory is concerned. The principles of terrorism as an instrument
of state policy, which emerged from the decade, were formulated
by radical republicans, notably Robespierre and Saint-Just.[1] Their
union of terror and revolutionary government made a permanent
impression on the theory of revolution, emerging in the interpretation of every modern, violent revolutionary crisis. Thus,
Mathiez, writing in 1928, claimed that the Robespierrist "terroristic dictatorship . . . today is called the dictatorship of the proletariat."[2]

The purpose of my essay is to explore the earliest intellectual
history of the modern link between terror and revolution. I in-

[1] References to their work are from *Discours et Rapports de Robespierre*,
ed. Charles Vellay, Paris, 1908 (cited below as DR) and *Oeuvres Complètes de Saint-Just*, ed. Charles Valley, 2 vols., Paris, 1908 (cited below as
OC). All translations, unless otherwise indicated, are my own.

[2] Mathiez, Albert, "La terreur: Instrument de la politique sociale des
robespierristes," *Annales Historiques de la Révolution Française*, Vol. 5,
1928, p. 219.

tend to show first that Robespierre and Saint-Just based their theory of revolutionary government on concepts taken from Montesquieu's political sociology; second, that they reorganized these concepts in a new theoretical structure; and, third, that at the height of the Terror they went further to recognize in the Revolution a social dynamic that was only inchoate in Montesquieu's work. Although I make no effort to deal with the extent or the limits of sociological understanding implicit in their work, I shall indicate in passing that the idea of wilful conspiracy demanded by their theory of terror — not to speak of the requirements of their forensic style — contradicted and overshadowed their sociological conception of the revolutionary process.

Robespierre and Saint-Just forged their theory of revolutionary government chiefly from Greek and Roman materials transmuted in the crucible of modern revolutionary experience, but Montesquieu was the catalyst in the process. For the revolutionary thinkers, the political histories of Sparta, Athens, and Rome were more than sources of information about political structures and the metamorphoses of power. They were a vivid political experience — not a remote past, but a mythical presence. In the trial of Louis XVI, for example, Saint-Just condemned the monarch politically as the despot of the French, and mythically as Tarquin, the last king of the Romans. The ancient sources provided vicarious experience; Montesquieu provided a philosophical interpretation of that experience and a theoretical analysis of the principles of monarchy, republic, and despotism.

The spell of classical writers on the revolutionary thinkers is familiar knowledge. The influence of Montesquieu is also well known,[3] but the exact nature of that influence is not clearly understood. It is taken for granted that his ideas helped shape the early phase of the Revolution and that they pervaded the Constitution of 1791, but it is also presumed that, after monarchy was overthrown, Montesquieu's influence grew less important and more vague because the revolutionaries — especially the Terrorists — abandoned his work to turn wholeheartedly to the ideas of

[3] Cf. Parker, Harold T., *The Cult of Antiquity and the French Revolutionaries*, Chicago, 1937. This study traces specific influences of the ancient writers and also records public references to Montesquieu.

Rousseau.[4] To be sure, Saint-Just's longest work, *The Spirit of the Revolution*, published in 1791, imitates in many ways *The Spirit of the Laws*, but one may contend that when, in the brief space of two years, he leaped from constitutional monarchism to terroristic republicanism he might have discarded Montesquieu. Superficially, it may seem odd that radical republicans like Robespierre and Saint-Just would have retained the ideas of a conservative aristocrat like Montesquieu.

The precise nature of Montesquieu's influence, then, is obscured because his work has been viewed from several perspectives. His politics were unthinkable to a patriot in the Year II. Furthermore, his theoretical system contains the seeds of modern pluralism—especially through its influence on Tocqueville—and it is also associated with constitutional restraints such as checks and balances. Therefore, narrow identifications of his work with the defense of privilege or with pluralist ideas or with constitutional restraints would indeed remove him from any suspected influence on the theory of terror. What must be taken into account is the perspective of his political sociology. It suffered no eclipse and was at least as important as the moral ideas of Rousseau in providing orientation and framework for the theory of terror developed by Robespierre and Saint-Just.

The Antithesis of Terror and Virtue in Montesquieu's System

In his report on the principles of revolutionary government, Robespierre announced that "the theory of revolutionary govern-

[4] Crane Brinton, to give one example, tends to make Rousseau *the* philosopher of the Terror. See Brinton, C. C., *The Jacobins*, New York, 1961. In the only reference to Montesquieu in this book, p. 142, Brinton observes, "In spite of the centralization of the Terror, there remained in Jacobin politics a certain strain of Montesquieu — or at least, a certain distrust of strong executive power." Thus, Montesquieu's influence is restricted to the idea of checks and balances. In an earlier essay Brinton recognizes Montesquieu's influence on Saint-Just, but claims that "it quite drops out before the omnipotence of the sovereign people . . ." and argues that "St. Just's justification of the Terror is . . . merely an aphoristic version" of Rousseau's ideas. See "The Political Ideas of St. Just," *Politica*, February, 1934, pp. 39, 45.

ment is as new as the revolution which brought it and not to be found in the books of the political writers. . . ." Nevertheless a political writer's book, namely, *The Spirit of the Laws*, provided the concepts on which the new theory was based. The ideas of virtue and terror, originally separate and contrary principles in Montesquieu's work, were joined together in a novel way, for in a report on the principles of political morality that ought to guide the Convention, Robespierre declared, "If the spring of popular government in peace is virtue, the spring of popular government in revolution is simultaneously virtue and terror: virtue, without which terror is deadly, and terror without which virtue is powerless."[5] In order to understand the full meaning of the new theory, it is necessary to grasp the logic of Montesquieu's concepts.

Montesquieu had developed a theory of political systems based on three archetypal forms, each integrated by a constitutive principle, namely, "despotic governments, whose principle is terror"; monarchy, which depends on honor; and the republic, which has for its principle, virtue.[6] The principle of each form is the typical "passion" which integrates the policy and also energizes the political structure, as the mainspring of a clock sets the mechanism in motion.

The three typical systems may be perceived as mechanisms or as organisms,[7] but they may also be understood — in the classical way — as moral structures as well. They may be located on a continuum stretched between the extremes of selfishness and selflessness, or they may be arranged in a hierarchy of value, with despotism the worst, republic the best, and monarchy intermediate. Despotism is the selfish rule of a solitary individual; the republic depends on the selflessness of the people; monarchy needs rank, which originates in selfish privileges dispensed as rewards for selfless acts. The hierarchy may also be constructed accord-

[5] DR, 311, 332. (See note 1.)

[6] Montesquieu, *The Spirit of the Laws*, trans. Thomas Nugent, New York, 1949, Vol. I, p. 81.

[7] Isaiah Berlin has recognized the forms as biological models, each regulated by its inner, dynamic force or principle. See his essay, "Montesquieu," *Proceedings of the British Academy*, Vol. XLI, 1955, p. 277.

ing to the moral content of each principle. Terror, the lowest of the three passions, is raw affect with no moral value. Honor, the intermediate principle, is a mixed passion, combining impulses with moral sentiment. Virtue, the highest, is a moral passion.

In a republic, the selfless restraint associated with virtue is necessary to maintain the integrity of the structure — indispensable in a democracy. In aristocratic republics, where nobles and people are not on the same level, the soul of the government is moderation, which is a virtue inferior to that of democracy. In both cases, a chaotic state created by ambition, avarice, and corruption is the alternative to virtue. But virtue is not necessary to a monarchy, for the structure is preserved by the force of laws and by the mutual restraints in the relation between the monarch and intermediate bodies such as the nobility. In despotism, virtue is absent — so are rationality and liberty; the structure is regulated by caprice and preserved by terror.

Only in despotism is terror consistent with the political structure. The purpose of terror is tranquillity, "but this tranquillity cannot be called a peace; no, it is only the silence of those towns which the enemy is ready to invade."[8] Terror eliminates resistance, prevents disorder, and holds together an expansive area, for it is the natural disposition of a despotic government to organize vast domains. Montesquieu thinks of despotism as an inherently "corrupt" form, according to moral standards, but corruption is not always unstable. Extrinsic factors such as climate, religion, situation, or genius of the people may lend a despotic government stability at least for a time.[9] Under those conditions, presumably, the despot "ought" to maintain the terror to keep the system intact, for, unless it is directed by its specific principle, "the government is imperfect."[10] He describes political acts and strategies consistent with each principle, assuming a hypothetical imperative similar to Machiavelli's, indicating that, if one wants to get a certain result, then one needs to use a specific technique.

One function of terror in a despotism is to suppress the tendency to form intermediate powers between the ruler and the

[8] Montesquieu, *Spirit*, I, 59.
[9] Ibid., pp. 115 – 116.
[10] Ibid., p. 28.

people. All officers must remain mere instruments of the despot, and their privileges and powers held in precarious possession, never amounting to anything more than rewards dispensed at his will. Were these men to develop a sense of honor and self-respect, and were they able to wrest a degree of independent power and privilege, then they would become in effect a nobility. Under such conditions the integrity of the despotism is destroyed, for the system would be transforming itself into a monarchy. Thus, Montesquieu writes:

> the immense power of the prince devolves entirely upon those whom he is pleased to intrust with the administration. Persons capable of setting a value upon themselves would be likely to create disturbances. Fear must therefore depress their spirits, and extinguish even the least sense of ambition.[11]

Montesquieu anticipates Max Weber's insight that historical reality involves a continuous, latent conflict between chiefs and their administrative staffs over the control of privileges and material rewards. The outcome of the struggle for political and economic independence by lieutenants, and the outcome of efforts by heads of states to suppress this drive for independence, has been crucial for the destiny of political systems and for the development of civilization as a whole.[12]

Ironically, Montesquieu continues, the absolute power of the despot may have advantages for the people, for it prevents their being oppressed by lesser powers:

> when a despotic prince ceases for one single moment to uplift his arm, when he cannot instantly demolish those whom he has intrusted with the first employments, all is over: for as fear, the spring of this government, no longer subsists, the people are left without a protector. . . . History informs us that the horrid cruelties of Domitian struck such a terror into the governors, that the people recovered themselves a little during his reign.[13]

[11] Ibid., p. 26.
[12] See Weber, Max, *The Theory of Social and Economic Organization*, trans. Henderson and Parsons, New York, 1947, pp. 383 – 384.
[13] Montesquieu, *Spirit*, I, 26 – 27.

Control from the center must be maintained by the threat of swift military violence against signs of resistance:

> There should be always a body of faithful troops near the prince, ready to fall instantly upon any part of the empire that may chance to waver. This military corps ought to awe the rest, and to strike terror into those who through necessity have been intrusted with any authority in the empire.[14]

Great distances make necessary the use of violent techniques, and, conversely, it is the natural property of large empires to be controlled by a despot:

> A large empire supposes a despotic authority in the person who governs. It is necessary that the quickness of the prince's resolutions should supply the distance of the places they are sent to; that fear should prevent the remissness of the distant governor or magistrate; that the law should be derived from a single person, and should shift continually, according to the accidents which incessantly multiply in a state in proportion to its extent.[15]

The idea that terror was best suited for the control of large numbers endured. A century after Montesquieu, James Mill observed "that the range of obedience, obtained by fear, is capable of much greater enlargement, than that which obtained by hope. The means any man has of paying for the service of others, extends at most to some thousands; the means which some men have had of imposing their commands on other men, through fear, has extended to many millions."[16]

The simplicity of despotism explains its adaptation to the control of large areas and its durability, but this simplicity is also responsible for the large number of despotic regimes in history, Montesquieu claims. Even though it is natural for mankind to detest violence and to love liberty, men do not perpetually rise up against despotism because it is such an easy system to establish and to maintain. Moderate governments are much more complex.

[14] Ibid., p. 147.
[15] Ibid., p. 122.
[16] Mill, James, *Analysis of the Phenomena of the Human Mind*, 2 vols., London, 1829, I, 166 – 167.

"On the contrary, a despotic government offers itself, as it were, at first sight; it is uniform throughout; and as passions only are requisite to establish it, this is what every capacity may reach."[17]

The system is effective because resistance is eliminated swiftly and decisively:

> In despotic states, the nature of government requires the most passive obedience; and when once the prince's will is made known, it ought infallibly to produce its effect.
>
> Here they have no limitations or restrictions, no mediums, terms, equivalents, or remonstrances; no change to propose: man is a creature that blindly submits to the absolute will of the sovereign. . . . Man's portion here, like that of the beasts, is instinct, compliance, and punishment.
>
> Little does it then avail to plead the sentiments of nature, filial respect, conjugal or parental tenderness, the laws of honor, or want of health; the order is given, and that is sufficient.[18]

All governments work toward the same general end, which is self-preservation, but each has a particular object as well. The object of despotic states is the pleasures of the prince. It pursues this object at great cost, for in the violence necessary to obtain it, "A despotic government does all the mischief to itself that could be committed by a cruel enemy, whose arms it were unable to resist."[19] Besides, "the terror of despotic power is so great that it recoils upon those who exercise it."[20] The depressed state of the people reduces their motivations so that action must be stimulated by bribes and presents, for "in a despotic government, where there is neither honor nor virtue, people cannot be determined to act but through hope of the conveniences of life."[21] Since "the customs of an enslaved people are part of their servitude," a culture of despotism is necessary to reinforce governmental controls, and cultural changes would carry the danger of fundamental political change:

17 Montesquieu, *Spirit*, I, 62.
18 Ibid., p. 27.
19 Ibid., p. 129.
20 Ibid., pp. 192 – 193.
21 Ibid., p. 65.

It is a capital maxim, that the manners and customs of a despotic empire ought never to be changed; for nothing would more speedily produce a revolution. The reason is, that in these states there are no laws, that is, none that can be properly called so; there are only manners and customs; and if you overturn these you overturn all.[22]

The political tranquillity of despotic systems, which Montesquieu says depends on the perpetual insecurity established by terror, is entirely different from the tranquillity of mind to be found in systems that ensure political liberty. "The political liberty of the subject is a tranquillity of mind arising from the opinion each person has of his safety. In order to have this liberty, it is requisite the government be so constituted as one man need not be afraid of another."[23]

Nevertheless, even though Montesquieu argued that only in a despotism is terror consistent with the political structure, it might appear briefly from time to time in the history of other systems. In republics its usefulness is limited: "As soon as a republic has compassed the destruction of those who wanted to subvert it, there should be an end of terrors, punishments, and even of rewards."[24] The limitations are imposed by the laws:

when an impression of terror has no certain object, it produces only clamor and abuse; it has, however, this good effect, that it puts all the springs of government into motion, and fixes the attention of every citizen. But if it arises from a violation of the fundamental laws, it is sullen, cruel, and produces the most dreadful catastrophes.

Soon we should see a frightful calm, during which everyone would unite against that power which had violated the laws.[25]

Although Montesquieu argued that in republics and monarchies bounds should be set to violence, he recognized that in extreme situations, "Great punishments, and consequently great changes, cannot take place without investing some citizens with an ex-

[22] Ibid., pp. 307, 297.
[23] Ibid., p. 151.
[24] Ibid., p. 197.
[25] Ibid., p. 309.

orbitant power," and that "there are cases in which a veil should be drawn for a while over liberty, as it was customary to cover the statues of the gods."[26]

It is perhaps this side of Montesquieu, observing that even in republics liberty must sometimes be sacrificed to the public safety, that most obviously lends itself to the theory of revolutionary or emergency government developed by Robespierre and Saint-Just. Less obvious but more important were Montesquieu's conception of the function of terror in despotic governments and his idea of the nature of virtue in republics.

Revolutionary Government: The Synthesis of Virtue and Terror

The notion of terror was not confined to the party of the republic, for in July 1792, Montmorin, the Prime Minister and the Queen's confidant, wrote to the Comte de la Marck, "I believe it to be necessary to punish the Parisians by terrorism."[27] Mathiez is undoubtedly correct — contra the opinion of Burke and others that terror was a function of republican ideology and fanaticism — in arguing that circumstances made the terror inevitable, so that the royalists would have instituted it had they prevailed. The White Terrors that succeeded the demise of the Republic would support that judgment.

The republicans instituted terrorism in 1793: on August 30, a member proclaimed at the Jacobins, "Let Terror (*la Terreur*) become the order of the day! It is the only way to alarm the people and force them to save themselves!"[28] The utterance recalls Montesquieu's statement that the good effect of a republican terror is that "it puts all the springs of government into motion, and fixes the attention of every citizen." On September 5, on the initiative of Barère, the Convention decreed, "Terror is the order of the day." A rationale for it was not explicitly developed until Saint-Just's report of 10 October 1793 and two famous

[26] Ibid., pp. 197, 199.

[27] Mathiez, Albert, *The French Revolution*, trans. C. A. Phillips, New York, 1964, p. 403.

[28] Ibid., p. 366.

speeches of Robespierre on 25 December 1793 and 5 February 1794. Robespierre's theoretical statements were drawn up to meet the challenges of the Dantonists on the right and the Hébertists on the left.

In using terror, Robespierre argues, the Republic is enlisting the weapon of the despot in the war against despotism. Wielded by royalist or patriot, a blade is a blade.

> It was said that terror was the spring of despotic government. Therefore, is yours like despotism? Yes, as the blade that shines in the hands of the heroes of liberty is like the one with which the satellites of tyranny are armed. As the despot governs his brutalized subjects by terror, he is right as a despot. Subdue the enemies of liberty by terror and you will be right as founders of the Republic. The government of the Revolution is the despotism of liberty against tyranny. Was force meant only to protect crime? And thunderbolts not destined to strike arrogant heads?
>
> Nature imposes on every physical and moral being the law of providing for its preservation. Crime slaughters innocence in order to reign; and innocence struggles with all its strength in the hands of crime.[29]

In the service of the Republic, terror defends the revolution, but it becomes something more than an instrument of war. It is also a means of vengeance for centuries of kings, as well as a form of justice, and after *ventôse* (March 1794), we shall see, an instrument of preparation for great social change. In the revolutionary republic, the spring of despotism is united with the spring of the republic. Robespierre explains to the Convention:

> It is necessary to stamp out the internal and external enemies of the Republic or perish with it. However, in this situation the first maxim of your policy ought to be to lead the people by reason and to manage the enemies of the people by terror.
>
> If the spring of popular government in peace is virtue, the spring of popular government in revolution is simultaneously virtue and terror: virtue, without which terror is deadly, and terror without which virtue is powerless. Terror is only another form of prompt, severe, inflexible justice. It is therefore

[29] DR, 332–333.

an emanation of virtue; it is less a specific principle than a consequence of the general principle of democracy applied to the most pressing needs of the fatherland.[30]

The only government that can realize the great social goals of the revolution is democratic or republican, synonymous terms for Robespierre, for aristocracy is no more republican than monarchy. Thus Robespierre's typology of forms is even more condensed than Montesquieu's. Despotism, tyranny, monarchy, and aristocracy were all evil; the democratic republic was the only good government.

> Democracy is a state in which the sovereign people, guided by laws which are its work, does for itself everything that it can do well and through delegates everything that it cannot do for itself.
>   It is therefore in the principles of democratic government that you [the Convention] ought to seek the rules of your political conduct.
>   But to found and consolidate democracy among ourselves, to reach the peaceful reign of constitutional laws it is necessary to end the war of liberty against tyranny, and to get through the storms of revolution successfully: such is the goal of the revolutionary system which you have regularized. Therefore you ought to regulate your conduct by the stormy circumstances in which the republic finds itself, and the plan of your administration ought to be the result of the spirit of revolutionary government combined with the general principles of democracy.

And the essential spring which supports popular government and makes it move is virtue: "I mean the public virtue which performed so many wonders in Greece and Rome, and which ought to produce even more astonishing ones in republican France – this virtue which is only another form of the love of country and its laws." In a democracy, to carry the argument one step further, love of country implies love of equality. Since the soul of the republic is virtue and equality, the responsibility of legislators in founding it is to nourish these qualities and to destroy what threatens them. The first responsibility of the legislator is to fortify the principle of government. "In the system of the French

[30] Ibid., p. 327.

Revolution what is immoral is unpolitical, what is corrupt is counterrevolutionary." One may conclude, then, that the Robespierrist phobia of corruption and preoccupation with virtue is not merely a displaced puritanism, as it is sometimes frivolously maintained, but an attitude consistent with the theory derived from Montesquieu.

If virtue and the political behavior associated with it are the very soul of the republic — its "spring" or vital source of energy — then anyone guilty of corruption, which is the opposite of virtue, carries within him a quality which may destroy the republic. The *patrie*, or fatherland, therefore, is menaced by two dangers: the first is despotism, the league of kings and aristocrats who are devoted to crushing the republic; the second is the danger that its formation will be defective because of insufficient virtue. Thus the war must be waged against conspiracy and corruption — against the enemies of France and the enemy within. Fortunately, virtue is natural for the people, unless they are led astray. "Republican virtue ought to be considered in relation to the people and in relation to the government: it is necessary in one and in the other. When the government lacks it, there remains a resource in that of the people; but when the people itself is corrupt, liberty is already lost."

Since conspiracy and corruption would destroy it, the constitutional republic cannot be founded immediately. It must be preceded by a transitional stage of revolutionary government. The function of a government is to direct the moral and physical forces of the nation toward its primary goal. The goal of constitutional government is to preserve the republic; that of revolutionary government is to found it. The revolution is the war of liberty against its enemies; the constitution is the regime of liberty victorious and peaceful. Constitutional government is principally interested in civil liberty and revolutionary government in public liberty. Under constitutional order it is enough to protect individuals against the abuses of public power; under the revolutionary regime the public power is obliged to defend itself against all the factions that attack it. To good citizens, the revolutionary government owes protection, but to its enemies it owes only death.

For Robespierre, revolutionary government seems to be based

on the Roman institution of constitutional dictatorship — absolute power within a rational framework to meet the needs of an emergency. He distinguishes it from tyranny and from anarchy. It has nothing in common with arbitrariness, he claims, for it is not particular passions that direct it but the public interest. Revolutionary government is justified if it is directed by good faith and remains in clean hands. The greater its power, the more free and rapid its action, and the more it must be guided by good faith. The day it falls into unclean or treacherous hands, liberty will be lost; its name will become the pretext and the excuse of counter-revolution. Its energy will be that of a violent poison.[31]

Saint-Just agreed that, in the circumstances in which the republic found itself, the constitution could not be established for it would be destroyed by itself. On 10 October 1793, he drew up measures for extreme centralization, placing everything under the surveillance of the Committee of Public Safety, and at his initiative the Convention declared, "The provisional government of France is revolutionary until the peace."[32] If those who want a republic do not also want what constitutes it, the people will be buried in its debris. What constitutes a republic is the total destruction of what is opposed to it. Those who make revolutions in the world — those who want to do it well — ought to sleep only in the grave. Indeed, those who make revolutions by halves do no more than to dig themselves a grave. The republic will be founded only when the sovereign will curbs the monarchical minority and reigns over it by right of conquest.[33]

If anyone complains of revolutionary measures, Saint-Just exclaims, let him know that in comparison to all other governments we are moderates. The monarchy, jealous of its authority, swam in the blood of 30 generations. In 1788 Louis XVI had 8,000 persons of all ages and of each sex immolated in Paris on the Rue Mêlée and on the Pont-Neuf. The court repeated these scenes on the Champ-de-Mars; men were hung in the prisons; drowned victims were picked up in the Seine. There were 400,000 prisoners; 15,000 smugglers were hanged each year; 3,000 men were broken

31 Ibid., p. 315.
32 OC, II, 75. (See note 1.)
33 Ibid., pp. 231, 84, 238.

people should be indivisible. Each faction, therefore, was a crime against sovereignty. Their conflict was a struggle between the forces of good and the forces of evil. "There are two factions in Europe," he said, "that of the people, children of nature, and that of the kings, children of crime." Likewise, Robespierre saw it as a global struggle, proclaiming, "There are two powers on earth, that of reason and that of tyranny; in every place where one rules the other is banished." Before the revolution, factions were good because they isolated despotism and diminished the influence of tyranny. Now they were a crime because they isolated liberty and diminished the influence of the people. When factions disappeared, the internal troubles of the revolution would come to an end, leaving an indivisible, happy people and a virtuous government. In Saint-Just's words:

> Our goal is to create an order of things so that one universal inclination toward·the goal is established, so that factions find themselves hurled on the scaffold, so that one virile energy inclines the spirit of the nation toward justice, so that we obtain in the interior the calm necessary to found the happiness of the people . . . . Our aim is to establish a sincere government, so that the people may be happy, so that finally, wisdom and eternal Providence alone presiding over the establishment of the Republic, it may no longer be each day shaken by a new transgression.[44]

Factionalism was encouraging the enemies of France. As Robespierre claimed, "aristocracy and royalty have begun to raise again an insolent head . . . and the national authority has experienced a *resistance* of which the schemers were beginning to lose the habit."[45] It is clear, however, that the central government was concerned not only with active hostility against the state but also with various kinds of passivity and noncooperation, which were also interpreted as resistance. The well-known Law of Suspects, one of the stipulated foundations of the Terror, marked as subject to arrest not only émigrés and unreconstructed persons associated with the nobility but also anyone who by conduct, connections, remarks, or writing showed himself a partisan

[44] OC, II, 235.
[45] DR, 345, italics added.

of tyranny, federalism, and the enemies of liberty, as well as anyone who could not demonstrate civism, meaning signs of active
patriotism, and a positive contribution to the revolution. The
theory behind this measure, Saint-Just indicated, was that the republic would not be founded as long as an enemy of liberty
existed, and that the government should punish not only traitors
but even the indifferent ones, including anyone in the Republic
who was passive and did nothing for it. "Since the French people
has manifested its will everyone who is opposed to it is outside
the sovereign, and everyone who is outside the sovereign is an
enemy. . . . Between the people and its enemies there is nothing
in common save the sword." Furthermore, "A patriot is one who
supports the Republic *en masse;* whoever fights it piecemeal is a
traitor."[46]

The revolution must combat active resistance on the one hand
and indolence and egoism on the other hand, but the greatest
danger was corruption — the active fomenting of selfishness by
bribery and propaganda, which would destroy the natural virtue
of the people, disassociate them from the revolution, and plunge
them into a state of immorality. The scheme of corruption, Saint-
Just believed, was more pernicious than the violence of the con-
spirators. The enemy has only one way to destroy us, he said,
and that is to pervert and corrupt us, since a republic can rest
only on nature and on habits. He insisted to the Convention, "you
have done nothing in immolating the tyrant if you do not im-
molate corruption, by which the party of the foreign power
brings you back to royalty. Immorality is a federalism in the civil
state."[47] By this social federalism he meant all forms of selfishness
and disassociation from the *patrie* and the government. On 23
ventôse he proposed a decree in which those who were convicted
of favoring a scheme corrupting the citizens of the Republic were
declared traitors, and in the same decree stated that resistance to
the revolutionary government, of which the National Convention was the center, was an offence against public liberty and
punishable by death.[48] To arrest the evil of corruption, there

[46] OC, II, 74, 275.
[47] Ibid., pp. 276, 230, 271.
[48] Ibid., p. 277.

was only one way, Saint-Just insisted — to carry the revolution into the civil state, that is, not to stop with constitutional or political changes but to use the revolution to transform the social structure.

André Malraux, in the preface to a book on Saint-Just, has called him "passionately totalitarian," pointing out his conviction that ultimately the republic should encompass "all relations, all interests, all laws, all duties," and give "a common direction to all parts of the state."[49] However, the precise nature of his totalitarianism is not always understood, for it is closer to the world of Sparta than to the world of Hitler or Stalin. Although Saint-Just was a terrorist, the totalitarian society of his dream was neither terroristic nor produced by terror, for it implied his disillusionment with terrorism as a technique for bringing about social change. Terror was necessary to produce initial conditions for the republic to exist — to ,abolish the monarchy and establish a republican *government*. But his idea of the republic was that of a *polis* — a society as well as a state. The power of government was limited, but the power of society limitless: his totalitarianism was social but not governmental. After a republican government was established, he believed, its dictatorial powers would be set aside, and social power would regulate the lives of men. Republican society must be preserved not by terror but by what he called "institutions." The further course of terrorism would only freeze the revolution and prevent it from transforming the civil state. Saint-Just declared: "The Revolution is congealed; all principles are weakened; there remain only the red caps worn by intrigue. The exercise of terror has dulled crime as strong liquors dull the palate. . . . Terror can free us from monarchy and aristocracy, but who will deliver us from corruption? Institutions."[50] By their nature the effects of terror are limited:

> Terror is a two-edged weapon, of which one serves to avenge the people, and the other serves tyranny; the terror has filled the prisons, but the guilty ones are not punished; the terror

[49] Malraux, André, "On Saint-Just," trans. Lionel Abel, *Partisan Review*, XXII, 1955, p. 473, from Ollivier, Albert, *Saint-Just et la Force des Choses*.
[50] OC, II, 508, 501.

has passed as a storm. Expect lasting severity in the public character only in the force of institutions; a frightful calm always follows our storms, and we are also always more indulgent after than before the terror.

Moreover, as a result of the work of the factions, the terror could get out of control and even reverse itself: "Friendship was no longer known; the terror had turned about against the national representation and against the *patrie;* crime pursued the judges, and violence in conflict with . . . decrees, oppressed each district through a power yet independent of the French people." In the absence of institutions, men lacked virtue, and this deficiency split off terror from justice, and through men's awareness of their lack of virtue, weakened the Terror:

> The vigor of the revolutionary government, which established the dictatorship of justice, has declined; one would believe that the hearts of the guilty and the judges, frightened by example, have come to terms secretly to freeze justice and to escape it.
> One would believe that each person, frightened by his conscience and by the inflexibility of the laws, has said to himself: We are not virtuous enough to be so terrible; philosophic legislators, sympathize with my weakness; I dare not tell you: I am vicious; I would rather tell you: You are cruel.

Institutions must begin where terror left off, consolidating their gains by stages, and the revolution must continue: "The revolution ought to stop at the perfection through the laws of happiness and public liberty. Its transports have no other object and ought to upset everything opposed to it; and each period, each victory over monarchy ought to bring and consecrate a republican institution."[51]

In his October 10 speech, in the early stages of the Terror, Saint-Just had cried out that the republic lacked institutions. The problem remained with him, but it was not a solitary preoccupation, for he was charged with the responsibility of drawing

[51] Ibid., pp. 239 – 240, 377, 237, 508.

up for the Committee of Public Safety a "code of social institutions." This work was never finished and the notes for it were not published until after his death. On 9 *thermidor*, they were in the hands of his secretary, Thuillier, and after the fall of the Robespierrists were published as "Fragments on Republican Institutions." As Mathiez has observed, Saint-Just believed that "civil institutions" were the "moral and social armature" that would render the republic indestructible, founding it in souls, in laws, and in customs.[52] Through institutions, the republic would be internalized and perpetuated as a way of life. He thought of them as a form of *paideia*, to use Werner Jaeger's term, which is appropriate to Saint-Just's understanding of Greek culture. This understanding is revealed in a statement among the notes found on Saint-Just on the fateful 9 *thermidor*: "Execute the laws on education — there is the secret."[53]

Saint-Just's statement about the compound, terror and virtue, is subtly different from that of Robespierre, although it is consistent with it. Robespierre had said that virtue *and* terror were the principles of revolutionary government, which was necessary before the republic could be established. Saint-Just added that "A republican government has virtue for its principle; *or else* terror."[54] Thus terror is generated by the absence of virtue. Supply the institutions that will guarantee virtue, and terror becomes unnecessary. "Institutions are the guarantee of a free people against the corruption of morals, and the guarantee of the people and of the citizen against the corruption of the government." Monarchy lacks social institutions altogether, thereby lacking virtue. The corruption of the old regime must be purified before republican society can be constructed:

> In a monarchy there is only a government; in a Republic, there are, besides, institutions to restrain habits, to halt the corruption of laws or men. A state in which these institutions are lacking is only an illusory Republic; and as each person

[52] Mathiez, "La terreur: Instrument de la politique sociale des robespierristes," loc. cit., p. 210.

[53] OC, II, 538.

[54] Ibid., p. 506, italics added.

in it understands by his liberty the independence of his passions and avarice, the spirit of acquisition and egoism is set up between the citizens, and the particular idea that each makes his liberty according to his self-interest produces the slavery of all. . . . *Institutions, which are the soul of the Republic, we are lacking.*[55]

The solidity of great empires is in immortal institutions, unmoved and sheltered from the violence of factions. Institutions are the guarantee of public liberty, moralizing the government and the civil state, suppressing the jealousies that produce factions, making the delicate distinction between truth and hypocrisy, innocence and crime, and establishing the reign of justice. Without them, the strength of a republic rests either on the merit of frail mortals or on precarious means. When personal influence is replaced by inflexible justice, then the revolution is consolidated and jealousies, factions, pretensions, and slanders disappear. The ascendancy of morals replaces the ascendancy of men. Institutions are the only means of bearing up the love of country and the revolutionary spirit when the revolution has passed. Thus, Saint-Just specified the social means of establishing the goal of the revolution which had been described in moral terms by Robespierre as follows:

What is the goal to which we are heading? The peaceful enjoyment of liberty and equality; the reign of that eternal justice of which the laws are graven not on marble and stone but in the hearts of all men, even that of the slave who forgets them and of the tyrant who denies them.

We want an order of things in which base and cruel passions are restrained, all the benevolent and generous passions awakened by the laws, where ambition is the desire to glorify and to serve the homeland, where distinctions are born only from equality itself; where the citizen is subordinate to the magistrate, the magistrate to the people, and the people to justice, where the homeland ensures the well-being of each individual, and where each individual enjoys with pride the prosperity and the glory of the *patrie;* where every soul expands through the continual communication of republican

[55] Ibid., p. 230, italics in the original.

feelings, and through the need to earn the esteem of a great people, where the arts are the decorations of liberty which ennoble it, commerce the source of public riches and not only of the monstrous opulence of several houses.[56]

Before social institutions could be established to do the work of constructing and preserving republican *society*, however, it was necessary to reconstruct the social base on which the republican *government* must rest. To overthrow the monarchy and remove the aristocrats from political power was insufficient if the aristocrats retained social and economic power. Saint-Just complained, "The government rests on liberty, the civil state on aristocracy." He also observed, "The bread given by the rich is bitter; it compromises liberty: bread belongs by right to the people in a state that is ruled wisely." Political power should not have to contend with social power that opposes it: "Opulence is in the hands of a large enough number of enemies of the Revolution; need makes the people who work dependent on their enemies. Do you think dominion is possible if civil relations radiate from those who oppose the form of government?"[57] The experience of the revolution urged the principle that those who showed themselves to be enemies of the country should not own property in it. The laws of *ventôse*, therefore, were issued to bring social power into harmony with political power and to establish a firm social base for republican government. With these decrees, Mathiez has pointed out,

> The Terror was assuming an unforeseen and impressive character. It was no longer a question of temporarily holding down a hostile party by force; but of dispossessing it for good, annihilating its means of subsistence, and, by means of the property of which it had been despoiled, promoting to social life the class of the perpetually disinherited.[58]

The *ventôse* decrees, if implemented, would have meant a vast expropriation, redistributing the property confiscated from persons named as suspects to the class of indigent patriots. Since

[56] DR, 325 – 326.
[57] OC, II, 240, 79, 238.
[58] Mathiez, *The French Revolution*, p. 451.

the decrees were not carried out, some historians have not taken them seriously. Others, led by Mathiez, have associated them with the other major decrees of the Terror and with Saint-Just's scheme of civil institutions, and these writers have insisted that the *ventôse* decrees were the heart of a definite social policy designed to elevate the economic position of the sans-culottes by enriching them with confiscated property in order to build a new class and to make it the republic's social base. Jaurès in his socialist history of the revolution, found the policy of the decrees "a terrorism blended with socialism," and Vellay, editor of the works of Robespierre and of Saint-Just, believed that Robespierre, along with Marat and Saint-Just, held a communist ideal that separated them from their colleagues of the revolution and ultimately led to their downfall. This point of view would find in Jacobinism the seeds of revolutionary socialism — in contrast to the judgment of Marx, who said that in the French Revolution the interests of the proletariat were fused with that of the bourgeoisie and that the Terror merely tried to carry out the interests of the latter. The whole French terror, Marx insisted, was nothing more than a plebeian way to get rid of absolutism, feudalism, and the petty bourgeoisie — that is, the enemies of the bourgeoisie.[59]

Socialist historians and theorists who draw a line of development from Robespierrists to Babouvists to the Paris communards to Lenin will meet with few objections, but to find anything more than socialist *intimations* in the Year II is to stretch Jacobinism beyond recognition. Malraux has suggested that "The Robespierrists were not [even] defenders of the bourgeoisie. They were defenders of the Republic, that is to say of the state."[60] That is true as far as it goes, but the state was the *patrie*, which was a *polis* — a society as well as a state. To found the government of the Republic was only a stage in the creation of republican society. The spell of eighteenth-century utopianism may be taken for granted, but Jacobin thought does not anticipate crucial ideas formulated by Marx, not even hinting at industrial society, the historic class struggle, or the industrial proletariat. The outrage

[59] See Karl Marx and Friedrich Engels, *Correspondence 1846 – 1895*, New York, n.d., p. 459.

[60] Malraux, loc. cit., p. 471.

at the plight of indigent patriots was more like the lament of
Tiberius Gracchus for the Roman veterans who wandered without refuge than like an analysis of the conditions of the working
class. Neither wealth nor poverty was necessary, said Saint-Just,
but his notion of equality recalled that of the Spartan peers, and
independence meant to him something like the independence of
the Spartan citizen whose subsistence was guaranteed. The levelling proposed in the *ventôse* laws was not expected to have any
effect on the systems of production or exchange; it would diminish the inequality of fortunes, remove a political threat, and
reduce the menace of counterrevolution. In the decree of 8 *ventôse*, Saint-Just announced: "The property of patriots is inviolable
and sacred. The wealth of persons acknowledged as enemies of
the revolution will be confiscated for the profit of the Republic. . . ." The poor who were struggling for liberty would receive the wealth of those who were menacing it.

Malraux recognizes that "Saint-Just's theories anticipate neither
communism nor fascism," yet he insists, "he does anticipate *the*
communists and *the* fascists, the single and all-powerful party."[61]
This charge misses the mark because, as we have already seen,
Saint-Just believed that total transformation, which he desired,
could not be produced by political organization or by the use of
force. Techniques of great change must wait for the right moment:

> Without doubt it is not yet time to do The Good. The
> particular good that one does is a palliative. It is necessary
> to wait for a general evil great enough for general opinion to
> experience the need of proper measures to do The Good.
> What produces the general good is always terrible, or appears
> bizarre when begun too soon.[62]

It would be false, therefore, to think of Jacobin terror as a
precursor of terroristic totalitarianism, which denies moral limits,
destroys primary relations, and atomizes individuals in order to
force social change. In theory at least, terror is limited to the
political stages and excluded from the last stages, which are pri-

[61] Ibid., p. 473.
[62] OC, II, 508.

marily social. Thus the end of the terror is not promised for a time after society is totally transformed but for the time when the revolution shifts from political to social power. The following outline, drawn from the theory of revolutionary stages implicit in the work of Robespierre and Saint-Just, makes clear the function and limits of the Terror:

1. The revolution overthrows the monarchy and drives out the aristocrats.

2. The revolutionary government wages war against its enemies and initiates the Terror to suppress the counterrevolution.

3. The government extends terror to all forms of resistance, active and passive, to the revolution. (The republic depends on "the total destruction of that which is opposed to it.")

4. The government would use the Terror to dispossess the classes hostile to the revolution, destroying their economic base and building up the economic strength of the sans-culottes, who would become the social foundation of the republican government (the *ventôse* decrees).

5. The Terror would end and civil institutions take over the work of reconstruction, inaugurating republican society.

6. In the new world of republican society, life would be regulated by social power, and government would assume a minor role.

Mathiez declared that the Republic of the Year II was an "accident," held together by force and fervor and doomed because the triumvirate in the Committee of Public Safety, Robespierre, Couthon, and Saint-Just, destroyed the political and social supports on which their power had to rest. Born in turmoil, he observed, the young republic was "cast in the mould of terrorism in opposition to its own basic principle." This fundamental contradiction was well understood by these men, but they resolved it by the shrewd theoretical stroke of making virtue and terror the dynamic principles of revolutionary government.

The concept of virtue, by suggesting its opposite, corruption, provided further theoretical justification for broadening the Terror to strike at passive as well as active resistance to the Revolution. Furthermore, the coupling of the two principles, virtue and terror, going beyond Montesquieu's static and detached political categories, marked a theoretical advance, opening up a new approach: the social theory of revolution, although at the time it was overshadowed by the idea of conspiracy. According to Montesquieu, if a despotism or a republic mixed its vital principle it was simply an imperfect system subject to decay and not worth examining. The new approach made it possible to see that a system — especially societies in the travail of social change — may contain opposing principles in dialectical tension. The despotism of liberty did not in fact cancel out the despotism of kings to liberate a republic of virtue, but the struggle of the republic did change the shape of social organization, and, having elevated the idea of equality, it generated new forms of inequality.

Stoically, Mathiez concluded that the First Republic was "A memorable example of the limitations of the human will in its struggle against the resistance of material things."[63] Perhaps he is right. Nevertheless, the record of that memorable example has also expanded the understanding of those limitations and deepened the meaning of the struggle.

[63] Mathiez, *The French Revolution*, p. 510.

Thirty-Nine Articles:
Toward a Theory of Social Theory

J O H N R . S E E L E Y

IN SPITE OF SKEPTICISM encountered here or there, sometimes combined with the imputation true-but-trivial, I am going to submit that all of the following propositions about social theories are true and material.

By a social theory, I mean here for the time being any proposition of the sort "Delinquency is due to broken homes,"[1] "The superego is the internalized parent or parent-surrogate,"[2] "Every society is characterized by mores that make everything right,"[3] "Some institutions are more basic than others. The economic are most basic,"[4] "The personality system is a unit of (part in) the social system,"[5] " 'Orientations' are the most stable of the pattern variables in a system of social action,"[6] "Social character is closely tied to (is a function of) the population cycle."[7]

By "true" propositions I mean simply non-false ones, i.e., those whose contradictories are untrue. I do not mean that what I assert to be true is all the truth, or a fair and proper representation of all the things that could or should be said.

By "material" I mean that, if true, they matter.

What I would like to submit as credible propositions are the following:

[1] Almost anyone, *circa* 1920.
[2] Roughly, Freudian.
[3] Summary Sumner.
[4] Walter Goldschmidt and, very roughly, Marx.
[5] Very Parsonian.
[6] Recent Parsons; probably, original Parsons too.
[7] Riesman, though not core Riesman.

Social Science is heard talk.

1   The propositions we, social scientists, put forward are (hopefully) heard or overheard by at least someone.

Beliefs structure action.

2   Insofar as they are believed (or even taken account of, but disbelieved or counter-believed) they, like any belief, are or may be part of the subsequent structure of action. If "action" is extended to include non-action (decision to refrain from an act contemplated) and also "internal action" ("restructuring" of dispositions and the like), such propositions act to restructure action for all who have access.

Knowings and feelings and integrations interact.

3   "Cognitive" alterations affect "cathectic" balances, and alter "evaluative" problems.[8] For example, an assertion that "men are almost wholly at the mercy of instinct," may alter the affect-investment we have in men, in rationality, or in instinct. It must, taken as belief, alter what is the problem of "integration" (the evaluative criterion)[9] for the person and the "collectivity."

Beliefs about society alter society.

4   At least some propositions about person or society, if credited, alter person or society. A society believing that society is necessarily naturally a *bellum omnia contra omnes* will not (cannot) operate as a society that believes that "disorder" is a "pathology" in relation to a more or less easily attained normal state. A society that believes that delinquents are requisite to a social system to mark its own boundary-zone[10] cannot act (especially with whole heart) like a society that believes delinquency to be a non-eliminable but abnormal state, or an abnormal and eliminable one. A society that does not (cannot) act in the same way *is* an altered society (or a new one).

Things become what they are said to be.

5   Persons (and social "units" and "societies") become what they are in virtue (very largely) of what they are said or taken to be, i.e., the theory of what we are is always a necessary

[8] The terms are Parsons', though the ideas are older.
[9] *Ibid.*
[10] Kai Erikson, for instance.

and sometimes a sufficient condition for becoming what we are said to be. Thus a child, as we now understand the term, is invented, not discovered.[11] The "recognition" that he is not a big doll or pet, or a little adult, is the pre-picking-out of one set of possibilities, which are realized at the expense of others. They are realized by virtue of a representation to him of what he "is" (a theory) including a context of what an adult consequently is and a representation accordingly of what his future is. Theory, identity, program are co-emergents. A "teenager" is an invention inside living memory; a new category and type of human being comes into existence with a theory that asserts a distinction and ascribes properties to what is distinguished.

Such alterations are social science problems.

6   Alterations in society (including those we aid, assist, procure, counter or prevent) are matter for social scientific study — as alterations in society procured by physical science invention are *not* matters for physical study.

Social findings now are social data later.

7   As, and to the degree that, social scientific propositions justify one set of our hopes, and are taken widely with the seriousness that science as against guesswork merits, they play or will come to play a crucial role in altering the beliefs on which action is based, and therefore action, and therefore society; *and*, since one generation's "findings" are the next generation's presuppositions, the very inner or "first" nature of human nature in subsequent cycles of the generation of society will be more or less radically affected.

Unmasking alters advantages.

8   Since description of social phenomena from a "detached" point of view constitutes or may constitute a species of unmasking, depriving going groups, practices, beliefs, etc., of their effectiveness insofar as that depends (as commonly) on a suitable cloud of operative illusion, we actively intervene thereby in the competitive or conflictive or cooperative or accommodative

[11] See Philippe Aries, *Centuries of Childhood.*

balances in which select persons or groups have vested interests. Hence in a complex competitive, conflictful, etc., situation, we deal unplanned blows or give uncalculated aids, now to one participant, now to another. By removing camouflage here, shining a searchlight there, providing a map of this bit of territory or that, we decisively but in no determinate way, act virtually as co-combatants, without the need to locate our "side" anywhere at any time, let alone permanently.

Probative studies alter morale bases.

9   Even apart from our effect in affecting the external chances of relative victory or self-defense, probative studies in terms of their theoretical conclusions affect or may seriously affect internal possibilities of self-esteem, morale, the support of self-comforting legend or illusion, and the like.

The taken-for-granted is legislatively exempted.

10   The *ceteris paribus* intellectual proviso, under which we operate, in effect generally leaves the taken-for-granted immune, while what is examined is brought under potential attack. A theory as to "how the market operates," taking non-interference by governments for granted, is different from and has different social consequences from a theory as to how a market operates with the state "recognized" as a unique party to transactions.

Cause-labeling alters responsibility - imputations.

11   Whatever we allege to be the cause of something will be seen as (and was meant to be) that which, if changed, would yield a desired change in something else. If poor teachers are the cause of poor teaching one political predisposition will likely be indicated; if poor administration (given such teachers as there are), then another line is indicated; if the penury of taxpayers (given the market supply and demand of teachers), then another policy opens up.

If we "try to do justice to the complexity of the situation" by naming "all the causes," we set ourselves an impossible task (their number is infinite), we point mostly to what cannot be changed (the past) and we invite paralysis by confusing policy. We confuse policy because policy requires a relatively small number of factors to be regarded as causes, so that a line of action or small fan of action is sketched in.

Analytic stopping-points arbitrarily assign special weights.

12   More particularly, as we trace out a chain of causation, the point where we (arbitrarily) stop, is thereby presented as a special point — in a graph, not one more articulation point, but a root point — and will be responded to socially in a way that depends not on its intrinsic quality but on the accidents of our sketching.

Problem-selection is attention-disruption.

13   The very locating and dealing with a problem has a diversionary or "Look here!" effect, that focuses attention selectively for others, and thereby alters both their image and their concurrent and subsequent action. It is not quite right, but nearly enough the case, that every article on Berkeley means one less on Selma, and every one on either, one less on Viet Nam or Poverty.

Available explanations preclude possibles.

14   The provision of a satisfactory account or a satisfying solution at one level of analysis is likely, in general, to delay or preclude the solution at another. Thus an answer to the question how to get our own soldiers to fight unjust wars (or just any kind of war) is likely to bar a question as to how to keep militarily strong by committing our soldiers only to just ones.

Findings – distributions alter incomes.

15   The differential distribution of our findings (selective cultural diffusion) is affected of course by the social structure and the pre-existent cultural differential distribution. The manner, place, time and language of our input, however, will itself be consequential for the social structure and for the distribution of these and other such goods and life-chances as there are. We cannot much console ourselves with the existence of middlemen or filtering-down-eventually. In the first place, by the time much has filtered down far, it has become wrong on up-to-date

views. In the second place, order is important: whether to spill the secret of the Manhattan Project *first* to Russia or Germany in the last great war might have made quite some difference.

Analysis accelerates social change.

16   The matter, manner and volume and depth of such theory as is released is or may be a prime cause or accelerator of social change — while the rate of social change is problematic for our society and a principal cause, perhaps, of many if not most social problems. (If Durkheim is to be credited, the pains are proportioned roughly to the extent of the change, and not to its for-better-or-for-worse character).[12]

Belief-changing is crucial for culture.

17   Since the changes procured by theory are in the realm of beliefs, and since credibly beliefs are nearer the core of the culture (and the personality) than practices,[13] and since many of our theorizings touch on core beliefs, there is every likelihood that such changes as are thus procured will be central rather than superficial. See, for example, the whole wave of virtually psychologically abandoned children[14] raised in the light of (a misapprehension of) Freud's discoveries as to some effects of repression and suppression.

"Validity" is not enough.

18   The best that we can guarantee with respect to any theory is non-falseness in the restricted sense. When Merton, quoting and evidently approving Rickert and Dilthey, says that value considerations enter into the selection of a problem and the admission of evidence, but not into validity (which he distinguishes from completeness),[15] it is at best this restricted validity we can claim. If A killed B, then "A killed B" is a valid statement of the kind we can provide. That B had killed fifty others first, and was at the moment trying to kill A and his family,

[12] Durkheim on norms and anomie.
[13] See Linton, Ogburn, etc.
[14] See, e.g., Seeley et al., *Crestwood Heights*.
[15] See Merton, *Social Theory and Social Structure*.

can be set aside, if our values incline us not to ask the question to which it would be a cogent answer, or if our canons for the admission of evidence rule it out.

The context of theory is judgment.

19   The context into which theorizing, explaining, accounting for, etc., socially fall is, quite generally, in effect a judicial context, i.e., one in which, on the basis of representations made, a decision will be rendered which is a guide for further action. Thus a guarantee (even if valid) to tell nothing but the truth, out of the classic threesome "the truth, the whole truth, and nothing but the truth," is small help. Of course, no one can tell the whole truth about anything, and, what *is* required, the whole relevant truth, depends for possibility on known canons of relevance, and hence on agreed purpose.

Terms determine outlooks.

20   The very terminology (the term, and the act of naming) we use has substantial, largely unforeseen, effects on what we purport to study. I cannot readily imagine a greater change than is involved, for instance, in people's generally coming to think of the thought-ways and act-ways somehow taken together as "the culture." Apart from its coming to be seen, and hence to operate, as something set over against man or men, apart from the utterly fictitious unity introduced *glissando* into a vast variety of disparate enterprises never the same from moment to moment, apart from the seeming provision of a new locus for causal ascription, the parallel emergence of a term like "the subculture" sets forth a system of images and sets free a series of action-dispositions that were never there before and that are only dubiously to be desired. Similarly, as indicated, with "the social system" and "the personality system" as a "part," or "unit," of it.[16]

Classifications reorganize events.

21   As for terminology, so *a fortiori* for classification. Everything *is* a case of an infinity of possible classes. Everything is, even significantly, interestingly and legitimately subsumed

[16] Parsons.

under many headings. Is alcoholism a moral failure, a deviation, self-comforting behavior, a dietary anomaly, an addiction, a disease, a disorder, a crime or misdemeanor, a cultural pattern, a defect of socialization . . . ? Perhaps, every one of these. But what we decide to assimilate it to, and the rubric under which we elect to study and describe it, affect sensibly what it is, both in consequence of what the alcoholic may then take himself to be and (for both reasons) what he is culturally or by "significant others" defined to be.[17]

General terms program alternative futures.

22   At the other extreme, perhaps, from "mere terminology," the most general terms in which we represent men would, I should think, have consequences of considerable consequence. If we represent men primarily or exclusively as within history, system or drama — to take Maurice Stein's treble classification — or perhaps natural history, we invite them, I suggest, by indirection, to participate in radically differently conceived enterprises, and therewith to be quite other sorts of persons.

Passive-active constructions alter dispositions.

23   And if within each of these, we depict them passively or actively, we should expect quite different results: as history-made or history-makers; as system-spinning or system-spun; as central to the drama, in effect dwarfing scene and agency; or as peripheral to it (more actors-out than actors) restricted by agency, agitated by scene, structured in act, and having even purpose "determined" by what is, in effect, scene to the actor (e.g., birth-chances or historic period).[18]

Assigned motives function polemically.

24   Closely related, again, to these passivity-activity nuances are the delicate balances preserved or destroyed between "because" and "in order to" lines of explanation.[19]

Almost any act or scheme of action can be resolved into or assimilated to either type of explana-

---

[17] See W. I. Thomas.
[18] The terms are Kenneth Burke's.
[19] Alfred Schutz' terms.

tion or a mixture of both. Compare: "Because he was a responsible bank officer he called in all loans" with "In order to protect his position in the bank, he chose to bankrupt debtors by calling in loans." The second line can be restated "Because of his inner insecurity he had to protect his own position . . ."; which may, in turn, be resolved into "In order to avoid minor anxiety. . . ." A common type of "explanation" would either consist of a chain or a network made up of both elements.

What I am concerned to point out here is only that the generalized effect of the respective lines is to direct attention differentially. Insofar as the "in order to" line is followed, we in effect invite action toward the reconstruction of motives, or we invoke in effect praise and blame, punishment and reward. "The cadet cheated in order to get ahead of his classmates." Insofar as the "because" line is followed, we invite either inaction or action directed toward something or someone other than the actor. "Because of the unreasonable pressure of institutional demands, the cadet cheated" has a different force and effect — and is probably intended to.

I only want to maintain here that it seems to me that every "in order to" can credibly be resolved into a "because" and left, there; and that nearly every "because" can be restated in terms of an "in order to"; and that the net effect of choices between these lines, or end-points of theorizing in these terms, is essentially reallocations of responsibility (and concurrently, of praise, blame, esteem, disesteem and the like). We practise this delicate redistribution, I believe, according to no explicit canons of procedure or outcome desired.

I would add further that the balance of such "explanations" (as a consequent characteristic of the culture of everyman, that we are thus creating or recreating) like alterations in the atmosphere in reference to the biological organism, affects sensibly the weight of the burden of responsibility subjectively carried, and indeed the sense of potency, and hence the potency, brought thereto.[20]

Cultural inno-vation lacks criteria.

25   The culture we thus weave or help weave, like any culture, opens up some further cultural and personal possibilities while it necessarily thereby closes off others. Beyond the level of satisfying "primary needs," we seem to have no criterion of the goodness of cultures in terms of satisfying "secondary needs," since it is in effect the culture in question that defines or brings these into being. The very basis for judging the culture (the first-order culture engendered by our progenitors and predecessors or the one we are reconstituting as we go) is (at least in large measure) culturally given. We may see ourselves, ambiguously, as developing the culture or changing it. Indeed, in any given innovative act we do both. The manner of securing for ourselves a sufficient or substantial extrication from the culture in order that possibilities to be desired are not needlessly foreclosed is unclear. It is a matter of more or less, of course. But there seems to exist neither a theory of what is to be desired, nor, insofar as that may be surmised, what is to be done to secure it.

Mastery as misleading motive.

26   As things are going, perhaps unavoidably, perhaps not, our enterprise as a whole is both rooted in and branches back into a generalized program of "mastery" that is one of the cul-

[20] Let me set up for later examination a more complex model. (1) *Because* of population pressure on scarce space and resources, the Japanese went to war; (2) *In order to* glorify Japan, the government encouraged a rising birthrate; (3) *Because* of the late emergence of Japanese power, constant glorification was needed to maintain national morale; (4) *In order to* defeat feared and hated competition, the Japanese elected morale over safety; (5) *Because* of the humiliation involved in Western penetration, a passionate devotion that deprecated safety was set loose in Japan; (6) *In order to* avoid the pains of cultural assimilation, the Japanese sought and found a different, less calculating, value-pattern, . . . and so on, at will.

ture's leading strands. (This is probably not the same strand as Parsons' "instrumental activism," because mastery is or is by way of becoming a good in itself, a "consummatory" experience.)[21] All talk of prediction and control[22] roots in and feeds this orientation.

But the most elementary question as to what these concepts *could* mean in reference to human affairs has been largely bypassed. A program that would permit me to control others is a proposal for a slave-master society. A program that would permit us together to control us severally, or permit us severally to control us collectively, is so badly stated as to be without evident meaning or, certainly, self-evident desirability. A program that would permit each of us to increase his control over himself suggests and commonly means a program to arrogate to a part of a human being a hegemony over another part such that the claims of that part or aspect — let alone the whole — are slighted with momentary impunity and, I believe, long-term sure disaster. Most commonly it is a program for bringing "impulse" under the dominion, or increasingly close supervision, of calculation or "reason." That this is a very special view of the natural or desirable construction of the self, it is difficult to doubt. Why the imposition of an alien (or any) will from outside should be resisted, while its internalization in the person is desired; why consensus should be sought outside, but control within; why segmental interests are *not* wholly to be regulated by comprehensive ones externally but are to be *so* governed internally — all this seems obscure to me, and not a little repulsive and frightening.

In any case, I think, unless we take especial pains to the contrary we foster and further such, probably misplaced, hopes and misguided orientations.

21 Again, Parsonian terms.
22 Appears in most theory of theory discussions.

Social Science as aid to administration.

27   In fact what we do may further most what may be called the administrative frame of mind, the leading component of which is the preference for doing and using, over being, becoming, having and other modalities.[23] Even the self may come to be thought of as something to be used[24] (or used up) in doing, particularly doing that makes possible still more doing (e.g., "organizing"). The basic functional schema of analysis — that a thing is what it does, more particularly the use it has, or that which it does that is useful — falls into and favors this select emphasis.

Social theory "represents" reality.

28   Social theory appears negligibly capable of being viewed as physical theory is. Few people are at a disadvantage with reference to the things that they must do or vitally want to do for want of direct personal knowledge of the substance of physical theory. But all must daily deal with, indeed live by and live in and by means of what social theory asserts. Whether the light's going on is a consequence of the relative resistance of some wires to the "passage" of "electricity" is generally a matter of operational consequence to few; we need only know which switch to throw. But whether Johnny's "No" is, on theory, likely to be a needed step in his discovering his identity, a slip of the tongue, a "phase" he must be helped through, a covert indication he wants to be punished, or a "test for bounds and limits," is a crucial matter for all parties (and perhaps for Johnny's social descendants to the *n*th generation).

For this reason (and perhaps other reasons) it is difficult for social theory to function in society on an *as if* basis.[25] Physical theory, as we know, asserts nothing about what something is.

[23] With apologies to Kluckhohn.

[24] Cf. "You learn how to use yourself in a relation" (in social work theory). For the basic theory of self-abuse, see Dale Carnegie.

[25] Cf. Hans Vaihinger, *Die Philosophie des als obs.*

Even without the current difficulty about the wave-particle models for light behavior, physics does not purport to say at all what light *is*. Anything said on this score is well understood to be only scaffolding, an *aide-mémoire* or perhaps an *aide-imagination*. But "this is a community" or "that is a folkway" is, unavoidably, I think, taken to be more than a "theoretical construct," pointing to some invariances in the relations among select measures.

Basic models carry radical implications.

29   All, or nearly all, models carry with them most particular, peculiar, perhaps unintended (and often awful) consequences.

Thus almost all talk of class, and whether the classes are numbered[26] or designated,[27] carries with it and reinforces almost inevitably the notion of an upper and a lower class with all the cathectic-evaluative implications of up = good = superior and down = bad = inferior. If we say "the most perverted pervert" we do not appear so evidently to convey implicit praise for the perfection of perversity undoubtedly involved. But we mean by an "upper class," at most, those who are held by a society best to incorporate its values, which they themselves have had a predominant role in defining *to be* values. This could well mean the most fraudulent of the fraudulent or the most exploitative of the exploitative. But the "upperness" we correctly ascribe in description we cannot help virtually prescribing, unwillingly and unwittingly, as prescription — if only because we take the word and locus over from those who have so defined it as cause and consequence of their "income."

Or, to take another model, Parsons' hierarchical systems of systems. At first blush, it may seem self-evident that it is proper, fruitful, and safe to view the system of the person as a part (constituent system) of the "more inclusive system" of society. It is then evident that the surrounding

[26] Hollingshead and others.
[27] Warner and others.

or more inclusive system must appear and function as a set of means and conditions for the function of the personality system.[28] Indeed, does not the cell-organ-body organization furnish us with a familiar example of the model in operation?

Let me bypass, for now, the aptness and effect of the whole *system* vocabulary, for the sake of directing attention to the effects of the hierarchy postulated, supposed, or rather taken as self-evident.

It may be easier to see what is fantastic about it, if we momentarily restrict the social system had in mind to a pair of friends. Is it at all obvious that the friendship includes the friends while the friends do not include the friendship? Is it not rather clear that the friends and the friendship are two abstractions from one phenomenon: friends are friends in virtue of the friendship; the friendship exists in virtue of their being friends. (Does a triangle have, include, three sides — or do three sides of a triangle have, include, a triangle?) And is the friendship a set of means and conditions to the friends or their "action"; or are the friends not, if one can talk of a collectivity "acting" at all, equally means and conditions for the friendship? What is "in" what — in what sense of "in"? Is the society not a society to the extent that it is "in" the members, and are they not correlatively members to the extent that they are "in" the society — like being *in* communion or *in* grace, not a locative term at all, but a poetic image like "the soup was so good because Mother put her heart into it," or "Her child was in her heart at all times." The "in" is an "in" of identity: "My father dwells in me; and I, in him" is an elementary aspect of a good filial relation; but neither father nor son is, insofar, means or condition to the other, nor — God forbid! — *inclusive* of the other.

But what is the harm in talking so?

[28] A very rough, but not distorting, Parsonian schema.

The harm is — and this "Conservative" effect continues to mystify Parsons, a most liberal and person-oriented man[29] — that inescapably (in his mind too, I believe, when he is theorizing) the "including" system seems to have paramount importance, as in Durkheim the society came "naturally" to be viewed as exerting constraint.[30] But if it is no more natural to say that society sets conditions for personal action than that persons set (constitute) conditions for societal action, then a one-sided representation is an invitation to a submission that is not lightly to be recommended.

Basic terms:
"the learnéd
knife."

30   In fact, more basically, the function and effect of our most basic terms such as "person" and "society" are themselves open to question.

I do not wish to — cannot — open up this large question now. But it seems self-evident to me that there is no society as a datum, and that we mean in every case that which is a society-to-a-person, i.e., the (numerous) societies that each of us — and even so in the most primitive tribe — lives in. The society I live in varies from moment to moment as — using one turn of speech, I shift my attention and identification and location (personalistically who, what, where I "am," and what I am about) — or using the alternative form, as one or the other relation or society claims me. Moreover, I also stand in a social relation to myself, relating now thus, now so, and shifting about the bound of what is relatively egoid or alien, "internal" or "external" in (but also, to) myself as I do so. So the unities on both sides of the alleged units are factitious and fictitious.

If there is any reality to which the term Society (taken as a whole) can refer for me, it is, at least *prima facie*, some "sum and organization" of all those societies in which I sensibly "partici-

[29] See Parsons, in Max Black, *The Social Theories of Talcott Parsons.*

[30] See *Les Règles.* . . .

pate" — or perhaps I should say that participate in me. But this participation of them in me (and me in them, necessarily correlatively) is in large part (if not altogether from a "social" conceptual viewpoint) what I "am" — just as committee being and action are defined by the interaction (explicit and implicit, actual and virtual) of the committeemen as committeemen, and *vice versa.*

I should note perhaps that this view neither makes of society a psychological construct, nor of personality a social construct, but leaves both not merely co-emergent[31] in Mead's happy phrase, but co-constitutive — conceptually *and* in experience.

The reification and separation of personality and society, a perhaps not inevitable but altogether likely outcome of our practice, thrusts, I think, in the direction of drawing and causing others to draw a peculiar and arbitrary identity and ego boundary. It tends to generalize what is a sometimes momentarily useful perspectival glimpse into a normal *modus observandi:* the posture in which occasionally, say, I distinguish "my body" as over against "me," or my established tastes or weaknesses as a set of means or conditions within which the "real I" must operate. That this makes for "alienation," and indeed *converts* what otherwise is sizably egoid into a set of idoid means and conditions, with far-reaching consequences both for the species of selves then possible and the sorts of societies (or reciprocal or mutually oriented participations in each other) I find hard to doubt. If "our marriage" is perennially stood over against the us who are married (i.e., personalistically interpenetrated, so that the pre-existing I's are now other I's "in" an other us) then, I think, that conception of marriage has acted to bring a new and different sort of marriage into being.

[31] See *Mind, Self and Society.*

Knowledge is ambiguously good.

31   The underlying fundamental theorem on which we frequently formally justify our proceedings is itself false: that, in matters human, it is good to know. (Again, for the physical sciences, to the extent that mastery is desired, it *is* apt to secure unlimitedly limited knowledge of some kinds.) That "knowing more" — merely knowing more — about human behavior is in some unrestricted sense good is as little obvious — to me, at least — as the corresponding assertions in NASA about putting a man on the moon, or the fundamental medical-practice theorem involving the multiplication and duration-extension of living forms.

The matter seems so obvious in reference to other cultures, especially the "primitive" ones to which we feel protective, that we would not willingly convince their bearers, if we could, that tabu X served merely to protect them against dangers of incest that would largely cease to exist by an alteration in child-raising or by simple disaccreditation (like the risk of becoming mentally ill by adolescent masturbating, a risk destroyed largely by simple disavowal in our own times).

"Ignorance is comfort is viability" — is indeed a precondition to satisfactory living — covers a wide domain.

Matter and manner of mediation matter.

32   Even if and where we may take it that over some span of time there is warrant in the resultant goodness of life for the diminution of ignorance and error, and/or the increase of knowledge, the questions of the matter, manner and order of the mediation of such knowledge are crucial for the likely balance between help and hindrance or worse. We know this when we bring up or teach a child: not any proposition, in any random or unexamined order, mediated just anyhow at any arbitrary moment is useful to him. A decent and reasonable protectiveness while not too rigidly screening him from every random or noxious input, nevertheless ensures that his learn-

ing (and hence he) is structured, by attending to his needs and possibilities and welfare balance as they change under such inputs as occur. (Even though it is really not inputs but takeups that count, we know that the screening and takeup capacity are affected by violative inputs attempted.)

Reference frame should be history-making.

33   It is not only that we must consult "state" data to assess the relevance, utilizability and noxity-innoxity-benity balances, but that the evaluation cannot be made outside the context of the "career" possible and to be desired for the child in question. So a sense of where "he" is going and where "we" (he and we) want him to go, at an appropriate level of generality or specificity, is requisite in order to permit us to rest calm that we do at least no unnecessary harm.

Correspondingly, I believe, we need, if we are to be anywise responsible professionals, to proceed in a sense of history in clear vision of ourselves as history-makers, small or large, for better or worse. What this requires beyond the blind effort to give effect to unexamined personal will — what it requires "personally" and "socially," — is well worth examination. Whatever it is, it is not purely "cognitive" (if that were possible), nor "cathectic," nor "evaluative."

Intellectual gap strategy will not serve.

34   The filling-the-intellectual-gap strategy of theorizing is, I think, of dubious merit, for us. I know this is supposed to distinguish the theoretically oriented from the practically oriented sociologist. But, as I have tried to indicate, it is precisely theory that has the most far-reaching practical consequence. In any case, the test is an insufficient guide: I do not think we have now sufficient structure in theory to permit us to define where the gaps of consequence are.[32]

[32] If sociology is, as I believe, the conduct of politics by other means, the gaps identified are *intelligence* deficits in the military sense.

*System-
hierarchy
theory
underwrites
centralism.*

35   I would like to draw attention at another level to still another consequence of hierarchy of systems theorizing. *Volens nolens*, it
nurtures nationalism and tends to tyranny —
whether the "more inclusive" system thought of
is social — the "larger society" — cultural, *the*
culture versus a "variant" or "subculture," actually, necessarily, then a "deviation" from a "norm"
— or personal — the idolatry of the whole person
over "component" (save the mark!) impulses or
part-goals. It is a vocabulary of and virtual, if
covert, invitation to centralism. What is less than
clear is that form follows faith — or, more forcefully, fiction. The "larger system" is lost to sight
for what it is: something brought into being afresh
each day[33] by the acts of the (presumably) "lesser
systems." An ecological network may just naturally exist in a niche, and impose its constraints
on breeding, locomotion and the like on species
and "individual forms," who are not required to
take it into account symbolically in order for it
to have its effects. But "American society," "the
Army," "our firm" are not only invented by but
owe their moment-to-moment existence to avow-
als (symbolic recognitions) that in principle can
be disavowed on sufficient provocation (as Americans did indeed disavow the British "larger system" of which they were, before defection, on
the system view, a "part"). What is lost from
sight in this way of talking is again that the principle of inclusion is not *given* (like the liver-cell's
relation to that liver and that body in which the
liver lies) but *enacted;* that what is involved is a
loyalty, not a locus; that while there are two-way
consequences, so that neither the soldiers nor the
army are conceptually or practically independent,
the relations are not those of logical implication
(as in the parts of triangles) nor necessity (as in

[33] See Stanley Diamond, "What History Is" in R. A.
Manners, ed., *Process and Pattern in Culture* (Chicago:
Aldine, 1964).

the body-cell) nor even undying convenience. Even seeming retention by force is not limiting: force or the threat of it can "make" a child live in his parents' house; it cannot make him live *at home* nor remain "in the family."

"Reciprocal system needs" favors fixity.

36   Nor is it other than misleading, I think, to save the situation by stipulating "system needs" of the higher and lower, larger and lesser systems, recognizing their reciprocity, and speaking of the necessary exchanges across "boundaries." As I have pointed out, the boundaries are themselves movable (over at least large ranges) at will or wish or whim. And the "needs," such as there are, are functions of the faiths sustained by and sustaining them. What is hidden or distorted thus is the conditionality: *if* (and for as long as) you and I want to play a duet we must (rather, will naturally) attend to promptings from "within" our (partly) separate selves; and also within (but subjectively less within, perhaps), ourselves: the promptings that are for each the reflections and representations of the other. Just that. To say the duet has "needs" is a figure of speech that has limited utility, but only so long as it is not held to be a necessary or paramount representation.

Defenses don't justify disregards.

37   It may be thought — or wish-thought — that persons and societies are well enough defended against any sizable or substantial risks from the propositions (and implicit programs and proposals) that we put about. This is consoling. But we do not know it to be so, and I suspect that it is not. (The fact that we know very little on this score is itself significant.) All the evidence that we have from operations that have been halfway decently observed in this respect should give us ground for adaptive anxiety. In psychotherapy — the essence of which is the putting of "data" into new "cognitive-cathectic-evaluative" contexts and structures — we know that there are both massive defenses and vulnerabilities of such an order that the relatively independent opera-

bility of either "system" (patient, or patient-therapist) can be virtually destroyed, temporarily or permanently. So, I believe, with the growing child. And so also, I believe, for such "small groups" as we have studied.

I do not doubt — though I do not know much about — a general, societal capacity for selective inattention, for distortion of perception to preserve comfort or safety, for denial, for forgetting or burying or other analogues functionally of repression in the person. But I do not think we may wantonly, blindly count on the effect, efficiency and efficacy of such defenses to protect us against the consequences of our operations, any more than a surgeon may needlessly count on the "defenses of the body" to guard against the risks of unnecessary sepsis.

I would not say that people had been properly or safely proof against Marx or Adam Smith or Freud or Spencer — or even, on a smaller scale, against Riesman, Bettelheim, Sumner, Skinner or Wiener.

Open market serves only so far.

38   Nor do I think we may comfort ourselves or each other with the open market theory. The open market in ideas is a necessary, but not a sufficient, condition for beneficent effect, and in any case is only very roughly approximated.

Where, even in the most limited fashion people get news about drugs or operations out of *Time* or *Newsweek* so that they proceed thus to self-medication or to making irresistible demands on their doctors, so that biological theory enters more directly into biology, the free market in ideas of scientific-professional communication among biologists and doctors ceases to have an exclusively beneficial winnowing effect.

Where, as in our case, everyman virtually is his own doctor, and where the theory either *is* the medication or the condition for medicamental choice, there is in a sense no free market in ideas, anyway, that is independent of that which the ideas are about.

Non-monopoly doesn't excuse non-policy.

39   I realize that social scientists are by no means the only social theory (or innovative myth) makers. (Indeed, I sometimes think that we resurrect, reclothe and reanimate a limited number of myths, themselves timeless and deathless.) We compete in a sense with journalists, pundits, poets, princes and other powers, secular and sacred. But, I believe that, unless and until science itself as an object (for obscure reasons) of veneration is itself "discrown'd and disannointed," as long as we claim and are held to be social *scientists*, what we say and do falls with peculiar force on those who so call us or who give recognition to our claims to speak with authenticity and authority. For better or worse we are cast as Wise Men; would that we could be surer that we are, within tolerable limits, wise men.

History as Private Enterprise

HOWARD ZINN

FOR A LONG TIME, the historian has been embarrassed by his own humanity. Touched by the sight of poverty, horrified by war, revolted by racism, indignant at the strangling of dissent, he has nevertheless tried his best to keep his tie straight, his voice unruffled, and his emotions to himself. True, he has often slyly attuned his research to his feelings, but *so* slyly, and with such scholarly skill, that only close friends and investigators for congressional committees might suspect him of compassion.

Historians worry that a deep concern with current affairs may lead to twisting the truth about the past. And indeed it may, under conditions which I will discuss below. But non-concern results in another kind of distortion, in which the ore of history is beaten neither into a ploughshare nor a sword, but is melted down and sold. For the historian is a specialist who makes his living by writing and teaching, and Rousseau foresaw the problem of professional specialization: "We have physicists, geometricians, chemists, astronomers, poets, musicians, and painters in plenty, but we have no longer a citizen among us."

The tension between human drives and professional mores leads many to a schizophrenic separation of scholarly work from other activities; thus, research on Carolingian foreign policy is interrupted momentarily to sign a petition on civil rights. Sometimes the separation is harder to maintain, and so the specialist on Asia scrupulously stays away from teach-ins on Vietnam, and seeks to keep his work unsullied by application to the current situation. One overall result is that common American phenomenon — the secret liberal.

There is more than a fifty-fifty chance that the academic historian will lose what vital organs of social concern he has in the process of acquiring a doctorate, where the primary requirement of finding an untouched decade or person or topic almost assures that several years of intense labor will end in some monstrous irrelevancy. And after that, the considerations of rank, tenure, and salary, while not absolutely excluding either personal activism or socially pertinent scholarship, tend to discourage either.

We find, of course, oddities of academic behavior: Henry Steele Commager writing letters to the *Times* defending Communists; Martin Duberman putting the nation's shame on stage; Staughton Lynd flying to Hanoi. And to the rule of scholarly caution, the exceptions have been glorious:

Beard's *An Economic Interpretation of the Constitution* was muckraking history, not because it splattered mud on past heroes, but because it made several generations of readers worry about the working of economic interest in the politics of their own time. The senior Arthur Schlesinger, in an essay in *New Viewpoints in American History*, so flattened pretensions of "states' rights" that no reader could hear that phrase again without smiling. DuBois' *Black Reconstruction* was as close as a scholar could get to a demonstration, in the deepest sense of that term, puncturing a long and destructive innocence. Matthew Josephson's *The Robber Barons* and Henry David's *History of the Haymarket Affair* were unabashed in their sympathies. Walter Millis' *The Road to War* was a deliberate and effective counter to romantic nonsense about the first World War. Arthur Weinberg's *Manifest Destiny* quietly exposed the hypocrisy of both conservatives and liberals in the idealization of American expansion. Richard Hofstadter's *The American Political Tradition* made us wonder about *now,* by brilliantly deflating the liberal heroes — Jefferson, Jackson, Wilson, the two Roosevelts. And C. Vann Woodward gently reminded the nation, in *The Strange Career of Jim Crow,* that racism might be deeply embedded, yet it could change its ways in remarkably short time. There are many others.

But with all this, the dominant mood in historical writing in the United States (look at the pages of the historical reviews) avoids direct confrontation of contemporary problems, apologizes for any sign of departure from "objectivity," spurns a liaison with social action. Introducing a recent collection of writings on *American History and the Social Sciences*, historian Edward N. Saveth asserts that the social science approach to history "was confused" by "the teleology of presentism." (In the space of three pages, Saveth uses three variations of the word "confusion" to discuss the effect of presentism.)

What is presentism? It was defined by Carl Becker in 1912 as "the imperative command that knowledge shall serve purpose, and learning be applied to the solution of the problem of human life." Saveth, speaking for so many of his colleagues, shakes his head: "The fires surrounding the issues of reform and relativism had to be banked before the relationship between history and social science could come under objective scrutiny."

They were not really fires, but only devilishly persistent sparks, struck by Charles Beard, James Harvey Robinson (in *The New History*) and Carl Becker. There was no need to "bank" them, only to smother them under thousands of volumes of "objective" trivia, which became the trade mark of academic history, revealed to fellow members of the profession in papers delivered at meetings, doctoral dissertations, and articles in professional journals.

In *Knowledge for What?*, Robert S. Lynd questioned the relevance of a detailed analysis of "The Shield Signal at Marathon" which appeared in the *American Historical Review* in 1937. He wondered if it was a "warranted expenditure of scientific energy." Twenty-six years later (in the issue of July, 1965), the lead article in the *American Historical Review* is "William of Malmesbury's Robert of Gloucester: a Reevaluation of the *Historia Novella*." In 1959, we find historians at a meeting of the Southern Historical Association (the same meeting which tabled a resolution asking an immediate end to the practice of holding sessions at hotels that barred Negroes) presenting long papers on "British Men of War in Southern Waters, 1793 – 1802," "Textiles: A Period of Sturm und Drang," and "Bampson of Bampson's Raiders."

As Professor Lynd put it long ago: "History, thus voyaging forth with no pole star except the objective recovery of the past, becomes a vast, wandering enterprise." And in its essence, I would add, it is *private* enterprise. This is not to deny that there are many excellent historical studies only one or two degrees removed from immediate applicability to crucial social problems. The problem is in the proportion.

There is immense intellectual energy in the United States devoted to inspecting the past, but only a tiny amount of this is deliberately directed to the solution of vital problems: racism, poverty, war, repression, loneliness, alienation, imprisonment. Where historical research has been useful, it has often been by chance rather than by design, in accord with a kind of trickle-down theory which holds that if only you fill the libraries to bursting with enough processed pulpwood, something useful will eventually reach a society desperate for understanding.

While scholars do have a vague, general desire to serve a social purpose, the production of historical works is largely motivated by profit (promotion, prestige, and even a bit of money) rather than by use. Although this does not mean that use-values are not produced (or that what is produced is not of excellent quality in its own terms, as our society constructs excellent office buildings while people live in slums), it does mean that their production is incidental, more often than not. In a rich economy, not in some significant degree directed towards social reform, waste is bound to be huge, measured in lost opportunities and misdirected effort.

True, the writing of history is really a mixed economy, but an inspection of the mixture shows that the social sector is only a small portion of the mass. What I am suggesting is not a totalistic direction of scholarship but (leaving complete freedom to all who want to analyze The Shield Signal at Marathon or Bampson of Bampson's Raiders) an enlargement of the social sector by encouragement, persuasion, and demonstration.

I am not directing my criticism against these few works labeled "history" which are really works of art, which make no claim to illuminate a social problem, but instead capture the mood, the color, the reality of an age, an incident, or an individual, conveying pleasure and the warmth of genuine emotion. This needs no justification, for it is, after all, the ultimate purpose of social change to enlarge human happiness.

Too much work in history is neither art nor science. It is sometimes defended as "pure research" like that of the mathematician, whose formulas have no knowable immediate use. However, the pure scientist is working on data which opens towards infinity in its possible future uses. This is not true of the historian working on a dead battle or an obscure figure. Also, the proportion of scientists working on "pure research" is quite small. The historian's situation is the reverse; the proportion working on applied data is tiny. Only when the pendulum swings the other way will the historian be able justly to complain that pure research is being crowded out.

Enlarging the social sector of historiography requires, as a start, removing the shame from "subjectivity." Benedetto Croce undertook this, as far back as 1920, reacting against the strict claims of "scientific history": what von Ranke called history "as it actually was," and what Bury called "simply a science, no less and no more." Croce openly avowed that what he chose to investigate in the past was determined by "an interest in the life of the present" and that past facts must answer "to a present interest." In America, James Harvey Robinson said: "The present has hitherto been the willing victim of the past; the time has now come when it should turn on the past and exploit it in the interests of advance."

But this confession of concern for current problems made other scholars uneasy. Philosopher Arthur O. Lovejoy, for instance, said the aims of the historian must not be confused with those of the "social reformer," and that the more a historian based his research on problems of "the period in which he writes" then "the worse historian he is likely to be." The job of the historian, he declared (this was in the era of the Memorial Day Massacre, Guernica, and the Nuremberg Laws) is "to know whether . . . certain events, or sequences of events, happened at certain past times, and what . . . the characters of those events were." When philosophers suggest this is not the first business of a historian, Lovejoy said, "they merely tend to undermine his morals as a historian."

At the bottom of the fear of engagement, it seems to me, is a confusion between ultimate values and instrumental ones. To start historical enquiry with frank adherence to a small set of ultimate values — that war, poverty, race hatred, prisons should be abolished; that mankind constitutes a single species; that affection and cooperation should replace violence and hostility — such a set of commitments places no pressure on its advocates to tamper with the truth. The claim of Hume and his successors among the logical positivists, that no moral *should* can be proved by what *is*, has its useful side, for neither can the moral absolute be disproved by any factual discovery.

For an American historian with an ultimate commitment to racial equality there is no compulsion to ignore the facts that many slaveholders did not use whips on their slaves, that most slaves did not revolt, that some Negro officeholders in the Reconstruction period were corrupt, or that the homicide rate has been higher among Negroes than whites. But with such a commitment, and more concerned to shape the future than to recount the past for its own sake, the historian would be driven to point out what slavery meant for the "well-treated" slave; to explain how corruption was bi-racial in the 1870's as in all periods; to discuss Uncle Tomism along with the passivity of Jews in the concentration camp and the inertia of thirty million poor in an affluent America; to discuss the relationship between poverty and crime of a certain sort.

Unyielding dedication to certain *instrumental* values, on the other hand — to specific nations, organizations, leaders, social systems, religions, or techniques, all of which claim their own efficacy in advancing the ultimate values — creates powerful pressures for hiding or distorting historical events. A relentless commitment to his own country may cause an American to glide over the elements of brutality in American "diplomatic history" (the term itself manufactures a certain aura of gentility). Compare, for instance, James Reston's pious column for Easter Sunday, 1965, on the loftiness of American behavior towards other countries, with Edmund Wilson's harsh, accurate summary of American expansionism in his introduction to *Patriotic Gore*.

It was rigid devotion to Stalin, rather than to the ultimate concerns of a humane Marxism, that led to fabrication of history in the Soviet Union about the purges and other things. After 1956, a shift in instrumental gods led to counter-fabrication. With the advent of the cold war the United States began to match the Soviet Union in the large-scale development of government-supported social science research which took an instrumental value

—the nation's foreign policy—and *assumed* this was identical with peace and freedom.

Thus, teams of social scientists under contract to the armed forces took without question the U.S. government's premise that the Soviet Union planned to invade Western Europe, and from this worked out all sorts of deductions for policy. Now it turns out (and we are told this by the same analysts) that that premise was incorrect. This is replaced not by the overthrow of dogma itself, but by substituting a new assumption—that Communist China intends to take over all of Asia and eventually the world—and so the computers have begun to click out policy again. The absolutization of an instrumental value—in this case, current U.S. foreign policy; in other cases, Soviet policy or Ghanaian policy or whatever—distorts the results of research from the beginning.

Knowing that commitments to instrumental values distort the facts often leads scholars to avoid commitment of any kind. Boyd Schafer, reporting for the American Historical Association on the international congress of historians held in Vienna in the summer of 1965, notes an attempt at one session to introduce the question of Vietnam. The executive body of the Congress "firmly opposed the introduction of any current political question," saying the organization "had been and could only be devoted to scientific historical studies." Here were 2400 historians from forty nations, presumably an enormous assembly of data and insights from all branches of history; if this body could not throw any light on the problem of Vietnam, what claim can anyone make that history is studied to help us understand the present?

It testifies to the professionalization, and therefore the dehumanization, of the scholar that, while tens of thousands of them gather annually in the United States alone, to hear hundreds of papers on scattered topics of varying significance, there has been no move to select a problem—poverty, race prejudice, the war in Vietnam, alternative methods of social change—for concentrated attention by some one conference.

But if a set of "ultimate values"—peace, racial equality, economic security, freedom of expression—are to guide our questioning, without distorting our answers, what is the source of these values? Can we prove their validity?

It is only when "proof" is identified with academic research that we are at a loss to justify our values. The experiences of millions of lives over centuries of time, relived by each of us in those aspects common to all men, *prove* to us that love is preferable to hate, peace to war, brotherhood to enmity, joy to sorrow, health to sickness, nourishment to hunger, life to death. And enough people recognize these values (in all countries, and inside all social systems) so that further academic disputation is only a stumbling block to action. What we see and feel (is not human emotion often a crystallized, ineffable rationality?) is more formally stated as a fact of social psychology in Freud's Eros, and in Erik Erikson's idea of "the more inclusive identity."

How should all this affect the actual work of the historian? For one thing, it calls for an emphasis on those historical facts which have hitherto been obscured, and whose recall would serve to enhance justice and brotherhood. It is by now a truism that all historical writing involves a selection of facts out of those which are available. But what standards should govern this selection?

Harvard philosopher Morton White (in *Social Thought in America*), anxious to defend "historical objectivity" against "the hurried flight to relativism," says that the "ideal purpose of history" is "to tell the whole truth." But since it is impossible to have historical accounts list all that has taken place, White says, the historian's job is to give a shorter, "representative" list. White values "impersonal standards" and "a neutral standpoint." The crux of his argument is based on the notion that the fundamental aim of the historian is to tell as much of the story of the past as he can.

Even if it were possible to list *all* the events of a given historical period, would this really capture the human reality of this period? Can starvation, war, suffering, joy be given their due, even in the most complete historical recounting? Is not the *quality* of events more important than their quantity? Is there not something inherent in setting the past on paper which robs human encounter of its meaning? Does not the attention to either completeness or representativeness of "the facts" only guarantee that the cool jelly of neutrality will spread over it all, and that the reader will be left in the mood of the writer — that is, the mood of detached scholarship? And if this is so, does not the historian, concerned with the quality of an era or an event because he wants to affect the quality of his own time, need to work on the list in such a way as to try to restore its human content?

In a world where justice is maldistributed, historically and now, there is no such thing as a "neutral" or "representative" recapitulation of the facts, any more than one is dealing "equally" with a starving beggar and a millionaire by giving each a piece of bread. The condition of the recipient is crucial in determining whether the distribution is just.

Our best historians, whether or not they acknowledge it, take this into account. Beard's story of the making of the Constitution was hardly a representative list of the events connected with the Philadelphia Convention. He singled out the economic and political backgrounds of the Founding Fathers to illustrate the force of economic interest in political affairs, and he did it because (as he put it later) "this realistic view of the Constitution had been largely submerged in abstract discussion of states' rights and national sovereignty and in formal, logical, and discriminative analyses of judicial opinions."

When C. Vann Woodward wrote *The Strange Career of Jim Crow* he chose instances of equal treatment for Southern Negroes in public facilities, voting, transportation, in the 1880's. These were certainly not "representative." But he chose to emphasize them because he was writing in a time (1954) when much of the American nation, North and South, seemed to believe that segregation was so long and deeply entrenched in the South that it could not be changed. Woodward's intent was "to indicate that things have not always been the same in the South."

Similarly, the "Freedom Primer," now being used in the deep South by the Student Nonviolent Coordinating Committee, carefully selects from the mass of facts about the Negro in America those stories of heroism and rebellion which would give a Mississippi Negro child a sense of pride and worth, precisely because those are the feelings which everything around him tries to crush. (Yet I would not hesitate to point out, to a Negro child who developed the notion that Negroes could do no wrong, that history also showed some unheroic Negroes.)

The examples I have given are not "neutral" or "representative," but they are *true* to the ideal of man's oneness and to the reality of his separateness. Truth only in relation to what is or was is one-dimensional. Historical writing is most true when it is appropriate simultaneously to what was in the past, to the condition of the present, and to what should be in the future.

How can a historian portray the Twenties? It was a time of glittering "prosperity," with several million unemployed. There were floods of new consumer goods in the stores, with poverty on the farm. There was a new class of millionaires, while people in city slums struggled to pay the rent and gas bills. The two hundred largest corporations were doubling their assets, but Congressman Fiorello LaGuardia, representing a working-class district in East Harlem, wrote in 1928:

> It is true that Mr. Mellon, Mr. Ford, Mr. Rosenwald, Mr. Schwab, Mr. Morgan and a great many others not only manage to keep their enormous fortunes intact, but increase their fortunes every year. . . . But can any one of them improve on the financial genius of Mrs. Maria Esposito or Mrs. Rebecca Epstein or Mrs. Maggie Flynn who is keeping house in a New York tenement raising five or six children on a weekly envelope of thirty dollars . . . ?

A "comprehensive" picture of the Twenties, the kind most often found in American history textbooks, emphasizes the prosperity, along with amusing instances of governmental corruption, a summary of foreign policy, a dash of literature, and a bit on the K.K.K. and the Scopes Trial. This would seem to be "representative"; it leaves the reader with an unfocused mishmash, fogged over by a general aura of well-being. But wouldn't a history of the Twenties be most true to both past facts and future values if it stressed the plight of many millions of poor behind the façade of prosperity? Might not such an emphasis on the Twenties, if widespread, have hastened the nation's discovery (not made until the 1960's) of poverty amidst plenty?

To carry the point even further, would not an account of the New Deal which stressed the inadequacy of its measures in solving the problem of unemployment and maldistribution of wealth be more true — for the Sixties, when "poverty programs" pretend to so much — than some of the saccharine, romantic accounts of the Roosevelt years written by liberal historians? (The closest we have to such a future-oriented picture of the New Deal are two penetrating studies: William E. Leuchtenburg's *F.D.R. and the New Deal*, and James M. Burns' *Roosevelt: The Lion and the Fox*.)

There is still another flaw in the exhortation to the historian to give a "representative" account of his subject: he is not writing in an empty field, thousands have preceded him and have weighted the story in certain directions. When the Marxist historian Herbert Aptheker wrote *American Negro Slave Revolts*, he was giving heavy emphasis to a phenomenon in which only a small minority of slaves had participated. But he was writing in an atmosphere dominated by the writings on slavery of men like Ulrich Phillips, when textbooks spoke of the happy slave. Both southern and northern publics needed a sharp reminder of the inhumanity of the slave system. And perhaps the knowledge that such reminders are still necessary stimulated Kenneth Stampp to write *The Peculiar Institution*.

The earth has for so long been so sharply tilted on behalf of the rich, the white-skinned, the male, the powerful, that it will take enormous effort to set it right. A biography of Eugene Debs (Ray Ginger's *The Bending Cross*) is a deliberate focusing on the heroic qualities of a man who devoted his life to the idea that "while there is a lower class, I am in it; while there is a criminal element, I am of it; while there is a soul in prison, I am not free." But how many biographies of the radical Debs are there, compared to biographies of John D. Rockefeller, or Theodore Roosevelt? The selection of the topic for study is the first step in the weighting of the social scales for one value or another.

The usual distinction between "narrative" and "interpretive" history is not really pertinent to the criterion I have suggested for writing history in the public sector. It has often been assumed that narrative history, the simple description of an event or period, is "low-level" history, while the interpretation of events, periods, individuals is "high-level" and thus closer to the heart of a socially-concerned historian. But the narration of the Haymarket

Affair, or the Sacco-Vanzetti Case, to someone with a rosy picture of the American court system, has far more powerful effect on the present than an interpretation of the reasons for the War of 1812. A factual recounting of the addresses of Wendell Phillips constitutes (in a time when young people have begun to be captivated by the idea of joining social movements) a far more positive action on behalf of social reform than a sophisticated "interpretation" of the abolitionists which concludes that they were motivated by psychological feelings of insecurity. So much of the newer work on "concepts" in history gives up both the forest and the trees for the stratosphere.

If the historian is to approach the data of the past with a deliberate intent to further certain fundamental values in the present, then he can adopt several approaches. He may search at random in documents and publications to find material relevant to those values (this would rule out data of purely antiquarian or trivial interest). He can pursue the traditional lines of research (certain periods, people, topics: the Progressive period, Lincoln, the Bank War, the Labor Movement) with an avowed "presentist" objective. Or, as the least wasteful method, he can use a problem-centered approach to the American past. This approach, used only occasionally in American historiography, deserves some discussion.

The starting point, it should be emphasized, is a *present* problem. Many so-called "problem approaches" in American history have been based on problems of the past. Some of these may be extended by analogy to a present problem (like Beard's concern with economic motive behind political events of the 18th century), but many of them are quite dead (the tariff debates of the 1820's; the character of the Southern Whigs; Turner's frontier thesis, which has occupied an incredible amount of attention). Not that bits of relevant wisdom cannot be extracted from these old problems, but the reward is small for the attention paid. Too often, the historian fits Tolstoy's description of him as a deaf man responding to questions no one has asked.

Teachers and writers of history almost always speak warmly (and vaguely) of how "studying history will help you understand our own time." This usually means the teacher will make the point quickly in his opening lecture, or the textbook will dispose of this in an opening sentence, after which the student is treated to an encyclopedic, chronological recapitulation of the past. In effect, he is told: "The past is useful to the present. Now you figure out how."

Barrington Moore (in *Political Power and Social Theory*), discussing the reluctance of the historian to draw upon his knowledge for suggestive explanations of the present, says: "Most frequently of all he will retreat from such pressures into literary snobbishness and pseudo-cultivation. This takes the form of airy generalizations about the way history provides 'wisdom' or 'real understanding.' . . . Anyone who wants to know how this wisdom can be effectively used, amplified, and corrected, will find that his questions usually elicit no more than irritation."

To start historical enquiry with a present concern requires ignoring the customary chronological fracture of the American past: the Colonial Period; the Revolutionary Period; the Jacksonian Period; and so on, down to the New Deal, the War, and the Atomic Age. Instead, a problem must be followed where it leads, back and forth across the centuries if necessary.

David Potter has pointed (in his essay in the volume *Generalization in the Writing of History*) to the unconfessed theoretical assumptions of historians who claim they are not theorizing. I would carry his point further: all historians, by their writing, have some effect on the present social situation, whether they choose to be presentists or not. Therefore the real choice is not between shaping the world or not, but between doing it deliberately based on certain values, or unconsciously.

Psychology has contributed several vital ideas to our understanding of the role of the historian. In the first place, the psychologist is not recording the events of the patient's life simply to add to his files, or because they are "interesting," or because they will enable the building of complex theories. He is a therapist, devoted to the notion of curing people's problems, so that all the data he discovers are evaluated in accord with the single objective of therapy. This is the kind of commitment historians, as a group, have not yet made to society.

Second, there is Harry Stack Sullivan's notion of the psychologist as "participant." Whether the psychologist likes it or not, he is more than a listener. He has an effect on his patient. Similarly, the historian is a participant in history by his writing. Even when he claims neutrality he has an effect — if only, with his voluminous production of irrelevant data, to clog the social passages. So it is now a matter of consciously recognizing his participation, and deciding in which direction his energies will be expended.

An especially potent way of leading the historian towards a presentist, value-directed history is the binding power of social action itself. When a group of American historians in the Spring of 1965 joined the Negroes marching from Selma to Montgomery they were performing an unusual act. Social scientists sometimes speak and write on public policy; rarely do they bodily join in action to make contact with those whose motivation comes not from thought and empathy but from the direct pain of deprivation. Such contact, such engagement in action, generates an emotional attachment to the agents of social change which even long hours in the stacks can hardly injure.

Surely there is some relationship between the relative well-being of professors, their isolation in middle-class communities, their predictable patterns of sociality (the dinner party, summer at the seashore), and the tendency to remain distant, both personally and in scholarship, from the political battles of the day. The scholar does vaguely aim to serve some social purpose, but there is an undiscussed conflict between problem-solving and safety for a man earning $10,000 a year. There is no deliberate, conscious avoidance of social issues, but some quiet gyroscopic mechanism of survival operates to steer the scholar towards research within the academic consensus.

Engagement in social action is not indispensable for a scholar to direct his scholarship towards humane concerns; it is part of the wonder of people that they can transcend their immediate circumstances by leaps of emotion and imagination. But contact with the underground of society, in addition to spurring the historian to act out his value-system, might also open him to new data: the experiences, thoughts, feelings of the invisible folk all around us. This is the kind of data so often missed in official histories, manuscript collections of famous personalities, diaries of the literate, newspaper accounts, government documents.

I don't want to exaggerate the potency of the scholar as activist. But it may be that his role is especially important in a liberal society, where there is a smaller force available for social change, and the paralysis of the middle class is an important factor in delaying change. Fact can only buttress passion, not create it, but where passion is strained through the Madisonian constitutional sieve, it badly needs support.

The Negro revolution has taught us that indignation stays alive in the secret crannies of even the most complacent society. Niebuhr was right in chiding Dewey that intellectual persuasion was not enough of a force to create a just America. He spoke (in *Moral Man and Immoral Society*) of his hope that reason would not destroy that "sublime madness" of social passion before its work was done. Perhaps reason may even help focus this passion.

Except for a scattered, eloquent, conscience-torn few, historians in America have enjoyed a long period of luxury, corresponding to that of a nation spared war, famine, and (beyond recent memory) imperial rule. But now, those peoples who were not so spared are rising, stirring, on all sides — and even, of late, in our midst. The rioting Negro poor, the student-teacher critics on Vietnam, the silent walls around state prisons and city jails — all are reminders in this, the most luxurious of nations, that here, as well as abroad, is an exclusiveness based on race, or class, or nationality, or ideology, or monopolies of power.

In this way, we are forced apart from one another, from other people in the world, and from our freedom. To study this exclusiveness critically, and with unashamed feeling, is to act in some small way against it. And to act against it helps us to study it, with more than sharpness of eye and brain, with all that we are as total human beings.

From Socrates to Plato

HANS MEYERHOFF

I

WHAT I CALL THE MOVE "from Socrates to Plato" refers to a distinction that is familiar to every reader of Plato. It is the distinction between the earlier and so-called Socratic dialogues, on the one hand, and the later dialogues, on the other. This development, in turn, corresponds to the difference between Plato's earlier and later dialectics; and this difference, as I shall try to show, reflects two types of thinking in philosophy, which I call Socratic and Platonic, respectively.

For my purposes, it is not necessary to discuss the historical question of what is Socratic and what is Platonic in Plato's philosophy. The move from "Socrates to Plato" was made by Plato himself; and the two types that I distinguish are both "Platonic" in the obvious sense that Plato, not Socrates, developed them. More importantly, both are "Platonic" in that they are still mixed even in Plato's late works. They are not yet separated as I separate them in this paper.

Before I do so, however, I wish to consider the mixture itself. It is possible to show, I think, that in some dialogues, e.g., in the *Meno* or in the *Republic*, the mixing of types — a Socratic and a Platonic type of thinking — may be observed in a particularly striking manner. In these dialogues, the two types confront each other directly in the same work. Let me, therefore, first say something about this confrontation.

The Editors wish to thank Mrs. Mary Meyerhoff for permitting them to print this posthumous draft of an essay which Hans Meyerhoff had written for THE CRITICAL SPIRIT but which he had not had time to rewrite.

187

The first part of the *Meno* is typically "Socratic": It deals with the Socratic "what is . . ." question; it proceeds by way of examining a series of definitions; and it ends aporetically. This failure then leads to an exchange between Meno and Socrates that also reminds us of what we have heard in earlier dialogues. There is the familiar complaint: Socrates is like a poisoned fish that stings and paralyzes upon contact. Then there is the familiar reply: The reason that Socrates has this effect on others is that he is perplexed and paralyzed himself. In short, he does not know either. After this exchange, however, Meno raises a more serious matter. Why, then, inquire? Why pursue a truth that forever eludes us? It seems to be both hopeless and useless to look for something that we can never find. Worse, even if we did find it, how would we know that we found what we were looking for?

To deal with this "trick argument," as every commentator has noted, the dialogue changes in tone, style, and substance; and the second part of the *Meno* is quite different from the first. Perhaps it is Plato's first step beyond Socrates. At any rate, it is a definite attempt to get out of the aporetic impasse reached in Part I — and in other "Socratic" dialogues.

How does Plato make the transition from Part I to Part II? First, he appeals to religion — i.e., to the "priests and priestesses" of the Orphic mystery cults. More specifically, he derives from this source a doctrine of the soul: the "truth" that the soul is immortal and reborn many times. It is this hypothesis provisionally accepted as "true" that provides the basis for Plato's own doctrine of knowledge as recollection. Next, Plato appeals to mathematics. There follows the geometrical experiment. It supports Plato's doctrine of knowledge and, implicitly, the "truth" of the Orphic doctrine of the soul. More importantly, it disposes of the "trick argument" by showing that there is true knowledge and that it is demonstrable by a formal proof. There is such knowledge (as Socrates never claimed to have) in mathematics: i.e., knowledge *a priori* consisting of universal and necessary truths, and these truths can be discovered though the slave-boy did not know what he was looking for. Finally, and not surprisingly, this transition is completed by appropriating the methods of geometry for philosophy. Not surprisingly because this is the method by which we have just obtained a proof that is absolutely certain. Hence, a man "will behave in the same way with all geometrical knowledge, and every other subject." Whether this be so or not, the formal method of proof employed in geometry (a hypothetical-deductive method, as we say) is quite different from the type of cross-examination that Socrates conducted in the marketplace and that never yielded any certainty.

There is another transition — from Book I to Book II of the *Republic* — where this confrontation of two ways of thinking comes to the fore. Though Book I, an independent Socratic dialogue sometimes called the *Thrasymachus*, was probably revised when Plato decided to use it as a prelude to the *Republic*, its content and style of thought are still typically "Socratic": Again, it deals with a "what is . . . ?" question; again, it consists of a series of definitions that are examined and refuted; again, as in the *Protagoras* or in the *Gorgias*, the presence of the Sophist is an integral part of the dramatic structure of the dialogue.

What happens as we move from Book I to Book II? Thrasymachus drops out of the dialogue; and the style and method of presentation change considerably. First, we get two long speeches by Glaukon and Adeimantus restating the case of Thrasymachus. This is not "dialogue" in the form of conversation; it's a formal, didactic summary as in a treatise; and after Plato's brothers have served this purpose, they never again function as true interlocutors in the remainder of the dialogue. They say yes or no; they expand or qualify certain views advanced by Socrates; but they never *challenge* any of them as Thrasymachus would or Protagoras or Parmenides. They are intellectual satellites as it were, not dialectical antagonists. Next, we get the demand voiced by Adeimantus at the end of his speech: "Prove to us. . . ." In the *Crito* Socrates invites his friend to inquire into a mutual problem by saying, "Let us then jointly investigate. . . ." Not so here: what is called for is not a "dialogical" exchange, or examination, of opposing views; what is called for is a proof or a demonstration. How? Presumably, as we prove conclusions in the exact sciences. And how does Socrates proceed in order to satisfy this demand for proof?

Not by cross-examination, but by a long formal exposition

that strains the dramatic structure of the dialogue to a breaking point. And this formal exposition employs a characteristic type of reasoning: setting up an abstract hypothetical model and deriving consequences from it. So we first construct a model of a primitive society, a "community of pigs," and see what follows. Then we construct the model of an advanced society and see what follows: production for profit, instead of use, the threat of war, both civil and foreign, and the need for a special class in society called "guardians." Then we educate the guardians, not under conditions of actual life, but in the context of the abstract, "ideal" model we have constructed. And, finally, we apply (by analogy) this model of society to the self, again on a completely abstract, theoretical level, and show how both models combined provide the kind of proof that Adeimantus demanded. All this may be of the highest importance — it may even be true — but it is *not* the kind of dialectics practiced by Socrates, alas, without positive results.

In both these cases, the move "from Socrates to Plato" is made in the same dialogue. In the *Parmenides*, I think, we find a similar situation, but let me add a third example of a more general kind. It refers to the way in which the same subject matter is treated differently in the earlier and later dialogues. Plato, of course, waged a continuous battle with, and against, the "Sophists." Now compare the treatment of the Sophists in the earlier dialogues with the late dialogue called the *Sophist*. In the *Protagoras*, this portrait is even favorable to the Sophist and, one might say, Socrates looks, and acts, much more like a "Sophist" than Protagoras does. Be that as it may, in the *Protagoras*, the *Euthyphro*, the *Gorgias*, or the *Thrasymachus*, the theoretical structure of these dialogues is always an integral part of their dramatic structure. There are dramatic human encounters; the Sophists are present and make their presence felt; they are depicted, or caricatured, as live human beings acting in and reacting to concrete situations.

In the dialogue called the *Sophist*, however, there is no Sophist at all and there is no human encounter. Instead, the Eleatic stranger gives a formal demonstration for the benefit of the young Theaetetus, with Socrates standing by without saying a word. Here the pursuit of the elusive Sophist is an exercise in definitions exemplifying the new logical method Plato introduced in his later dialogues — the method of division, as it is called. It is true that the dialogue still contains rich material derived from social life (all of Plato's dialogues do), but it is also true that all this concrete material is subordinated to a repetitive logical exercise producing an elaborate conceptual schema. Thus when the Sophist is finally "tracked down" he has a definite place on the conceptual map constructed by the Eleatic stranger, but this is an abstract place, not a grasp of the reality of the Sophist as in the "Socratic" dialogues.

II

These introductory remarks were designed to show that the move "from Socrates to Plato" may be located in some of the dialogues themselves. I will now follow Plato's lead and abstract from the actual context in which these two ways of thought appear in his own works. In other words, I will construct two models, or "ideal types," for a purpose that goes beyond an interest in Plato. Though they generally appear in a mixed state even in the late works, this mixture, I contend, *can* be separated.

I should add, however, that even this relatively modest claim would not be acceptable to every reader of Plato. For example, there are some scholars (including an old teacher of mine) who argue that even in those dialogues, say the *Sophist* or the *Statesman,* where Socrates is merely present listening silently to the discussion without participating in it, this presence alone makes all the difference in interpreting these dialogues. Whether this is so or not, it is surely possible to take another line. We may also say that the fact that Socrates is no more than a silent listener in these dialogues indicates that Socrates is, or would be, a stranger in the intellectual world of the late Plato. He would not feel at home in it, I submit, because his thinking differed from Plato's later dialectics (1) in subject matter, (2) in method, and (3) in purpose. Let me expand upon this theme by describing some of the characteristic features of what I have called a Socratic and a Platonic type of thinking in philosophy.

First, what did Socrates do in the name of philosophy? He

asked questions, "what is . . . ?" questions. What is courage?
What is piety? What is love, or friendship? What is the good life
of man in society? Apparently, he was interested in any question
that might arise in the context of actual life, whether it was a matter of public policy or personal conduct, whether it was the problem of drinking or homoerotism, whether it was the exegesis of
a poem or the relationship between tragedy and comedy. But
these were invariably problems encountered in the human world.
Socrates did not concern himself with problems of science; and,
Aristotle to the contrary, he did not deal with problems of ethics
or epistemology, for these special fields in philosophy did not yet
exist for Socrates.

Next, how did Socrates approach this general field of inquiry?
Here several points are worth noting: (1) Socrates talked about
these problems of life in an informal, social setting, not in an
Academy, not *ex cathedra*, but barefoot in Athens, at a banquet,
at the banks of a river, at the house of a rich merchant, at a court
hearing, even in prison. (2) He used a common type of evidence
in support of his arguments, not evidence derived from any technical knowledge, but evidence supplied by the concrete facts of
life familiar to everybody, then and now. (3) He always discussed
philosophical problems, not on an abstract level, but in the context of a concrete human situation — fathers asking for advice
on how to educate their sons (as in the *Laches*), a son prosecuting
his father for manslaughter (as in the *Euthyphro*), a friend trying
to persuade Socrates to escape from prison (as in the *Crito*),
friends celebrating the blessings of love in life (as in the *Symposium*), or friends downcast and depressed at the impending death
of Socrates (as in the *Phaedo*).

Finally, (4) the logic Socrates used in this kind of inquiry was
neither scientific nor formal. It was an informal method of reasoning. Collingwood called it a question-and-answer method. In Plato
it is called "cross-examination." This is the so-called earlier dialectics, or *elenchus*. Generally, it consists of two major steps:
first, clarifying the meaning of a view that is advanced; secondly,
refuting this view by citing concrete counter-instances or by
pointing to logical flaws in it. Instead of refutation, I think, it

would be better to say that view and counter-view are examined to show that both are defective, inadequate, or deceptive. Be that as it may, the logic here employed is not formal. Basically it consists of arguing back and forth, pro and con; and this "dialogue" rarely, if ever, produces a formal proof or a formal refutation as in logic or in mathematics. It is an informal dialectics, not unlike the way we still argue the merits of a case of law, cross-examine witnesses, or debate the pros and cons of a political issue or a private decision.

So much for what Socrates did in the name of philosophy, and how he did it. There remains the question, why did he practice this kind of analysis? Apparently, for a rather simple and limited purpose: to expose ignorance, or false beliefs, in others and in himself. The process of self-examination was an end in itself because it expressed a way of life; hence, "the unexamined life is not worth living." This is a strange view because, in Socrates, the examination never seems to get anywhere. It is never completed. It is "interminable," as Freud said of some cases of psychoanalysis. Why, then, pursue a project that seems to be both frustrating and disappointing as far as the goal of attaining truth, or certainty, is concerned? The answer is twofold: (1) Though the process be interminable, it is the only means of gaining self-knowledge; and (2) self-knowledge, though forever incomplete, is the only means of knowing what we are doing and how we are living.

This conception of knowledge may be called "practical" — or "existential," if you like. It is existential in the simple sense I just mentioned: truth is expressed in a way of life. It is not necessarily put into propositional form. Thus true knowledge is not yet defined as the correspondence between thoughts and things, or words and things. It is not yet an *adaequatio intellectus et rei*, as the traditional formula reads. Instead, it is more like an *adaequatio* of thinking and feeling, thinking and willing, or thinking and doing. Truth refers to a correlation between consciousness and life. It means that theory and practice, consciousness and action are conjoined in a conception of life. Put differently, (true) knowledge in the primary sense is an attribute of life; it is not necessarily an attribute of beliefs or propositions as in later logic. Hence, Socrates could legitimately claim he was ignorant and still display (true) knowledge in life. That has been the perennial paradox, and fascination, he has presented to posterity.

*   *   *

I now turn to the Platonic type of thinking in philosophy: Plato's later dialectics. In order to make this move "from Socrates to Plato," we must take a few preliminary — though again familiar — steps:

First, we must note that Plato developed a theory of his own — the theory of Forms. It is this theory that provides a way out of the epistemological impasse reached in the so-called Socratic dialogues. In other words, the Forms are the basis for a positive theory of truth. True knowledge, in the words of the *Meno*, may now be firmly "tethered" to the reality of Forms; and, by means of this break-through, we arrive at the traditional definition of truth. It now consists in the correspondence between words and things or between reason and reality — the only "true" reality being the Forms, or essences, of things.

Secondly, we must note that, in the Academy, philosophy was practiced in closest possible conjunction with the exact sciences — of which mathematics was the most advanced at the time.

Thirdly, we must note that, according to Plato, the closest approximation to a knowledge of Forms is a knowledge of mathematical objects, relations, and equations.

Finally, we must note that, in the later dialogues, Plato is increasingly preoccupied with a new problem. It is not the Socratic question, "what is . . . ?"; it is not even Plato's earlier problem of how things in this world participate in the Forms beyond. It is the new problem of how these Forms, or essences of things, are logically related to each other in an ascending order of abstraction.

With these preliminaries in mind, we can sketch a model of the Platonic type of analysis. What is analyzed? Some formal language — whether this be the language of Plato's own Forms, the formal language of mathematics, or the abstract language of some other science. The important thing is that this is not the language of life. Forms, as Plato kept repeating, are timeless and unchanging. They are essences distilled, or abstracted, from "process and reality," i.e., from the world of time, change, and history in which we live, act, and suffer as human beings. It is this realm of abstract essences into which the philosopher ascends from the human world of the cave. In the schema of the "Divided Line" in the *Republic*, it is the intelligible world comprised of mathematical and dialectical reasoning where true knowledge dwells. Again, it is mathematics and dialectics that complete the education of the philosopher-king — an "education" Socrates never had. In the penultimate stage of this education, the philosopher studies the five mathematical disciplines, arithmetic, plane geometry, solid geometry, astronomy, and harmonics. The final stage is dialectics.

What, then, is this later dialectics? Not a method of mutual cross-examination, but a different method. In the *Republic* it consists of an inquiry into the foundations of mathematics, or the derivation of mathematics from "first principles." In the later dialogues, it is generally called the method of division (*diaeresis*). This is a method of studying the logical relations, both combinations and divisions, that are possible in the universe of Forms. The reasoning employed in this dialectics is modeled after geometry. Thus there must be "first principles" — definitions, axioms, or hypotheses, e.g., the One and the indefinite Dyad — and the Forms must be so organized that they constitute a logical system, a system in which we may descend downward from first principles or upward from species and genera to the "greatest of the kinds" as outlined in the *Sophist*. In addition to correspondence, this method employs another criterion of truth: coherence. Coherence, however, not as expressed in a way of life, but as defined in the context of a scientific theory or a logical system.

The purpose, or goal, of this later dialectics is obvious. It is not self-knowledge, but something else. The aim is to convert philosophy into the "queen of the sciences," providing both the logical foundation and a supreme *Summa* of the exact sciences. Self-knowledge may still be a by-product of this inquiry, but it is not the main object. The primary task of philosophy is to reconstruct *more geometrico* — i.e., in the form and language of a logical, or deductive, system — the body of *general* knowledge about man's place in the universe and in society. That was Plato's secret dream, as it were.

III

It is evident that these two types that I have abstracted from Plato differ in significant respects. They differ in what they analyze, in how they analyze, and in why they analyze. These differences, in turn, give rise to divided views about the nature and function of philosophy itself. They reflect divided loyalties in Plato's own mind; more simply, two different views of philosophy may be seen at work in the development of Plato's thought from the early to the late dialogues. This distinction is not only of historical interest as far as Plato is concerned. Curiously enough, it also provides a clue to the contemporary situation in philosophy; for it is possible to look at this situation in the light of the move "from Socrates to Plato." I need not add that this is a restricted view to take, and over-simplified, but if we take such a view, the two types of philosophy acquire a historical significance that goes beyond Plato. In looking back upon them from the perspective of our own time, we may distinguish a twofold trend: (1) The Platonic type has been the dominant tradition in the history of philosophy. (2) This tradition has suffered a decline in modern thought. More precisely, there has been a definite reaction against it, a "revolt against formalism," and a return to a Socratic type of thinking in philosophy. In other words, there has been a counter-move "from Plato to Socrates" in recent philosophy.

Obviously, it is impossible to treat a theme of this scope and magnitude in a few concluding remarks. All I can do is to indicate briefly what I have in mind.

In saying that the Platonic type became the dominant tradition in Western philosophy I do not mean, of course, that later philosophers have all been Platonists or crypto-Platonists. I am not even saying, as Whitehead did, that the history of Western philosophy consists of a series of footnotes to Plato. What I mean is that the type of thinking expressed in "Plato's dream" became the dominant historical model in determining what was to be done in the name of philosophy — even among thinkers who were not Platonists. Again, I cannot even deal with the complex ramifications of this historical model; I can only select a few features by way of illustrating the reaction against it and the reasons for the re-instatement of Socrates in modern thought.

To begin with, let me take a relatively simple matter — the reaction against the "Platonic" view of philosophy as the crowning *Summa* of the sciences. It is clear that, however influential this view was in the past, there is no future for philosophy along these lines. All the sciences have moved out of the Academy — the natural, or exact, sciences a long time ago, the social and human disciplines more recently. Even logic — i.e., formal logic, since Aristotle the special prerogative of philosophy — has now become a branch of higher mathematics. In short, all the sciences have broken away from philosophy and have become autonomous. In such a situation, it would seem to be futile, and pretentious as well, for any philosopher to set himself up as the "king" of the sciences. And, in such a situation, it is perhaps not surprising that, for some time now, philosophers have been looking for a subject matter that they can still call their own and have found it in something like the human world, the language of life that Socrates chose as his primary field of investigation — not the language of science.

Similarly, the "Platonic" view of philosophy as the rational reconstruction of human knowledge in the form of an axiomatic, or deductive, system has suffered a sharp decline, though it was of preeminent influence in the past. All the great systems developed in modern philosophy, e.g., by Descartes, Spinoza, or Leibniz, were "Platonic" in my sense of the word. They were "Platonic" (1) in that they claimed to be based on the exact sciences, (2) in that they claimed to discover metaphysical essences, and (3) in that they were patterned after the Platonic model of a deductive system. Descartes dreamed of a deductive physics derived from "first principles" in philosophy; Spinoza proceeded *more geometrico;* and Leibniz shared Plato's dream that philosophy would, and should, be converted into a "universal mathematics," i.e., into a logically perfect language and system. Even Locke and Hume, empirical or skeptical as they were, subscribed to a similar model. They, too, tried to provide a logical reconstruction of the sciences on the basis of "first principles" — called sensations, impressions, ideas, or the "principle" of association.

I do not wish to disparage these great thinkers in saying that this tradition has also run its course. I simply mean that, after Hume and Kant, there is little, or no, future for philosophy along these lines. Hegel once said that the owl of Minerva only takes flight at dusk. He meant that philosophy had reached its maturity in the gathering dusk of its history. (In other words, in Hegel's own philosophy.) If Hegel still developed a philosophical system — and I don't believe he did — this was the end of system-building in philosophy. This era, too, is over.

Most importantly, however, modern philosophers, at least since Kierkegaard and Nietzsche, have challenged the basic principle employed in Plato's reconstruction. This principle is that what is logically prior (first) — i.e., most general and abstract — is also ontologically prior (first). Hence, the most general science, like mathematics, is not only closer to truth, but to reality as well. Again, the most abstract concept, say, Being *qua* Being, which is farthest removed from actual life, approximates most closely an ideal type of reality. This is perhaps the most un-Socratic feature of Plato's later dialectics — an explicit turning-away from the human world in which Socrates, barefoot in Athens, lived and thought. (In the *Republic*, the philosopher must be *compelled* to return to this world in which Socrates was at home all his life.)

Now it is true that today this "Socratic" field is also studied by the sciences; and it would make no sense to say that we have learned nothing about the human world since the days of Socrates. A return to Socrates, therefore, cannot mean that we discard the knowledge we have gained in biology, psychology, sociology, economics, or history. (That is a "romantic" fallacy.) What it does mean is that an increasing number of philosophers in the modern world have felt that something remains to be done along Socratic lines in two respects:

(1) As Ionesco said, mathematics leads to philology, and philology leads to calamity. Put less dramatically, this means that abstractions are not reality, not the reality of human life. The more

abstract the concept, or the law we deal with, the farther removed we are, yes, alienated, from the actual life-processes in society and history. Thus, Plato to the contrary, there is a need, as Whitehead insisted, "to reverse this process" of abstraction to which we owe the progress of knowledge in the general sciences in order to return to the concrete — the concrete situations and problems in actual life. There is a need, as Gabriel Marcel has said, to re-affirm "the primacy of the concrete." There is a need to affirm, as Brecht did, the principle that "the truth is concrete" — meaning the "truth" as discovered in the context of one's own life. This principle is the very opposite from that affirmed by Plato.

(2) The sciences themselves are now an integral part of the human world as they were not in the days of Socrates. Yet, today, as I have indicated, a philosopher can do little in contributing to the actual progress of knowledge that is made in the Academies. Let me add, without arguing the case, that it is also a fact that all the sciences (and the humane studies as well) are now moving in the direction of a logical autonomy corresponding to their autonomy in practice. As they do so, philosophy is deprived of another monopoly it has enjoyed since the days of Plato: a conceptual analysis of the language in the sciences and elsewhere. Yet, despite these losses, a philosopher can still ask a question, a "Socratic" question, rarely, if ever, put by the sciences themselves. He can critically examine the meaning and function of science, both pure and applied, in man's life and in society.

In conclusion, let me mention another significant feature associated with the "Platonic" tradition and challenged in recent philosophy: the "quest for certainty," as Dewey called it. In the *Meno*, it was the "certainty" of religious and/or mathematical truths that helped Plato out of the *aporia* induced by Socrates; and ever since Plato, philosophers have followed his example, whether they are called rationalists or empiricists. Both believed, as did Plato, that philosophy must be based on certainty. It must rest firmly and securely on foundations, premises, or principles that are absolutely certain, indubitable, incorrigible, or infallible, whether these be "truths" of reason or of experience. A philosophical system was worth its weight only if constructed on such premises.

Again, there has been a noticeable trend away from this time-honored tradition. "The pursuit of the incorrigible," to cite a contemporary English philosopher of considerable influence (John Austin in *Sense and Sensibilia*), "is one of the most venerable bugbears in the history of philosophy." I could cite many other thinkers in our time (including Dewey) who have expressed similar sentiments. Why? For several reasons: (1) There has been an increasing awareness over the last hundred years that all the "truths" discovered and proclaimed in the human Republic are not timeless, not absolute, but temporary, changing, and fallible. (2) In a contextual type of analysis such as Socrates conducted, there may be clarification and enlightenment, but there are no final answers. The analysis may clarify meanings and truths as they arise in different linguistic contexts or in different human situations, but there are no final answers because there is nothing fixed or final about the contexts or situations that we encounter in actual life. The case of Laches differs from the case of Lysander. Finally, (3) if the truth be concrete, i.e., the truth of one's own life at a specific time and place, there is no end to the existential project of "being in the truth." Self-analysis is interminable — or terminated by death. For these reasons, a "Socratic" pursuit of truth breaks the "Platonic" spell that there must be certainty in life as there is certainty in mathematics.

Why, then, follow Socrates? In this age of analysis, whether Freudian or Wittgensteinian, I need not insist that self-examination may have a "therapeutic" value. It may remove "mental cramps," as an English writer has put it, or mental disturbances, as we say, that are due to ignorance, confusion, repression, or — more simply — to a lack of consciousness with regard to the things we say and do in actual life. Thus this type of analysis may help to recover a sense of "truth in the concrete" that is lost in the abstractions, or general "laws," in science and society. It may contribute to a sense of "true" being that is expressed in the *adaequatio* of thinking and feeling or thinking and doing as in the life of Socrates; and in doing so, it may help to restore a sense of individual identity, integrity, and autonomy that is increasingly impaired in the life of The Great Society.

Nevertheless, this loss of certainty is perhaps the most serious offense of a Socratic view. It is an offense to the undialectical disjunction: Either philosophy is the Truth (with a capital T) or it is nothing — (or it is "Sophistry"). Hence, a Socratic view does not appeal to those who yearn, as Plato did, for certainty. Yet a confession of ignorance in the Socratic spirit need not signify the failure of philosophy. On the contrary, it may be an affirmation of something positive in the life and thought of man; for it also signifies that there are no limits to the pursuit of self-knowledge, no limits set by any system, religious or scientific, no limits set by any authority, social or political, no limits set by any language, logical or ordinary. All these limits that we encounter in the human world may be overcome, or overthrown, by a Socratic dialectics — i.e., in the dialectics of man's consciousness, not in the logic of science. In making a confession of "ignorance," therefore, we may affirm that which makes man most human and that which is most valuable in life: his own freedom.

What is demonstrable is necessary, and belongs to science. What is non-demonstrable, or questionable, is free, and belongs to philosophy. Thus in saying, as Socrates did, that there are no limits to the questions and answers encountered in our own life, we are also saying there are no limits to human freedom, and we call upon philosophy to defend the cause of this freedom. Plato did not.

These are some of the connections I had in mind when I suggested that the situation in recent philosophy may be viewed as a countermove from Plato to Socrates.

PART TWO

Art, Literature, and Society

Rational Society and Irrational Art

HERBERT READ

EXPLANATIONS OF THE PLACE AND FUNCTION of art in society offered by sociologists are so multifarious and contradictory that a mere philosopher of art like myself tends to fall back on formalism as the only logical basis for a discussion of the subject. It is true that such tactics involve a redefinition of form, but this has in any case been made necessary by our expanding knowledge of the many varieties of art prevailing in the past and manifested in our own time. This revolution in aesthetics has not been a concession to external influences such as those of social science or technology, but a recognition that a philosophy of art based on the evidence provided by the Graeco-Roman tradition was no longer adequate to account for the aesthetic values of quite other traditions, such as the Oriental, the African, the Pre-Columbian, nor can it account for those new traditions, partly inspired by the discovery of exotic art, to which we give the generic name of "modernism."

All these separate traditions can, of course, be *described* in terms of climatic conditions, of economic and social structures, but description is not explanation and art remains a distinct entity, often, as Marx realized, in flagrant opposition to the norms of economic production. This opposition can be interpreted in Hegelian terms as alienation, and this, for the art of the past, is the interpretation favoured by Herbert Marcuse. Literature and art were devised (consciously or unconsciously) as a cover for the contradictions of a divided world — "the defeated possibilities, the hopes unfulfilled, and the promises betrayed."

Let us accept for the moment this description of the art of the past, merely noting in passing the emphasis on form. Marcuse then proceeds to an original and contentious statement about the art of our present technological era. "The developing technological reality undermines not only the traditional forms but the very basis of the artistic alienation — that is, it tends to invalidate not only certain 'styles' but also the very substance of art." In accordance with the general trend of "one-dimensional society," "in the realm of culture, the new totalitarianism manifests itself precisely in a harmonizing pluralism, where the most contradictory works and truths peacefully coexist in indifference." Even the traditional images of artistic alienation, the "classics" of the past, are, so to speak, de-alienated — they are "incorporated into this society and circulate as part and parcel of the equipment which adorns and psychoanalyzes the prevailing state of affairs. Thus they become commercials — they sell, comfort, or excite." And coming to life as other than themselves "they are deprived of their antagonistic force, of the estrangement which was the very dimension of their truth."[1]

I do not wish to question this analysis of what is actually happening in our society. As culture is popularized, is "mediated" to the masses, it is necessarily diluted, castrated, de-formed (in the precise sense that the form the artist gave to his work is destroyed in order to comply with the technological demands of the medium, whether film or radio, and with the supposed "level of appreciation" for which these media cater). As a consequence of this "process of technological rationality" the whole basis of aesthetic judgement is subtly perverted and the pre-technological images lose their power.

This change is particularly noticeable in academic circles, where the masterpieces of the past are not so much subject to revaluation — a process which is always necessary on other, namely, aesthetic grounds — as dismissed as no longer relevant in a technological society. I have myself in the past called for such a revaluation of the art of the past on the basis of the new aesthetic values — for example, in an essay on "Surrealism and the Romantic Principle."[2] I even proposed that such a revaluation should be

[1] The quotations in this paragraph come from pages 61–4 of Herbert Marcuse, *One-Dimensional Man* (Boston and London, 1964).

[2] *Surrealism and the Romantic Principle* (1936), reprinted in *The Philosophy of Modern Art* (London and New York, 1952).

based on Hegel's dialectics! But it is one thing to question traditional aesthetic judgements on the grounds that they have become
conventional, that is to say, no longer organically aesthetic, and
quite another thing to question such judgements on grounds that
are extra-aesthetic — namely social, political, moral or technological. The work of art, the intellectual function of form apart, is
always a physical syndrome — it exists within a complex of emotion and feeling, and for its proper appreciation it may demand
selective channels of communication — a fact which Marcuse fully
recognizes. But when an academic critic, a professor of English
Literature in one of the new English universities, tells us that the
poetry of Shelley is no longer viable (Donald Davie in *The New
Statesman* recently) one suspects he is merely asserting that Shelley's images are pre-technological: in other words, since technological man is already "good, great and joyous, beautiful and
free" he no longer needs ·

> To suffer woes which Hope thinks infinite;
> To forgive wrongs darker than death or night;
>   To defy Power, which seems omnipotent;
> To love, and bear; to hope till Hope creates
> From its own wreck the thing it contemplates . . .

Suffering and forgiveness, love and hope are part of the terminology of estrangement and the images associated with such feelings have lost their power because technological man no longer
has such feelings.[3] He does not suffer so how can he forgive; he
does not love and therefore has no need to hope.

   Herbert Marcuse seems to accept the possibility that the physical transformation of the world entails the mental transformation
of man's symbols, images, and ideas, but "since contradiction is
the work of the Logos" (a gnomic utterance I do not quite understand) he concludes that a technological culture must have its
own medium of communication. "The struggle for this medium,
or rather the struggle against its absorption into the predominant
one-dimensionality, shows forth in the avant-garde efforts to cre-

   [3] I was once told by a member of an audience I was addressing in Zagreb,
Jugoslavia, that my remarks were incomprehensible to him because man in
a communist economy does not suffer from *Angst.* That was before an
earthquake had destroyed his city.

ate an estrangement which would make the artistic truth again communicable." In other words, since art demands for its vitality a condition of estrangement, and since our one-dimensional society does not provide such a condition, it must be artificially created (or imagined).

To what extent does contemporary art exhibit such a tendency? Marcuse relies on Brecht as a conscious exponent of such an artificial *Verfremdungseffekt*. According to Marcuse, Brecht's *Schriften zum Theater* reveal him as consciously aware of the need for mental conflict as a basis for art. The things of everyday must be lifted out of the realm of the self-evident — "That which is 'natural' must assume the features of the extraordinary. Only in this manner can the laws of cause and effect reveal themselves."[4] On such grounds not only the work of Brecht, but the whole "theater of the absurd" can be justified in a rational society. Even the whole Surrealist movement, which is not so *passé* as some of its critics assume (it died as a movement when it became acceptable as a social phenomenon, that is to say, when it was absorbed into the predominant one-dimensionality), has been comfortably adapted to our technological culture — witness the "surreality" of the James Bond films. But the process, Marcuse points out, is one of "desublimation." The aim of tragic art of the past was a sublimation of the instincts — "mediated gratification" or catharsis. Replace this effect by immediate gratification and the whole exercise loses its point. The tragedy becomes a farce.

Everything in Brecht's theater, observes one of Brecht's most perceptive critics, "is dedicated to the same end: replacing a magical theatre with a scientific one, a childish theatre with an adult one."[5] Admirable as this may be as a social ideal, it is not a possible ideal for art: art is basically irrational and even infantile, and to require the artist, as does Brecht (and I believe Marxist critics such as Lukács), to "deny himself the methods of hypnosis and even at need the customary empathy,"[6] is to require him to deny art itself as a medium of communication. To deprive the

---

[4] *Schriften zum Theater* (Berlin and Frankfurt, 1957), p. 63.

[5] Eric Bentley, *The Life of the Drama* (New York, 1965), p. 163.

[6] Quoted from Brecht's "Prospectus of the Diderot Society" by Bentley, *op. cit.*, p. 162.

artist of magic and empathy is to deprive him of the essential processes of the creative or imaginative activity that have characterized art from Homer and Aeschylus to Brecht himself (who luckily does not always practice what he preaches).

Admittedly the ideal of "becoming independent of the primitive side of his own nature" is one that has been characteristic of many schools of art and many individual artists. It is the classical ideal itself, and the result, in its perfection and severity, is as "alienated" as any other kind of art. In a very real sense *Phèdre* is as super-real as *King Lear:* what distinguishes such typical representatives of the classical and romantic imagination is not their attitude to reality (much less their attitude to "the actual world we live in," "the things of everyday life," etc.) but simply their different conceptions of artistic form. The point is even better illustrated in the visual arts, for even a David and a Delacroix, a Cézanne and a Monet, do not differ in their choice of subject-matter, but only in their different treatment of the same subject-matter. Even a formal classicist such as Paul Valéry in the end admits, as Marcuse notes, "the inescapable commitment of the poetic language to the negation" (of the real, of the actual). Or, as Marcuse phrases the same thought: "Creating and moving in a medium which presents the absent, the poetic language is a language of cognition — but a cognition which subverts the positive. In its cognitive function, poetry performs the great task of *thought:* le travail qui fait vivre en nous ce qui n'existe pas."[7]

To return to the actual condition of the arts in our technological civilization, I would suggest in the first place that it is a mistake to generalize their characteristics. Apart from the artificial division between bourgeois "free" art and a regimented socialist realism (a division that disappears as soon as the restrictions are removed, as in Poland and Jugoslavia), there is no real unity among the various schools of Western art. Surrealism may be stretched as a category to include not only the systematic alienation of the Surrealists proper (the systematic *dérèglement* of the senses, or, to quote from Breton's definition, "thought's dictation, in the absence of all control exercised by the reason and outside all aesthetic and moral preoccupations"), but also all those

[7] Marcuse, *One-Dimensional Man* (Boston and London, 1964), p. 67.

distortions of the images of the "actual world" that characterize expressionistic art of all kinds, from Picasso to Max Beckmann (I would propose the latter as a rough equivalent to Brecht). But outside such a comprehensive category we find, not only various examples of constructivism or neo-plasticism (perhaps the rough equivalents of Paul Valéry's poetry, for theirs too is "le travail qui fait vivre en nous ce qui n'existe pas") but also, still distinct, those forms of "action painting" so prevalent in the United States, Japan and Germany which are realistic in the sense that they project immediate sensations, trace gestures which are not so much symbolic as dynamic, an overflow not of emotions but of energies, muscular exertions that have style only in the sense that a boxer or a bull-fighter has style. As for "pop art" and "op art," these are significant only as secondary phenomena, as attempts to "desublimate" art and thus bring it onto the plane of one-dimensional society, pop art by destroying the boundaries between art and the images of mass-communication (ads and comics), op art by destroying the boundaries between art and the scientific "sign."

If nevertheless the technological ideal is, in spite of all temporary divisions of economic policy and social structure, the attainment of a "pacified existence," a human society without conflicts or unsatisfied needs, then, as Marcuse seems to indicate, art may well take on a new function and become distorted in the process. One may perhaps see the prototypes of such an art in science-fiction. The scientist, though a slave to reason, is well aware of the power of the imagination. Indeed, in a certain sense of which Marcuse is well aware, imagination is easily confused with invention, and the more the imagination abdicates to technological realism, the more ingenious become the inventive faculties. Marcuse speaks of "the obscene merger of aesthetics and reality," but what is accomplished by technological progress is not so much "a progressive rationalization and even realization of the imaginary" but rather a perversion of fancy, which Coleridge carefully distinguished from the imagination. Imagination was recognized by Coleridge as an essentially *vital* function of the mind, "the living power and prime agent of all human perception," whereas fancy is a mode of memory "emancipated from the order of time and space; while it is blended with, and modified by that empirical

phenomenon of the will, which we express by the word CHOICE."
Fancy, like science itself, deals in "fixities and definites" and there
is no limit to its power to convert illusion into reality—the space
flight is no sooner a fancy than it becomes a reality. The final
paradox would be to accept "the specific rationality of the irrational"; the comprehended imagination (that is to say, in
Coleridge's meaning, the fancy) then becomes, as Marcuse says,
redirected, "a therapeutic force." Art is then indeed in the service
of the revolution, but not in the sense of the phrase invented by
the Surrealists; the revolution remains in the sphere of technological rationality. The imagination becomes almost totally
atrophied.

The "historical alternative," as described by Marcuse, is "the
planned utilization of resources for the satisfaction of vital needs
with a minimum of toil, the transformation of leisure into free
time, the pacification of the struggle for existence." I confess that
this ideal still leaves me dissatisfied because no vital role is assigned to the imagination, unless such a role, therapeutic in intention, is implied in the pacification of the struggle for existence.
But art is not concerned with the struggle for existence in the
economic sense of the phrase, but rather with the mystery of
existence in the human and metaphysical sense. *This is the fundamental reason why no imaginable society of the future, however
free from material need, can ever dispense with art.* Though one
can easily equate "pacification" and art's traditional role of catharsis, catharsis was never envisaged (by Aristotle or anyone else)
as merely an aid in "the struggle for existence"; on the contrary, it
was always envisaged as a stoical acceptance of man's tragic destiny. The struggle for "existence" is within the mind of man; in
its highest intensity what art is concerned with is not existence
but essence. Technology has so far failed to dissipate the tragic
sense of life, and we may suspect that this is one achievement that
is beyond its powers. It is art and not science that gives a meaning
to life, not merely in the sense of overcoming alienation (from
nature, from society, from self), but in the sense of reconciling
man to his destiny, which is death. Not merely death in the
physical sense, but that form of death which is indifference,
spiritual *accidie*. In this sense art is committed to an illusion, and

the greatest illusion is the demand for reason and clarity, for a resolution in ontological myth of the paradox of existence. This truth about the role of art in society has been perfectly stated by Lucien Goldmann in *The Hidden God:*

> Man is a contradictory being, a mixture of strength and weakness, greatness and poverty, living in a world which, like himself, is made up of opposites, of antagonistic forces that fight against one another without hope of truce or victory, of elements that are complementary but permanently unable to form a whole. The greatness of tragic man lies in the fact that he sees and recognizes these opposites and inimical elements in the clear light of absolute truth, and yet never accepts that this shall be so. For if he were to accept them, he would destroy the paradox, he would give up his greatness and make do with his poverty and wretchedness [*misère*]. Fortunately, however, man remains to the very end both paradoxical and contradictory, "man goes infinitely beyond man", and he confronts the radical and irredeemable ambiguity of the world with his own equal and opposite demand for clarity.[8]

In *Soviet Marxism* (London and New York, 1958) Marcuse acknowledges that when Soviet aesthetics "attacks the notion of the 'unsurmountable antagonism between essence and existence' as the theoretical principle of 'formalism,' it thereby attacks the principle of art itself." He admits that, in outlawing the transcendental function of art, Soviet aesthetics "wants art that is not art, and it gets what it asks for." Marcuse's nearest approach to a positive definition of the function of art is to be found in another book, *Eros and Civilization* (Boston and London, 1956), where after an interesting discussion of Schiller's aesthetics he admits that Schiller's ideas on this subject "represent one of the most advanced positions of thought." But "it must be understood that the liberation from the reality which is here envisaged is not transcendental, 'inner,' or merely intellectual freedom (as Schiller explicitly emphasizes) but freedom *in* the reality. The reality that

_____

[8] *The Hidden God: A Study of Tragic Vision in the Pensées of Pascal and the Tragedies of Racine*, trans. by Philip Thody (London, 1964), p. 60. For "clarity" in this passage we may substitute Coleridge's "unity" or Valéry's "form."

'loses its seriousness' is the inhumane reality of want and need, and it loses its seriousness when wants and needs can be satisfied without alienated labour" (p. 188) — the same "historical alternative," therefore, as that presented in *One-Dimensional Man*. But Schiller's formulations "would be irresponsible 'aestheticism' if the realm of play were one of ornament, luxury, holiday, in an otherwise repressive world. . . . here the aesthetic function is conceived as a principle governing the entire human existence, and it can do so only if it becomes 'universal.' Aesthetic culture presupposes 'a total revolution in the mode of perception and feeling,' and such revolution becomes possible only if civilization has reached the highest physical and intellectual maturity" (pp. 188–9). Under such conditions, again the conditions of the "historical alternative," "man will be restored into the 'freedom to be what he ought to be.' But what 'ought' to be is freedom itself: the freedom to play. The mental faculty exercising this freedom is that of the *imagination*."

So once again we are thrown back on this undefined faculty, the imagination. Schiller's definition of the imagination is akin to Coleridge's and may have inspired it: it is essentially vital and irrational, it dissolves, diffuses, dissipates in order to recreate (? in play), or, where this process is rendered impossible . . . it struggles to idealize and to unify. Unification — there's the rub! Schiller's notion of unification was formalistic — "the aesthetic form is sensuous form — constituted by the *order of sensuousness*." The Platonic ideal is implied, for what can the "order" of sensuousness be but the paradigms of physical harmony. But this is getting a long way from Hegel and Marx and I suspect from Marcuse himself. The final choice is between form (which is neither rational nor irrational, but a "thing-in-itself") and what the Soviet theorists call "realism," which again is neither rational nor irrational, but "the given facts" (and what is a "fact"?) The "pacification" which Marcuse sees as the achievement of a technological civilization "presupposes mastery of Nature." "History is the negation of Nature. What is only natural is overcome and recreated by the power of Reason." Nature is not merely subdued: it is transcended, and the result is (or will be) an epoch of joy and happiness. All this is the result of *conscious* mediation (science and

technology). Technics becomes "the organon of the 'art of life.'
The function of Reason then converges with the function of
Art." This essential relation "points up the specific *rationality* of
art."

But is a *rational* art possible, now or in the future? It is at this
point that I find Marcuse's answer ambiguous. He affirms, quite
correctly, that "the artistic universe is one of illusion, semblance,
Schein." This world of art in the past has represented the dark
forces of the unconscious, the resolution of psychic conflicts. Art
and Reason have been alternative and even antagonistic methods
of confronting Nature. But now "the formerly antagonistic
realms merge on technical and political grounds – magic and
science, life and death, joy and misery."

"The obscene merger of aesthetics and reality refutes the
philosophies which oppose 'poetic' imagination to scientific and
empirical Reason. Technological progress is accompanied by a
progressive rationalization and even realization of the imaginary.
The archetypes of horror as well as of joy, of war as well as of
peace, lose their catastrophic character." A science of art allied
to a science of the psyche *comprehends* the processes of artistic
creation, and "the comprehended imagination becomes, redirected, a therapeutic force."[9]

If this is the inevitable fate of art in a one-dimensional society,
in what sense does art survive? Marcuse predicts a society in
which the imagination is released from all aesthetic control, and
it is a vision of unmitigated horror. In its place he calls for a
planned society which would be "rational and free to the extent
to which it is organized, sustained, and reproduced by an essentially new historical Subject." This new entity (Subject with a
capital S) remains a vague concept, transcending the dialectics of
the situation. But what is the situation? The one-dimensional society is not a universal society, and has no certain future. ". . .
underneath the conservative popular base is the substratum of the
outcasts and outsiders, the exploited and persecuted of other races
and other colours, the unemployed and the unemployable." The
economic and technical capabilities of the established societies
may be strong enough to contain this threat, but only at a cost

[9] *One-Dimensional Man*, pp. 248 – 9.

that destroys the liberties of the individual: "the second period of barbarism may well be the continued empire of civilization itself." With such a gloomy prospect Marcuse closes his study of "one-dimensional society." Such a society, offering "no concepts which could bridge the gap between the present and its future; holding no promise and showing no success," remains negative. The purpose of life remains a mystery.

Art has fallen by the way and is indeed impotent in such a situation, unless it is to be the instrument that ensures "the emergence of a new Subject." This chiliastic concept, introduced at the end of *One-Dimensional Man*, remains vague, but I doubt if Marcuse envisages a Messiah. In *Eros and Civilization* he remarked that "the discipline of aesthetics installs the *order of sensuousness* as against the *order of reason*" and this notion (which comes from Schiller), "aims at a liberation of the senses which, far from destroying civilization, would give it a firmer basis and would greatly enhance its potentialities." But can the senses be liberated to create their own order in a society that has achieved "the pacification of the struggle for existence"? Is there not some final contradiction between an irrational art and a rational society, between the paradoxical man who insists on going "infinitely beyond man" and the technological man who plans "the utilization of resources for the satisfaction of vital needs with a minimum of toil"? If pacification and sublimation are contradictory processes, what then is the difference between the new Subject and the old Myth?

The Quest for the Grail:
Wagner and Morris

CARL E. SCHORSKE

Is IT JUSTIFIED to yoke together two artists so different as Richard
Wagner and William Morris? By what warrant shall one compare
a musician with a designer and craftsman, a German nationalist
with an English socialist, a child of the age of Metternich with a
son of the Victorian era twenty-one years his junior? All these
incomparabilities make an effort at reciprocal illumination suspect. Yet history often reveals patterns in seemingly disparate
phenomena. Although Wagner and Morris were indifferent to
each other's work and even to each other's existence, they were
joined by many ties. Both became artists in an era when art was
changing its function in European culture; when, no longer expressing the dominant values of society, art began to advance its
own values, sometimes in the guise of a vanished past, sometimes
in the garb of a hoped-for future. Wagner and Morris both
quested for the future in the relics of the past.

There was scarcely a fund of tradition drawn upon by Wagner
as poet-musician which his younger contemporary did not also
appropriate as poet-designer. Arthurian legend, Minnesang, Norse
or Germanic myth, and — more concretely historical — the medieval guild ideal: both men exploited all of these in confronting the
problems of modernity. Although children of the so-called Age of
Realism, they scrupulously avoided contemporary materials as a
subject of their art. Revolutionaries in aesthetic expression, they
were conservatives in their search for spiritual anchorage. Wag-

Valuable assistance and suggestions in the preparation of this essay were
provided by my wife, Elizabeth, and Mr. John Rockwell.

ner and Morris rang their German and English variations on a common theme of 19th century culture: disenchantment with modern civilization. Each sought for a vision by which the ills of his age might be cured.

In their quest for that vision, these two romantics traveled the same road in reverse directions. Wagner and Morris began their intellectual journeys at what seem like opposite ends of the road, crossed in a dead center of historical despair, and continued to the starting point of the other voyager. To trace that course may perhaps reveal a few of the hidden threads which bind together art and social change in the dense texture of 19th century life.

I

William Morris (1834–1896) began his intellectual career where Wagner was to end: infatuated with medieval Christianity. When Morris went up to Oxford in 1853, the Catholicizing tendencies of the Oxford Movement had just reached their height. Swept out of what he called the "rich establishmentarian Puritanism" of his family by a new-found friend, Edward Burne-Jones, Morris developed a passion for medieval Christendom. An aspirant to Anglican Holy Orders, Morris avidly read the new Oxford theology, and in 1854 almost took the fashionable and fateful step to Rome. He joined the Plain Song Society, devoured medieval history, and became engrossed in medieval art. Culture soon began to speak more strongly than Faith. Ruskin's *Stones of Venice*, demonstrating the superiority of free Gothic work-forms over the tyranny of ancient and modern rational design, provided a theoretical basis for the late romantic medievalism of Morris and his friends.

Morris' group, which, in college style, had begun informally and was known as "the set," reorganized itself more earnestly as "the Brotherhood." The members, most of whom were destined for the clergy, pledged themselves to celibacy and the conventual life. The religious bond among them, however, was ambiguous. They loved the holy more because it was beautiful than because it was true. They saw the ills of the world not in the Christian fashion as the perduring consequence of sin, but as the special product of modern history, the result of commercial civilization. Most of the Brotherhood were sons of industrial Birmingham (Morris himself was the child of a well-to-do London business-man), and as such perhaps in quite normal revolt against their utilitarian parents. Whatever their motives, the brothers launched what Burne-Jones called "a crusade and holy warfare against the age." The knights of the grail offered them a peculiarly appealing model, combining religious idealism and aestheticism, aristocratic style and romantic service. Burne-Jones advised Morris to learn "Sir Galahad" — presumably Tennyson's — by heart, "as he is to be the patron of our order."[1]

In his writings, young Morris idealized the middle ages as a romantic refuge for the starved modern imagination. G. B. Shaw, a devoted admirer of Morris, was always uneasy about his literary archaism. Shaw characterized Morris' energetic and life-long me-dieval story-writing as an attempt to restore Don Quixote's burnt library. There was justice in the charge. Morris and the pre-Raphaelites despised Cervantes as "an abominable Philistine" who destroyed medieval romance by creating Don Quixote, "an in-sult to beauty and chivalry."[2] Morris' writing, however, reflects only the romantic and less original part of his quest.

More fruitfully, Morris interpreted medievalism as committing him to rejuvenate the modern environment by reviving craft culture. A kind of aesthetic Luddite, he directed his "holy war-fare" against the factory and its products, against the whole wretched environment of industrial England. He set out to re-store the medieval unity between artist and artisan, art and craft, beauty and utility. On leaving college, he first studied architec-ture, then turned, under Rossetti's influence, to painting, and finally to an incredible range of handicrafts — house furnishings, wall-papers, textiles and the like — to restore imaginative handi-work. Through the revival of crafts Morris hoped both to restore joy to the worker and beauty to the scene of modern life. With

[1] The best account of Morris' Oxford years is given in J. W. Mackail, *The Life of William Morris,* 2 vols. (London, New York, Bombay, 1901), I, 28 – 66.

[2] George Bernard Shaw, "William Morris as I Knew Him," in May Morris, *William Morris, Artist, Writer, Socialist,* 2 vols. (Oxford, 1936), II, xxviii.

prodigious energy, Morris instructed himself in the decorative crafts. Like Diderot when he worked on the great dictionary of arts and crafts for his Encyclopedia a century before, Morris went to the workroom as well as to the library to learn the skills he sought. Where Diderot looked for the most modern mechanized techniques that he might spread them, Morris pursued the dying arts that he might save them. Diderot fought for an economically liberating technology against an inhibiting ancient way of work; Morris, for a psychologically gratifying ancient way against an enslaving new technology. Both were equally zealous learners of the crafts that would redeem.

From religion to the romantic-aesthetic brotherhood, to the workshop: so Morris' journey ran. With some of his friends, Morris in 1859 built a model home for himself, the Red House on Bexley Heath. His first and last *Gesamtkunstwerk*, Morris embodied in it his medieval ideal of a unified, simple house, posited against what he called "the age of makeshift" and the eclectic Victorian home. The architect Philip Webb planned the building on simple, spacious lines, and assisted Morris in designing the furniture, from cabinets to candlesticks. Burne-Jones, Ford Maddox Brown and Rossetti painted walls and cupboards with illustrations from classical and medieval romance, while the ladies of the circle embroidered tapestries. Though medieval in aspiration, the Red House was modern in conception: a bold precursor of unified design — from floor plan to ashtray in a single, almost tyrannically harmonious conception of the house beautiful.

In 1861, Morris established the Firm, a partnership to produce craft products on a paying basis. For two decades, the Firm's products sold well, and influenced the taste of the well-to-do.[3] But Morris drew decreasing psychological satisfaction from this sort of success. For every Morris chair or tapestry sold, England was stained by another gerry-built housing development. The fair vision of the grail, of an England redeemed by revived crafts, seemed incommunicable. Like Don Quixote's windmill, the factory was too strong. Morris fell into personal depression and social pessimism.

"Dreamer of dreams, born out of my due time, why should

---

[3] The Firm decorated rooms in St. James' Palace and a model dining room for the Victoria and Albert Museum.

I strive to set the crooked straight?"[4] In this mood, Morris took refuge in poetic fantasy. In the late sixties, he produced a collection of tales entitled *The Earthly Paradise*. The collection expressed, as his perceptive daughter observed, "the melancholy of an unquiet mind, standing on the verge of some infinitude, waiting and listening."[5] The tales are far removed from reality. Ifor Evans has described well the author's approach to capture the remote quality of the life of fantasy: "He himself dreams that a group of men set out for a distant dreamland, and then within that scheme they tell tales to each other, many of them dreams, some dreams within dreams."[6]

Among the tales that Morris tells is *The Hill of Venus*. It is the same story which Wagner set to music in *Tannhäuser*, celebrating the triumph of profane love over the consciousness of sin.

Most of *The Earthly Paradise*, however, is dominated by a more sombre mood, one reflected in a line which came to epitomize Morris in the Victorian mind, "the idle singer of an empty day." The usually vital Morris here came uncommonly close to Baudelaire's *ennui*, or to Wagner's musical rendering of Schopenhauer's deathly metaphysical dream-reality in *Tristan und Isolde*. By the end of the 1860's, the holy crusader against the ugliness of his age seemed to be seeking refuge in art rather than in transforming his world by means of it.

II

Wagner's development in the equivalent part of his career ran a different course but terminated in a similarly airless dead center of ontic malaise. Born in 1813, two decades before Morris, Wagner grew up in a society whose problem was not social justice but personal liberty; his target accordingly was not the factory, but the state. Though Wagner and Morris built their heavens out of much the same materials, they had quite different hells.

Wagner began as a late-born child of the *Sturm und Drang*, the Promethean flamboyance of which had psychological rele-

[4] *The Earthly Paradise*, in William Morris, *Collected Works* (London, 1910 – 15), III, 1.

[5] May Morris, *Morris*, I, 399.

[6] B. Ifor Evans, *William Morris and His Poetry* (London, 1925), 97.

vance in the stillness of Metternich's Germany. The young musician's enemies were the traditional ones of the creative German intellectual: the philistines of his own burgher class and the rationalistic, absolute state. These two enemies joined in upholding convention, and convention was what the young Wagner attacked on every front. He fought it in music and in literature, in politics and in love. Because he saw convention as having in Reason its strongest ally, Wagner became the lifelong enemy of Reason. Accordingly, he began his revolt not, like Morris, for the beautification of life, but for the liberation of instinct; not as a medievalizing romantic conservative, but as a semi-Bohemian revolutionary. In one of his earliest operas, *Das Liebesverbot*, Wagner celebrated the rehabilitation of the flesh in a vindication of "unrestrained sensuality" against "puritanical hypocrisy." Shakespeare's *Measure for Measure* gave Wagner his plot; but he altered it to allow the victory of love over law to be accomplished by a revolution rather than by a princely judgment.[7] In *Rienzi*, he glorified the Renaissance tribune of the people as a Promethean democrat and revolutionary hero.

In *Lohengrin* (1845), Wagner brought together three themes which dominated his early concerns: sexual fulfillment, folk freedom and the redeeming hero. Lohengrin, son of Parsifal the grail-knight, is the artist as self-conscious redeemer. He *has* the grail and its vision; his quest is for fulfillment through serving others and being loved. It is politics which makes this possible: corruption in the court of Brabant results in injustice to Elsa, the embodiment of womanhood. "Elsa," Wagner tells us, "is the unconscious, the unvolitional, in which Lohengrin's conscious, volitional being yearns to redeem itself." As woman, she is "the *un*conscious, *un*volitional in Lohengrin"; but, as princess, she is a political victim. "Elsa the Woman . . . ," Wagner says, "made me a full-fledged revolutionary. She was the spirit of the folk, in whom I too, as artistic human being, was yearning for my redemption."[8]

What shall we make of this astonishing identification of the

---

[7] Richard Wagner, *My Life*, 2 vols. (New York, 1911) I, 101 – 102; *idem*, "Eine Mitteilung an meine Freunde," in *Gesammelte Schriften und Dichtungen*, Wolfgang Golther, ed., 10 vols. (Berlin, etc. [1913]), IV, 254 – 255.

[8] Wagner, *Gesammelte Schriften*, IV, 301 – 302.

female and the folk? Both were the inactive element, the victims, and at the same time potential receivers of the seed. The folk, like the woman, had healthy instinct and the capacity to become ennobled, but lacked conscious will. The folk, like the woman, was passive, held in thrall by the political order, awaiting a redeemer. Lohengrin is that redeemer, but he can accomplish his work only on his own terms: that he be unconditionally loved, like a child, regardless of his origins or attributes. Neither the woman nor the folk are ready to accept the artist knight of the grail. The redeeming mission of the artist in society fails; he is the frustrated victim of incomprehension. But Wagner tells us that, through writing the tragedy, he shifted his own identification from the rejected Lohengrin to the fallible but unfulfilled Elsa-folk.[9] The self-pitying male egoist found the link between eros and society.

Wagner's early years, in pre-1848 Germany, allowed him to relate the fate of art to folk-revolution in ways not possible for an Englishman in the mid-century. Intellectually advanced but socially retarded, Germany had no concrete mass movements of the lower classes before the Revolution of 1848. Hence the as-yet-unconscious masses — for Wagner no less than for Marx — could be assigned universal historical tasks and characters without reference to their sleepy present. The lack of dynamic popular reality allowed the fantasy of the radical intelligentsia full sway. For Wagner, this meant that the folk would provide the social material to realize the artist's dreams of a restoration of "wholeness" to man. In mid-century England, on the other hand, the working classes had already acquired a sufficient clarity of definition and consciousness of aim to be something more than the stuff that dreams are made on. Trade-unionism and Chartism appeared on the stage even before Morris went to school. In the 1870's and 1880's, when Morris sought to relate his art to politics, he both could and necessarily had to reckon with social forces already formed and organized. While English conditions imposed narrower limits on the political imagination than did German ones, they also gave Morris a social base for the active realization of his values. And in his early years, the more homogeneous social climate among intellectuals in England gave Morris a Brotherhood

[9] *Ibid.*, 302.

in his crusade. Young Wagner as redeeming grail-knight, like so many intellectuals in his fragmented country, wandered and served alone.

Still committed to a heroic concept of individuality, Wagner was swept up in the rising tide of democratic nationalism in the late 1840's. His most important ideas on the nature of drama and its relation to society took shape during the Revolution of 1848. Wagner welcomed the Revolution with the most naive confidence that a new and happier world would spring from it. Falling under the influence of Feuerbach, Wagner turned from the grail to the Greeks to find the right relationship between art and society. Like Schiller and Hegel, Hölderlin and Marx, Wagner saw the Greek polis as the historical archetype of community, a lost paradise to be regained. Greek drama expressed the oneness, the wholeness of that community: ". . . [T]he drama was the sum and substance of all that could be expressed in the Greek nature; it was — in intimate connection with its history — the nation that stood facing itself in the art-work, that became conscious of itself."[10] The Greek polis and Greek drama rose and fell together. When the polis fell, the drama fragmented into the many arts which had composed it: music, poetry, dance, and the visual arts. These all then acquired their separate existence, just as the individuals in an atomized polis did. Wagner set himself the task of reviving holistic drama, which was part of the larger task of making a community out of coldly rationalistic modern society. That is the origin of his *Gesamtkunstwerk*, less simple and far more pretentious than Morris' archaizing house beautiful.

Greek drama, in Wagner's view, was conservative because it reflected the community and its experience of life. Modern art must be revolutionary: it must present in ideal form a unified community which does not exist in broken modern society. Drama in Greece reflected community; drama today can only live in opposition to society. It must *create* community by serving as model for it. Only "the great revolution" can restore the unified art-work as a mirror of society. Both art and politics must strive

[10] Quoted in Ernest Newman, *Wagner as Man and Artist* (New York, 1924), 184.

for the same end: "the strong and beautiful man, to whom revolution shall give his strength and art his beauty."[11]

What Morris aimed at only in his last, Socialist years, Wagner proposed in 1848: to link the political future of mankind and the future of art in indissoluble union. The drama was the only possible model to make of enslaved mankind a community of artists. Morris' crafts could be practiced in the here-and-now, insinuated into present-day society. Wagner's ideal drama could only live in constant contradiction with contemporary social reality. Drama must be an art of the future; with a disordered present, it could only live in tension. It would have to cut through the external realities of an age of false authority and materialism to the suppressed folk, to the buried communal consciousness, the spirit of the people.

In the pursuit of this subliminal folk-soul, Wagner was drawn to German myth, and especially to the *Nibelungenlied*. Shaw, who admired Wagner as much as Morris, interpreted the Ring operas simply as an allegory of revolutionary radicalism. Siegfried, said Shaw, is Wagner's friend Bakunin.[12] If this interpretation is too pat, certainly Shaw's larger, central thesis holds firm: that the ancient myth pointed an accusing finger at the materialistic and hypocritical order of present-day society. In the person of a vital, young and innocent folk-hero from the past, Wagner celebrated a German *renovatio* in the future.

The defeat of 1849 left Wagner profoundly disillusioned. He reworked his *Nibelungen* materials in more pessimistic directions. He replaced the heroic optimism of the early version of the Ring with an ending in doom and gloom. The *Gesamtkunstwerk* lost its paradigmatic and specifically social character. Wagner's later works relate less to historical possibility than to passional necessity. He shifted from history to metaphysics. From other defeated exiles, Wagner discovered Schopenhauer, who sealed the development in him which, as he was himself aware, the revolution *manqué* had prepared.[13] Wagner transformed the metaphysi-

---

[11] *Ibid.*, 183 – 184.

[12] [George] Bernard Shaw, *The Perfect Wagnerite* (Chicago and New York, 1905), 57.

[13] Wagner, *My Life*, II, 614 – 617.

cal conception of Schopenhauer's Will — blind cosmic energy — into a psychological one: compulsive instinct. *Tristan und Isolde* was conceived in this mood of post-political ontic despair, in which only the claims of libido have life. The communal eros has become confined to the personal, sexual. One can feel the birth of depth psychology out of the spirit of frustrated liberal idealism. In *Tristan*, music drama becomes a theater of the psyche.[14] Id and ego, eros and reality are in hostile array. The state appears not as unjust or corrupt, as in Lohengrin or Siegfried, but as a symbol of eternal social restraint upon our emotional life. Fulfillment lies not in regeneration, but in death. The whole drama is a farewell to time and space, and thus to history. Nietzsche's phrase, "*Und alle Lust will Ewigkeit*," suits *Tristan und Isolde* well. In no work of art is the organized world of reality so drastically contraposed to the world of wish and of dream, of instinct and of love. The linkage of instinct and folk, so strong in Lohengrin and Siegfried, has disappeared without a trace. Psyche and society are in hopeless disjuncture, in absolute opposition.

Tristan und Isolde is one of the most sophisticated works of European art, and it is perhaps not right to relate it to Morris' rather simple *Earthly Paradise*. Yet the moods of the two are strikingly similar. Wagner's disillusion with politics and Morris' disappointment with the results of his aesthetic crusade had produced similar states of mind in both men. Morris' description of his own intention is like the plight of Tristan and Isolde in the realm of King Mark:

> . . . Pardon me
> Who strive to build a shadowy isle of bliss
> Midmost the beating of the steely sea.[15]

The heavy feeling of doom, the sweet scent of death the dreamy quality of life, the affirmation of night from which Morris' lovers, like Wagner's, wake "from delight unto the real day void

[14] See especially Francis Fergusson, *The Idea of a Theater* (Princeton, 1949), chapter III, "*Tristan und Isolde*: the Action and Theater of Passion," *passim;* Joseph Kerman, *Opera as Drama* (New York, 1959), 192 – 216.

[15] Morris, *Works*, III, 2. For the best analysis of Morris' "poetry of despair," see E. P. Thompson, *William Morris* (New York, 1961), 140 – 162.

and white";[16] above all, the total abandonment of the historical world as a field of action: these join the German composer of metaphysical despair with England's idle singer of an empty day. This was their common *mezzo del camin'*.

III

Norse mythology served Wagner as the vehicle for his most massive commitment as artist to the revitalization of political and cultural life in 1848. Under the impact of defeat, his modification of the Ring's libretto in the direction of political pessimism marked Wagner's transition from social politics to psychological metaphysics. In William Morris' intellectual development, Norse mythology played just the opposite part: instead of the last stage before the plunge into despair, it was the first step out of defeat and world-weariness.

In 1868, Morris took up the Icelandic language, and became enamored of Norse sagas. Henceforth he devoted years to translating and reworking them. Even more than Wagner, Morris found in Old Norse life the model of community existence. Here was a culture which had learned to face poverty and adversity with directness, courage and good-humored acceptance. And the ancient heroism still survived! Visiting modern Iceland, Morris found it still undistorted by the crippling machine, by ugliness and slums. The Icelanders faced grinding poverty, but, said Morris, that "is a trifling evil compared to inequality of classes."[17]

There was no "aristocracy" here. Even kings in the Norse sagas shared the common life, making sails and working in the fields. Morris' enthusiasm knew no bounds: "glorious simplicity of the terrible and tragic. . . ." "Delightful freshness and independence of thought of them, the air of freedom which breathes through them, their worship of courage (the great virtue of the

[16] Thompson, *William Morris*, 156. In *Tristan und Isolde*, the persistent problem of the lovers is to banish the day-world. Act II, where they succeed in this, is a night-act; Act III opens with the victory of day: a shepherd's plaintive song; a hot, still air; an empty sea; an atmosphere heavy with foreboding.

[17] *Ibid.*, 222.

human race), their utter unconventionality took my heart by storm."[18]

The discovery of community, of collective, heroic folk strength smoothed the transition for Morris, as Shaw observed, from "the facile troubadour of love and beauty into the minstrel of strife and guile, of battle, murder and death."[19] There was a contemporary ingredient too. Like Wagner, Morris moved the problem of gold and greed into the center of *Sigurd the Volsung*, his version of the Siegfried saga. Iceland, ancient and modern, had shown him the value of collective struggle over the aesthetic isolation of the Brotherhood and the Firm. The erstwhile knight-errant of "the holy, the beautiful and the true" thus girded himself for the *vita activa* of democratic working-class politics.

As Morris passed from his metaphysical despair into Wagner's world of myth and politics, Wagner for his part was passing back over Morris' earlier course. In *Die Meistersinger von Nüremberg* (completed in 1867) Wagner returned to history once more, seeking relief from the pain of life so sorely felt in *Tristan*. The model was neither chivalric nor heroic now, but medieval burgher. Like Morris in the period of the Firm, Wagner was drawn to the medieval commune, where social, economic and aesthetic life were one. This model allowed Wagner a new form of archaizing critique of the modern world. But again, as in *Lohengrin*, the misunderstood artist is at the center of the world. His old enemy, convention, appeared once more, in the character of Beckmesser, who represented the classical, contrapuntal tradition in music. *Die Meistersinger* also conjoined historical nostalgia with a new brutality against the establishment in scenes of brawling apprentices and the "healthy" mauling of Beckmesser. Small wonder that this was Hitler's favorite opera!

If Wagner, like Morris, extolled the medieval guild, he embraced it for different reasons. Morris' crusade was for creative work, Wagner's for the artist's right to social recognition for his personal genius. Morris' medieval heroes of art were, like Ruskin's, anonymous workers. In *Die Meistersinger*, the hero is the artist as *Führer* of the artisan; Wagner honors the guildsmen only because

[18] *Ibid.*, 219–220.
[19] Shaw, in May Morris, *Morris*, II, xxxvii.

they recognized that German art must be an élite, personal expression, and *not* merely a socal craft. For Wagner the gap between art and the common life was widening at the same time as it was narrowing for Morris.

IV

In his final phase, Morris went out into the modern social arena. Wagner turned inward to explore the modern soul. Both remained the dreamers their romantic heritage had made of them. But as each in old age assumed something of the youthful concerns of the other, he illuminated those concerns in a new and modern light. Wagner in his last decade reached the point whence Morris had begun his quest: the redemption of the world through art, as expressed quasi-religiously in the legends of the grail. In the late 1870's Morris finally arrived at Wagner's conviction of the forties: that art could be regenerated only by revolution. Each artist found an appropriate institution to project his final vision. What the Bayreuth Festival was to Wagner, the Hammersmith Socialist Society was to Morris: a center for a brotherhood of redeemers.

Since his first years of exile after 1848, Wagner had projected a theater for the German people, through which it could become conscious of its own essential nature. As the project grew, he came to think of it, as he said, as "an art-Washington," "something absolutely new," deliberately remote from the workaday cities and the corruption of materialistic German culture. Finally, in 1876, the Bayreuth summer opera house was opened. Here Wagner's great dramas, mirrors of the German spirit, would restore wholeness to divided modern man. Here the magic of art would weld together a mythical, archetypal community which allowed the audience of votaries to escape, as Wagner said, "this world of lying, fraud, hypocrisy and legalized murder," . . . "the toil and trouble of life, for the sake of its loftiest ends."[20]

Like the customers of the craft products of Morris's Firm, those of Bayreuth were too often wealthy followers of fashion rather than true believers. At the opening in 1876, Nietzsche recoiled in

[20] P. A. Loos, *Richard Wagner* (Bern, 1952), 487 – 88; Ernest Newman, *Life of Richard Wagner*, 4 vols. (New York, 1933 – 1946), IV, 705, 101.

disgust at the audience, well-to-do middle-brows: "The whole idle rabble of Europe had been brought together. . . . I recognized nothing any more . . . not even Wagner."[21] Wagner became high priest of a cult. His patron, Ludwig II of Bavaria, hailed him as such in fitting language at the opening of the first festival: "an artist by the grace of God, who came into this world to purify, bless and redeem it."[22] Wagner himself accepted the assignment.

He provided not restoration of "wholeness" to all classes of society, but a theatrical psychotherapy for the cultivated opera-goer. Bayreuth became not the model of a new society, a restored Greek theater, but the center of a new cult. As in Morris' early Oxford Brotherhood, art was the center of the faith, rather than faith the center of the art. Wagner the artist offered a communal rite to remove the votary from the pressures of space and time, from the pain and corruption of modern life.

> Beyond all that is thinkable as concept, the tone-poet seer reveals the inexpressible to us: we [dimly] sense, yes, we feel and see that even this seemingly inescapable world of Will is only a [transient] condition, disappearing before the one [truth]: "I know that my redeemer liveth."[23]

In "the knowledge of the decadence of the human race," we purify ourselves and restore our innocence by "submerging ourselves in the element of . . . symphonic revelation which can count as a consecrated, purifying religious act."[24]

As once the Greeks had developed community drama out of religious ritual, so at Bayreuth Wagner developed a religious community out of theatrical ritual. Even the strongest myths he used — those of Siegfried and Parsifal — did not incorporate a belief held by the society. They only posed suggestively a truth of wholeness which modern man could accept as aspiration but not embrace as creed. Wagner's art could no more posit a surrogate religion than it could earlier create a new community. All the depth-psychological shock-tactics of modern musical stagecraft

[21] Quoted in Loos, *Wagner*, 489.
[22] Newman, *Life*, IV, 482.
[23] Wagner, *Gesammelte Schriften*, X, 250–251.
[24] *Ibid.*, 250.

could not transcend the limits of virtuality to which art is by its nature condemned. The grail in the theater could enchant and bewitch but it could not redeem.

Wagner's last glorious achievement, *Parsifal*, is redolent with the pseudo-religiosity of Bayreuth, but it far transcends it. Nietzsche truly missed the mark when he cried out in anger, "What you hear is Rome: Rome's faith without words!"[25] What in fact you hear is the opposite: Rome's words without faith. *Parsifal* illuminates modern man neither through social message nor religious faith, but through a musical statement of depth psychology. Parsifal, the innocent fool, redeems the guilty world by discovering his oedipal self.

The political world is completely absent from *Parsifal* — for the first time in any Wagner opera. In all his previous works, Wagner rendered the ordered world of the state in a specific musical idiom. In *Tristan* its character is especially sharply drawn: a diatonic world of space, a marked and metrical world of time. Against the strong grid of this harmonic, tonal, regular day-world, the lovers' life of passion plays, chromatic and almost keyless, surging and rhythmic. *Tristan* dramatizes a battle between personal, instinctual wish and social, rational reality; within Tristan and Isolde, the struggle eventuates in a total victory of id over ego, even unto death. Conscience, super-ego, plays almost no role. In *Parsifal*, by contrast, there is no political state; in fact, no outer reality at all, i.e., no world of ego; the only society is the mystical Brotherhood of the Grail. The dualities in *Parsifal* are not Wagner's earlier ones: heart and reason, freedom and slavery, love and social greed, love and the state, id and ego. His dramatic tension is now both more archaic and more modern: in religious terms, which dominate the text, between guilt and redemption; in Freudian terms — and these dominate the music — between super-ego and id. The social scene of action has been narrowed to a brotherhood whose members are spiritually sick and psychologically paralyzed. The drama has no external action, only internal transfiguration. Even the scenery dissolves the coordinates of spatial reality. In dream-like transmutations deserts become gardens, a scenic analogue of transubstantiation, the mystery of the grail.

[25] Loos, *Wagner*, 205.

The drama of Parsifal is not a religious exploration but a depth-psychological one. It centers upon the ambiguous relationship of love as sexual drive and love as social conscience. The technique of the seductress, Kundry, is to exploit mother-love, the oedipal vulnerabilities of Parsifal, to undermine the childish innocence of her victim. In some of the sweetest yet most penetratingly sickish music ever written — *luxe, calme et volupté*, Wagner's admirer Baudelaire might have called it — the temptress almost ensnares Parsifal by identifying herself dream-like with his mother. Asking Parsifal to think of his father, she implants her nearly fateful kiss as "the last greeting of maternal blessing: love's first kiss." In resisting the oedipal crime, Parsifal's sexual temptation becomes transfigured into diffused libido, socially redemptive rather than instinctually gratifying. The ecstasy of sex and the ecstasy of religious passion are shown to be convertible; the magic of art works the transformation.

In the deep psychological world of *Parsifal*, there are virtually no deeds. History is left off the stage; only psychic states have life, in shifting planes of memory and hope. Leaden music represents the guilt-sick present and its cure lies in regression. One goes forward only by going back: historical regression into the medieval past for the ideal of redeeming service; psychological regression into pre-oedipal innocence for the strength to purify the fallen brotherhood with a diffuse and oceanic sense of love. Wagner-Parsifal becomes the psycho-therapeutic artist-redeemer. No wonder Thomas Mann's and Freud's contemporaries worshiped at Wagner's shrine. No wonder that, despite the cult of Bayreuth, they stood in awe of him, both for his insight into the modern condition of moral pessimism and psychological introversion, and for his powers in translating the ancient arts of religious redeemers into the modern religion of aesthetic redemption.

* * *

The end of Morris is more simply told. The young religious aesthete became an old revolutionary — just the reverse of Wagner. Morris spent his last decade as *spiritus rector* of the Hammersmith Socialist Society. He turned over the large weaving-room of his Hammersmith house as a meeting-hall for the Society. After

the meetings on Sunday night, Morris entertained the votaries of
the new religion of Marxian socialism. Burly workers would join
young intellectuals such as Yeats or Shaw for a supper at the
broad bare oaken table of the great designer. Agitation became
the center of the old man's life.

Did Morris' dream of medieval beauty evaporate in the strenu-
ous years of socialist struggle? For the answer one need only read
his utopian novel, *News from Nowhere* (1890). Here again is the
"dreamer of dreams, born out of my due time." Morris fills out
the socialist future with that romanticized picture of the Middle
Ages so characteristic of the era of his youth. He imagines future
London, the London of 1962: a congeries of small villages again.
Factories are no more. There is salmon running in the Thames,
and men spend their time in the creative play of happy artisans.
The Houses of Parliament are a dung-market, their erstwhile
powers taken over by local motes. The costumes are fourteenth
century and charming; the language of the good folk is Morris'
own neo-Chaucerian. Above all, socialist England is a community
— a community such as Morris discovered in Norse mythology,
but gentler; a community such as the early Wagner loved to
dream of, but more playful; a community such as English new-
town planners today, children of Morris, still hope to create to
redeem industrial civilization.

Neither Wagner nor Morris succeeded in conquering the drag-
ons they had sallied forth to slay: the English factory or the
German state. But the visions they had on their Quixotic quest,
penetrating visions into the social and psychological needs of 19th
century civilization, live into our own day.

Valéry: *Monsieur Teste*

LUCIEN GOLDMANN

En 1956, j'écrivais dans un rapide aperçu que les trois grandes étapes du rationalisme français caractérisé par les noms de Descartes, Voltaire et Valéry pourraient être distingués entre autres par la conception que ces écrivains se faisaient des relations entre la pensée et l'action, relations certaines mais implicites pour Descartes, souhaitables et réalisables pour Voltaire et, enfin, problématiques et irréalisables pour Valéry. Et j'ajoutais que cette évolution correspondait dans ses grandes lignes à celle du Tiers Etat français dont le rationalisme constituait — et constitue encore — la principale expression idéologique: Tiers Etat qui se trouvait en plein essor au 17e siècle, à la veille de la prise du pouvoir politique au 18e et plus ou moins touché par la crise de la société occidentale dans la première moitié du 20e siècle.

C'est à partir de cette définition que j'ai, par la suite, analysé dans *Mon Faust*, la discussion de Valéry avec Goethe et Nietzsche et c'est encore à partir d'elle que l'on peut, me semble-t-il, comprendre ce chef-d'oeuvre d'élégance, de concision et de rigueur qu'est *Monsieur Teste*.

Or, cette analyse marque de manière assez rigoureuse, à la fois la grandeur et les limites de la pensée de Valéry. Grandeur, d'avoir vu clairement les obstacles que la crise du capitalisme a suscités à l'efficacité et au pouvoir d'action de la pensée rationnelle, d'avoir compris la rupture radicale qui s'est établie dans la société occidentale entre la raison et la réalité pendant toute la première moitié du 20e siècle et d'avoir néanmoins, au moment du grand essor du romantisme et de l'irrationalisme, sous leurs diverses formes, depuis Bergson jusqu'à l'existentialisme, maintenu fermement l'affirmation de la valeur unique et suprême de la raison, même si cette raison ne pouvait plus rien ni pour l'homme ni pour la vie. Grandeur réelle certainement, mais limitée aussi par le fait que Valéry n'a jamais envisagé la possibilité de dépasser la raison discursive des Lumières, de passer comme l'ont exigé les grands dialecticiens, du *Verstand* à la *Vernunft*, de la raison cartésienne à la raison dialectique pour essayer de défendre la place de l'homme et de l'espoir dans un siècle qui les avait, plus peut-être que tout autre et plus que ses propres penseurs n'en avaient conscience, mises en danger.

Le seul complément dans cette situation que Valéry ait accepté à la raison — et il a toujours considéré cette acceptation comme une faiblesse — a été la poésie, l'image sensible qui, tout en appartenant au monde de l'obscur, du rêve et de l'enfance, permet néanmoins un contact avec la réalité que la raison avait, selon Valéry, entièrement et définitivement perdu.

Monsieur Teste se sait, se veut une continuation du cartésianisme. Valéry l'annonce dès la première ligne "*Vita Cartesii est simplicissima*," la vie de Descartes est la plus simple . . . et sans doute Monsieur Teste est-il cartésien à outrance, il a radicalement séparé l'esprit de "la marionnette." Il veut:

> . . . tout reconstruire en matériaux purs: rien que d'éléments définis, rien que de contacts et de contours dessinés, rien que de formes conquises, et pas de vague.

Et pourtant, quoi qu'en dise Valéry, il est aussi essentiellement différent de Descartes. Il lui manque, en effet, l'optimisme cartésien, la calme tranquillité d'un penseur qui sait que la pensée claire est en train de maîtriser le monde. Car le problème de Monsieur Teste réside dans le fait que la société, l'action, le vouloir, la passion, autrui et même le Moi, échappent entièrement à la prise et à l'action de la raison. C'est pourquoi dans la mesure où il est exigence absolue de rigueur, Monsieur Teste abandonne toute communauté avec le monde et tout engagement dans celui-ci. Il n'est plus que la tête lucide qui s'intéresse aux définitions claires et rigoureuses, et le *testis*, le témoin d'un monde dans lequel il ne peut rien changer. Sur ce point d'ailleurs, — et c'est rare — Valéry a écrit deux phrases qui, si elles ne sont pas contradictions, ne coïncident pour le moins pas; il nous dit, en effet:

. . . si cet homme avait changé l'objet de ses méditations fermées, s'il eût tourné contre le monde la puissance régulière de son esprit, rien ne lui eût résisté.

On pourrait ainsi croire que pour Valéry l'esprit de Monsieur Teste s'est librement et par une décision voulue, séparé d'un monde qu'il aurait pu facilement et sans difficulté maîtriser. Mais, à un autre endroit du même livre, et c'en est un des plus pathétiques, parlant de la même rupture entre la poésie et le monde, Valéry dit d'abord la même chose:

Le regard étrange sur les choses, ce regard d'un homme qui ne *reconnaît pas,* qui est hors de ce monde, oeil frontière entre l'être et le non-être, — appartient au *penseur.* Et c'est aussi un regard d'agonisant, d'homme qui perd la connaissance. En quoi le penseur est un agonisant, ou un Lazare, facultatif.

mais il rectifie aussitôt:

Pas si facultatif.

Une autre différence sépare Descartes de Monsieur Teste. Pour le premier, la raison était la chose du monde la mieux partagée; elle était, virtuellement tout au moins, égale en tous les hommes, alors que Monsieur Teste se sait différent des autres et seul. Descartes se savait partie du monde et c'est pourquoi il a pu écrire, sans voir en cela une concession ou une faiblesse, alors que Monsieur Teste (qui n'est pas Valéry lui-même, mais son idéal) ne s'abaisserait jamais à le faire.

. . . Il n'était, nous dit-on, non plus philosophe, ni rien de ce genre, ni même littérateur; et, pour cela, il pensait beaucoup, — car plus on écrit, moins on pense.

— Jaloux donc de ses clartés séparées, — Teste pensait: qu'est-ce qu'une idée à laquelle on n'attache pas la valeur d'un secret d'Etat ou d'un secret de l'art? . . .

. . . les têtes les plus fortes, les inventeurs les plus sagaces, les connaisseurs le plus exactement de la pensée devaient être des inconnus, des avares, des hommes qui meurent sans avouer . . . avec le dédain de livrer leurs chances et leurs résultats particuliers.

Aussi Monsieur Teste se sent-il essentiellement différent des autres hommes pour lesquels, en dernière instance, il n'a qu'ironie. Dans la *Soirée à l'Opéra,* on nous dit que

. . . tout ce qui respirait dans ce cube, allait suivre ses lois, flamber de rires par grands cercles, s'émouvoir par plaques, ressentir par *masses*, des choses *intimes*, — *uniques*. . . .

Et pour parler d'eux, Monsieur Teste dira, de sa voix basse et vite:

. . . qu'ils jouissent et obéissent.

La stupidité de tous les autres nous révélait qu'il se passait n'importe quoi de sublime. . . . Monsieur Teste dit: le suprême *les* simplifie. Je parie qu'ils pensent tous de plus en plus *vers* la même chose.

Mais en face de ces êtres régis par une loi extérieure, il se sait essentiellement différent.

Du reste, la loi n'est pas si simple . . . puisqu'elle me néglige, — et — je suis ici.

Un autre fois, Valéry nous dit qu'en se promenant avec Monsieur Teste:

. . . Nous nous taisons, nous nous fixons, anxieux de n'être pas un fragment de foule.

Mais, nous l'avons déjà dit, Valéry ne s'identifie pas avec Monsieur Teste; il y a entre les deux la même différence qu'entre Faust et le Solitaire, dans la discussion avec Nietzsche. A la solitude rigoureuse du penseur, s'oppose la faiblesse de celui qui garde malgré tout le contact avec le monde à travers la sensation, le rêve et la poésie. Aussi le texte continue-t-il:

Mais moi, l'immense autrui me presse de toutes parts. Il respire pour moi dans sa propre substance impénétrable. Si je souris, c'est un peu de sa pulpe enchantée qui, non loin de mon idée, se tord; et, par ce changement dans mes lèvres, je me sens tout à coup, subtil.

Enfin, pour terminer ce dessin trop bref, ajoutons qu'

. . . il n'y a pas un grain d'espérance dans toute la substance de Monsieur Teste. . . .

On voit la grandeur, la rigidité, le caractère radical, le refus de toute concession qui caractérisent la pensée de Valéry. Et pourtant, il a ressenti et — au nom de cette même rigueur — il a indiqué l'existence possible de limites à sa position, limites qu'il ne pouvait pas reconnaître et accepter mais qu'il n'entrevoyait pas moins.

Nous avons déjà cité le passage hautement caractéristique selon lequel "le penseur est un agonisant, un Lazare, facultatif. Pas si facultatif." Ou bien l'autre passage où Monsieur Teste et Valéry sont *anxieux* de ne pas faire partie du monde des promeneurs. C'est le même sentiment qui a amené Valéry à écrire *Mon Faust*, la discussion avec Goethe, le poète de l'action et de l'espoir universels, et avec Nietzsche, le philosophe de l'espoir solitaire et héroïque. En face du premier, en éliminant l'amour et l'histoire, en transformant Marguerite en *Lust*, ce qui veut dire plaisir, et en plaçant la discussion sur son propre terrain, Valéry a maintenu rigoureusement le rationalisme de Monsieur Teste; en face du second, il a affirmé le contact avec le monde qu'apportent encore, même en tant que faiblesses, le rêve, l'enfance, la poésie. Et dans un cas comme dans l'autre, bien qu'il ait dit d'une manière remarquable tout ce qu'il avait à dire et qu'il ait publié ces textes, les désignant comme suffisamment complets pour être livrés au public, il les a intitulés *Fragments*, ce qui suggère que peut-être la décision, le choix de Monsieur Teste n'étaient pas tout à fait volontaires, que la discussion restait ouverte et que la conclusion dépendait de l'avenir et de l'histoire.

Depuis, l'histoire a-t-elle tranché? Si l'on se place au niveau mondial, où se situent aujourd'hui les problèmes, certainement pas de manière définitive. Mais si nous restons dans le cadre du monde occidental, de ce que les sociologues appellent les sociétés industrielles, alors, il est de plus en plus à craindre que l'évolution historique ne soit en train de donner tort non seulement à Goethe et à Nietzsche, mais aussi à Descartes, à Voltaire et à Valéry. Quelles que soient les différences qui opposaient les grands penseurs et les grands écrivains du monde occidental, leurs oppositions et leurs discussions se situaient sur une base commune, celle de la défense de l'homme, de l'inquiétude pour son destin. *Maturare* était le mot essentiel de Monsieur Teste, et, d'une manière plus ou moins modifiée, on pourrait en faire le mot-clef de plusieurs siècles de culture occidentale. Or, pour la première

fois, les sociétés industrielles et technocratiques sont en train de
créer une civilisation fondée sans doute sur une pensée rationaliste,
qui maîtrise la nature, mais sur une pensée qui est aussi en train
de rompre d'une manière radicale avec la tradition humaniste et
d'assimiler progressivement les hommes aux choses. La vie de
Descartes était la plus simple, écrivait Valéry, opposant à la
simplicité extérieure la richesse et l'activité de l'esprit. Mais si,
dans le monde moderne, la vie des hommes devient sur le plan de la
consommation de plus en plus variée et spectaculaire, la simplicité
ne se généralise pas moins sur le plan de la pensée et de l'esprit.
Une culture rationaliste et une civilisation technocratique qui se
désintéressent de l'homme risquent de créer une production de
masse non seulement de voitures et de frigidaires, mais surtout de
gens auxquels sans doute on a donné la possibilité de faire des
études, mais qu'on a transformés en ignorants et en analphabètes
diplômés. Contre ce danger, la résistance est difficile et une sorte
de solidarité s'établit entre des pensées qui, il y a quelques dizaines
d'années encore, paraissaient opposées.

Il y a peu de temps, si j'avais eu à parler de Valéry, j'aurais
probablement mis en avant des réserves et des critiques. Aujourd'hui, je ressens — et j'espère que nous serons nombreux à le
faire — avant tout la solidarité de toute la tradition culturelle eu-
ropéenne devant l'essor d'une société qui tend à ignorer de plus
en plus tout aussi bien les espoirs de Goethe, de Hegel ou de
Marx, que les inquiétudes de Kierkegaard et les questions de
Valéry.

Et c'est pourquoi je voudrais terminer en disant à quel point
l'oeuvre de Valéry est non seulement rigoureuse et importante,
mais à quel point il est urgent de tout faire pour qu'un nombre
aussi grand que possible de lecteurs continuent encore — ou bien
apprennent maintenant — à la lire, non pas comme un document
historique, comme une pensée qu'il faut connaître pour parfaire
sa culture générale, mais comme la parole vivante d'un inter-
locuteur sérieux et perspicace, dans une discussion qui concerne
les problèmes les plus urgents et les plus sérieux que soulève
l'existence de chacun d'entre nous.

History and Existentialism in Sartre

LEONARD KRIEGER

EXISTENTIALISM POSES both subjective and objective problems for history. As subjects, existentialists espouse positions that are often antithetical to the historical dimension; as objects, they have exhibited ideas and activities that are often opaque to historical knowledge. In Sartre both kinds of problems are joined, and, in what follows, through him a joint solution will be essayed.

The figure of Sartre — philosopher, novelist, playwright, essayist — raises the objective question first: how is a mere historian, as an historian, to set about understanding him? Clearly, this is not much of a problem for an historian who happens to have a special genius for philosophy, the novel, the drama, or the belleslettres in general, but when we posit, as we do here, an historian without such distinctive character and with only the common method of his craft — such as it is — what then? There are three things that he is equipped to do — things that perhaps only he can do and that may therefore not only perform the service function of making Sartre accessible to historians but even contribute a new dimension to the general comprehension of him.

First, obviously, we can look for the history that is in his work and thought. Who better than the historian can understand and interpret another man's treatment of history and who better than an historian can exploit this treatment for the light it sheds upon the work and thought as a whole? The methodological principle here is: it takes one to know one.

A simple principle. Would that its application were as simple. But it is not. Sartre has written in many fields, but the one field

An earlier version of this essay was read at the 1965 meeting of the Society for French Historical Studies. I am particularly indebted to Kenneth Douglas for his generous counsel on Sartre's bibliography.

in which he has not written is — unfortunately — history. Even when he has written *about* history, he has tended to disguise it, enveloping it initially in facticity and latterly in dialectic. As its guises have changed, moreover, so have the quality and the quantity of its function. To recognize history in Sartre, the historian must don some cloaks of his own. And so his simple principle acquires a corollary: to wit, it takes one to catch one.

The apparent simplicity of the second prescription — the explanation of Sartre by his historical context — is again deceptive. For if we proceed to ask, "what historical context?" we find ourselves confronted with a situation constituted by two radically different dimensions of history. First, there is the philosophical tradition to which Sartre has attached himself and in which the idea of history forms part of the general structure of thought. Secondly, there is the reality of contemporary history, vital, actual, eventful, factual, extra-philosophical. To understand Sartre, we must first give each of these dimensions its separate substantive identity in order to project the distinctive demands which his logic and his experience made upon him.

Our final and most crucial task is to understand how Sartre put these two dimensions together — that is, how he opened his philosophical system to ingest immediate experience — and it is to this end that the historian can employ a third characteristic device, the historisation of Sartre himself. Whatever the logic of his final synthesis may be, we can at least trace the chronology of the stages in the development of his thought at which his idea of history invoked the fruitful appropriation of the reality of history.

Our prospectus, then, is this: first to set up the problem of history in the general existentialist mentality; then — and this will engross the bulk of. our attention — to illuminate the problem through Sartre's specification of it and to follow his successive attempts to resolve it under the dual influences of the logical dynamics within his existentialist philosophy and the impact of events outside it; and finally to indicate the bearing of his developing solution upon the role of history in western culture.

*   *   *

Most of the intellectual movements with which we are familiar have developed in two stages, which we may denominate formally as adjectival and substantive. There were conservative, liberal,

idealist, historicist individuals and groups before there was conservatism, liberalism, idealism, or historicism. The distinction is
not a mere matter of nomenclature, or of self-consciousness, or
of stylistic degeneration. It is a matter of distinguishing between
the stage in which a tendency develops as part and in the shelter
of an already established set of ideas and the stage in which it
sets itself up as an independent doctrine or philosophy on its own.
At least some of the ambiguities in existentialism stem from the
indiscriminate application of the term to both stages of its development and may be clarified by distinguishing them. In its
adjectival stage it goes back at least to Hegel's *Phenomenology*
and it contributes subordinately to such 19th century stalwarts, in
addition to Hegel, as Marx and Nietzsche. In its substantive stage
it became an autonomous and characteristic 20th century philosophy, with Husserl its main forbear and Jaspers, Heidegger,
and Sartre its primary exponents.[1] On the basis of this pattern we
may attempt to define, in general terms, the problematical relationship between existentialism and history.

The nub of this relationship consists in the paradoxical combination of congruity and indifference — at times, indeed, even
repulsion — in the existentialist posture toward history. The paradox is visible in both the external and internal relations of these
two approaches to reality.

Externally, the relationship between existentialism and historical
mindedness is one of rival siblings, spawned in the same cultural
matrix and developing through separate but homologous cycles of
growth. Both came first to the fore as parallel responses to the
demand of early 19th century Europeans for the intellectual
recognition and cultivation of the heterogeneous, particularized
facts of natural and social reality. Both tendencies, the existentialist
and the historical, initially attended to this level of reality within
one variant or another of the traditional philosophical systems to
which they succeeded in attaching themselves before participating
with equal filial impiety in the decomposition of those systems.
When both, finally, undertook, around the turn of the century,
to make their related view of reality the ultimate reality, they did

---

[1] Kierkegaard, as the one 19th century substantive existentialist, occupies
a special place in this roster. Appropriately, the life of his ideas belongs
rather to the 20th century than to his own.

it by developing the mutually exclusive philosophies of existentialism and historicism.

The internal relations between the two intellectual movements, as evinced in the attitude of existentially-minded thinkers toward history, yields a more definite formulation of the problem. In the 19th century, during the adjectival phase of existentialism, its thinkers simply split on their orientation toward history. One group, led by Hegel and Marx, integrated history and existence into a single temporal process. It seemed a logical enough division of labor between the two collateral categories: history was simply the past of existence and revealed its direction. But another group, equally representative — their outstanding exemplar is Nietzsche — found history indifferent or hostile to the free act that creates existence. The best-known of the judgments in this genre are those of Nietzsche, who condemned as "excess of history," "unrestrained historical sense," and as "the tyranny of the actual," everything that was objective and influential in history and who admitted it in the derivative and emasculated form of "a knowledge of the past desired only for the service of the future and the present." For his own time, he would cure "the malady of history" by frank resort to the "unhistorical" and the "super-historical": "The unhistorical and the super-historical are the natural antidotes against the overpowering of life by history; they are the cures for the historical disease."[2] But for both 19th century groups, the relationship between existence and history, whether of the positive or negative type, was not a necessary one, since existence and history were equally subordinate to an overriding metaphysical, ethical, religious, aesthetic, or social principle which permitted flexiblity and variation in their respective assignments. With the derogation of this kind of principle from an absolute to a relational status during our own century, however, and with the concomitant rise of existence and history to the status of independent categories of reality, as signalized in the parallel growths of existential*ism* and historic*ism*, the relationship between these two categories became necessary and the problem of it critical.

[2] Friedrich Nietzsche, *Use and Abuse of History* (tr. by A. Collins, New York, 1957), pp. 12, 22, 42, 69 – 70.

It is for insight into this problem that we turn to Sartre, with the knowledge that the ambiguities of the relationship that we find in him are not idiosyncratic but reflective of a fundamental dilemma in a characteristic intellectual movement of our age. Sartre is a uniquely qualified subject for two reasons. First, as a first-rate philosopher and simultaneously as a participant in a 20th century French intellectual class which, like the German intellectuals of the 19th century and the French of the 18th, has been particularly open to the broadest range of social influences, he combines a rigor of thought with a responsiveness to the world in a way that makes his performance at once cogent and representative. Secondly, in his development he has traversed the whole spectrum of possibilities from the anti- to the pro-historical postures of existentialism. Consequently, he holds out to us not only the advantages of a bargain rate — the understanding of two types at the cost of only one study — but, if we can discover an historical logic in his development, the prospect of uncovering the function of history in contemporary thinking. For Sartre's development involves a philosophical shift that is larger than the change in his evaluation of history, and the growing centrality of history is the key to it. We may view this development in terms of two main phases, joined by the cataclysmic experience of the war. Consonant with the historical approach, we shall consider his second main phase — since it occupies the approximate present — as the given which needs to be explained, and we shall concentrate upon the early Sartre and the subsequent break which serve as the explanation.

Our starting-point must be Sartre's pre-war novel, *La Nausée*, for it is the vehicle of as dramatic and as categorical a rejection of history as was ever penned. A philosophical novel cast in the form of a journal, its diarist is an amateur historian who seeks to escape the sporadic onslaughts of an undiagnosed nausea by writing the life of a Marquis de Rollebon, vicious attendant at the court of Louis XVI and murderous conspirator at the court of Paul I. Unable to establish any meaningful connection with the world about him, including his historical documents — "I understand nothing more about his conduct. . . . Slow, lazy, sulky, the facts adapt themselves to the rigor or the order I wish to give them;

but it remains outside of them"[3] — the protagonist suddenly discovers, at the climax of the book, the meaning — that is, the meaninglessness — of all existence, including his own, and at that very
moment throws history from him as antithetical to his existence
and indeed to existence in general.

> M. de Rollebon was my partner; he needed me in order to
> exist and I needed him so as not to feel my existence. I fur-
> nished the raw material, the material I had to resell, which I
> didn't know what to do with: existence, *my* existence. His
> part was to have an imposing appearance. . . . I no longer
> existed in myself, but in him.[4]

> Only M. de Rollebon has just died for the second time. . . .
> Nothing existed but a bundle of yellow pages which I clasped
> in my hands. . . . Rollebon was no more. No more at all.
> . . . The great Rollebon affair was over, like a great passion.
> I must find something else. . . . The thing which was wait-
> ing was on the alert, it has pounced on me, it flows through
> me, I am filled with it. . . . Existence, liberated, detached,
> floods over me. I exist.[5]

Why this antithesis? Because of the two primary qualities of
existence impressed upon the fictionized Sartre in these moments
of revelation. First, its absolute contingency. Existent things are
simply here, with no ground for their being and no connection
among them save friction — "things exist one against the other."[6]
"Existence everywhere, infinitely, in excess, for ever and everywhere; existence — which is limited only by existence. . . . Every
existing thing is born without reason, prolongs itself out of weakness and dies by chance."[7] Nausea, superfluity, absurdity: these
notorious Sartrean terms are simply responses to this incomprehensible and groundless plethora of unmeaning existence. Obviously, such qualities undercut any relationship between an
historian and his object, and Sartre explicitly makes the point.

[3] Jean-Paul Sartre, *Nausea* (tr. by Lloyd Alexander, Norfolk, Conn.,
1949), pp. 22 – 3.
[4] *Ibid.*, p. 133.
[5] *Ibid.*, pp. 131 – 4.
[6] *Ibid.*, p. 137.
[7] *Ibid.*, pp. 178 – 80.

Even in the denouement of *La Nausée*, when the protagonist spies a glimmer of hope, he projects the writing of a book, "but not a history book," because "history talks about what has existed" and "an existant [sic] can never justify the existence of another exist-ant."[8]

But the second quality of Sartre's existence cuts even deeper, for it goes beyond history to destroy the larger dimension of reality which it inhabits — the past. Existence has no dimensions: it is "the very paste of things," composed of "soft, monstrous masses, all in disorder," and the apparent individuality of things in only "a veneer."[9] "Without memory," "existence . . . falls from one present to another, without a past, without a future."[10] "All that was not present did not exist. Not at all. Not in things, not even in my thoughts. . . . For me the past (had been) only a pensioning off: . . . another way of existing, a state of vacation and inaction."[11] And once again Sartre did not hesitate to associate a fundamental ontological position with a negative judgment upon history: "How can I, who have not the strength to hold to my own past, hope to save the past of someone else?"[12]

From this initial exposé of brute existence as the ubiquitous condition of what Sartre will later call "human reality" we may then derive three propositions about the initial status of history for him. First, even in the sense of its raw material, of historical objects, history is no part of original existence. Secondly, in the sense both of historical events and of historical knowledge the denial of history is associated with the denial of meaning, and by implication we must look for its subsequent affirmation, if such there be, in conjunction with the general affirmation of meaning. Thirdly, in his denial of meaning Sartre lumps together three levels of historicity which are usually distinguished: individual memory or past, which we do not call historical; actions in the past taken by individuals in reference to other individuals, which we do call historical; and the knowledge the historian has of such

[8] *Ibid.*, p. 237.
[9] *Ibid.*, pp. 171 – 2.
[10] *Ibid.*, pp. 178, 234 – 5.
[11] *Ibid.*, pp. 130 – 1.
[12] *Ibid.*, p. 130.

actions. As we follow Sartre's reconstruction of meaning in the world, we shall, accordingly, have both to look for the internal relationship and even interpenetration which Sartre deliberately maintains across these levels and to distinguish, as he does not explicitly, among these levels as separate stages, each with its distinct problems, in the tortuous reconstruction of meaning out of nothingness.

Sartre's reconstruction of meaning must be viewed as the obverse side of its destruction, and he began it in the initial phase of his development, simultaneously with the doctrine of existence which cleared the ground for it. In form — although not in content — the lines along which Sartre undertook the exposition of meaning during his first phase served as a model for his second as well. In each case, an insight into contemporary existence spurred him to transcend it immediately in the form of artistic creation and then gradually, through the slow and painful accumulation of ideas, in the form of a fundamental philosophical application of meaning to reality which closed out the phase. The aesthetic dimension of the first phase is traceable in *La Nausée* itself as well as in *L'Imaginaire*, its philosophy in *L'Être et le néant*. The hallmarks of this phase are the elemental character of the reconstruction, its individualistic basis and limit, its seeming indifference to history, its provision of what we may call "cognate history," and its provisional failure.

Sartre's immediate response to the opacity of existence was aesthetic. The note of hope on which *La Nausée* ends holds forth the prospect of escaping "the sin of existence" not by penetrating it but by going "behind" it and "above" it to create an intangible something to which existence refers but which itself has being, duration, meaning, and therefore no existence.[13] This something, exemplified in *La Nausée* by a tune and a novel, is generalized in *L'Imaginaire* into any work of art. Sartre here revealed the function of art through the less dramatic but more authentic analysis — at once philosophical and psychological — of the mental process that produces it; by making art the most notable activity of the imagination, he cast a fundamental vehicle of human meaning into the form of a basic unreality. For imagination is an activity of

---

[13] *Ibid.*, pp. 234–8.

consciousness which creates "unreal" objects out of "analogues" or "substitutes" intentionally directed to that purpose.[14] Imagination and knowledge of the real are indeed mutually exclusive modes of consciousness: "For the real and the imaginary cannot co-exist by their very nature. It is a matter of two types of objects, of feelings and actions that are completely irreducible. . . . The work of art is an unreality. . . . It is outside of the real, outside of existence. . . . The real is never beautiful. Beauty is a value applicable only to the imaginary. . . ."[15] Although alienated from reality, the imagination — and the work of art that is its fullest product — has a crucial function in reference to reality. By denying the real in order to create the unreal, not only is the imagination "the whole of consciousness as it realizes its freedom . . . and the necessary condition for the freedom of empirical man in the midst of the world" but, because imagination must "hold the real at a distance, . . . to deny it," the imaginary consciousness makes man able "to posit reality as a synthetic whole . . . from a certain point of view."[16] Simone de Beauvoir recognized the central position of art for Sartre in the 30's but misread its function when she wrote that "the work of art or literature was, in his view, an absolute end in itself; . . . a law unto itself, and its creator . . . a law unto himself."[17] Actually, it was not, even then, for Sartre, an end in itself, for it had an essential, if as yet unexamined, relation to the real. "The imaginary thus represents at each moment the implicit meaning of the real," that is, the way in which consciousness grasps reality as a whole in order to surpass it.[18]

Thus Sartre initiated his fundamental doctrine of a split at the

---

[14] Jean-Paul Sartre, *The Psychology of Imagination* (New York, 1948), pp. 20, 117, 200. This is a translation of *L'Imaginaire: Psychologie phénoménologique de l'imagination* (Paris, 1940), which should be distinguished from Sartre's *L'Imagination* (Paris, 1936), recently translated by Forrest Williams as *Imagination: a Psychological Critique* (Ann Arbor, 1962). The latter work has not been used in this essay.

[15] Sartre, *Psychology of Imagination*, pp. 210, 274, 280 – 1.

[16] *Ibid.*, pp. 267 – 71.

[17] Simone de Beauvoir, *Memoirs of a Dutiful Daughter* (tr. by James Kirkup, Cleveland, 1959), p. 334.

[18] Sartre, *Psychology of Imagination*, p. 272.

very heart of being, and at this stage he assigned its dynamic mode to the imaginary and the aesthetic. In *La Nausée* he drama-tized the inception of this mode; in *L'Imaginaire* he analyzed its operation after inception. The role of history in this syndrome is merely derivative and incidental. Like the general category of the past under which it is subsumed, history, as *La Nausée* has shown us, has no existence before the activation of the aesthetic imagina-tion, and, as *L'Imaginaire* shows us, the existence that it acquires by exercise of the activated imagination is only as a dimension of inert, passive reality. Memory, the past, is "one mode of real existence among others"; as such, it has nothing in common with the time of the imagination, which is arbitrary, reversible, un-real.[19]

The dichotomy seems decisive enough, and yet there are, even at this stage, signs that Sartre was reaching for a more positive valuation of the past and of history, and these signs betrayed the general needs of his thinking that the more positive valuation was to help fill. In *La Nausée* Sartre's alter ego gropes toward a union of imagination and history in the inchoate notion that his proper genre is the historical novel. "I have the feeling," he wrote anent his incapacity to find any rationale in the historical facts, "of doing a work of pure imagination. . . . I could imagine him so well if I let myself go. . . . But if this is where it all leads me, I'd be better off writing a novel on the Marquis de Rollebon."[20] And in the denouement, after his definitive discovery of art, he supplemented this premonition that art could penetrate the past with the hope that, thus penetrated, the past could provide a ground for, could justify, the present. After the projected novel was written, he wrote at the end, "I think that a little of its clarity might fall over my past. . . . And I might succeed — in the past, nothing but the past — in accepting myself."[21] And, as a matter of fact, the closest thing to history which Sartre has written was the series of contemporary historical novels published as *Les Chemins de la liberté*, of which more anon.

In *L'Imaginaire*, similarly, the explicit relegation of the past to

[19] *Ibid.*, pp. 184 – 8, 263 – 4.
[20] Sartre, *Nausea*, pp. 23, 82.
[21] *Ibid.*, p. 238.

a reality which serves as a mere foil to the free play of the imagination does not ban the nagging recognition that, whatever Sartre said or failed to say, his description of the imaginary act as the construction of unreal objects out of real analogues is suspiciously close to what an historian does with his documents. Nor must we content ourselves with mere suspicion, for in *L'Imaginaire* itself Sartre, without recognizing the principle of it, applies valid acts of the imagination to historical reconstruction. Works of art become *de facto* historical sources. The imagination is capable of making Michelangelo's David a "symbolic scheme . . . of the historical period known as the Renaissance," in terms of which we can define it and "consider the Renaissance itself as present in person."[22] But we may glimpse the reason why Sartre could not rise from the illustration to the principle, nor from the historical novel to history proper, when we understand the problem that he has even with this historical illustration, a problem that opens out into the fundamental irresolution of this stage of his thought. For Sartre admits that the symbolic apprehension of *David* requires two progressive acts of imagination, since the image is first formed for its own sake "as the first gropings of a lower thought" and only by "a further creative effort" represents the larger scheme of the Renaissance.[23] But Sartre did not, at this stage, indicate what was ingredient in this further effort. His inability to demonstrate the movement from historical perception to historical synthesis, moreover, was irremediable so long as he associated historical knowledge with the aesthetic imagination. For he generalized this incompatibility between what the real analogue is and what it represents into an "inherent contradiction" and "ambiguity" of all images.[24]

The problem which thus invaded the very core of the imagination, and incidentally attracted Sartre toward but not into history, was twofold. First, his approach to being and meaning through art and imagination, which surrounded and surpassed reality but did not penetrate it, raised the problem of the relations between existence and consciousness in general — that is, consciousness of

[22] Sartre, *Psychology of Imagination*, pp. 155 – 9.
[23] *Ibid.*, pp. 158 – 9.
[24] *Ibid.*, pp. 169 – 71.

the real as well as of the image. His aesthetic emphasis upon the image postulated the necessary complementarity of reality, which helped dialectically to define the image and shared both consciousness and existence with it. Indeed, Sartre's reading and thinking along the lines of the complement accompanied his aesthetic approach throughout the 30's. What crystallized this parallel activity into a comprehensive formal work was, externally, his awareness of political and social reality and, internally, the ungrounded connections which he made, willy-nilly, between reality and the aesthetic imagination.[25] For since the imaginative consciousness must grasp reality in order to deny it, we are left with the apparent paradox that what Sartre calls "human reality" is constituted by the faculty that constitutes the unreal. Since, moreover, the imaginary is for Sartre "a fact" and he confers on it the status of existence — "unreal existence" — an unstated generic notion of being underlies this two-dimensional existence.[26] It was this tendency of Sartre's art and imagination to slide over into reality that explains his tenuous attraction to the history he denied. It was to resolve the general problem of relating reality and creation that he rounded out his first stage with the writing of *L'Être et le néant*, in which he articulated the doctrine of history appropriate to this first stage.

The second problem adumbrated in his early work on art and imagination was, if anything, even more fundamental to Sartre: it went straight through *L'Être et le néant* to dominate his second stage. This problem was the problem of synthesis and integration — of what Sartre calls "totality." Objects of the imagination, works of art, are themselves "indivisible wholes," but each one is "independent, isolated," without relations to one another or to their milieu: they form no organized world.[27] It is true, as we have seen, that the imaginative consciousness posits reality as a world, but it is always from the point of view of the particular image, and this real totality is always collapsed by the imagination which transcends it toward a particular end dominated by that

25 On Sartre's early political interests, see Simone de Beauvoir, *Memoirs*, p. 344.
26 Sartre, *Psychology of Imagination*, pp. 200, 271 – 2.
27 *Ibid.*, pp. 188, 193.

point of view. For art and the imagination, in short, the world is always being dissolved into what is discontinuous and individual. Simone de Beauvoir's judgment that Sartre was, at this stage, something of an "anarchist" has a more profound reference than she perhaps intended.[28] His persistent dedication to art and psychology, so pronounced during this first phase, was the consistent expression of his individualizing mentality. And yet, as *L'Être et le néant* reveals, this dedication was balanced, and ultimately over-balanced, by the compensatory passion for totality. He overcame, in *L'Être et le néant*, the problem of discontinuity and, in the service of this measure of integration, established the elemental basis for history. But he remained, in this work, within the framework of individuality. It was the internal drive to overcome this limitation upon unity that pushed him finally into the second stage of his thought in search of a supra-individual totality, and it was in the process of this search that history became central to him.

And so *L'Être et le néant* becomes, for us, the pivotal work. Not that there is much in it about what we would recognize as history: there is, indeed, very little. It concludes, as I have indicated, the phase of Sartre's thought in which his existentialism ranges only from the hostile to the indifferent in its orientation toward history. Yet, as the most profound, systematic, and coherent exposition of Sartre's philosophy it is crucial for the revelation of the inescapable limits and problems of that thought — limits and problems which created intellectual needs that history was later brought in to fill. Moreover, since Sartre has never departed from the main foundations of his thought, *L'Être et le néant* also set forth the assumptions which molded the subsequent form of his historical doctrine.

Published in 1943, the work has been interpreted in terms of the impact of war and occupation. But Sartre himself has denied the relevance of these conditions, indicating the slow gestation of the work through the whole decade of the 30's and its virtual completion, in the sense of its "method and principal conclusions," by the winter of '39 – '40.[29] We have, then, empirical confirmation of

[28] Simone de Beauvoir, *Memoirs,* p. 344.
[29] Jean-Paul Sartre, *Critique de la raison dialectique* (vol. I, Paris, 1960), p. 34.

what should be clear from the substance of the book — it is the philosophical foundation of the ideas and attitudes that we have been reviewing, the ideas and attitudes of Sartre's first stage. The work is long, the terminology special and precise, the structure tightly joined. I propose here to hack it up, to appropriate only what is pertinent to our purpose, and to translate it into the grosser terms of general usage. Let us simply look for the general theme of *L'Être et le néant* and then list, as select propositions frankly torn from context, the discrete positions which have a coherence in their common reference to the problem of history.

The theme is the relationship of existence and consciousness for the particular kind of being which Sartre calls "human reality." These two sub-types of being manifest a radical rift in the heart of human being as such. This rift manifests itself in the striving of consciousness to create a ground, a reason for being, and to re-join existence in a unitary, or, in Sartre's term, "totalized" being whose contingency would now be replaced by meaning. The pattern for the action of this consciousness of the real is analogous to the previously developed consciousness of the image — the spontaneous withdrawal from and denial of the existent, the simul-taneous organization of the existent into a world to be tran-scended, and the surpassing of it by the individual consciousness' projection of itself toward its freely chosen end. But the changes of scene entail a process quite different from that of the imaginary arena, for now consciousness is engaged continuously in and with real existence and its vehicle is moral action rather than art. Since this consciousness emerges from existence and seeks to return to synthesis with existence, its primary function is not imagining nor even knowing — but doing.

Sartre's theme was thus the immanent unity of being, and he articulated it by turning existence into a process. He showed con-sciousness surging out of existence, planting a ladder made of recalcitrant existent materials firmly upon nothing, attaching it to a hand-made star, and climbing with the whole weight of exist-ence upon its back toward that blessed landing where the exist-ence would be justified and the consciousness realized. In the course of the trip Sartre had to bring consciousness to terms with all dimensions of human reality. Yet the historical dimension of this reality, obvious as it is, gets short shrift, and Sartre's orientation of his theme against detached knowledge as an activity and detached particulars as objects — both the stock-in-trade of historians — makes it clear that this was no mere oversight. But his position was more intricate than the specific neglect implied. If we arrange six of his pre-historical propositions — that is, propositions on time and society, the two main constituents of the historical dimension — in the form of a cumulative argument, the bases of both the actual indifference toward and the potential usefulness of history for the pre-war Sartre should stand revealed:

1. Neither consciousness nor existence are *in* time. Time is created by consciousness as the medium through which consciousness transforms existence into a world for which it can take responsibility. All the dimensions of time, consequently, including the past, are derivatives of the "original synthesis" of time and are internally related to one another through it.[30]

2. The three dimensions of time correspond to the three facets of the creative act of consciousness. The present is the free consciousness' withdrawal from and negation of existence; the future is the freely chosen end toward which consciousness projects itself; the past is existence itself, as it exists for consciousness. The past, then, is the "facticity," "the given," the "contingent," the "essence" and "substance" of what we are. It is the unalterable, irremediable, factual necessity that "haunts" consciousness; it is the world that consciousness determines itself to transcend.[31]

3. The role of the past in the constitution of "human reality" is admittedly "a paradox."[32] Consciousness must be *both* its own past — since the past is by definition the substance of what anything is — *and* at the same time it must deny, negate, "nihilate" this very past, for this is consciousness' very reason for being. The past must be *both* continuous with the present — "the origin and springboard of all my actions" — *and* ruptured from it. The past must *both* supply *to* the future the terms in which possibilities are projected and choices made *and* be "illuminated" — that is,

[30] Jean-Paul Sartre, *Being and Nothingness* (tr. by Hazel E. Barnes, New York, 1956), p. 107.
[31] *Ibid.*, 35, 83 – 4, 118 – 9, 140 – 1.
[32] *Ibid.*, 489, 496. For this paragraph see also pp. 141, 436, 453, 465 – 7, 478.

offered its "meaning" — *by* the future, since it is in the light of its possibilities and choices that consciousness determines what the past is. In Sartre's trenchant expression of the paradox: "All my past is there, pressing urgent, imperious, but its meanings and the orders which it gives me I choose by the very project of my end."

As a matter of fact, if not of logic, Sartre did break through the paradox, but he did it now by deciding for the present and future over the past. The past includes both "unchangeable" and "variable" elements — that is, facts and meanings — but "the meaning of the past fact penetrates it through and through," with the effect that unchangeable fact cannot be distinguished as such but must lie "beyond reach" within its layers of variable meaning. The priority of meaning over fact *in* the past entails the priority of present and future over past, "for the meaning of the past is strictly dependent upon my present project" for the future.[33] Consciousness decides now, in accord with its projected ends, what parts of the past it will maintain in continuity with the present and what parts of the past it will in varying degrees break off from the present and leave for dead or in varying degrees of death throes. The past, then, becomes irremediable and effective only in the form that consciousness decides to make it so. The past becomes "the actually revealed materialization of the end which we are." Thus Sartre resolved the paradox at the cost of the past, but he paid for it in ambiguity. "We choose our past in the light of a certain end, but from then on it imposes itself upon us and devours us."[34]

4. The past, as a dimension of temporality, is the basis of history but it does not by itself constitute history. For the past, as such, is a structure of the individual consciousness — it is "my past," of "my consciousness" — whereas history begins only with a social past. The "event" that is "a condition of all history" — that has the effect of "making history possible" — is the "fact," absolute, contingent, inexplicable, of the birth of social consciousness out of individual consciousness — Sartre's terms, "the upsurge" of "being-for-others" out of "being-for-itself."[35] The time

[33] *Ibid.*, pp. 497 – 8.
[34] *Ibid.*, p. 503.
[35] *Ibid.*, p. 282.

dimension which history inhabits is, accordingly, an addition upon original time: it is "universal time," composed by the succession of simultaneous intersections of "my" time and "the Other's."[36] But — and this is the crucial fourth proposition, although it is an interpretation of Sartre rather than Sartre's own interpretation — history is in fact reduced to the individual past, is indeed a mere function of it, and the entire third proposition on the past, with all its ambiguities, applies equally to history. For the Sartre of *L'Être et le néant*, history has no autonomous status whatsoever; what small status it does have derives from its existence as a special case of the individual past. Although he did not bother to define it, he identified as "history" those sections of the past and of the knowledge of the past that had a social reference, but his approach to history in both these senses was such as to make these sections minuscule subsets within the generic past created by individual consciousness. Sartre's quantitative neglect of history — in *L'Être et le néant*'s six hundred pages the two brief excursions into history comprise some six pages devoted to actual history and a mere five sentences to the historian — thus reflected a parenthetical view of history, and this view was, in turn, faithfully reflected in what he did with it on the few occasions he troubled to discuss it.[37]

Sartre could conceive of history in the terms and on the pattern of the individual and his past because he refused to make either of the two distinctions that usually define history. He would not distinguish in principle either between the two senses of history — history as the reality of the past and history as the knowledge of the past — or between history as such and the past. This deliberate ambiguity, moreover, had a tendency, for Sartre used the confusion between real history and known history to make the agents of history act like historians and he used the confusion between history and the generic past to make historians act like any past-creating individuals. Thus when Sartre recalled historical situations it was to adduce in each case an "historical agent," assessing his own past in the manner of an historian, as an example in a larger analysis of individual choice. On the one occasion when Sartre raised history beyond the level of a convenient illustrative

[36] *Ibid.*, pp. 267, 282.
[37] *Ibid.*, pp. 446 – 9, 500 – 3.

individual who happened to live in the past, he simply assumed societies to obey precisely the same rules in the relationship to their past as individuals do. Thus the pattern which he had worked out for individual consciousness whereby its present project decides "the value, the order, and the nature of our past" "is simply the historical choice in general."[38] It applies therefore to societies in the same way as to individuals. "If human societies are historical, this does not stem simply from the fact that they have a past but from the fact that they reassume the past by making it a memorial."[39]

Obviously, if historical agents become indistinguishable from individuals in general by becoming their own historians, then the pattern applies *a fortiori* to historians as such. ". . . The historian is himself historical; . . . he historicizes himself by illuminating 'history' in the light of his projects and those of his society."[40] Neither the society nor the historian has any more right to claim a definitive status for their historical pasts than the individual does for his temporal past: for all these agents alike the meaning of the past will change in the tow of their changing projects.[41] And if there be any lingering doubt about Sartre's reduction of history, it may be removed by his inconsistent but revealing use of the term to characterize the individual's view of his own past, apart from any social consciousness, when he reflects upon it.[42]

5. Behind Sartre's inability to people the historical arena which he defined was his more fundamental — and this time admitted — failure to go beyond the individual and to constitute the society that was to inhabit it. For Sartre, always "the question is of *my* freedom," of "only *my* particular consciousness."[43] This did not mean solipsism but rather the inherent impossibility of discovering or establishing any kind of relationships among individuals that would be reasonable or meaningful and hence that could constitute any kind of group. "Human reality remains alone because the Other's existence has the nature of a contingent and

[38] *Ibid.*, p. 500.
[39] *Ibid.*
[40] *Ibid.*, p. 501.
[41] *Ibid.*, pp. 501 – 2.
[42] *Ibid.*, pp. 158 – 9.
[43] *Ibid.*, p. 438. Sartre's emphasis.

irreducible fact. . . . It is therefore useless for human reality to seek to get out of his dilemma: one must either transcend the Other or be transcended by him. The essence of the relations between consciousness is not the *Mitsein;* it is conflict."[44] This is because individuals apply their isolated temporal processes to a common world: each consciousness knows other individuals as objects in its world to be used and transcended; it experiences the fact of other individuals as consciousnesses — that is, as free beings — only by feeling itself demeaned to an object for them, to be used and transcended. Thus there are only "us objects," that is, common objects for a third party, but this is no union, for each individual here "feels trapped, among an infinity of strange existences . . . and alienated radically."[45]

But this insulated, individualized kind of existence was not, for Sartre, simply a fact; it was a failure. Our awareness of others, our development of a social consciousness, tells us not only that a plurality of consciousnesses exist but that this plurality "is a totality." And yet, so imprisoned is each within himself that we can neither know nor do anything about it. "The multiplicity of consciousness appears to us as a synthesis and not as a collection, but it is a synthesis whose totality is inconceivable."[46]

6. Here we have the key to the final and summary proposition of *L'Être et le néant*. It is a philosophy of "perpetual failure."[47] This proposition, be it noted, is not a judgment upon Sartre; it is Sartre's explicit thesis. Repeatedly, at the critical points of his analysis, Sartre affirms failure, not on the part of Sartre but on the part of being, of "human reality." As we have seen above, the individual consciousness cannot realize any union with a community of consciousnesses. Again, the individual consciousness, which, it should be recalled, is in its primary structure an active rather than a knowing consciousness, fails when it tries to unite itself with existence through knowledge, which the active consciousness produces as a secondary mode of its being. For knowledge, operated through "reflection," literally reflects the original dis-

[44] *Ibid.*, pp. 250, 429.
[45] *Ibid.*, p. 419.
[46] *Ibid.*, pp. 252, 301.
[47] *Ibid.*, p. 623.

junction between existence and consciousness in the duality of the known and the knower.[48] Consciousness as such, finally, whatever its structure, fails in its practical effort to rejoin existence by attaining for "the real . . . the dignity of the self-cause."[49]

All these failures are aspects of one generic failure inherent in reality: the failure of its parts to achieve a unity that is actually impossible but is just as actually a target, indicated by reality itself, for their striving. A paradox? Of course. But also an intolerable torment. "The being of human reality is suffering because it rises in being as perpetually haunted by a totality which it is without being able to be it. . . . Human reality therefore is by nature an unhappy consciousness with no possibility of surpassing its unhappy state. . . . Everything happens as if the world, man, and man-in-the-world succeeded in realizing only a missing God. Everything happens therefore as if existence and consciousness were presented in a state of disintegration in relation to an ideal synthesis."[50]

These six propositions are, of course, related, and their connection epitomizes Sartre's position at the conclusion of his first stage. Everywhere he looked he saw isolation and frustration, and, as a corollary, the desired unity and fulfillment of which the frustration was a function. Between the two, nothing. The most tangible block was man's inability to relate to other men and thereby to direct common action to a total human goal. The corollary of *this* inability was the absence of any effective history beyond the type of past that lived and died with each individual or social cognate of individuals and contributed nothing but transient matter to the transcendent goal.[51] And yet, though the denigration of history was a consequence of the inviability of the group, the same philosophy implied history's potential as a power for synthesis. The deprecation of history was a function both of the dependent status of the past and the unreality of the group. But the past and the group were the only possible forces that could form a continuum. If history could be recognized, it could exercise a

[48] *Ibid.*, pp. 218, 624.
[49] *Ibid.*, p. 623.
[50] *Ibid.*, pp. 90, 623.
[51] E.g., *ibid.*, pp. 502, 623.

reverse effect as the medium for the realization of both past and society by internally relating them. Here was the need and here was the possibility that cradled Sartre's growth.

*   *   *

Since Sartre had reached the limits of his own resources in *L'Être et le néant* he obviously could not grow from within. But he was philosophically prepared to absorb actively what came to him from without. What came was the war, the occupation, the resistance — and the effect upon him was cataclysmic. But what, precisely, was the effect? What filtered through the fine mesh, so carefully manufactured, of his thought? According to Simone de Beauvoir, the effect was dual. First, "we discovered the reality of history and its weight."[52] Secondly, the experience taught Sartre "solidarity": whereas he had thought to attain the absolute through art, he now "discovered, with his historicity, his dependence; . . . the universality to which, as a bourgeois intellectual, he aspired, only those men who embodied it on earth could give him" — that is, the proletariat, "the universal class."[53] Now this has the ring of authenticity. As we have seen, history and social solidarity were precisely what the pre-war Sartre needed. But the question is not only *what* were added. It is also *how* they were added, since, as we have seen, Sartre seemed closed to both history and society by necessary paradoxes of his thought. The "how" really involves two questions. In what forms did he perceive the cataclysm of his times? And how did he translate the experience into concepts at least coherent to if not entirely consistent with his philosophy?

For the first question we have the evidence from the trilogy of novels — *Les Chemins de la liberté* — which embody the contemporary expression of his attitudes for the critical war-time interval spanning the break between the two stages of his thought. For the second question we have Sartre's own direct retrospective testimony.

The trilogy — which is not strictly a trilogy since there is a projected fourth volume that has not appeared — may be viewed

[52] Simone de Beauvoir, *La Force des choses* (Paris, 1963), p. 47.
[53] *Ibid.*, pp. 15 – 7.

as the incomplete representation of Sartre's progressive grasp of the inevitable participation by originally isolated individuals in the life and time of larger complexes of individuals. *L'Age de raison* — the first volume — represents the point of departure, the fictional equivalent of *L'Être et le néant*, but told now from the point of view, not of existence, as in *La Nausée*, but of consciousness. It is, indeed, an account of "unhappy consciousness."

The actors are a set of individuals in Paris, revolving loosely in various confrontations around Mathieu, a teacher of philosophy, but each in his or her own orbit — what Sartre calls "an unbarred cage" — seeking in vain for a meaning in it.[54] The time is presumably during the 30's, but there is no reference to the larger society to date it. Each has his own life and, though these lives "interlace and intersect," they "remain as vigorously personal as a toothbrush"; each has his own past, which offers no support because it "was in continual process of retouching by the present."[55] The want of meaning within each life is internally associated with the incapacity to break out of it toward others. Mathieu, the reflective consciousness who incorporates the age of reason, is "empty," "a negation" because he thinks rather than acts and can find no reason for acting. He feeds upon himself, but sporadically he breaks through to a momentary vision of "above his life a pure consciousness, . . . without ego, . . . unlinked to any person."[56] Concretely, his vision of a meaning is embodied in the Communist, Brunet, whose life has "meaning," is "a destiny" because he has "a whole world in common" with his comrades. "His age, his class, his time — he had deliberately assumed them all. . . . He had joined up, he had renounced his freedom. . . . And everything had been rendered to him, even his freedom. 'He is freer than I: he is in harmony with himself and with the party.' "[57] Mathieu yearns for this kind of solidarity, but his sympathy remains "abstract."[58] He cannot make the leap from his individuality to this extreme pole of solidarity; in the light of this standard his reason

[54] Jean-Paul Sartre, *The Age of Reason* (tr. by Eric Sutton, New York, 1947), p. 146.
[55] *Ibid.*, pp. 242, 272.
[56] *Ibid.*, pp. 64, 245, 395.
[57] *Ibid.*, pp. 155, 159.
[58] *Ibid.*, p. 137.

can only demonstrate to him, at the end, "the failure of a life."[59] But we must remember Brunet, for the trilogy will end with him as a central character and a real figure. In a sense his passage — the passage of the solidarity that he stands for — from abstraction to reality is the theme of the work.

The passage leads through the second volume — *Sursis* — for our purposes the most important of the three. Ostensibly it is a sequel which follows the experiences of these characters, plus a few new ones, during the week of the Munich crisis and the partial mobilization that accompanied it. Actually, it signified a radical change in point of view, reflected in the dramatically changed technique of the novel. Gone was the mechanical unity of place and of middle class. The familiar individuals are scattered through France, the newer ones extend the scene from north Africa to Czechoslovakia and the types from Neville Chamberlain to an illiterate shepherd. Not only are the encounters between these individuals now fortuitous — most of them never meet — but even their individual orbits are broken, discontinuous.

And yet there is a strong coherence in the work, a coherence now constituted by time, by what we may call social time. The chapters are capped by the calendar days of the Munich crisis, but it is not this device that registers the full impact of the innovation. The scenes shift, from situation to situation, from individual to individual, within the chapter, within the paragraph, within the sentence, led by the logic of a common time which is the measure of the social crisis. Through the medium of time the world, in the form of the imminent war, invaded individuality and smashed it. "The sum" of all individual futures "is peace."[60] But "now the war is there; my life is dead. . . . I own nothing any more, not even my past. It was indeed a spurious past, and I don't regret it. . . . They have rid me of my life."[61] The events of Mathieu's past "belonged to the world's past, together with the peace; his life had been put away in the archives of the Third Republic. . . . This man had shaped a future to his measure: the

[59] *Ibid.*, p. 395.
[60] Jean-Paul Sartre, *The Reprieve* (tr. by Eric Sutton, New York, 1947), pp. 47 – 8.
[61] *Ibid.*, pp. 86 – 7.

war had thundered down upon it and crushed it to powder."[62]
Thus, through participation in the invisible time of a war that
was not yet, the circuit of self-hood was broken. The individual
was opened to the world, but still only negatively, recognizing his
existence as a thing in a world made by the war into an organization of things. "Myself a nondescript entity beneath that vast indifferent arc: that's war. . . . A new world was coming into
being: the austere and practical world of functional objects. . . .
Outside. Everything is outside: . . . solid objects, all of them.
Inside, nothing. . . . Myself, nothing. . . . Inseparable from the
world as light, and yet exiled, gliding like light over the surface of
stones and water: freedom is exile. . . ."[63] Individuality had lost
its substance, its integrity. In a grim climax Sartre makes his point
by describing the reluctant submission of the virgin Ivich to an
anonymity in precise synchronization with the rape of Czechoslovakia.

Thus opened forcibly, cataclysmically, to the world through
membership in the world's time, Sartre initiated his characters to
the humanizing of the relationship in *La Mort dans l'âme*. It was
the story now of the real war, of the experience of his characters
under the impact of the French military defeat in 1940. As the
title indicates, the theme once again was of the violation of the
individual, but this time by reality and in a more positive sense.
The continuity was still supplied by social time, the temporal pattern of the defeat, but no longer were the individual destinies
simply chopped up by it: once again they pursued their projects
through solid blocks of life. The attenuation of their individuality
now served their membership in an inchoate, homogenized, face-
less association, for they lived in its time and were unified by its
historian. "I can break the shell that separates us only if I wish
for myself no other future than his, . . . share his time and his
minutes."[64] The association, a society of defeat, was passive, an
object rather than a subject, and yet even in this spiritless form
it was born into history as a group. " 'We're being looked at.' A

[62] *Ibid.*, pp. 341, 352.

[63] *Ibid.*, pp. 348 – 9, 362 – 3.

[64] Jean-Paul Sartre, *Troubled Sleep* (tr. by Gerard Hopkins, New York,
1951), p. 200.

crowd growing more and more dense was watching them swallow
this bitter pill of history. . . . There they stood, guilty forever in
the eyes of their sons, of their grandsons, and of their great-
grandsons, they, the conquered of 1940 to all eternity. . . . He
looked at his comrades, and his mortal eyes met the timeless,
petrified eyes of history."[65]

And yet they were also something more than the mere "us
object" of *L'Être et le néant*. "At one and the same time they
were less than human and more than human."[66] For they had participated in the creation of this general destiny whose embodiment was this defeated army. The war was "each and every one
of us, war made in the image of all of us."[67] Thus the community
in which individuals lose their individuality is nonetheless one
which they have made and which reflects them all. "At once . . .
part of the general whole yet rejected by each individual, perfectly lucid yet utterly deceived, enslaved yet sovereign, I'm just
like everybody else."[68] Mathieu, standing for those who cannot
accept the immersion of their individuality chooses to die (and
when we leave him, he is about to). He has finally made the decision that fulfills his own destiny, but it means "firing on his fellow
men, on Virtue, the whole world: Liberty is Terror."[69] Sartre's
focus then becomes the group, defined now by the common
status of prisoners of war, and personified by Brunet, the Communist organizer, the group man, and Schneider, a socialized
Mathieu and clearly the surrogate of Sartre himself. By the standards of the dissatisfied and uncomprehending Brunet we feel the
inertia of the group. In Schneider's understanding of the death in
the group soul and his collaboration with Brunet simply to give
"the boys . . . something to live for" we feel the first glimmer-
ings of the group as an agency for meaning.[70]

If we project the direction of the fourth volume which Sartre
has been as yet unable to finish from the angle of the trilogy we
may anticipate the growth of an active group consciousness in the

[65] *Ibid.*, pp. 85–6.
[66] *Ibid.*, p. 87.
[67] *Ibid.*, p. 196.
[68] *Ibid.*, p. 193.
[69] *Ibid.*, pp. 255–6.
[70] *Ibid.*, p. 339.

Resistance. But, as we shall soon see, it is characteristic of Sartre's second stage that he has as yet not been able to clinch the synthesis of the individual and the group. Involving as it does not only the coherence of an idea but the capstone of a system, this synthesis is itself a becoming, a movement along the dimension of time.

And so the answer to our first question — in what form did Sartre perceive the cataclysm? — is simply this: he absorbed the contemporary experience in the form of contemporary history. That is, he took the break-through of social cataclysm into individual lives and the response of individuals in the form of joint action as proof of a collective reality that was created and knowable through the synthesizing force of a common temporal process upon the activities of individuals participating in it. And because he saw history — which is composed precisely of the relationships which individuals create with one another through time — because he saw history being made, he came to understand how history was made. Because he saw in their possession of a common time the basis of meaningful relations among individuals, he came to see in the succession of these relations a meaning not only within but through history.

This illumination lies behind Sartre's own retrospective testimony that the cataclysm marked the decisive turn not only in his life but in his philosophy. According to this testimony, "the war, the occupation, the resistance, the years that followed," "exploded the former framework of our thought. We now desired to fight at the side of the working class, we understood finally that the concrete is history and dialectical action. We denied pluralist realism by recognizing it in the fascists and we discovered the world."[71] This "pluralist realism" of his first stage he now characterized as "a confusion of the individual and the total, . . . a description of artificially isolated essences and types" appropriate to the critical revelation of "the contradictions of reality" but not to its deeper unity. The "reality" that "the whole bloody history of this half-century" suddenly revealed to him, initiating his second stage, he called "the reality of Marxism," but he meant Marxism in the sense of "the only valid interpretation of history," "the conception of concrete syntheses . . . within a moving and

[71] Sartre, *Critique de la raison dialectique*, p. 24.

dialectical totalization which is nothing else but history" — "the historical process in its totality."[72] In short, what replaced the individualistic temporal paradoxes and failures of his first stage was the conviction, mediated by contemporary history, that individuals could join with their fellows in an *historical* process in which they could recover their integrity. He subscribed to Marxism because Marxism provided both the historical schema and, in the proletariat, the social group to realize it.

This second stage of Sartre's, philosophically grounded in his massive *Critique de la raison dialectique* of 1960, is thus not so much Marxist as historicist, and the work might well have been titled the Critique of Historical Reason that so many philosophers since Kant have been tempted to write. He set as his aim: "to test, criticize, and ground . . . the instruments of thought by which history is thought in so far as they are also the practical instruments by which it is made."[73] Marxism, for Sartre, does indeed reveal the general process through which men make a unity out of human reality through history, but for him, too, Marxists do not know how the process works and, more important, contemporary Marxists have lost the sense of the movement, the dialectic, the real history in the process. The role of existentialism within Marxism then, according to Sartre, is precisely to restore authentic history to it as the only means of knowing and ultimately realizing the "totalization" that is history.[74] Existenialism contributes the appreciation of the individual — the event — views history as the succession of creative moments, and commands the dialectical method that consists in the internal relation of individuality and totality through time. Thereby Sartre means to resolve his own paradoxes through history: practise gets integrated into knowledge as intelligibility, the historical agent into the historian as "the historical man," the individual into society as "the group."[75]

Of this synthetic labor, Sartre has thus far performed half (the *Critique* is labeled volume one). He has integrated, to his own satisfaction, individuals, groups, and the historian into an "intelli-

[72] *Ibid.*, pp. 24 – 9.
[73] *Ibid.*, p. 135.
[74] *Ibid.*, pp. 28 – 59, 152.
[75] *Ibid.*, p. 143.

gible totalization" through the unity of "synchronous" time — that is, the lateral unity at any particular moment of historical time. What he has still to do but has not yet done — and perhaps will never do — is to complete the synthesis by demonstrating the intelligible, "progressive" movement toward human integrity through time.[76] For so tight a system the reach may well exceed the grasp. Nonetheless, the philosophy of perpetual failure has become the philosophy of continuous success.

*   *   *

If we grant to Sartre any kind of representative status in contemporary thought, the implications of his conversion to history are profound.

Because the material of history is the specific, the concrete, and the unique, its function in the cosmos of knowledge is usually characterized or assumed to be the provision of particular information or, at most, particular truths, on a level as close as possible to the original variety of human existence. Our forbears warn us to align particular events with as much indifference as we can muster to any order of general truths. Our social scientific friends adjure us to supply the test of particular information for *their* general truths. Our revisionist colleagues are having great sport using the heterogeneity of grass-roots history to dismantle every general truth in sight.

All these positions deny a synthetic role for history, either by assuming a pre-existing structure of general truths to be merely particularized in history or by rejecting the relevance of general truths to the historical enterprise. But, if Sartre is an even approximately faithful expression of contemporary culture, then these relationships and, with them, our familiar notion of history's function, are anachronisms. If neither logic, nor science, nor art any longer furnish general truths pertinent to human conduct, if their meanings are also utterly fragmented, then history must use the patterns of synchronization and succession of human actions in the common medium of time to link *their* particular fragments and to construct whatever general truths about man we must have. If we do not apply our history to this end we fail both as the historians and as the historical agents of our age.

[76] *Ibid.*, pp. 754–5.

German Popular Biographies: Culture's Bargain Counter

LEO LOWENTHAL

I

THE BIOGRAPHY (we are here excluding scholarly works of history), which in the period after the First World War rapidly took its place alongside the traditional species of fiction as an article for literary mass consumption, reminds us of the interior in large department stores. There, in the rambling basements, heaps of merchandise have been gathered from all sections of the establishment. These goods have become out-dated and now whether they were originally offered for sale on the overcrowded notion counters or in the lofty silence of the luxury-furniture halls, are being indiscriminately remaindered for relatively little money. In these basements we find everything; the only common principle is the necessity for fast sales. The biography is the bargain basement of all fashionable cultural goods; they are all a bit shop-worn, they no longer quite fulfill their original purpose, and it is no longer particularly important whether there is relatively much or little of one or the other item.

With almost statistical accuracy, the same material has been collected and displayed in about the same package. To be sure, from the outside it looks quite different. The biographies are presented as if in the intellectual realm they represent that which the exclusive and specialty stores represent in the realm of consumer goods. This comparison designates the social atmosphere in which the popular biography belongs: one of apparent wealth. It lays claim to the philosopher's stone, as it were, for all contingencies of history of life situations, but it turns out that the motley mix-

ture of generalizations and recipes is actually an expression of
utter bewilderment.

Since 1918, the political biography has become the classical literature of the German middle-brow. To be sure, it is not restricted
to German language, nor did it make its first appearance after the
First World War — Nietzsche, years before, spoke of "our time so
accustomed to the biographical contamination."[1] The best-selling
German biographical writers were able to record great successes
outside of the boundaries of their country and language, and the
French and English tongues made many contributions of their
own during the twenties and thirties. But nowhere did the social
role of this literature become so visible as in the German material.

An analysis of the popular biography is first of all an analysis of
its reading public, and as such it comprises a critique of late European liberalism. Arbitrariness and contradiction have destroyed
any claim to theory; ultimately this literature is a caricature of
theory. During the ascendancy of the middle classes, when the
educational novel characterizes narrative literature, the individual
vacillated between his own potentials and the demands of his environment. The author drew material, which represented the substance of each individual destiny, from imagination; in only rare
exceptions were data used for surface decoration and coloration.
But, while imaginative, the educational novel was at the same time
exact, because, as a product of poetic imagination, social and psychological reality were mirrored as they were observed within the
social stratum of the author and his public. *Wilhelm Meister, Illusions Perdues, David Copperfield, Éducation Sentimentale, Der
Gruene Heinrich, Anna Karenina* — these novels not only evoked
the readers' experience of *"déjà vu,"* but confirmed the salvation of
the individual by demonstrating the burdens and good fortunes of
an invented individual existence in such a way as to permit the
reader to experience them for himself. In these works of art, specific individuals, consistent within themselves and living within a
concrete world, are represented as a complex of subjects closely
connected with the fate of living and reading contemporaries.
This is "reality" conceived as historians have conceived it since

[1] Nietzsche, *Werke*, second section, vol. 10, *Die Philosophie im tragischen
Zeitalter der Griechen* (Fragment, Spring, 1873), Stuttgart, 1922, p. 26.

the Enlightenment, and in this sense there exists a direct relation between scientific and literary realism and the theory of society: one formulates the concern about the individual, the other tries to sketch the conditions for his happiness.

The biography is both a continuation and an inversion of the novel. Documentation in the middle-class novel had the function of background — raw material as it were. Quite otherwise in the popular biography: there documentation, the pompous display of fixed dates, events, names, letters, etc., serves in lieu of social conditions. The individual who is fettered by these paraphernalia is reduced to a typographical element which winds itself through the narrative as a convenient device for arranging material. Whatever the biographies proclaim about their heroes, they are heroes no longer. They have no fate, they are merely variables of the historic process.

II

History and time have become reified in biography — as in a kind of petrified anthropology.

Consider, e.g., "The stronger will of history is indifferent to the innermost will of individuals, often involving persons and powers, despite themselves, in her murderous game" (34/p. 117),[2] or else: "the sublime breaths of history sometimes determine the rhythm of a period at times even contrary to the will of the genius that animates it" (20/p. 424), or history, "the sternest of the goddesses, unmoved and with an incorruptible glance" looks over "the depths of the times and . . . with an iron hand, without a smile or compassion" brings "events into being" (29/p. 147), or history, "possibly the most terrible and most depriving sea journey, . . . the eternal chronicle of human sufferings" (33/p. 373), "almost always justifies the victor and not the vanquished" (33/p. 217), when she "in the ultimate sense is based on force"; or, history acts "neither morally nor immorally" (28/p. 270); "one comes to term with her", so decrees the biographer personifying world-reason which, however, does not deter him from

---

[2] The numbers in parentheses refer to the biographies quoted; they are listed at the end of this essay.

occasionally calling history also "the supreme judge of human actions" (34/p. 476). At times history even permits herself to choose "from the million-masses of humanity a single person in order to demonstrate plastically with him a dispute of *Weltanschauungen*" (28/p. 134).

In statements of this kind history acquires the traits of an overpowering robot, who, however, hardly seems to be the result of human production, but with considerable stamping and with incomprehensible arbitrariness drives mankind before it.

To be sure, compared with the imagination of film producers and technocratic dreamers, this robot is rather paltry. The enumeration of its qualities is its appropriate interpretation: This is a cliché-robot — even with regard to concrete things.

> For instance, concerning Erasmus, "Instinctively time chose correctly", in him: "time saw the symbol of calm but unceasingly operating reason" (37/p. 98); during his life: "the times forced him into the tumult to the right and to the left" (37/p. 20), and in the end: "but don't deceive yourself, old man, your true time is over . . ." (37/p. 165). Needless to say, the period-cliché and the century-cliché are used extensively. The Middle Ages, "a gloomier period" (34/p. 34), were "a cruel and violent age" (34/p. 510); when they are over, we have "a turn of the century which becomes a turn of the times" (37/p. 32). There is the "great and contradictory nineteenth century" (4/p. 10), with "the people of the nineteenth century" (4/p. 22), which "does not love its youth" (29/p. 25); and it is said of the seventeenth century: "the curious century, whose child she [Christine of Sweden] was in good and ill, died with her" (25/p. 410).

The serious European historians of ideas had neither place nor time for such pomp. These intellectuals wanted to be educators, to delve into the past to better understand the present, in which definite tasks had to be done — even if it was only the task of equipping new philologists or historians with sharper tools. True, historiography was exposed to the wrath of Nietzsche, who often tortured himself with the idea that mankind was actually doomed, that "one can recognize the basically evil nature of every human being in the fact that none of them can bear to be scrutinized carefully and closely."[3] An historical fatalism, which had taken hold of European middle classes long before the authoritarian state practiced it, led him to remark that none "who today consider themselves 'good,'" are able to tolerate "a biography."[4] He thus evaluated in advance present-day biographers who magically produce a historical sphere, about which they profess to know everything. They assure us that "history" or "the century" does this or that or has this or that quality, and the historical person appears as a mere product. With this device the popular biography — although in a distorted form — mirrors reality: the literati and the consumers of their products were becoming subjected to the "rigid rhythm of world history," the pitiless *Zeitgeist*, and the general expressed in these high-sounding phrases destroys the particular of individuality. In the biographies this is glossed over; although the mirror into which the reader looks hangs crookedly, he nevertheless finds reflected there something of his own historical substance. The qualities of "history" are here described somewhat in the way the person of the authoritarian "leader" and the co-ruling elite would have to be characterized: pitiless, indifferent, only intent on success; equipped with the will and the necessary apparatus to pronounce and execute decisions affecting the overwhelming majority. Such historical philosophy betrays a social attitude toward life — which at all times acknowledges its subjugation to the highest power in command. The rules of this power, so to say the drill book of history, are contained in innumerable generalizing assertions with which biographical literature abounds.

III

The biographer is the supplier of sociology for mass consumption. What is happening here is a caricature of that inductive method which attempts to develop from empirical observations reliable rules of the game of human life across the ages. The political sociology of the biographers is the "sunken cultural herit-

---

[3] Nietzsche, *loc. cit.*, note 1.
[4] Nietzsche, *The Genealogy of Morals*, Anchor Books, p. 275.

age" of social research concerned with laws. A cue for this sociology is the little word "always," a favorite in Stefan Zweig's vocabulary, which bestows upon accidental data the dignity of the normative. Whatever was, was always that way, is that way, and so it will remain — this is the wisdom of all generalizing methods and of their popular offspring as well.

The favorite themes of popular biography are politics, power, and the leader. The new point from which the political power-apparatus and its mechanisms are discussed is that of the spectator who cannot do anything about them and who contents himself with observation. These biographers behave as if actually the whole matter was of no concern to them, as if in their wildest dreams it would not occur to them that they themselves had a stake in the matter.

> In recompense they offer the general consolation: "one who has committed himself to politics is no longer a free agent and must obey other laws than the holy ones of his nature" (34/p. 42). A philistine impotence hides behind the at times grandiose, at times cynical, words, that politics ruin the character. Politics "has always been a science of contradiction. It is forever in conflict with simple, natural, sensible solutions" (34/p. 28). It has been reified like the concept of history: "The individual man or woman simply does not exist for history; they amount to nothing when compared with tangible and practical values in the great game of world affairs" (34/p. 25). Whoever is in touch with politics, touches a dubious realm: "As always with politicians he made a compromise with God" (3/p. 253). From such types one cannot expect anything else but actions in accordance with not very lofty standards; we experience "The eternal and always recurrent spectacle . . . that politicians always become cowards as soon as they sense that the wind is turning" (35/p. 493). It is a pitiful trade: for instance, "the cleverest thing that a shrewd politician can do — he vanishes" (34/p. 146).

Behind the jaundiced view of politics hides the psychological corollary of infatuation with success, consciously decried: to study the politician requires a preoccupation with the phenomenology of power.

The reflexion concerning the Russo-Napoleonic treaty is intelligible from the perspective of empathy with power: "it is plain that when two men are dividing the world between them, they will in the long run come to blows" (20/p. 271). "It is an eternal fate of mankind that its most memorable actions are almost always spattered with blood and that the greatest success comes to the toughest" (33/p. 318); but power is such a convincing phenomenon that it demands recognition.

The same social repression mechanism, which constructs reifications out of concepts such as history, time, and politics so that they are no longer recognizable as a reflex of social relationships, also affects the concept of power. Thus we read: "Power promises, even when it is silent and does not promise anything" (22/p. 23); ". . . a power can persevere, but not reveal" (3/p. 175).

The language is equally eloquent when it deals with the favorite topic of the individual in relation to society. For here is the opportunity to speak about the universal laws of the leader.

Impartiality is self-evident: "Mussolini is a man of the most refined politeness, like all genuine dictators" (19/p. 35). It is really not a simple business: "It is part of the tragedy of all despots that they fear the independent man even after they have rendered him politically powerless and speechless" (28/p. 273). This is particularly true of the revolutionary leaders, including religious fanatics: "This is one of the secrets of almost all revolutions and the tragic fate of their leaders: none of them likes blood, but they are nevertheless forced to spill it" (32/p. 61).

Regarding the relationship of society to a dictatorship, there are certain rules for the prehistory, for the beginning, for the climax, and for the decline.

Before: "Every world renewal, every complete recultivation first experiments with the moderate reformers instead of with the rabid revolutionaries" (37/p. 98 f.). A little later: "All dictatorships start with an idea" (28/p. 65). When it really arrives: "Always in the beginning of a dictatorship . . . the resistance has a certain impetus" (28/p. 49). Later on: "After

the restless victory, dictators can always give humanity its
due and more readily permit free speech after their power
has been secured" (28/p. 239). But in the end: "Never can
humanity or a part of it, a single group, tolerate the dictatorship of a single person for very long without hating him"
(32/p. 96); "dictatorships represent in the over-all plan of
humanity only corrections of short duration" (28/p. 327).

Here in this spiritual department store we find a Machiavellian sociology of politics and, in the next moment, a utopian conception of history. It is particularly characteristic for the social
function of these biographers that they combine both of these
concepts. From the sixteenth to the nineteenth century, materialistic or idealistic as well as optimistic or pessimistic interpretations of the course of history were clearly related to the goals
of different social groups. But in the lukewarm and tired-out
political and moral climate, in which the biographies thrive,
everything goes: one puts up with the pessimistic perspective
partly by exorcising it with magic and by categorizing it, as if
the knowledge of its eternal recurrent formulas would make it
harmless to the individual involved, or by playing the role of the
cynical observer, who really is not affected. Optimism is created
by the assurance that in the end the good will win. We encounter
this pluralism of viewpoints time and again; it belongs to an attitude which takes nothing seriously, least of all the intellect. Its
ultimate wisdom is relativism.

As far as we encounter the optimistic philosophy, it runs on
many tracks. One of its versions is a "theory" of two different
human types: the bad one, the politician — the good one, the
moralist. "Regardless of what one calls the poles of this constant
tension — . . . their names express basically an ultimate innermost and personal decision, as to what is more appropriate for
each individual — the human or the political, the Ethos or the
Logos, the individuality or the collectivity. This inexorable de-
marcation between freedom and authority no people, no period,
and no thinking man can escape" (28/p. 14). A sidetrack is
created by the idea that perhaps after all there might be such
a thing as a conciliation between the "political" and the "moral"
attitude. Emil Ludwig, who specialized in Goethe-mottoes and in

realpolitisch common sense, must be cited foremost in this connection. Here we read: "In the long run one can rule as little with the will for power without the idea of the times, as with the ideas without the will for power" (16/p. 335).

However, the overriding theme of the biographers' political sociology, when they speak about the social fate of morality, is that after all the good will always be victorious. This is recited in such a stereotype and pathetic manner that it is reminiscent of the moralizing consolation verses in certain popular tunes, namely, that it cannot go on much longer in this way and that eventually things will improve. In the light of what actually has happened it is brutally funny to be told by Ludwig that "one can read the logic in a destiny [we are dealing with Masaryk] whereby an honest man reaps what he sows" (15/p. 15). However, particularly Zweig has yet a richer list. As in a song entitled "Reason" we hear: "Sometimes when the others rage drunkenly, reason must be silent and lose her voice. But her time will come, it always returns" (37/p. 25). "All fanaticism directed against reason aims necessarily into the void" (27/p. 410).

Just as the moral philosophical systems, which can turn into a critical weapon against the existing, are characteristic for progressive tendencies of liberalistic thinking, so is the contention that truth and freedom always come out on top characteristic for the retreat from the sphere of action. "Toscana defended the eternal feeling of freedom. This ideal of freedom survives the existence of all powers at large. One day of freedom topples pyramids of slavery, which seem to rise into the sky for all eternity. Freedom always returns, caresses humanity, shows it its dignity, God in her bosom, and tests the swords" (23/p. 341); or quite monumentally: "Truth always wins again. . . . Truth in the end always wins! Only those who know this are immune against the apparent eternally victorious infamy" (8/p. 326).

IV

Finally, the relationship between nature and history belongs in the general section of this pseudosystem of a social philosophy. It is treated in the spirit of a bad monism. It corresponds to the malaise, the ruin of initiative, which characterized the condition of the broadest strata of the middle class, particularly in Central Europe, during the period just before Fascism. The history of the middle classes started as the history of accelerated conquest of extra-human nature in the service of man; but mastery over nature became increasingly harnessed into the service of mastery over man, of his subjugation and destruction. I have pointed out elsewhere that important trends in literature around the turn of the century, particularly the concept of nature, reflected the resignation of the ruled confronted with a technical apparatus from which the population at large became increasingly alienated.[5] When biographical literature at times speaks of the alleged identity of natural and historical laws and at times uses natural phenomena for cliché-like comparisons with human life, it creates thereby an atmosphere of a tired-out pantheism.

This literature takes on almost mystical traits in which anything and everything merges into a great gray sameness. This is the mystique of relativism, which is shared by victims and masters alike.[6] To the latter it is the appropriate expression for the conservation of power at any price; the former confess almost masochistically how little they still value their own thoughts or the application of their minds to serious intentions. This is the place where the ideological origin of modern biography reveals itself. It hails from that *Lebensphilosophie* (philosophy of life) which, with its radical rejection of the severe rules of philosophical system, and its equally decisive opposition to any criticism of political economy, helped to prepare for the brutal vitalism of authoritarian practice in a typical manner. At times it hides behind assurances that what the biographers deal with are ultimates — a rhetoric of make-believe grandeur and magnanimity which in truth hides their own uncertainty. As in speaking about the everlasting stream of life, eternally in motion and yet always the same, one chatters about the original, the eternal, and the ultimate. We hear of "the eternal man" (30/p. 377), of "the eternal march

[5] See Leo Lowenthal, "Knut Hamsun," in his: *Literature and the Image of Man*, Beacon, 1957, pp. 190 ff.

[6] See Max Horkheimer, "Der neueste Angriff an die Metaphysik," *Zeitschrift fuer Sozialforschung*, vol. VI (1937), p. 33.

of mankind toward the eternal goal" (6/p. 26), of "the arch-eternal man issued from the mortal body of cultural man" (31/p. 148), of freedom and justice, "the two archetypal forces" (36/p. 254), "the archetypal instincts of the human instinct world" (37/p. 18).

But there are also expressions which are taken yet directly from the relativistic thought-and-language-style of the *Lebens-philosophie*. "Man is a ceaseless wanderer" (6/p. 24); for man "in the last analysis the highest goal is limitless abundance of life" (29/p. 70). This irrationalism glorifies sentiment at the cost of thinking, and hence also at the cost of morality. It is downright senseless "to sit in moral judgment upon an individual [Mary Stuart] who happens to be a prey to an overwhelming passion" (34/p. 223). The stream of life at times is also called destiny: "But it is the tendency of destiny to mold the life particularly of the great into tragic forms. It tests its powers on the strongest, steeply it pitches the paradox of events against their strength, interweaves their lifespan with mysterious allegories, obstructs their paths, in order to confirm them in the right action. How-ever, it plays with them an exalted game: because experience is always profit" (36/p. 11). The rhetoric about the game is re-vealing. It belongs to the relativistic aesthetization of history. It too is a disguise of impotence, of the enforced role of the spec-tator. Emil Ludwig revealed it most naively: "When the destinies of intrepid people begin to become confused the beauty of their aspect doubles" (10/p. 245).

The biographers ventured forth to conquer the kingdom of highest wisdom. They did not tarry for trifles — they aimed for the imperium of the intellect in which the riddles of history, time, nature, politics, morals, of life as such are solved. They returned with an herb and bottle collection. They feel as at home in the sphere of highest abstraction as the positivist in the realm of so-called facts. With them generalities supplant facts; they hurry from observation to observation gathering the most divergent generalizing statements from the well-known pastures of philoso-phy and the social sciences. Out of these phony facts, which nei-ther reflect empirical reality nor sketch its theoretical picture, a veil is woven which transforms history into a mythology of no

significance. Quite the opposite is true of the school of Stefan
George: in its esoteric cult of heroes and prophets there comes to
the fore a moment of social rootedness: the dedication to an objective canon of esthetic and moral taste. This school produced
luxurious "culture" articles of such a kind that it was acceptable to
an elite of social status or philosophical stature. It still fed on the
great heritage of middle-class ideology and was directed to and
fighting for stated goals, and could not be deterred from its original intent; it made its drive in the face of alternatives and knew
when to open and when to close a door. On the other hand, modern biography is indiscriminate because it is perplexed. As numerous as are its myths of universality, as casual are its delvings into
the reservoir of past human lives. As if anyone and everyone, gen-
erals, poets, chiefs of police, rulers, composers, inventors, and religious founders, were good enough to justify a consistency of the
individual in which one no longer believes. History and its contents become the occasion for world historical chatter; its banner
is a relativism which takes nothing seriously and which no longer
is taken seriously.

V

Paradoxically, this relativistic mentality of the biographers is also
present when they turn from perplexing generalities about the
individual as merely a variable of the pace of "history" to his
specificity and uniqueness. According to Hegel, the work of reason consisted in encasing the phenomena of nature and man in
adequate concepts by searching for precise and "determined
negation," i.e., the unequivocal designation of a phenomenon by
excluding all the moments which are neither generically nor
genuinely attached to it. The biographers, however, whose overt
business is the exact portrayal of the essence and activity of a
given human being, pervert Hegel's conceptual model into a
muddy stew where nothing and nobody is conceived in terms of
specific characteristics. True, at first sight the biographers seem
to pay the greatest honor to their subjects, and, alongside the
speculation about the general as the truly powerful, we find at
the same time the praise of the individual. Alongside a conviction

of the radical determinism of cosmic-historical laws and socio-logical rules, stands, in smooth and unobtrusive irreconcilability the hymn of individuality. But closer inspection reveals that the categories within which individual uniqueness is described are closely related to universal phrases which negate the autonomous nature of man. The hymn to the individual is a mere pretence, and reflects a convulsive attempt to conjure up a wish dream of the individual's autonomy and steadfastness. But this realm of freedom is deceptive, for the biographer handles the person in the same way that he handles events and objects, and under his fingers the individual is inflated into an artificial colossus. One browses through the index of a mail-order house which depends on a large turnover. Everything is the best and the most expen-sive, the opportunity of a lifetime. People are described as "unique" in terms of sameness, and everybody is marked by a pricetag and a sales plug making such outrageous claims that no single person in reality shows any specificity because the distinc-tion of uniqueness is conferred on all.

The outstanding quality of the "personality" merchandise (which turns out to be a mass article) is plugged by an indiscrimi-nate use of the superlative. Here are some examples:

Index of Superlatives

Barthou: "The most significant statesman of Europe" (5/p. 16).

Bismarck: "The two strongest German politicians of that epoch" (i.e., Bismarck and Lassalle) (9/p. 268).

Burckhardt: His "Greek cultural history, the most pro-found that we have on the Greeks" (12/p. 16 f.).

Calvin: "the darkest messenger of God in Europe" (4/p. 11).

Caesar: "The most sagacious Roman" (10/p. 49).

Cleopatra: "The shrewdest woman of her epoch" (10/p. 250).

Cosimo di Medici: "The mightiest man in civilian, non-military dress; the world's wealthiest banker" (23/p. 7).

Francis Drake: "one of the most ingenious of Magellan's heirs and successors" (33/p. 217).

Elizabeth of England: "this most remarkable of all women" (34/p. 457).

Erasmus: "the first — and really the only — German reformer" (37/p. 20).

Fouché: "the intellectual kind of all of this most remarkable of political beings" (32/p. 332); "the most perfect Machiavellian of modern times" (32/p. 10); "psychologically the most interesting person of his century" (32/p. 10); "the most accomplished intriguer of the political stage" (32/p. 29); "most unreliable character and most reliable diplomat" (32/p. 254).

Lloyd George: "most cunning, agile, and marvelous of contemporary statesmen" (13/p. 180).

Hindenburg: "most celebrated German soldier of the last epoch" (16/p. 9).

John Knox: "perhaps the most accomplished example of the religious fanatics" (34/p. 83).

Lenin: "the most sincere, yet at the same time the coldest fanatic of our epoch" (14/p. 96).

Leonardo da Vinci: "In abundance of faces, Leonardo remains unique" (14/p. 596).

Leopold of Belgium: "the only personality of first rank among all the crowned heads of Europe" (2/p. 215).

Ludendorff: "during the war the most interesting figure and the most dangerous" (16/p. 196).

Luther: "Of all ingenious men perhaps the most fanatical — the most indocile, unpliable, and discordant" (37/p. 190).

Magellan: "history's greatest seafarer" (33/p. 297); "the greatest deed of seafaring of all time" (33/p. 330).

Mary Stuart: Her deed, "perhaps the most perfect example of the crime of passion" (34/p. 259); "perhaps no woman who would have been sketched in such an irregular form" (34/p. 7).

Marie Antoinette: "one of the most beautiful" tragedies "of this undesired heroism" (35/p. 9).

Masaryk: "the great European man" (15/p. 8).

Mussolini: "in conversation the most natural man in the world" (19/p. 37).

Napoleon: "this foremost field commander of his time" (20/p. 171); "concerned for the smallest matters, because he wants the great" (20/p. 48); "the burning European youth finds no greater model of warning than he, whom, of all western men, created and suffered the greatest shocks" (20/p. 676).

Nietzsche: "the brightest genius of the intellect" (29/p. 243).

Plutarch: "the most modern of all portrait painters" (14/p. 11).

Rathenau: "as a critic of the times, after Nietzsche almost without competition"; of "the noblest taste" (14/p. 140).

Romain Rolland: "he will always be tied by his relation to the most powerful" (36/p. 28).

Stanley: "the clearest, most sensible example of a hero" (2/p. 95); "he accomplished the boldest and most successful reporting" (2/p. 85).

Freiherr vom Stein: "a German, the best whom the nation has produced in its fall and deliverance" (20/p. 403).

Talleyrand: "perfection of this life as the greatest achievement possible to man" (3/p. 347).

Tolstoi: "the most powerful . . . the mightiest of the Russian land" (30/p. 232); "the most human of all men" (30/p. 234); "the nineteenth century knows no counterpart of similar primeval vitality" (30/p. 242).

The index of greatness is at the same time an index of monads. Alienation hides behind a specificity which is no longer to be surpassed. The reification of man has been broken down into a roster of qualities on which this commodity, man, is being measured, and each then represents a particular kind of merchandise. What one happens to have in stock is offered as the incomparable. It is a travesty of the development of mankind.

This whole realm of the superlative is a wish dream of the free economy. For each one it is important to reach the summit of the pyramid; only when all competitors have been removed from the field has the highest imaginable goal for an individual existence been reached. The individualism of the superlative conveys the true social meaning of this view: individualism rests on the exclusiveness of possession of a quality.

The myths of earlier humanity express the dichotomy of the natural and the historical; the cliché-like myths which the biographers report of their darlings make of each man his own myth.

Relativism is only seldom the manifest belief of this literature — but it is always present in a latent form. It is presented as an arbitrary interchange between the general and the individual, thus making clear the function of relativism in late European liberalism: a cloak for the helplessness of the vanquished on the eve of the age of the "Leaders." The pace of world history, as well as the mythical shading of oversized individuals, do not join into one theory of man and his destiny. This biographical jungle amounts to an ideology of weariness and weakness; it is an ideology of tired epigoni who lost their way.

Bibliography

1. Heinrich Bauer, *Oliver Cromwell*, München/Berlin, 1937.
2. Ludwig Bauer, *Leopold der Ungeliebte*, Amsterdam, 1934.
3. Franz Blei, *Talleyrand*, Berlin, 1932.
4. Martin Gumpert, *Dunant*, New York/Toronto, 1938.
5. Wilhelm Herzog, *Barthou*, Zürich, 1938.
6. Hermann Kesser, *Beethoven der Europäer*, Zürich, 1937.
7. Hermann Kesten, *Ferdinand und Isabella*, Amsterdam, 1936.
8. Erich Kuttner, *Hans von Marées*, Zürich, 1937.
9. Emil Ludwig, *Bismarck*, Berlin, 1927.
10. Emil Ludwig, *Cleopatra*, Amsterdam, 1935.
11. Emil Ludwig, *Der Nil*, Amsterdam, 1935.
12. Emil Ludwig, *Die Kunst der Biographie*, Paris, 1936.
13. Emil Ludwig, *Führer Europas*, Amsterdam, 1935.
14. Emil Ludwig, *Genie und Charakter*, Berlin, 1925.
15. Emil Ludwig, *Gespräche mit Masaryk*, Amsterdam, 1935.
16. Emil Ludwig, *Hindenburg*, Amsterdam, 1935.
17. Emil Ludwig, *Kunst und Schicksal*, Berlin, 1927.
18. Emil Ludwig, *Lincoln*, Berlin, 1930.
19. Emil Ludwig, *Mussolinis Gespräche*, Berlin/Wien/Leipzig, 1932.
20. Emil Ludwig, *Napoleon*, Berlin, 1926.
21. Klaus Mann, *Symphonie Pathétique*, Amsterdam, 1935.
22. Valeriu Marcu, *Das grosse Kommando Scharnhorsts*, Leipzig, 1928.
23. Valeriu Marcu, *Machiavelli*, Amsterdam, 1937.
24. Walter von Molo, *Eugenio von Savoy*, Berlin, 1936.

25. Alfred Neumann, *Königin Christine von Schweden*, Amsterdam, 1936.

26. Franz Werfel, *Verdi*, Berlin/Wien/Leipzig, 1924.

27. Stefan Zweig, *Begegnung mit Menschen, Büchern, Städten;* Wien/Leipzig/Zürich, 1937.

28. Stefan Zweig, *Castello gegen Calvin*, Wien/Leipzig/Zürich, 1936.

29. Stefan Zweig, *Der Kampf mit dem Dämon*, Leipzig, 1925.

30. Stefan Zweig, *Drei Dichter ihres Lebens*, Leipzig, 1928.

31. Stefan Zweig, *Joseph Fouché*, Leipzig, 1929.

32. Stefan Zweig, *Drei Meister*, Leipzig, 1920.

33. Stefan Zweig, *Magellan*, Wien/Leipzig/Zürich, 1935.

34. Stefan Zweig, *Maria Stuart*, Wien/Leipzig/Zürich, 1935.

35. Stefan Zweig, *Marie Antoinette*, Leipzig, 1932.

36. Stefan Zweig, *Romain Rolland*, Frankfurt a. M., 1921.

37. Stefan Zweig, *Triumph und Tragik des Erasmus von Rotterdam*, Wien, 1935.

PART THREE

Industrial Society and Its Plight

The Rechtsstaat *as Magic Wall*

OTTO KIRCHHEIMER

I

I SHALL BEGIN with some remarks on the historical setting of the British Rule of Law and the German *Rechtsstaat.*[1] From there I shall proceed to show how these concepts have been transplanted and are still serviceable under conditions of present-day industrial society. Changes in the apparatus of government, and the substitution of executive and bureaucratic government for parliamentary government, bring about modifications of the rule of law without affecting the requirement that it serve the essential protective needs of the individual. The true yardsticks of legal devices, as of the regimes to which they belong, are their practices. It is the behavior of state officials, who along with their political elites are the creators and manipulators of institutions, that determines the effectiveness of available legal devices.

What types of claims is society willing to satisfy by putting legal machinery at everybody's disposal? How does society proceed when it is faced with the necessity of setting its course in uncharted or half-charted waters? What does it do with traditional formulas? Hide behind them, junk them, or try to adapt them to the purposes at hand?

A posthumous essay which the author intended for this volume but had not edited. The editors are grateful to Mrs. Anne Kirchheimer for submitting it and also wish to thank Fred Burin and John Herz for their editorial assistance.

[1] Speaking of Western countries, I treat "rule of law" here as a generic proposition. Its specific cases of historic application include Germany's *Rechtsstaat* and the British Rule of Law, which will be capitalized.

"*Ein Schelm gibt mehr als er hat.*" Questions are cheap and answers may be long in coming.

The career of concepts resembles that of established trade names. The good will attached to them is too precious, too much in the nature of mental first-aid kits, to be cast aside lightly. What matters then is to hold the gloss added by successive generations against the original text, thus helping them to analyze and provide for their own situation. But is there an original text in the concept of Rule of Law in Britain or the related German *Rechtsstaat?* I think that for all the differences in historical roots and particular legal traditions[2] their common denominator lies in the simple thought that the security of the individual is better served when specific claims can be addressed to institutions counting rules and permanency among their stock-in-trade than by reliance on transitory personal relations and situations. Beyond that, a good part of their common success probably lies in the mixture of implied promise and convenient vagueness. Who would not breathe more freely if told that the law can rule and that state and law may march hand in hand? Yet, rule may mean different things to different men. It may imply that the legal rule dominates the scene with a firm hand, but it may also mean an indefinite type of overlordship entrusting the actual running of things to those who minister to the needs of the customers. Such a state of affairs would leave the rules somehow in the position of the God of eighteenth-century deism, providing those in need with a certificate of correct origin, but little more. What is the nature of the law which rules or which, in the German version, enters into an indissoluble partnership with the state? What transformations does it experience in this union? If the state fathers the law, how and under what circumstances does it become a force of its own? Is it a center that directs or at least forms the conscience of the state? How much will rule-of-law concepts help us to answer these questions?

The British Rule of Law is a token of gratitude to a political success story. When formulated in 1885 by Dicey it connoted a safely established level of political civilization and a career of con-

[2] These differences are sharply emphasized in Ernst Fraenkel, *Das amerikanische Regierungssystem* (Köln and Opladen, 1960), pp. 196 – 200.

stitutionalism nearly 200 years old. Constitutional continuity is by
no means tantamount to social continuity. But the fact that the
political establishment did not snap out of order during the bitter
years of post-Napoleonic starvation and repression or during the
years of Chartist agitation lends some color to the asserted connection between the political success story and the constitutional
underpinning. What Dicey did was to fuse the timeless elements
of the story — the interest of all individuals to be hauled into court
only for specific breaches of law established by general propositions (Parliament) and under regular procedure — with the
particular concerns of a British Whig. Arbitrary power was thus
not only the policeman's knock on the door but also what we
might call the discretionary power of the administration to act in
the interest of public welfare. Conferring of such powers should
be maximally avoided and submitted to what Dicey, in a polemical
way and with a side glance at the contemporary French situation,
called "regular law courts."[3] Added to this was a somewhat
myopic view of the meaning of equality before the law. It had
nothing to do with the entry of new classes into the fold of the
community but instead was another paean to the virtues of middle-
class constitutionalism. The fact that a colonial governor, a secretary of state, or a military officer could be hailed into court like
any ordinary citizen was for Dicey both the necessary and sufficient content of legal equality. (This is not to deny that Dicey
was on firm ground when he established "equality before the
law" in the formal sense as an integral part of his Rule of Law.
What later generations criticized was the absence of any thought
that the formal concept of the Rule of Law would need to be
supplemented by an ever increasing body of legislative and cor-
relative administrative action.)

But where does this law come from? As common law it is the
judge's and his predecessors' own creation. As statute law it
originates in Parliament, formally omnipotent but which, as a corporate body, is thoroughly reasonable and "does not interfere
with the course of the law."[4] Dicey's *fin de siècle* formula mirrors

[3] See A. V. Dicey, *Introduction to the Study of the Law of the Constitution*, 7th ed. (London, 1908), p. 198.

[4] Dicey, *ibid.*, 10th ed., p. 415.

both the constitutional tradition and a social ambience. In the absence of a written constitution Parliament has a theoretical omnipotence which, given the careful doses of nineteenth-century enlargement of the franchise, raised few problems. To the extent that law was statute law, a "popularly revered judiciary,"[5] safely recruited from Oxbridge precincts, remained loyal to the emanations of Parliament. In case of need, however, the latter could be rendered harmless by a narrow interpretation of statutory intent.

In contrast to the placid career of the British Rule of Law throughout the nineteenth century, the German *Rechtsstaat* retained some elements of a snake charmer's performance, remaining an index of partly fulfilled and partly outstanding claims. How can a rising class, the bourgeoisie, gain entrance into the official setup without being able to make the requisite show of strength? In classical fashion, it will assert the universality of its demands. Thus, when the century was young, it protested against an eighteenth-century, police-state concept of individual freedom that would allow the state to busy itself with the personal happiness of the individual for which, according to Kant and Feuerbach, there was no general law. As long as the state apparatus was slated to stay in the hands of privileged groups, a *Rechtsstaat* concept featuring the state's limitation to legal purposes deriving from the moral freedom of the individual might provide the objective law which would miraculously bind ruler and ruled together in common observance. The *Rechtsstaat* idea might permeate the state apparatus and induce the state to observe as objective law what could not be postulated as subjective right.[6] A bureaucratic concept of duty might thus have to compensate for the absence of legally enforceable claims by individuals or groups. But what if the ruler were not willing to subscribe to the tenets of early constitutionalism? Kant could not find a right of revolution, though he would accommodate its results.[7]

When Bismarck undertook to fix the relations between army,

---

[5] *Ibid.*, p. 398.

[6] C. Welcker, *Letzte Gründe von Recht, Staat und Strafe* (Giessen, 1813), p. 95; see also L. Krieger, *The German Idea of Freedom* (Boston, 1957), p. 255.

[7] *Metaphysische Anfangsgründe der Rechtslehre*, par. 49a.

bureaucracy, and bourgeoisie, he did not hand over full legislative power to the bourgeoisie but rather conceived it as a unifying bond between relevant social forces. For the administration the legislative power circumscribed, as Gneist put it, the discretionary space within which it could continue to operate.[8] For the bourgeoisie it safeguarded its primordial role in the legislative machinery, jointly to be operated by the federal and state bureaucracies and itself. If Bismarck granted the bourgeoisie at best an indefinite share in what Gneist had called the Archimedean point of the *Rechtsstaat,* participation in local self-government,[9] he gave it its full share of legislative power. But at the same time he made the bourgeoisie uncomfortable by the introduction of universal suffrage which, in the words of its spokesman Gneist, "produces average opinions which cannot maintain the stability of legal principle."[10] The people at large, besides being admitted to the precincts of the *Reichstag,* became beneficiaries of a system of administration based on law (*Gesetzmässigkeit der Verwaltung*). Administrative action was subjected to legal scrutiny by courts, civil and administrative, whose members were somehow not completely integrated into either the bourgeoisie or the reigning regime but managed to maintain their own *esprit de corps.*

II

When the battle of concepts was again joined after the two world wars, the European political scene had changed. In the beginning of the century, practice had been concerned with supervision of a limited number of state functions and with the techniques of guaranteeing individual freedom and property. The more or less efficient carrying out of these tasks now made it quite evident that in a number of countries individual freedom was threatened more by those who controlled jobs and the necessities of life than by the official authorities of the day. Hence there arose increasing demands for positive governmental action, whether pertaining to town and country planning or health and welfare legislation.

[8] Rudolf von Gneist, *Der Rechtsstaat* (Berlin, 1873), p. 159.
[9] *Ibid.,* p. 160.
[10] *Ibid.,* p. 137.

These demands were facilitated by the fact that everywhere in the West the electoral franchise had become universal. The last remnants of more limited forms of representative government had by the end of World War I given way to political democracy. But the appearance on the parliamentary scene of mass parties committed to the speedy fulfillment of the above-mentioned welfare demands raised a new problem: how to relate the rule of law to the new output of the legislative body. Since the beginning of the twentieth century a practice, recognizable enough in its outlines even if not always tidily followed, had developed, requiring that general rules for identical case situations were to be issued by parliamentary legislation. Individual cases were to be dealt with by the administrative services on the basis of these statutory rules. Such cases were to be reviewed, upon application, by courts of law which scanned both the legal basis and, at least to some extent, the limits of discretion applied in administrative action. The criminal case and the civil claim continued to enjoy the benefit of direct access to the courts without need of prior administrative decision. Could the same general scheme which applied to the granting of professional licenses, building permits, etc., be transferred to the handling of an increasing body of legislation in the fields of city planning, health and welfare, agricultural subsidies, etc., which either conferred benefits on the individual or made some of his activities dependent on administrative agreement?

Attacks were now forthcoming in force, alleging that the extension of state activities to such an ever increasing number of fields was not compatible with the rule of law and would destroy its protective character. It was intimated that special legislation introducing numerous new administrative jurisdictions in the interest of a great variety of social and professional categories was incompatible with a concept of equality of law, which rested essentially on the existence of a body of common law to be uniformly applied by the judiciary to all groups. The French jurist Ripert had blazed the trail, and Swiss, Austrian, and Italian lawyers, economists, and social scientists followed suit.

Is not, for instance, legislation allowing the government to take away land for a compensation, fixed at prices substantially inferior to those prevailing on the free market, a violation of the rule of law?[11] This idea that the rule of law requires the state to restrict its activities to whatever is compatible with formal guarantees of legal equality, thus necessarily excluding the legislator from the welfare field, is a theorem which does not become more tenable by endless repetition. On the contrary, a more far-reaching measure of social equality, exemplified by some types of land legislation, while not required by the equality postulate of the rule of law, is in no way contradictory to it. Nobody will doubt the immense importance of land-use planning in densely settled areas after World War II. The almost uniform failure of the French, German, and Italian governments to deal comprehensively with the immense surplus profits accruing to proprietors of development land, and the consequent impossibility for the overwhelming majority of the population to acquire land of their own, has become one of the social characteristics of post-war Europe. Could it be seriously argued that the accident of physical proximity of land to urban agglomerations vests in the proprietor a right, attributable to the rule-of-law concept, to benefits toward which he has contributed nothing? In such cases remedial legislation, without doing violence to the concept of formal equality before the law, supplements it with a concept of social equality.

It has also been argued that any policy carrying out the substantive ideals of distributive justice must inevitably lead to the destruction of the rule of law as the impact of decisions becomes incalculable. Yet it is not intelligible why social-security rules cannot be as carefully framed, and the community burdens as well calculated, as rules concerning damage claims deriving from negligence actions. As to the chances of the foreseeability of results in yesterday's and today's social system, one might safely ask a French peasant of the 1960's whether he prefers the old-age pensions and government-fixed wheat prices of today or his grandfather's competitive freedom under Méline.

Such arguments are quite dated by now. More far-reaching contentions are made to uphold the link between economic liberalism and the rule of law. Doubts have been raised whether the law-making process by central authorities and the core of the

[11] See Bruno Leoni, *Freedom and the Law* (New York, 1961), p. 69.

rule of law are mutually compatible. Downgrading the importance of central legislation, according to this opinion, is justified
not only by the simultaneous prevalence of a free market economy and common law as the predominant source of law for private disputes in the nineteenth century, but also by the superiority
of economic over political choice. At the basis of the whole argument is mistrust of unwelcome majority decisions and an attempt
to seek refuge in the *fata morgana* of a society able to dispense
with intermediary public organizations, those mediating between
groups and between individuals and groups. A spontaneous law-
making process through voluntary cooperation of individuals as
loosely tied to each other as they were under the reign of the
trusted non-expert, the common-law judge, is recommended as
an alternative. But this is at best romanticism, at worst sheer evasion of the administrative tasks to be faced in order to make the
world a place worth living in for the majority of the population
in our age. One does not wish away the reality of the administrative state in mass society by reminiscing on the judges' social
role in bygone days.[12]

Economic liberalism's attacks on the compatibility of the rule
of law and collectivist forms of society are rearguard skirmishes.
The more intensively a particular state went through a period of
massive economic and social dislocation and the resultant abandoning of constitutionalism, the more urgent thereafter the insist-
ence that community planning for decent living not only has a
political priority, but constitutes a task postulated by the very
constitutional order. The *Rechtsstaat* is transformed into the *So-
zialrechtsstaat*. What previously might have been stated in purely
permissive terms may now become elevated to the dignity of a
constitutionally prescribed mission for the whole community.[13]

[12] R. Stevens, "Justiciability. The Restrictive Practices Court Reex-
amined," *Public Law*, 1961, p. 265, reports the astonished reaction of
English legal circles when judges were recently called upon to sit in implementation of the vague policy concepts of the 1956 Restrictive Trade
Practices Act. Their attitudes belie continued reliance on the judges as ex-
perts in non-expertise.

[13] Konrad Hesse, "Der Rechtsstaat in der Verfassungsordnung des
Grundgesetzes" in *Staatsverfassung und Kirchenordnung*, Smend Festgabe
(Tübingen, 1962), p. 78.

Thus legal protection is no longer only an appanage of conflicts concerning personal freedom and property titles. It becomes available for other claims to which the individual may be entitled in his various status capacities, whether this status derives from his own initiative or is a consequence of a merger of societal guidance and personal response. If social services may be produced for the purposes of mass consumption, the accompanying procedures guaranteeing these rights must be producible too.[14]

But the doubts expressed about the legislature's role in the rule-of-law scheme come not only from the ranks of those who deprecate the extension of community interest from commercial and penal codes to land speculation and social insurance. It is asserted that parliaments have for a long time been covering up for a job which in fact is being done by somebody else, namely the bureaucracy. Yet the relative weight given to the interest of the individuals in the forming of general rules does not depend on specific forms of representation. The individual's chances depend on organizational vigilance, multiplicity of points of access to respective decision-makers, and, closely connected, the existence of some form of intra-bureaucratic competition. Neither of these requirements is necessarily tied to the parliamentary institution, which, as experience has shown, is as prone to manipulation as any other body. Some of the rules formulated by the still powerful American legislature have been like bills of attainder, legislation as inequitable as decrees occasionally produced by de Gaulle's government.

There has been a merger of the authorities who make the general rules with those who apply them to the individual case. What about the possible dangers that application of rules may represent in the context of this administrative practice of post-parliamentary society? Is the individual ruling the citizen receives from an administrative office now more aleatory because the bureaucracy is likely to have had a decisive hand in forming the general rule thereafter applied to his case? Most countries provide a layer of isolation between the rule-making activity and the decision of individual cases — possibly as much in the interest of the effi-

[14] H. W. Jones, "The Rule of Law and the Welfare State," *Columbia Law Review,* 58 (1958), p. 155.

ciency of the establishment as in the asserted welfare of the customer or in deference to the doctrinal claims of the constitutional lawyer. They cannot rearrange the applicable categories each time to fit the particular purposes of the case. Even de Gaulle experienced resistance when he repeatedly reshuffled extraordinary military courts in order to obtain desirable policy results.[15]

Moreover, the substantive ends of justice require that the individual be able to make effective use of its procedural weapons. This has recently led to a remarkable diffusion of an institutional device originally domiciled in northern European countries, the Ombudsman. As supervisor-extraordinary in the interest of both the aggrieved citizen and administrative efficiency, he has been allowed to lift some of the veil of intra-bureaucratic case-handling[16] which a judge may only pierce with the heavy weapon of subpoena of documents and records. It may well be that the Ombudsman — as a non-formalized half-insider able to penetrate somewhat further into the mysteries of administrative discretion than a court bound by strict rules of evidence — will become a blessing for the little, organizationally unattached fellow pursuing a pension claim or chasing after a change-of-residence indemnity. To that extent he fills in for the member of parliament of old. For the petitioner, the certainty of a thorough examination is enhanced by exchanging a high-level parliamentary letter-carrier for a semi-detached bureaucratic representative; but the member of parliament by this token might lose his line of contact with the ordinary citizen.

Nevertheless the relative success of the Ombudsman — relative because only isolated success stories have been reported on inquiries of a more complicated nature pertaining to disputes involving larger socio-political complexes — brings only into sharper relief a large additional problem area. This area is exemplified by

15 See *Conseil d'état*, 19 octobre 1962, *Canal et autres*, and the remarks of François Mitterand in *Journal officiel* (Débats, Assemblée Nationale), 4 janvier 1963, p. 221.

16 The emphasis lies on "some." Intraoffice memos made in preparation of a case, even in the country where the institution originated, become available to the Ombudsman and his staff only after they have been placed into the permanent record, which is to say after the case has long been closed. Cf. N. Herlitz, "Publicity of Office Documents in Sweden," *Public Law*, 1958, pp. 50, 65.

pension or overtime claims of former employees where the social situation and the antecedent relations out of which the claim originated are relatively simple and clear-cut. This could explain why the rate of compliance with the respective judgments may be quite high, why in this type of case the legal determination of the claim and its realization (*Recht* and *Rechtsverwirklichung*) have a tendency to converge. The near certainty that many types of claims once established will in due course be satisfied makes it reasonable for many legal systems to take such great pains to build up foolproof procedures to establish claims. If adjudication of a claim is tantamount to final settlement, it is certainly worth the effort to equip the parties with the best available means to get to the decision stage. But does the assumption of a unity between law and its realization hold true in all cases? If it did, our job would be finished. For Rule of Law and *Rechtsstaat* would be truly identical with the availability of generous and impartial procedures for obtaining legal protection or pursuing legal claims. To what extent does this proposition hold true? Is the concept of the rule of law exhausted by the availability of legal redress?

III

In 1956, during the trial of the German Communist Party before the Constitutional Court, a discussion arose whether that party could claim a "right of resistance" against specific policies of the West German political leadership which in the Communist Party's opinion were violations of the Basic Law. In answering this line of argument, the reasoning of the court decision[17] insisted on the fundamental difference between what the court called an intact constitutional order, in which isolated violations of the Basic Law might happen, and an order in which the organs of the state show no respect at all for law and justice and therefore corrupt the constitution, the people, and the state as a whole. Only in the latter case, so argued the court, would legal remedies be of no use to the people, so that resistance might be justified.

From this dictum we might assume that a clear-cut dichotomy exists in the mind of the German court between good and bad

[17] Vol. 3, p. 737.

regimes. The good ones would provide effective and honest procedures of legal redress for any and all parties that might feel their position threatened by an abuse of public power. There is an implied premise that well-functioning means of legal redress, part of what we have recognized as the traditional armor of the rule of law, will always guarantee a balance between individual and public authority, thus arresting trends in a process of deterioration which would land the state in the "bad" column.

Is there such an easy way to sort out the good from the bad state? How does the problem of the "good" and the "bad" state present itself to the *homme situé*, the man trying to exist within the confines of modern society? Generally speaking, the state, "good" or "bad," remains an abstraction. People think in terms of subdivisions: politicians, tax collectors, welfare officers. Only in periods of turmoil does the day-to-day confrontation recede behind the expectations and fears directed toward larger entities. How do the men who constitute the state behave in the most acute and not infrequent situation when a break of continuity occurs and a new regime takes over?

For the officials or other dignitaries of the establishment, continuity, with its double sense of legal and social continuity, is the password. The first is elliptic and contains an element of necessary self-deception. The official is at one and the same time the witness to and the creator of this continuity. As a contemporary he watches the transition, the mixture of accidental or contrived emergency, of coercion and formal correctness, in the course of which the requirements theoretically set by the antecedent regime's constitutional documents are fulfilled. The official's continuing performance in his job constitutes the major certificate desired by the new regime to show that the fact of transition had all the hallmarks of regularity. The new regime thus hopes to earn the first credit toward transforming a shaky legality into legitimacy. Thus continuation in his job, immensely valuable for the incoming regime, both registers and by the same token creates the legality of the formal takeover. Yet the very nature of this transition also contains the official's absolution for his mode of acquiescence: passivity. Frequently the official in the exercise of his duties need not concern himself with the question of the legality of the regime. If he stopped running the trains or delivering the mail when the regime changes, he would be dubbed a partisan rather than an official. Insulation in correct jurisdictional grooves avoids such difficulties; yet the victims of extralegal violence that may accompany the changeover might still appeal to judicial official-dom, as did the bedraggled Prussian government after its ejection from office in 1932. But this appeal only proved that this particular government was not prepared to fight for its life. What could a judge do for a party unwilling to incur any risks in the service of its own cause? Its attitude only indicated that the cause was beyond rescue even before the chain of legality had snapped completely, and the case evaporated into thin air. Thus, when the chips are down, in the very process of maintaining or changing power the official must either join the fight, if there is anything or anybody to fight for, or, as he usually does, become a witness and passive but valuable co-creator of the new regime's legality.

But legality, whether representing true or barely contrived continuity, is a step, and no more than that, toward creating legitimacy. To behold legitimacy there must either be social continuity or the attractive promise of a new social system. This legitimacy is the business of the community as a whole, not only the official's. The official may have been instrumental in creating the penumbra of beneficial legality but, this job done, he steps back into the ranks and becomes a citizen, naive or skeptical, enthusiastic or matter-of-fact, reticent or correct, scheming against or joyfully participating in the regime. In contrast to the official, the citizen at large, unless he is one of the few declared partisans in politics, need not take a position at all, as nothing is asked of him but to continue to pay his taxes and give an occasional cheer from the sidelines. His act of registering events is steeped in ambiguity and less consequential than the official's behavior with its precedent-building quality. It is both these things at the same time, because the social continuity which the citizen's passivity helps to create could be endangered, lacerated, or cut through by many manifestly contrary acts.

If the regime engages in foreign wars and imperialist conquest, the legitimacy problem reaches new dimensions. The citizen's total identification with both internal and foreign policy, which hitherto might have been evaded, may now become inescapable. Unless the foe of the regime has made a clear-cut choice of rejecting the official ideology, the daily necessities that are seemingly unconnected with the larger purposes of the regime may take precedence. Alienated, he may continue the daily routine. Court opinions dealing with negative choices, naturally written only under a successor regime, are not a very reliable guide, especially if the judges themselves have to realign and rationalize their own record in this process. But at least they elucidate the dimensions of the problem and show that behind the neat differentiation between "good" and "bad" regimes there may lurk a number of additional problems. Complications arise from the fact that even "bad" regimes must run the mails and feed their citizens, in short, pursue the millions of transactions without which the civilized existence of millions of people would rapidly come to an end. The citizen who refuses to lend a hand separates himself not only from the regime, but perhaps also from his fellow citizens' intent to continue living as well.

Thus men's actions under any regime will have to be judged in the light of their own contribution. The record of the regime under which they serve establishes at best a rebuttable presumption as to their own behavior. There are few who will deny this truth when it concerns the record of what commonly is called a "bad" regime; indeed, much time has been spent in the courts of many a country to put the burden of a fallen regime on the broad shoulders of its principals if they are safely out of the way, thus by logical implication absolving all those acting in their and the regime's name. But the opposite contention is one which bears some additional inspection, i.e., that a regime which has some well established and well safeguarded channels for setting up general rules and universally accessible procedures to redress injustice is a perfect rule-of-law candidate.

There is no hard and fast line of separation between the formal remedies and the substantive goals of a social order. The availability of legal remedies for the citizens and the implantation of legal duties for the official world may, under favorable circumstances, lead to the attainment of individual or community goals. Whether available procedures are put in motion and whether legal rulings once obtained will be enforced or complied with has to be investigated for each category of cases. Without making

such an effort, a rule of law, resting only on the theoretical availability of legal remedies somehow resembles a modern house
whose glass wall, the major attraction for all visitors, already
stands, but whose wooden utility walls no one has so far bothered
to build.

From the fact that, in some cases, finding the law is almost
tantamount to executing its mandate, it is a big step to assuming
that such a situation must invariably prevail. Let me develop a
case whose interest centers not only on the psychology of the
players but on the intermeshing of many levels of participants.
Presumably all of them acted correctly within their understanding of the rules of the *Rechtsstaat* and yet never arrived at satisfactory results. What I have in mind are the antecedents of and
the 1965 German debate leading up to what in effect amounted to
a prorogation of the statute of limitations for National Socialist
murders. Official statements, as well as the course of the public
and parliamentary debate, have established beyond doubt that
until more than eight years after the Federal Republic was established no one in a responsible official position took the initiative
systematically to collect evidence and initiate proceedings against
the multitude of Nazi murderers. This does not mean that no one
against whom witnesses had preferred complaints, or whose anonymity was lifted by private or bureaucratic accident, was investigated and, if the evidence was sufficient, prosecuted by the
competent local authorities. But, as an official German report puts
it with unintentional irony — as if murder were something which
is only followed up upon specific complaints — "the survivors
were much too busy building up a new life to care to push criminal prosecutions in Germany."[18] As no agency coordinated these
individual local efforts, collected evidence, and systematically
searched through the mountains of documents dispersed over
many places at home and abroad, the outcome of these chance
proceedings was unsatisfactory. Of 12,882 persons indicted
between May 8, 1945, and January 1, 1964, only 5,445 were
convicted; 4,033 or 31.8% were acquitted, whereas the highest ac-

[18] *Die Verfolgung Nationalsozialistischer Straftaten im Gebiet der Bun-
desrepublik Deutschland seit 1945* (Bonn, Bundesjustizministerium, 1965),
p. 49.

quittal rate in German courts for all types of proceedings in the 1950's was 8.5%. The remaining persons were discharged without judicial proceedings.[19]

It is thus entirely clear that the German executive, administrative, and judicial authorities during the first decade of the new state did not perceive any connection between the *Rechtsstaat* concept and the need to look for ways of dealing effectively with the problem of the National Socialist murders. The relentless zeal which characterized the German federal government's handling of the reverse side of the Nazi criminal account, the energetic and successful pressure on the Western High Commissioners in 1951 for speedy release of war criminals sentenced by Western Occupation Courts, found no resonance in the field of settling accounts with Nazi murderers. It took eight years until in the wake of public pressure, following the revelations of the Ulm SS trial, the various federal and state administrations of justice founded an agency coordinating the collection of evidence and other documents. After another six years it became clear that the statute of limitations would run out before it became possible to start proceedings against all presumable participants in Nazi murder activities. Under the impact of new pressures from abroad, some of them mainly designed to embarrass the regime, the Bonn legislature then decided that the statute of limitations for murder, which had been presumed to have started running again in May 1945, would be deemed to have come into operation only in December 1949. Thus, sins of omission were followed by the sin of commission — depriving presumed, not yet adjudged, culprits of the mild type of protection which the statute of limitations furnishes against the abuse of bureaucratic routine and changing political pressures. Moreover, the new solution solves the problem as little as did the policy before 1958 of diffuse and hit-or-miss prosecution. Certainly the 750 proceedings, presently pending, with more than 7000 defendants which so far have not ripened into the trial stage, together with the new proceedings which may be opened in the next four years, would push the trials well into the 1970's. This not only would put a burden on the defendants called to task more than a quarter of a century after the incriminating acts, but also raises the question with what yardstick a new

[19] *Ibid.*, p. 43.

generation of judges, of jurors, and of the public, acting in a totally changed political situation, should measure the deeds of a
previous generation.

The whole episode shows that the *Rechtsstaat* concept can be
honored by scrupulous observation of all prescribed forms and
proceedings while its spirit is constantly violated by an unwillingness to initiate steps commensurate with the magnitude of the
problem at hand. In terms of the official rule books, the Law on
the Administration of Justice, and the Code of Criminal Procedure, every German authority was proceeding correctly within
its own jurisdiction. Many minor impediments to action (initial
remnants of the few Allied reservations on jurisdiction; partial
unavailability of records; access to records only under conditions
not in accord with the goals of inter-German or German foreign
policy, etc.) were allowed to stand in the way of facing the problem squarely, allowing it to be downgraded in this process to a
series of interminable individual cases. There is no discernible individual to whom responsibility can be assigned. Who is to be
blamed? The German Parliament, which in the 50's withstood
right-wing pressures to issue blanket amnesties for National Socialist crimes, but carefully refrained from checking up on the
positive performance of the bureaucracies involved? The political
and administrative heads of the federal and state ministries of justice who waited until 1958 to take the necessary coordinating
steps? The untold numbers of individual prosecutors and judges
who acted properly in terms of the cases before them, but never
transmitted doubts to their superiors nor aroused the public as to
the spotty and unsatisfactory results obtained?[20] They all acted
bureaucratically correctly in terms of their individual jobs and
yet eluded their responsibility when the occasion arose for showing that mass murder could be prosecuted in an administratively
and morally difficult situation, yet well within the safety margin
of the regime they were serving.

The example is instructive: not because it proves that the Federal Republic is not a *Rechtsstaat* — which obviously it does not —

[20] Admittedly, however, the very change of role of the German judicial
apparatus, from involvement in the legal politics of the National Socialist
regime to the handling of the latter's criminal legacy, made such an expectation largely illusory.

but rather because it shows that the implementation of the rule of law is a problematic affair and that the mere enumeration of available remedies and jurisdictions does not suffice. The case shows how compartmentalization of organizations, each of which acts correctly within its own jurisdiction, may lead to results which might satisfy the tactical needs of participants in the official game, but falls wide of the mark of what one might call a step toward solving the substantive problems involved. The German politicians, lawyers, and administrators must have been fully aware that buying four more years for initiating new criminal proceedings would take the spotlight off an unsatisfactory record while compounding old sins of omission by new iniquities. Quite probably a full parliamentary inquiry into the causes of failure, which, except for exculpatory arguments, were only evoked in the most cryptic terms, would have been more appropriate than the theorizing on the justifiability of proroguing the statute of limitations, a measure of which nobody knew the meaning in actual practice. An analysis of the shortcomings of case handling would have laid bare the need for a new approach to the problem of human dignity. Is the time of the subject at the unlimited disposal of the official, is it part of the suspect's preemptive punishment to be at the authority's disposal literally till his last judgment day? Or is an enforceable provision for "deliberate speed" part of the subject's inalienable legal rights? What comes to the fore, therefore, is the *Rechtsstaat's* need to strive for the attainment of substantive justice through procedures which are not liable to negate the very goal of the *Rechtsstaat* itself. The admixture of complementary elements of mass democracy and bureaucracy may create distortions at both ends.

IV

It is the title to glory of the *Rechtsstaat* and of the Rule of Law that remedies for all claims are provided. Implicit in the rule-of-law concept is the calculation that the mere availability of remedies will settle most claims out of court or enhance the chance of voluntary observation of the law, even though only a fraction of the offenders can ever be pursued. We ask more rarely whether a claim is always recognized where injury has been inflicted. Sup-

pose the injury has occurred in an area where the individual concerned has established no business or employment relations with
the agency involved. The jobholder who loses his employment
through mistaken withdrawal of his security clearance may have
avenues of redress; but the job seeker equipped with all necessary
professional qualifications who for security reasons is not permitted to pass beyond the interview stage never has a chance to
contest the report which deprives him of access to entire job
categories.[21]

Would it help in this connection if we introduced a differentiation separating the roles of the rule of law in conflicts involving
public law from those in private law? Recently an erstwhile official practitioner of international law has opined that the private
sphere is eminently related to courts, whereas law as a system allo-
cating public power is by no means the creation of judges and
courts. If judges go beyond the limits in which they can effectively exercise power, the result will be evasion rather than vindication of legal authority.[22] The statement reflects experience in a
field where the discrepancy between existing norms (above all,
art. 2, par. 4, art. 51, and art. 53 of the United Nations Charter)
and the unwillingness of the major powers to comply with these
norms makes it problematic how far the rule of law extends into
the field of major power relations. Increasingly we meet attempts
to deny that the rules in question are legally applicable to a specific situation or to reconstruct the meaning of the concept of
compliance. In the place of judging a state's willingness to comply
with a legal norm, it is now proposed that we consider compliance as a "spectrum, . . . a matter of degree varying with the
circumstances of the case."[23] But such an approach confounds the
job of the lawyer with that of the sociologist. The latter may try
to determine under what circumstances a rule is enforced or meets
with resistance. The lawyer, however, cannot turn doubts and

[21] For the most recent discussion of this problem, see J. Rottmann's review of H. U. Evers, *Verfassungsschutz im Rechtsstaat* (Tübingen, 1961) in
Archiv für öffentliches Recht, 88 (1964), pp. 227 – 244.

[22] A. Chayes, "A Common Lawyer Looks at International Law," *Harvard
Law Review*, 78 (1965), pp. 1396 – 1413.

[23] L. Gross, "Problems of International Adjudication and Compliance
with International Law," *American Journal of International Law*, 59 (1965),
p. 56.

considerations antedating his opinion into some sort of statement like the following: "Because of original doubts as to whether my country is acting in self-defense or committing an act of aggression, I am recommending the landing of a limited troop contingent only." Limited or unlimited troop commitment, his country either acted in self-defense or committed an act of aggression, i.e., if the problem is considered as a proposition of law, the action can only be classified as either aggression or self-defense, compliance with or violation of the rules of international law.

In so far as the rule of law enters international relations, it exists only at the sufferance of the major power holders and to the extent that the latter find it advantageous to submit to its working. Given the ever increasing importance of interpersonal and interorganizational exchanges on an interstate level, the absence of enforceable rules governing the behavior of the most powerful territorial units is fraught with the danger of a constant spillover into other fields. But while the spillover from international relations into the domestic field may be a constant threat in our times, it has relatively little to do with a differentiation between an acceptable rule of law for private violations and its unacceptability for the public sector.

Our world knows no magic wall separating the structure of private from that of public law. Non-justiciability in the one sphere can easily spill over into the other. Witness the situation already mentioned concerning the activities of agencies protecting the security of the state. If anyone is in public business, then these agencies are; yet they interfere with the chances for a private life of untold multitudes of people. Or take the matter of race relations, where the finding of meaningful solutions has become a matter of critical public concern and where one of the major difficulties lies in the permanent intermingling of public objectives and private decisions. The effectiveness of new state or federal policies is frequently predicated on a great variety of attitudes of private persons: the behavior of labor unions toward opening equal employment opportunities; the reaction of real-estate interests and their customers to fair housing regulations; or the degree of willingness of negro parents to submit their children to the tormenting experience of serving as guinea pigs for integration. Are the busloads of SNCC students traveling south engaged in a private trip? What then about the reception they will receive from the local sheriff? Or do we have to await how the sheriff's actions will be characterized, first in the state courts and then in the federal courts? Semantics may help to rationalize a court decision one way or another, though to harmonize federal decisions and those of southern states is beyond human ingenuity. But one interesting observation can be made: the (until recently) official U.S. practitioner of international law would call "public" the area from which he wanted the courts to be excluded, whereas in the realm of race relations the argument would go the other way. The U.S. Supreme Court rationalizes the right to interfere with a certain institution by referring to its public character, while it calls private relations those areas in which it does not feel entitled to interfere. The private-public dichotomy is thus largely a matter of the different manipulative concerns of various agencies. It offers no clue to the problem of which relationships should be left to private arrangements and what form necessary cooperative arrangements should take.

One can hide the magnitude of the enforcement problem as one of the touchstones of the rule of law, as, e.g., in Llewellyn's variant of legal realism. Only those legal rules may then be considered meaningful which involve solutions acceptable to major forces in the community. From this viewpoint, few enforcement problems are likely to arise. First, lawmakers are psychologically conditioned to issue norms compatible with the wishes of major clienteles; and secondly, if the lawmakers have somehow failed to take such ground rules into account (the motto being "where reason stops, there stops the enacted rule"), the duty of restrictive interpretation takes over.[24] As Llewellyn puts it, "even the machinery of the rightest of right *jus* is subject to limitations of human inventiveness."[25] In other words, few occasions arise for conflict between the will of the legislator and grass-roots obedience to his mandate, because the intermediate level of interpreters takes care of accommodation and excludes what to the legal realist must be "meaningless" conflicts. No doubt this has happened often enough.

[24] See K. N. Llewellyn, *Jurisprudence* (Chicago, 1962), p. 228.
[25] *Ibid.*, p. 486.

One might even add the numerous cases where the legislator is of such uncertain or divided mind that the called-for interpreter, be he judge or, as is more frequent, administrative agency, will have full freedom to evolve substantive decisions of his own with only a minimum of legislative guidelines.[26]

Yet legislative efforts, sometimes braced up by the executive, are not always uncertain about what they want to achieve, nor do judges invariably function as harmonizers or eternalizers of the existing group equilibrium. In other words, there may be situations where the question of enforcement of a definite policy may be inescapable. This was the case, for instance, in the United States in World War II when the Office of Price Administration was set up to ration all scarce but essential commodities. They were to be distributed fairly among customers at prices within inflation-preventing ranges. The allocation part of the system somehow worked. The number of commodities available outside rationed channels was curtailed, but not to the extent that the ethically relevant part of the goal, equality of sacrifice, could be sufficiently realized. Enough commodities, like gasoline or meat, moving in parallel channels, remained available for those willing and able to pay. Yet, the risk of suspension orders, injunctions, civil-damage suits, and to a very minor degree fines was reflected in premiums of various sorts. Now one might say, in the fashion of legal realism, that the authorities had neglected to calculate the magnitude of organized pressures against the system, which were simply too great to allow for anything but hit-or-miss enforcement.[27] Thus, in the nature of things, people would understand that punishment, i.e., prison sentences, remained mostly reserved for those in the business of counterfeiting ration coupons, while all other visitations by the authorities were simply reflected in the size of the risk premium.[28]

[26] Cf. M. Edelman, *The Symbolic Uses of Politics* (Urbana, 1964), ch. 3.

[27] Whole regional production lines, like Del-Mar poultry or Southern lumber, worked outside the system. See H. C. Mansfield, *A Short History of the OPA* (Washington, 1948), p. 257.

[28] M. B. Clinard, *The Black Market* (New York, 1952) reports that 88% of a sample of businessmen in 1945 simply did not understand the difference between criminal fines and payments which had to be made as the result of triple damage suits (p. 235), and quite justifiably so, since this was all included in the same risk premium.

The OPA case shows that the enforcement of legal sanctions is anything but automatic, even though in contrast to the German case it involved routine problems of a continuing political and social order — sanctions destined to keep goods out of undesirable channels and to further a reasonable price level and patriotic morale. Yet, enforcement not only presented the difficulty that businessmen against whom measures were to be taken were organized, in close contact, and therefore never broke ranks to help the prosecution; but the potentially much more numerous supporters of enforcement policy, the consumers at large, neither had an organization to speak of nor many voices to represent them in public. The outcome of the individual enforcement skirmishes may have been unpredictable. Trade associations, more often than not helped along by politicians, joined issue with the OPA staff. The latter was itself frequently split according to whether the division in question was more interested in the survival of the organization, with its important allocation function,[29] or in attempts to implement policies aimed at equality of sacrifice. If a conscious choice had ever been made, it would have been between symbolic enforcement as part of an educational bargaining drive and effective enforcement to obtain the goal of equality of sacrifice. Circumstances helped to avoid such a clear-cut choice. In essence, both sides, the government and the consumer, carried part of their points, because the concatenation of propaganda, compromise, and symbolic enforcement — and still more the reality of ample profits through a guaranteed mass market rather than through inflationary prices — kept price rises in bounds. And the chiseler won, in that attempts at enforcement, such as they were, were never able to stamp out the market in parallel-risk premiums. Seen from the viewpoint of legal organization and the rule of law, the outcome was at best dubious, for neither the substantive goal of equal sacrifice nor evenhandedness in enforcement procedure made a particularly strong showing. It demonstrates the difficulty of harnessing the legal system to the pursuit of nationally approved goals in the face of concerted resistance by major organizations in the Establishment.

The situations in law enforcement are too multifarious for even

[29] See V. A. Thompson, *The Regulatory Process in OPA Rationing* (New York, 1950).

a rudimentary attempt to catalogue them. Visualized as a continuum, at one end there would be adjudicated individual claims
for wages or damages — reinstatement claims of employees being
quite a different matter — deriving from contractual relations. At
the opposite end would lie situations such as that presented in
Korematsu v. *U.S.*, the case of Japanese exclusion during World
War II.[30] Here the government, by expelling citizens from their
homes and places of work and sending them into camps because
of their Japanese ancestry, committed direct and acute injury;
but the courts in trying to remedy the situation might have run
head-on into difficulties in enforcing their judgment against the
executive. They thus had to choose between covering up the impotence of the law by adducing a special war-time jurisdictional
scheme allowing security questions to be decided by the military
without outside interference; and — as done in Justice Jackson's
well-known dissent — establishing a dichotomy between the judicial power, which applies the law and the Constitution and must
judge accordingly, and the military power, telling the people at
the same time not to rely on the exercise of judicial power in such
circumstances.

A judgment first and above all renders a decision on the concrete situation which has been presented. To that extent the
administration as well as the private litigant must fashion their attitude so as to bring themselves into line with the specific order of
the court. But higher courts do not make their decisions merely
with regard to the particular case before them. They may want
to give directives to future actors in only partly charted fields or
to weed out malpractices not in conformity with their notions of
applicable law or constitutional rule. To what extent will they
succeed? A look at wiretapping, search and seizure, and utilization
of illegally obtained confessions, gives rise to the following observations.

Courts have no direct supervisory power over the police — federal, state, or local — except in relation to the individual case
under review. From the viewpoint of the administrator their decisions serve therefore primarily to introduce a new element of risk.
Politicians can be expected to make declarations showing defer-

[30] 323 U.S. 214 (1944).

ence to the court; yet in the absence of continuous organized political pressure the situation in the case directly under review will differ from the sum total of the practice falling under related headings. In the particular case under review, the Supreme Court in nine cases out of ten may be able to see its mandate through, even if the instrument through which it has to work is as unpromising as a state court in the deep South. But in later cases the lower courts, if they feel the urge or are exposed to sufficient pressure, may exercise the fine art of distinguishing some elements justifying a different outcome and, at the very best, requiring time-consuming new litigation in the higher courts. On the other hand, however, lower courts may also get tired of shielding police practices against criticism by higher courts that might possibly reflect a large segment of public opinion. In any case, from then on the administrators will have to face increased risks against which even legislative support is not invariably a permanent help.

Conformity of administrative practices with rules emanating from lawmakers and bodies interpreting the law has not the same meaning for administrative and judicial organizations. For the administrative organization, conformity to the law is one factor among many in its calculations. To obtain such conformity is essential, however, for courts, whose very impact is predicated on the community's willingness to abide by the rules set by courts. On the other hand, the fact that the courts are outside bodies which do not stand to the administration in a relationship of hierarchical superiority enhances the numerous factors of uncertainty in their relations to each other.

The facile idea that the availability of procedure for making claims or upholding the public order is tantamount to guaranteeing that these rules are effectively observed or put to work has little to recommend itself. Wherein then lie the benefits derived from rule-of-law concepts and from the institutions to which they correspond? For both procedural and substantive goals, rule-of-law concepts are best understood as yardsticks for performance. They connote law as observed regularities. Where the route is charted, and only there, there is a great advantage to drawing up formulas to be applied to both the object and the subject of power situations. The sheer need to avoid the eruption of chaos among the ever increasing masses of population, as much as the unheard-of increase in the productive capacity of the advanced nations, puts a premium on satisfying the expanding needs of such multitudes. The efficient handling of the host of recurring problems which make up their daily existence, pertaining to job conditions, living quarters, health arrangements, and the easy translatability of such typical needs into corresponding money equivalents, makes the operations involved smooth and calculable — up to a point. To the extent that the rule of law furthers these ends, it contributes elements of personal security and even of substantive justice. It may well be, however, that the historian of the twentieth century will be less impressed by diverse propagandistic claims of various regimes as to the reign of law under their dominion than with the close cohabitation between wide stretches of certainty for mass man's daily living conditions with unheard-of areas of oppression, lawlessness, and rewards for maximum aggressiveness. A generation which has lived through Auschwitz and Hiroshima and was indifferent or powerless to prevent them, and which is prepared to see bigger Hiroshimas, has no cause for complacency about its preservation or even enlargement of some orderly forms of living. It may have forgotten the essential: there must be life for life to be worth living.

Revolution from Above:
Some Notes on the Decision to Collectivize Soviet Agriculture

E. H. CARR

THE DECISION taken at the end of 1929 to proceed to the mass collectivization of Soviet agriculture was probably the most significant, and certainly the most revolutionary, decision taken by the regime in the first fifty years of its existence. Yet the way in which it was taken has always been something of a puzzle. Pronouncements of party leaders up to that time had given no reason to expect so far-reaching a measure. It was followed by disastrous consequences which had clearly not been foreseen and which for some years altogether nullified its advantages. Granted that we now approach the problem with the benefit of hindsight, it remains a matter of legitimate speculation why this drastic solution was so precipitately adopted.

Party Doctrine

Many writers[1] have suggested that ideology may have been responsible for driving the Soviet leaders into action inappropriate to the situation which confronted them. Marx undoubtedly believed in the efficiency of large-scale collective organization for agriculture as for industry; and he held that the peasant would eventually be obliged to abandon his reactionary role as a petty proprietor and enter the ranks of the proletariat. But he evidently regarded this not as something to be enforced on the peasant, but

[1] D. Mitrany, *Marx against the Peasant*, *passim*; A. Nove in *Soviet Studies*, April 1959, p. 386.

as a natural corollary of the revolutionary process. Engels, after Marx's death, in his pamphlet on *The Peasant Question in France and Germany*, explicitly ruled out the idea of "expropriating the small peasants [as opposed to the large landowners] by force, with or without compensation":

> Our task in relation to the small peasants will consist, first and foremost, in converting their private production and private ownership into collective production and ownership — not, however, by forcible means but by example and by offering social aid for this purpose.

This very specific passage was more than once quoted by Lenin both before and after the revolution, and was familiar to every Bolshevik. Even at the eighth party congress, held at the height of the civil war in March 1919, at which Lenin remarked that "we have been, are, and shall be in a state of direct civil war with the *kulaks*," he deplored the fact that blows intended for *kulaks* had sometimes fallen on middle peasants; and the resolution of the congress, drafted by Lenin, firmly enunciated the principle of non-violence in regard to the middle peasant:

> In encouraging associations of every kind, and also agricultural communes, of middle peasants, the representatives of the Soviet power should not permit the slightest compulsion in founding such bodies. . . . Those representatives of the Soviet power who allow themselves to apply not merely direct, but even indirect, compulsion in order to attach peasants to communes, should be held strictly accountable and removed from work in the countryside.

Throughout the middle nineteen-twenties, collectivization remained in the party programme, but as a distant and unrealizable goal; even Molotov is on record as referring in 1925[2] to "poor peasant illusions about the collectivization of the broad peasant masses." The opposition platform of September 1927 put forward, without special emphasis and without any hint of the use of force, its routine demand for a gradual advance towards a socialized agriculture.

With the turn to the Left at the end of 1927, more talk was

2 *Pravda*, May 9, 1925.

heard of collectivization, and the fifteenth party congress in December 1927 proclaimed "an offensive against the *kulak*." But this did not imply any intention to use force. When a foreign delegate asked Stalin in November 1927 how he hoped "to realize collectivism in the peasant question," he spoke of "measures of an economic, financial and cultural-political character," and concluded: "things are moving in that direction, but have not yet got, and will not soon get, so far." At the congress Stalin attacked "those comrades [presumably members of the opposition] who think it possible and necessary to finish with the *kulaks* by administrative measures, through the GPU"; and Molotov, explaining that the party was still faithful to NEP, went on:

> The affair can proceed only by way of the gradual development of large collective farms. . . . We can permit of no illusions, no coercion in regard to the peasantry in the transition to large-scale farming.

Even after the grain crisis of the first months of 1928 (see below), no thought of mass collectivization by force entered the mind even of the most ambitious planners. The framers of the first five-year plan, drafted in the autumn of 1928, made what were thought to be optimistic prognostications of the advance of the "socialized sector of agriculture," but frankly admitted that "we should deceive ourselves if we claimed that the socialized sector, in the dimensions in which it will exist at the end of the five-year period, will enable us to neglect the production which will be brought to the market by groups of middle peasants." *Pravda* on November 2, 1928, denounced "ignorant attempts to solve the complex question of the conquest of capitalist elements in the countryside by administrative measures," and as late as June 2, 1929, demanded in a banner headline "Neither terror nor dekulakization, but a socialist offensive along the paths of NEP." At the sixteenth party conference in April 1929 a sharp controversy occurred on the question whether to admit *kulaks* to the kolkhozy. If admitted, they might dominate and pervert the kolkhoz; if excluded, they would remain as independent producers in competition with the kolkhozy. No alternative was envisaged. A commentator in *Bol'shevik* remarked ironically: "We have heard no proposals to drive the *kulak* off the land, or to send him packing to desert frontier regions or to an uninhabited island." The aim of Soviet policy, Kalinin told the fifth union congress of Soviets in May 1929, was not only to promote collective agriculture, but to improve "the individual poor and middle peasant economy."[3]

Whatever prompted the decision abruptly taken in December 1929, nobody seriously contemplated it six months earlier or thought of it as required by party doctrine. It was only in December 1929 that Stalin tried to explain away the famous passage from Engels on the ground that it was written under a regime of private property in land; he did not mention Lenin's, or his own earlier, pronouncements on the subject. Marxist dogma favoured collectivization in principle. But it would be far-fetched to suggest that it was dogma which drove the politicians to act as they did.

Industrialization

Industrialization did not become an issue till 1925, when pre-war levels had been regained and most existing factories and machines brought back into production. The question of the rate of further expansion now became acute. 1926 was the year of the inception of Dnieprostroi, and 1927 of the Stalingrad tractor factory. Preobrazhensky had demonstrated in his famous article on "primitive socialist accumulation" at the end of 1924 that expansion could be financed only by extracting "surpluses" from the peasant; and, though this did not become official doctrine till 1928 (when Stalin spoke of exacting "tribute" from the peasantry), it was not seriously refuted. But in 1925–1926 it was assumed that industrialization would proceed at a pace which would not place too great a strain on the peasant, and that emphasis would fall on the production of consumer goods for the peasant market. Dzerzhinsky, who was president of Vesenkha till his death in July 1926, strongly upheld these principles, and Pyatakov, who wanted more intensive industrialization, was dismissed. An important factor was the international crisis and the war scare of the spring and

[3] *Bol'shevik*, No. 11, June 18, 1929, p. 345; 5 *S"ezd Sovetov SSSR* (1929), No. 15, p. 3.

summer of 1927 (disaster in China, breaking-off of relations by Great Britain), which focused attention on the need for rapid industrialization and for emphasis on the heavy capital industries which were the basis of military strength. From 1927 onwards industrialization was the over-riding official aim. It was affirmed by the fifteenth party congress in December 1927, and led to the rift with the Right wing in the party (Bukharin) in 1928–1929. The views of the Right, as Mr. Barrington Moore has remarked, "strongly resembled the gradualist views of western social-democracy";[4] and this doubtless explains the favour commonly shown to Bukharin by western writers. At a moment when the survival of the revolution seemed to be in jeopardy both from "capitalist" intervention from without and from the growing strength of "capitalist" elements in the economy, such a policy was unlikely to find acceptance. It was recalled that Bukharin had once in an incautious moment spoken of "snail's pace industrialization." This was now out of date. Nothing would suffice but intensive industrialization at all costs — even the cost of maximum pressure on the peasant (and on the industrial worker). Meanwhile every problem was aggravated by the growing imbalance between industry and agriculture. The value of the output of industry increased by 34.2 per cent in 1926, by 13.3 per cent in 1927, and 19 per cent in 1928; the corresponding figures for the output of agriculture were 7.5, 2.5, and 2.5 per cent (it actually fell by 2.4 per cent in 1929).[5] The facts were worse than these figures indicated; for the proportion of wheat and rye, the principal food crops, in the total output, and the proportion of these crops brought to the market, were both declining. While industry raced ahead, agriculture was not advancing fast enough even to take account of the basic needs of a rising population.

State v. Private Capital

While, however, much can be said for treating collectivization as a by-product or necessary condition of industrialization, this is not the whole story. NEP was a compromise between nationalized industry and individual peasant farming, between state control

[4] Barrington Moore, *Soviet Politics* (1950), p. 103.
[5] *Narodnoe khozyaistvo SSSR v 1958 godu* (1959), pp. 135, 351.

and a market economy based on the survival of private capital. It represented a balance of forces in which the revolution had carried the towns and factories and the urban proletariat, and had failed to carry the peasant countryside. Nobody expected the compromise to last for ever; the scissors crisis of 1923 and the persistent battle between controlled and "free" prices were symptoms of the intensity of the underlying struggle. Either the nationalized industry through the medium of planning would succeed in subordinating the peasant economy to itself and integrating it into a centrally planned and centrally controlled system; or peasant resistance would prove impregnable and would compel state industry to operate within the framework of a market economy in which even existing forms of control (e.g. the monopoly of foreign trade) might be progressively modified or dismantled.

If we free ourselves from the hindsight conferred by knowledge of the sequel, we can see that in the middle nineteen-twenties the issue was still open. In 1924 Zinoviev coined the slogan "Face to the Countryside"; and, when in 1925 Bukharin issued the injunction "Enrich yourselves" to "all the peasants," the phrase was disowned, but not the policy. Removal of controls (e.g. on the leasing of land and the hiring of labour) favoured the well-to-do and efficient peasant, exactly as the Stolypin reform had done; its logic was the creation of small rural capitalists. This policy was repeatedly challenged by the opposition, which Zinoviev had now joined; the so-called "declaration of the 83" of May 1927 alleged that the "real danger" to the regime now came from the *kulak* "under the brand-name of the economically strong peasant." As Trotsky put it, "the wager on the *capitalist farmer* (the European or Americanized *kulak*)" might well yield fruits, but they would be "capitalist fruits which at no distant stage will lead to the political downfall of the Soviet power."[6] This was the policy which was supported by the "expert" advisers of Narkomfin and Narkomzem, most of them pre-revolutionary professors or officials. These fell into two groups. The liberal-bourgeois group (Kondratiev, Litoshenko) sought to encourage investment in agriculture, as the sector of the economy likely to yield most rapid returns, rather than in heavy industry, to remove restric-

[6] *Byulleten' Oppozitsii* (Paris), No. 1–2, July 1929, p. 22.

tions designed to favour or protect the poor peasant, and to restore as much as possible of a free market economy; this would promote maximum production by the most efficient peasants. The neo-narodnik group (Chayanov, Chelintsev, Makarov) was against the *kulak* or the small rural capitalist, and in principle supported equalization of holdings, but believed that the small peasant farm was the only sound basis for agriculture, and resisted any policy designed to create large-scale units of cultivation. Both groups were united in their opposition to measures of state control and to collective forms of agriculture promoted by official action. These groups were put out of action early in 1928. Bukharin, when he took up the campaign against pressure on the peasant, followed a recognizably similar course, and, though he never made a clear choice between "liberal" and "neo-narodnik" lines of approach, and was stronger on the negative than on the positive side, was discredited by his association with these heretical doctrines. In this welter of opinion the need for some kind of action was apparent; and any action involved coming down on one side of the fence or the other.

The Battle of the Grain

The crisis occurred in the winter of 1927–1928, simultaneously with acceptance of the policy of rapid industrialization, and for reasons in part independent of it. The harvests of 1925 and 1926 were good. The official grain collections proceeded satisfactorily, and the needs of government, cities, and factories were met. Numerous private traders still operated in grain, but in relatively small amounts, and at prices not much higher than the official prices. It was assumed that better organization would make the official collections still more efficient and that the private trader would be gradually squeezed out. Some food shortages in the cities in the early summer of 1927 were attributed to increased consumption or to hoarding rather than to difficulties of supply. But another good harvest in 1927 (only slightly below the bumper harvest of 1926) underlined the deep-seated character of the difficulties. In the autumn shortages became chronic; the grain collections fell off catastrophically; and the opposition, now in the last stages of open activity, made capital out of the failure of the policy of support for the well-to-do peasant, *alias* the *kulak*. The two main elements in the problem were soon apparent, and were somewhat guardedly discussed at the fifteenth party congress in December 1927 (which expelled the opposition from the party).

In the first place the productivity of Soviet agriculture was too low; tables were circulated at this time showing how far it lagged behind that of the rest of Europe and of the Americas. It was difficult to think of raising productivity by mechanization or by scientific methods of farming unless the existing "fragmentation" of the land — its division among 25 million small peasant *dvors* — could be overcome. This could theoretically be achieved in two ways — by encouraging the "strong" peasant to acquire more land and more control of the tools of production (the "capitalist" solution), or by collective organization of agriculture (the "social-ist" solution). Secondly, the "marketability" (tovarnost') of the crop was too low. Of the 1926 harvest only 16.9 per cent was marketed, i.e., became available to feed the urban population, against a pre-war figure of 24 per cent. This was also the result of having too many too small holdings; it was the peasant who held most land and most machines who, like the former land-owner, brought most grain to the market. But in the grain col-lections of 1927–1928 a new and disturbing factor appeared. After the third good harvest in succession, the most efficient and well-to-do peasants, having complied with Bukharin's injunction "Enrichissez-vous," were more prosperous than at any time since the revolution. They had not only stocks of grain, but money; and, owing to the emphasis on capital goods production, the con-sumer goods on which the money might have been spent were in chronically short supply. With memories of past inflation they preferred to use money to pay their taxes and to hoard their grain; official grain prices were low, and they reasonably calculated that they could gain by waiting. The grain collections for November and December 1927 were only half those of the previous year.

Once the party congress was over, the gravity of the situation was realized, and the party leaders were seized with panic. Early in January 1928 an instruction was sent to party organizations everywhere to bring in the grain at any cost. The leaders themselves toured key regions; Stalin went to Siberia – the only such mission undertaken by him after Lenin's death. What were called "extraordinary measures" were applied. These included forced loans, "self-taxation," prosecutions under an article of the code imposing penalties for concealment of grain, allocation of quotas, and more or less open requisition, though any analogy with the methods of war communism was vigorously denied by the authorities, and some of the things done were afterwards described as abuses. It was proof of the large stocks of grain in peasant hands at this time that these methods were for the moment entirely successful. The grain collections of January – March 1928 were far in excess of any corresponding period, and wiped out the large deficits of the previous six months. When the agricultural year ended on June 30, 1928, the grain collections fell only a little below the total of 1926 – 1927, and the collections of wheat and rye (the main food crops) equalled it. But the costs were heavy. The peasants had been stripped of their reserves, so that the operation could never be repeated; few managed to keep more than was barely necessary to carry them through to the next harvest; some went hungry, or had to kill their animals. The operation was a declaration of war against the *kulak*,[7] who would henceforth fight the authorities by any means in his power. Moreover the blows had fallen on many who could not by any stretch of imagination be called *kulaks* – on middle peasants, on anyone who had some reserve of grain. On the other side, the authorities drew the short-sighted conclusion that strong-arm methods paid. This episode, more than any other single event, set in motion the process which ended in collectivization. It was a decisive turning-point.

In 1928 – 1929 a marked decline for the first time occurred in the sowings of wheat and rye, presumably owing to the reluctance of the well-to-do peasant to grow surpluses which were liable to confiscation. The prospects of the grain collections were

---

[7] No satisfactory definition of a *kulak* could be found, and the word was applied as a term of propaganda to any peasant holding, or believed to hold, grain surplus to his immediate requirements. Estimates of the total number of *kulaks*, and of the proportion of grain delivered by *kulaks* and middle peasants, vary widely and become almost meaningless.

The Critical Spirit

grim. Violent arguments were exchanged at the party central committee; and against the view of Stalin (who seems to have been converted to a tough line by his Siberian trip) it was decided in July 1928 to raise official grain prices by 10–15 per cent. The harvest was patchy — poor in the Ukraine and the northern Caucasus (important rye and wheat areas), good elsewhere. In the end the total yield was not far below that of 1928. The rise in official prices helped the collections at first. But private market prices again quickly overtook them. In the grain collections of 1928–1929 the private trader paid 2 or 3 times the official prices for wheat and rye. By April 1, 1929, private retail prices of foodstuffs were already double the prices in state or co-operative shops, and continued to soar. "We are entering a period," said Kalinin in May 1929, "in which capitalist elements oppose the most furious resistance to the advance of socialism."[8] By this time no peasant who had access to the private market would deliver grain to the official collectors except under compulsion; and the old "extraordinary measures" were again in use. But this time the results were trivial. The total of the grain collections for 1928–1929 (in round figures) was 8 million tons against 10 millions for 1927–1928, of wheat and rye 5 millions against 8 millions. This was near starvation level for the cities; nobody could survive any longer without paying the exorbitant prices of the private market. It became necessary to import 250,000 tons of grain. It should be emphasized that in the summer of 1929 the system of official grain collections had effectively broken down, though nobody would publicly admit it, and that, under existing conditions, no reasonable prospect existed of restoring it. A third successive annual crisis of the grain collections loomed ahead. The problem of supplying towns and factories had become completely untractable. Gradualism was not enough. This was the negative impulse behind the decision to collectivize.

Mechanization and Collectivization

Lenin's dictum about the 100,000 tractors which could convert the peasant to communism was the winged word which inspired the programme of mechanization plus collectivization. The im-

[8] 5 S"ezd Sovetov SSSR (1929), No. 15, p. 37.

portation of American tractors went on throughout the 1920s. The building of the Stalingrad tractor factory began in 1928. The year 1927 saw the foundation of the first large-scale grain-growing Sovkhozy and kolkhozy, mainly in the southern Ukraine and the northern Caucasus. The Shevchenko Sovkhoz in the Odessa province was the first "grain-factory" with its attached fleet of tractors; and here the first MTS was created in 1928 to serve not only the Sovkhoz itself but neighbouring peasant holdings. The programme was based on the correct calculation that higher yields could be obtained by these methods than from individual peasant holdings, and above all that the "marketability" of the crop would be substantially increased. This was a sensible policy. Belief in its potentialities was the positive impulse behind the materially premature decision to collectivize. The failure of the grain collections convinced the leaders that collectivization was necessary. Mechanization convinced them that it was possible. The desperation bred by the first conviction may have contributed to the optimism of the second.

The weakness of the policy was that, though a real beginning had been made, mechanization had scarcely progressed far enough to sustain the weight of widespread collectivization. The first tractors did not come off the production line in Stalingrad till 1930; another tractor factory was planned in Chelyabinsk, but was still in the future. A dozen or more large-scale Sovkhozy and kolkhozy were at work. But, even so, the total number of peasants incorporated in all Sovkhozy and kolkhozy together amounted in 1929 only to 5.4 per cent of the peasant population; they were responsible for 14 per cent of marketable production. This included many small Sovkhozy and kolkhozy whose productivity was little or no higher than that of peasant holdings. By and large, the country was still overwhelmingly dependent on primitive individual peasant agriculture. Peasants whose holdings were incorporated in the Shevchenko Sovkhoz retained vegetable and garden plots for their own use. Kalinin explained that this was because they had "a great deal of free time thanks to the complete mechanization" of farm work.[9] Moreover, all these institutions — notably the tractor and the MTS — were still in the stage of teething troubles. As a later commentator put it, "the road from the

[9] 5 *S"ezd Sovetov SSSR* (1929), No. 19, p. 3.

wooden plough to the tractor" had been "only half travelled" even at the end of the first five-year plan.[10] But, where there is only one way out of a desperate situation, it must be tried even with inadequate resources. This was the mood of the decision of December 1929.

"Revolution from Above"

The short history of the communist party published in 1938 and credited to Stalin described collectivization as a revolution carried out "from above, on the initiative of the State power, with direct support from below." (I have found no earlier use of the phrase in this context.) This has now been condemned as heretical on the ground that it relegates to a secondary place "the decisive force in the revolutionary transformation of the countryside — the movement of the toiling masses themselves."[11] Contemporary evidence is scarce. The existence of class divisions in the countryside, and the hostility of the poor peasant to the *kulak*, were postulates of party doctrine and policy from Lenin onwards: it was one of Bukharin's sins that he failed to recognize these divisions, and treated the peasantry as an undifferentiated mass. What was referred to as the policy of "kindling the class war in the countryside" was actively pursued, for the first time since the civil war, in the grain collections crisis of January – March 1928. It was promised that 25 per cent of all grain confiscated under the article of the code prohibiting concealment of grain would be handed over to the poor peasants in the form of long-term credits. This was designed to encourage informers, and doubtless did so; without local informers the large stocks collected during these months could hardly have been unearthed.

The expected result of deepening the rift between the *kulak* and the mass of the peasantry does not, however, seem to have followed to any significant extent. When hunger spread over the countryside, it was still the well-to-do peasant who had whatever

[10] *Istoriya Sovetskogo Krest'yanstva i Kolkhoznogo Stroitel'stva v SSSR* (1963), pp. 201 – 202.
[11] *Voprosy Istorii KPSS*, No. 11, 1964, pp. 134 – 135; on the other hand, Stalin is blamed *ibid.*, p. 137, for "an unjustified forcing of collectivization."

grain was left, and who was therefore in a dominant position vis-à-vis the rest of the peasantry. Frumkin, in his letter to the party central committee of June 1928, wrote that the peasantry with few exceptions had turned against the party. This was denounced as heresy. But Bauman, secretary of the Moscow party committee and a staunch Left-winger, also wrote in *Bol'shevik*[12] that "the poor peasant, having nothing to eat, has had to do obeisance to the *kulak*," and that recent changes in the village had been "not to our advantage, but to that of the *kulaks*." More serious was the alienation of the middle peasants on whom much of the weight of the extraordinary measures had fallen. This was the gist of Bukharin's argument at the party central committee in July 1928. The *kulak* himself was not dangerous: "We can shoot him down with machine-guns, and he cannot shake our country." The danger was that the middle peasant would follow the *kulak*. The coining of the word *podkulachniki* (little sub-*kulaks*) for hangers-on of the *kulaks* from other strata of the peasantry points to the frequency of the phenomenon. There is little doubt that the party, in drawing a largely imaginary line between the *kulak* and the middle peasant, underestimated the degree of solidarity among different strata of the peasantry. Far from being gratified by the penalization of their old enemies the *kulaks*, the middle and even the poor peasants had reason to fear that the same penalties would fall on them. The archives report the "spontaneous dekulakization" of 40 per cent of *kulak* holdings in the Lower Volga region in the winter of 1929 – 1930.[13] But this, whatever exactly it may mean, seems to have been a rare exception. The official thesis, voiced by Kalinin, that encouragement by the government of collective and cooperative activities had "implanted in the peasantry a consciousness of collectivization," and an awareness of its benefits, had little foundation.[14] In general, the party and the government proceeded to the work of collectivization with a minimum of assistance from any group of the peasantry. The human, as well as the mechanical, resources available were inadequate to the smooth performance of the task.

12 *Bol'shevik*, No. 13 – 14, July 31, 1928, pp. 46 – 47.
13 *Istoriya SSSR*, No. 6, 1958, p. 18.
14 *5 S"ezd Sovetov SSSR* (1929), No. 15, p. 28.

*   *   *

When the party central committee at its session of November
1929 declared that "the kolkhoz movement now presents to particular regions the task of wholesale collectivization," an early
advance in certain localities was evidently envisaged. A recent
article based on unpublished archives[15] gives some account of the
background of the decision of December 1929. On December 5, a
commission was set up by the party central committee to submit
to the Politburo a plan of collectivization. The commission worked
in eight sub-commissions, and on December 22 presented its report to the Politburo. This proposed collectivization by stages, to
be completed (except for Central Asia, Transcaucasia, and some
northern regions) within the period of the first five-year plan.
The Crimea and the Lower Volga Region were to be collectivized in 1930; the North Caucasian, Middle Volga, and Black Earth
Regions, and the steppe region of the Ukraine in 1931; Siberia,
Kazakhstan, the Moscow and Nizhny-Novgorod regions, and the
Ukraine on the left bank of the Dnieper in 1932. The collectives
were to take the form of artels; land, machines, and working animals were to be included, but the peasant was to retain small animals and milch-cows serving his own use. When the report came
before the Politburo Stalin demanded a speeding-up of the timetable, and the inclusion of all animals. On January 3, 1930, the
commission submitted to the Politburo a revised plan on these
lines. On this occasion Ryskulov, apparently with Stalin's support,
called for a further speeding up and collectivization "without any
limitations." A decision was taken in this sense and formed the
basis of the published decision of the central committee of January 5, 1930, in which only a trace of the old staging remained in
the provision that the Lower and Middle Volga regions, and the
North Caucasus, should be collectivized by the autumn of 1930
or the spring of 1931, and the rest a year later. This account is no

[15] *Voprosy Istorii KPSS*, No. 1, 1964, pp. 32 – 43; an article by N. A.
Ivnitsky, in a collective work not available to me when the present article
was written (*Istochnikovedenie Istorii Sovetskogo Obshchestva* (1964),
pp. 265 – 288), gives further details from the archives of the work of the
commission and its sub-commissions.

doubt correct as far as it goes. But nothing is quoted textually, and the selective use of unpublished archives can be misleading. What we have here is perhaps something less than the whole truth. It does, however, reveal the haphazard and impulsive character of the final decision.

Winston Churchill:
Power Politician and Counter-Revolutionary

ARNO J. MAYER

IN HIS SCHOLARLY CAPACITY a historian should not deliver eulogies; nor should he perpetuate or embellish legends. When reviewing an extraordinary life like Churchill's he has an obligation to examine this life critically in the context of its time. Historians hold that just as the greatness of a leader cannot be properly appreciated without a close look at the era on which he left his mark, so the forces agitating any given era cannot be understood without a careful evaluation of the great men who bent these forces to their will. In brief, great men and their times illuminate each other.

Let us begin by raising, but not answering, a question with which Churchill himself is likely to have wrestled: was his own leadership essential to the survival of Britain, the Western World, and Soviet Russia in 1940–41? Historians will forever speculate about this unanswerable question, so much more so because Churchill's life history prior to the invasion of France and the Low Countries did not commend or qualify him for his epochal historical assignment. He was anything but a modern man: he was guided by archaic ideas; his personality and conduct were remnants of a by-gone age; and he was consumed by nostalgia for a vanished elitist society and a faded imperial grandeur.

Indeed, he and de Gaulle have much in common. Both reconciled themselves to modernity in only one major sphere: in the technology of war. They were equally sensitive to the accelerated movement, time, and space of 20th century military battles. Whereas Churchill pushed the modernization and growth of naval, tank, and air power, de Gaulle pioneered in tank warfare and in the *force de frappe*. Both had a purely instrumental interest in industrial modernization, social reform, political stability, and administrative efficiency. Churchill and de Gaulle left others to plan and implement these improvements provided they dutifully placed themselves and their achievements under their command for the pursuit of the national interest, as they saw it.

In May 1940 Churchill became the man of the hour — not unlike de Gaulle in 1958 — because at home Britain's deadlocked political situation invited, if not demanded, the ascendancy of a resolute autocrat; while in international politics his vague and inconsistently held concepts of power and balance of power momentarily became relevant.

Let us consider first, Churchill the man and the politician; second, Churchill the counter-revolutionary; third, Churchill's foreign policy and effectiveness in the 1930's; and last, his ambivalent diplomatic role during and after the Second World War.

I

Throughout his public school days Churchill was consistently at the bottom of his class, while at the same time doing miserably in sports. Moreover, he was unpopular with his classmates. Worse still, in that sober pre-Freudian era, he refused to worry or brood about his unpopularity — quite the contrary. He relished the solitude in which he took his walks and read his books. Yet, his academic achievements and motivations were so low that he passed his entrance examination to the Sandhurst Military Academy only on his third try; and even then he barely qualified for the obsolete cavalry, "which accepted lower standards for men who had independent means."[1] But once he was in, and with the sudden explosion of his passion and interest in warfare, Churchill applied his stupendous intellectual gifts and energies to his studies.

No doubt the fascination for the study of military affairs, which stayed with him all through his life, suited Churchill's romantic and heroic view of political leadership. He was not cut out for harmonious teamwork; he never discovered the meaning of personal loyalty; and he cruelly severed relations even with long-time associates the moment they threatened to embarrass him

[1] Virginia Cowles, *Winston Churchill: The Era and the Man* (London, 1953), p. 37.

or his career. He had an artist's or a robber-baron's temperament, in that he was volatile, selfish, unreliable, and ambitious. For
relaxation he sought out the company of men of similar dispositions. He laughed, sang, drank, and recited poetry with self-made
men rather than with titled aristocrats who thrived on patronage,
provided these self-made men aspired to be part of the established
power elite and demonstrated their reverence for, and familiarity
with, Europe's, particularly Britain's, cultural heritage. In his personal relations, except with members of his family, Churchill
tended to be crude and boorish. At the same time, he belonged to
that rare species, i.e. the cultivated men of action: as an *engagé*
intellectual, he admired the historical style of Gibbon and Ma-
caulay; as a practising politician, he carried the English language
and rhetoric to new heights; and he incessantly recharged his vital
intellect and psyche by seeking repose and self-expression at his
writing desk and at his painting easel.

In brief, Churchill was a Renaissance man of exceptional gifts,
driven by one over-riding passion: and this passion — to which all
else was subordinated, harnessed, and attuned — was politics. Paradoxically, however, he was not a good politician. To be sure, he
would have excelled in an era of deferential politics. But precisely
because of his archaic temperament, outlook, conduct, and style,
he was unsuited for this modern age of mass, party, and pressure
politics. He had an elitist's contempt and distrust for the mass
electorate and a patrician's disdain for routinized party accommodation and discipline. That he was a great orator is beyond question. However, under conditions of mass literacy, universal
suffrage, and party competition, oratory is only one of many in-
gredients for political effectiveness. Except for a very brief spell,
throughout his political career he was never really popular with
the British electorate; nor did he ever enjoy solid party loyalty
and confidence in Commons. Moreover, he was not an outstanding parliamentarian, though on the floor of the House few Prime
Ministers ever surpassed him in repartee during the question
period.

This, then, was the man and the politician. What about his political vision, projects, and policy? Both friendly and critical students of Churchill persist in stressing his repeated party shifts as

evidence of an erratic and inconsistent but ultimately successful striving for leadership. Accordingly, in 1899, Churchill began his political career as a member of the Conservative Party. In less than six years he defected to the Liberal Party, where he soon joined the Radical faction. But within four years he moved back into the moderate wing of his newly adopted political home. During and immediately following the Great War he was a Lloyd George Liberal and cheerfully contributed to the fatal schism in the parent Liberal Party. Finally, in the mid-20s he returned to the Conservative fold, having toyed with the idea of starting his own center party both before and after this return. And within this Conservative Party he repeatedly was torn between the Tory, the center, and the progressive wings.

These shifts in party affiliations cannot be explained away. But how important were they? As I suggested, Churchill was not cut out to be a regular party man. He was a virtuoso, with a flaming sense of destiny. At the same time, to understand Churchill it will not do simply to attribute his changing party affiliations and postures to his inordinate political ambitions and pretensions. Such strivings are the stuff of which so many political leaders, and not only Churchill, are made.

Perhaps Churchill's political behavior emerges in a more consistent light once it is viewed in the broad context of the fundamental political encounter of his time. His career was co-extensive with the confrontation of revolution and counter-revolution in Europe, including Britain, during the first half of this century and with the related clash of nationalism and imperialism in the non-Western World.

Churchill was an equally resolute opponent of socialism and of anti-imperialist nationalism. Whatever his party affiliation may have been at any given moment, his purpose remained constant: to maintain Britain's political, social, and economic system at home while upholding her imperial glory in the international arena. But even his strategy and tactics were not that erratic. Except for a few years, 1904–10, when he experimentally championed timely reforms as the best antidote to revolutionary change, his policies stayed within a narrow spectrum ranging from congealed conservatism to outright reaction. That his flirtation with Radical reformism should have been so short-lived is not surprising, given his tradition-bound and orthodox values and behavior patterns as well as his fascination with warfare. Precisely because he never reconciled himself to the revolution of rising expectations in either Lancashire or Bengal, he was by far more interested and effective in the realm of foreign and military policy than in domestic affairs.

II

Let us look briefly at Churchill's political career in this context of the confrontation of revolution and counter-revolution. In 1899 (June) he fought his first election on the Conservative ticket in Oldham, a typical Lancashire working-class district. Ignoring Disraeli's and his father's injunction not to neglect social issues, he campaigned with slogans extolling the virtues of the High Church, of imperial unity, of the existing social system, and of Conservative rule. His thorough defeat at the polls came to him not only as a personal rebuff but also as a revelation of the ineffectiveness of conventional political appeals among the lower urban classes.

Almost by rebound he rushed off to South Africa to cover the Boer War as a special correspondent for the *Morning Post*, Britain's leading jingoist daily. On the strength of his stories and of his courageous bearing in captivity, he soon returned to England to stand once again as a Conservative candidate in Oldham. In this first khaki election of the 20th century a groundswell of super-patriotism carried the Conservative Party, including Churchill, to victory.

During his inaugural term in Commons, Churchill distinguished himself by the skillful rhetoric with which he expounded the wilting Conservative credo of the Victorian sunset. He advocated isolationism from Europe, military retrenchment, imperialism, free trade, and fiscal orthodoxy. Moreover, while the Boer War was in its guerrilla phase, Churchill rationalized the high military, moral, and diplomatic costs of counter-insurgency — such as concentration camps, the burning of farms of suspect guerrillas, and the censure of the entire civilized world.

Soon he began his move first to the back bench and then across the floor to the Liberal side of the House. Admittedly, in some measure, impatience with his own advancement in the Conservative Party motivated this defection. Nonetheless, he charged the Conservative high command with abandoning the time-honored policies of government economy and free trade. Still insensitive to the rising social unrest and unconcerned about the mounting Anglo-German trade and naval rivalry he could not join those Conservatives and Liberal Imperialists who meant to solve these problems through costly imperial ventures, navalism, and protectionism. In any event, ideas of fiscal and economic orthodoxy prompted Churchill to switch to the Liberal Party which, under the pressure of its own Radicals, was about to stage a frontal assault on the establishment.

It was not until after he fell under the spell of Lloyd George and Sidney Webb that he discovered labor and social problems; advocated spending less on guns in order to be able to afford more butter; and insisted that only daring social reforms could contain the fledgling Labour Party on the left. As an aristocrat, a soldier, and a renegade Tory he found it convenient to legitimize his shift to creeping welfarism with allusions to his father's abortive campaign for Tory Democracy in the 1880s. Once he succeeded Lloyd George at the Board of Trade in 1908 — his first Cabinet post — he was in a position to act on his strident criticism of sweated industries and unemployment by setting up Trade Boards and Labour Exchanges.

By 1910, his reformist zeal began to cool. Whereas he still favored small and gradual tax reforms to finance welfare measures, he was not prepared to undermine the foundations of existing class relations and political institutions. Specifically, he balked when Lloyd George set out to emasculate the powers and prerogatives of the House of Lords, that glorious citadel and symbol of Britain's traditional, stratified, and deferential society.

But he could not switch back to the Conservative Party for fear of further compounding distrust of himself in Westminster as well as in the clubs. Besides, Asquith made him Home Secretary, thereby charging him with the maintenance of law and order in a society shaken by labor disputes. His engrained conservatism and his flair for military action informed the repressive measures with which Churchill handled the coal strike in Wales in November 1910, the bogus anarchist scare on Sidney Street in January 1911, and the railway strike in August of that same year.

Presently Asquith moved Churchill to the Admiralty because his Home Secretary was under attack by Radicals and Labourites for reveling in precipitate police and military repression, and also because a man with martial talents and disposition was needed in that post.

Actually, the Panther incident at Agadir, which in July 1911 exposed Germany's hostile and offensive intentions, helped Churchill to disentangle himself from the internal social and labor struggles, struggles in which he was being ground up by the fast-growing polarization between the right and the left. Overnight he forgot about reform, retrenchment, and appeasement. From the Admiralty he pressed for a bigger navy, regardless of cost and fiscal burden. If he still backed Home Rule for Ireland, he did so both to win Radical votes for his high naval estimates and to promote civil peace in the face of external dangers.

In any case, in July – August 1914, at the age of 39, he was the most ardent interventionist in the Liberal Cabinet. He did not wait for the violation of Belgian neutrality to provide a moral purpose for war; his arguments for declaring war were couched in terms of balance of power, security, prestige, and the sanctity of England's commitment to France.

I need not elaborate on his brash but abortive pledge to hold Antwerp against the advancing Germans; on his share of the responsibility for the Gallipoli fiasco; and on his resignation from the Admiralty under Conservative pressure. Instead, let me emphasize that the war and the Bolshevik Revolution combined to push both the Conservative and the Liberal parties further to the right while radicalizing Labour, the Irish Nationalists, and the Indian Congress Party. In the second khaki election of the century, the one coming on the heels of victory in 1918, Churchill once again condoned and benefited from the upsurge of jingoist superpatriotism. With Lloyd George he intoned the Tory clamor for hanging the Kaiser, for exorbitant reparations, and for colonial booty. The new House was overwhelmingly dominated by those hard-faced men who had benefited so much from the war. Since the Liberal Party was in shambles, Labour became His Majesty's

Loyal Opposition. The wartime Coalition continued, with Prime Minister Lloyd George and his "coupon" Liberals beholden to the Tories.

Lloyd George repeatedly, though unsuccessfully, tried to disengage himself from these Tory shackles in order to secure a moderate peace, domestic reforms, and an accommodation with the Irish and Indian nationalists. Churchill not only failed to support his Chief in this endeavor; he actually sabotaged him. In his capacity as Secretary of State for War and Air he became the Government's most fiery advocate of direct and large-scale military intervention in Russia for the purpose of overthrowing rather than merely containing the Bolshevik Revolution. He was the first in high office to charge publicly that Russian Bolshevism was worse than German militarism, and as of 1919, not unlike after 1945, he urged that Germany be made into the principal continental bulwark against Communism. Not surprisingly, the Tories exploited Churchill's summons for a full-scale anti-Bolshevik crusade to press their own opposition to the recognition of the Soviet Government and to withdrawal from Russia. In turn, this opposition to peaceful co-existence with the revolutionary regime abroad was an integral part of a preemptive offensive against both Lloyd George reformism and the Labour Party at home.

In the election of 1922, Churchill again ran as a Lloyd George Liberal. However, he was defeated; the Lloyd George faction was reduced to 57 seats; and Labour rose to 142. Churchill now sought to return to the Conservative fold, without, however, breaking altogether with Liberalism. His stern treatment of strikers and anarchists before the war, his decisive advocacy of belligerency in July 1914, and his unremitting enthusiasm for intervention in Russia had done much to restore his credit with the Conservatives. Presently he decided that by agitating and magnifying the specter of Bolshevism he could complete his reconciliation with the Conservatives while at the same time frightening Liberals to rally behind him.[2]

Accordingly he set out to red-bait the Labour Party. In January 1924 he declared that "the enthronement in office of a Socialist Government would be a serious national misfortune such as has usually befallen great states only on the morrow of their defeat

[2] Cowles, *Winston Churchill*, p. 249 and p. 252.

in war . . . all . . . prospects [of a foreign policy consonant with the national interest and of social reform] will be destroyed by the accession to office of a minority party innately pledged to the fundamental subversion of the existing social and economic civilization and organized for that purpose and that purpose alone. Strife and tumult, deepening and darkening, will be the only consequence of minority socialist rule."[3] This was the first of a stream of broadsides warning that a Labour government would subvert Britain's political and social institutions. In 1924 he fought two elections on an outright anti-Socialist platform. Even though he lost both races to a Labour rival Churchill hereafter stood forth as Britain's leading counter-revolutionary.

In the fall of that year he returned to Commons as a Conservative in good standing. Partly because he feared Churchill's machinations if left outside the Government, Prime Minister Baldwin made him Chancellor of the Exchequer. As a member of the Baldwin Administration, he not only introduced a Budget which aggravated Britain's trade depression and unemployment; he also played a key role in the suppression of the general strike of 1926 — which was called in support of the coal miners — denouncing it as a sinister revolutionary plot. But even before this strike was over, he was off on a trip which, among other places, took him to Rome, where he conferred with Mussolini about Italy's new society. Before returning home he gave the Italian press the following statement:

> I could not help being charmed as so many other people have been by Signor Mussolini's gentle and simple bearing and by his calm detached poise in spite of so many burdens and dangers [he began]. If I had been an Italian I am sure that I should have been whole-heartedly with you from start to finish in your triumphant struggle against the bestial appetites and passions of Leninism. But in England we have not had to fight this danger in the same deadly form. We have our own way of doing things. But that we shall succeed in grappling with Communism and choking the life out of it — of that I am absolutely sure.
>
> I will, however, say a word on an international aspect of Fascism. Externally, your movement has rendered a service

[3] Cited in Cowles, *Winston Churchill*, p. 252.

to the whole world. The great fear which has always beset every democratic leader or working-class leader has been that of being undermined or overbid by someone more extreme than he. It seems that continued progression to the Left, a sort of inevitable landslide into the abyss, was the characteristic of all revolutions. Italy has shown that there is a way of fighting the subversive forces which can rally the mass of the people, properly led, to value and wish to defend the honour and stability of civilized society. She has provided the necessary antidote to the Russian poison. Hereafter, no great nation will be unprovided with an ultimate means of protection against cancerous growths, and every responsible labour leader in the country ought to feel his feet more firmly planted in resisting levelling and reckless doctrines. . . .[4]

Of course, in the early 30s he also held Labour and Radical influences responsible for the government's appeasement of Indian nationalism. In late 1930 he proclaimed that "Gandhism and all it stands for will, sooner or later, have to be grappled with and finally crushed. It is no use trying to satisfy a tiger by feeding it on cat's meat."[5] Shortly thereafter he was alarmed and nauseated by the sight of

Mr. Gandhi, a seditious middle-Temple lawyer, now posing as a fakir of a type well-known in the East, striding half-naked up the steps of the vice-regal palace while he is still organizing and conducting a defiant campaign of civil disobedience, to parley on equal terms with the representative of the king-emperor.[6]

Needless to say, the Government of India Bill of 1935 never produced any of the dire consequences predicted by Churchill.

III

The point I wish to make is that in the 30s the man who couched his warnings about the approaching international crisis in terms of power politics and military strength was England's foremost ideo-

[4] *The Times* (London), January 21, 1927, cited in Cowles, *Winston Churchill*, pp. 271–72.
[5] Cited in Cowles, *Winston Churchill*, p. 280.
[6] Cited in Cowles, *Winston Churchill*, p. 280.

logical warrior. On social and imperial questions he was not just a meek, bland Conservative; he was an aggressive, diehard Tory. Here, then, was Churchill, leading the battle against Bolshevism at home while, at the same time, trying to rally political support for a foreign policy designed to contain, if not overthrow, Europe's foremost anti-Bolshevik dictators and regimes.

Since many Tories and Conservatives sympathized with the counter-revolutionary regimes on the Continent, Churchill was not likely to gather support in that quarter. As for the Labourites and Radicals, they were not about to trust this Tory who was such a recent convert to bi-partisanship in the face of foreign danger. To be sure, even after the Labour Party recognized that international danger — and Labour did so as of 1933 — it remained opposed to rearmament.

Still, the Left continued to have good reasons to suspect Churchill. He never retracted his praise of Mussolini. Moreover, as late as September 17, 1937, he still declared that, while disliking the Nazi system, he nevertheless hoped that should Britain ever be defeated she would "find a champion as indomitable [as Hitler] to restore our courage and lead us back to our place among the nations."[7] Apparently he still preferred Nazism to Socialism, since at this late date he once again charged that Socialism could only make its way "in some semi-barbarian Asiatic country or in a nation ruined by defeat in war."[8] Then, in 1945, when on the morrow of victory — not of defeat — Labour was on the verge of gaining a majority, Churchill stuck to his guns, except that he now prophesied that Socialism would mean a "Nazi state" and "a Gestapo."[9]

Apart from never exposing the destructive political and ideological tap-roots and objectives of Fascism and National Socialism, Churchill equivocated on some of the major international crises of the 30s. Right down to the outbreak of war he favored the appeasement of Mussolini in the hope of tying Italy to Britain and France. He completely evaded the Abyssinian question. In sup-

[7] Winston S. Churchill, *Step by Step, 1936–1939* (London, 1939), p. 170.
[8] Churchill, *Step by Step*, p. 148.
[9] See Ronald B. McCallum, *The British General Election of 1945* (London and Oxford, 1947), p. 142.

porting the National government's do-nothing response to Italian aggression in Africa, he went so far as to declare that no one could "keep up the pretense that Abyssinia was a fit, worthy, and equal member of a league of civilized nations."[10]

Churchill was equally evasive with regard to the Spanish Civil War. He again backed the government's non-intervention policy, even though he knew that this policy benefited Franco. In his view, the Spanish welter was none of Britain's and France's business: these countries should simply "send charitable aid under the Red Cross to both sides, and for the rest, keep out of it and arm."[11] In other words, while he claimed not to want to make a choice between a Fascist and a Communist Spain, the net effect of non-intervention was to favor the cause of counter-revolution on the Iberian peninsula. And, incidentally, it is rather strange that, as a champion of the balance of power and of Britain's security needs, Churchill barely hinted at the danger to Gibraltar and the Western Mediterranean should Franco and Hitler join forces.

It should be stressed that whereas this appeasement of Mussolini and Franco was popular with the Conservatives, including the diehard Tories, it was scathingly criticized by the Labourites and Radicals. Churchill himself conceded that Britain's Spanish policy was not dictated by military unpreparedness but by internal political division over the question of intervention,[12] as was also the case in France. But, except for this casual admission, throughout most of the 30s Churchill deliberately created the impression that England's military unpreparedness, particularly in the air, was at the root of appeasement.

His position on Russia was also far from straightforward. To be sure, especially following the purges, there was room for doubt about the Red Army's military capability. Just the same, as early as September 1936, Churchill acknowledged that these purges were "less a manifestation of world propaganda than an act of self-preservation by a community which fears and has reason to

[10] Winston S. Churchill, *While England Slept: A Survey of World Affairs, 1932–1938* (New York, 1938), p. 233 (October 24, 1935).

[11] Churchill, *Step by Step*, p. 53 and p. 57 (August 10 and 21, 1936).

[12] Churchill, *Step by Step*, p. 228 (April 5, 1938).

fear, the sharp German sword."[13] But it was not until a few months before Munich that Churchill unequivocally called for diplomatic and military cooperation with the Soviet Union in order to resist Germany. Will it ever be known whether this delay was due to his low assessment of Russia's military capabilities rather than to his long-standing and bitter hatred of the Soviet regime? Meanwhile, he continued to play the Italian card while also invoking the "powerful military republic of Turkey."[14]

Obviously, Churchill was caught in a double bind. His own kind were reluctant to listen to him: they had hidden sympathies for the Axis dictators and were fearful that popular fronts as well as the Soviet Union would benefit from a successful anti-Nazi crusade. At the time of Munich, barely 40 Conservatives shared Churchill's sense of danger and urgency.

On the other hand, Labourites and Radicals were hostile to the Axis regimes precisely because of their counter-revolutionary objectives and methods. And yet, how could they rally behind Britain's foremost counter-revolutionary for this battle, particularly since Churchill appeased Mussolini and Franco and dragged his feet on cooperation with Soviet Russia?

Not that Churchill failed to work at overcoming Labour and Radical reticence. Since Labour claimed to oppose increasing armaments because the Tories could not be trusted to use them for democratic and progressive purposes, he advanced the formula "arms and the Covenant." Ever since Woodrow Wilson's days, the British Left and not Churchill had been loyal to the League of Nations. He now favored collective security within the framework of the Covenant in order to "secure a measure of unity at home among all classes and all parties, which is indispensable to the efficiency of our foreign policy as well as to the progress of our defense preparations."[15] And, indeed, as of the Fall of 1938 this wooing of the Left began to pay dividends.

I am suggesting, then, that the lack of popular, party, and parliamentary support for Churchill's foreign policy prescriptions cannot be traced to any significant extent to rancor over his party

---

[13] Churchill, *Step by Step*, p. 62 (September 4, 1936).

[14] Churchill, *Step by Step*, pp. 309–10 (December 15, 1938).

[15] Churchill, *While England Slept*, p. 373 (December 21, 1937).

infidelities; to immunity to his spurious prophesies of doom; or to misgivings about his personal eccentricities and his lust for power. Nor will it do to pin the responsibility for appeasement on the pacifism of the public at large; on the failure of the Foreign Office and Chamberlain to recognize the expansionist drive of the Nazi regime; or on the low level of military preparedness.

Instead, it would seem that Churchill remained isolated because most Conservatives hesitated to endorse a foreign policy which had progressive if not revolutionary overtones; because Labour distrusted a counter-revolutionary's advocacy of a progressive cause; because Churchill's equivocal attitudes toward Fascist Italy, Franco's Spain, and Soviet Russia reinforced this Labour distrust; and because right up until Munich Churchill's summons for a return to pure power politics was intermittently infused with ideological concerns.

This same intermingling of power and ideology reemerged during and after the Second World War. Accordingly, in October 1944, it was Churchill, the hard-headed power politician — and not Roosevelt, the naive idealist — who first recognized Russia's predominance in Rumania and Bulgaria, and her vital interests in Yugoslavia and Hungary, in exchange for British predominance in Greece. On the other hand, there was a strong ideological motivation behind Churchill's advocacy of an assault on the allegedly soft underbelly of Europe; behind his reluctant support of the leftist partisans in Yugoslavia; behind his battle against the guerillas in Greece; behind his hostile suspicion of the Italian and French partisans; and behind his defiant braggadocio that he had not been appointed by His Majesty the King to preside over the liquidation of the British Empire.

Similarly, his Fulton speech of March 5, 1946, which signaled the formal start of the Cold War, had an unmistakable ideological flavor. Churchill not only indicted Soviet Russia for lowering an "iron curtain . . . from Stettin in the Baltic to Trieste in the Adriatic," but also asserted that the Soviets were out for "the infinite expansion of their power and doctrines." And yet, at the time, as a student of power, he must have known that Russia was altogether exhausted; that there was no serious danger of the Red Army advancing into Central Europe; and that to the extent that there was a Communist danger in the Western World it was an out-growth of internal conditions, particularly in Italy and France.

Perhaps Churchill welcomed the Cold War because, not unlike the Red Scare after 1918, it could be used to dish the Labour Party which threatened permanently to disfigure his beloved traditional England. In any case, Churchill should be remembered as a champion of the balance of power as well as of counter-revolution. I have a hunch he himself would not mind this epitaph.

Brahmins and Business, 1870 – 1914:
A Hypothesis on the Social Basis of
Success in American History

GABRIEL   KOLKO

1

THE IMAGE OF AN AMERICAN SOCIAL ELITE alienated by the growth
of a society dominated by big business at the end of the nineteenth century has gained a firm, if not universal, place in recent
interpretations of post-Civil War American history. This conception has led historians to discuss a status tension or "status
revolution," to use Richard Hofstadter's expression, which led the
older social elites to agitate for progressive legislation designed to
extend political control over the new capitalists and restore, by
political means, the less acquisitive social values of a displaced social order losing its power.[1] The established elite was by-passed,
losing economic ground relative to the raw *arrivistes* who lacked
both scruples and a civic consciousness. "Seasoned wealth and seasoned conscience," most notable in a community such as Boston,
led to the Mugwump mentality that agitated for good government, civic reform, and the application of moral standards to the
consequences of an increasingly immoral, business-dominated
society.

Such a view has also sustained the notion of an American cultural crisis at the end of the nineteenth century, a crisis personified by alienated members of the Boston social aristocracy, such as

This essay is a shortened version of a paper presented in 1966 to the
Faculty Colloquium of the Department of History, Princeton University.

[1] Richard Hofstadter, *The Age of Reform: From Bryan to F. D. R.*
(New York, 1955), 135 – 40 is the clearest statement of this viewpoint.

Henry James or Henry Adams, who were perhaps the most brilliant representatives of this allegedly typical mood. "I have
known, and known tolerably well, a good many 'successful' men
— 'big' financially," Charles Francis Adams, Jr., has been frequently quoted as observing, ". . . and a less interesting crowd I
do not care to encounter. Not one that I have ever known would
I care to meet again . . . nor is one of them associated in my
mind with the idea of humor, thought or refinement."[2] To the
American historian it was the function of such American "aristocrats" as there were to be disengaged from the dynamic phases of
economic development and alienated. The quantity of the literature on this disenchantment now staggers the imagination, and it
is virtually a standard theme to be restated again and again.

This conception of a tension and conflict between the social
elite and the economic elite at the end of the nineteenth century
has remained essentially unchallenged notwithstanding Weber's
logical arguments on the impossibility of a long-term conflict between the two elements, and despite the extremely valuable research by William Miller, Mabel Newcomer, C. Wright Mills,
and others on the social origins of the American business elite.
The general conclusions of these studies have been unanimous for
the period 1870–1910, the data varying only slightly. The most
important businessmen during that period overwhelmingly were
the sons of well-to-do or middle income families, highly educated
by contemporary standards, Protestants, and with important economic assets which utterly disprove the Horatio Alger myth.
These men were the sons of businessmen and professionals able
to give them every advantage in life, including high status.[3]

Granting the great value of such research on the social origins of
the American business elite, the fact remains that it is largely cir-

[2] Charles Francis Adams, Jr., *An Autobiography, 1835–1915* (Boston,
1916), 190.

[3] William Miller, ed., *Men in Business* (New York, 1962); Mabel Newcomer, *The Big Business Executive* (New York, 1955); Reinhard Bendix
and Frank W. Howton, "Social Mobility and the American Business Elite,"
British Journal of Sociology, VIII (December 1957), 357–69; IX (March
1958), 1–14. Hofstadter, *Age of Reform*, 140, cites this data but fails to
integrate it into his theory of a status revolution. Indeed, he really ignores its
practical meaning.

cumstantial in regard to the problem of the status elite and the economic elite, which can only be resolved by precisely identifying both groups and the extent to which they overlap. For practical purposes this can only be done on community levels, where, in key urban areas, it can have as much political and economic significance as a national sample. The research of Miller and this school also slights the gradients within income and occupational categories they described as "upper" or "businessmen," since it does not exclude the possibility of decisive mobility within such all-inclusive categories. A well-educated son of a grain merchant may have high status in a community but also be a *parvenu* among the sons of millionaires; and the fact that such an individual may also make a great sum of money, but still fall into the same occupational or income designation as his father (Rockefeller is a good example), should not obscure the fact of significant mobility or changes in relative status. Without specific descriptions of the functional operations of key social and economic elites in the crucial urban areas — New York, Boston, and Philadelphia are the three most important at the beginning of this century — the existing research is too oblique. Despite this, such work also happens to be valid, for the reasons argued by its authors and also because of the corroboration that follows. In this paper I shall define some of the general theoretical issues involved and indicate certain types of evidence necessary to bring theory and reality closer together, concentrating on the Boston Brahmins for specific illustrations.

Boston is especially interesting because it also illustrates the problem of uncritically projecting the insights of intellectual history onto economic and political reality, and the limitations of the assumption that the more measurable cultural moods permit one to understand in a more sensitive fashion the essential quality of an age. I shall not argue that this technique cannot be employed with profit for different places and periods, for the value of such an approach can only be determined by attempting to apply it in each particular instance, but in the case of Boston it has been seriously misleading, if not disastrous. Evidence for this disparaging view will also be offered.

My thesis, in its barest outline, is that economic development in the United States after the Civil War took place largely in the hands of existing and long established social and economic elites—not merely in the hands of the broader occupational class of "businessmen"—save where transitory factors of recent settlement created an economic vacuum where more-or-less constituted traditional elites were lacking. In this sense Schumpeter's notion of entrepreneurial innovation must be radically modified, for it is not so much innovation—it existed everywhere, among men from all strata—that explains who succeeded in economic competition, or how, but status and access to existing power. Given the fact that the crucial groups in economic development were to a very significant degree extended families that recruited within their own ranks, and that these high status families had access to capital, Boston Brahmins could control local economic growth and extend their power westward, especially in mining and railroads, to help determine the criteria for success elsewhere as well. Status for many led to economic power even when it did not begin with it, and the men who commanded the economy were also dominant in society. The economic structure failed to conform to any traditional model of development, whether conservative or radical, simply because historians and economic theorists were insufficiently aware of the reality that not all men entered the economic process as equals utilizing impersonally available tools, but that some men had, so to speak, a "head start" that was to define the distribution of future economic and political power in crucial new fashions which conventional economic theory did not anticipate.

II

Historians of recent America for the most part tend to describe the Brahmins as living outside the major currents of American economic and political life in the decades following the Civil War, alienated by the emerging new society and full of expressions of hostility towards it. Living off "inherited wealth from commerce," the Brahmins became critics and reformers apart from the rest of society.[4] "The genteel reformers were as much alienated from

[4] Arthur Mann, *Yankee Reformers in the Urban Age* (Cambridge, 1954), 7; and chap. I.

the general public as they were from the main centers of power in the business corporations and the political machines."[5] "Bostonian, Harvard man, Unitarian, Congregationalist, old family — these had been the signs of power, wealth, and prestige proudly worn by the New England aristocracy. As the nineteenth century came to a close, however, newcomers had wrested leadership from the old order."[6]

There can be no question that among the nineteenth-century Brahmins could be found alienated, culturally accomplished, and pretentious elements, probably more than in any other city in the United States at the time. When one passes from the intellectual luminaries among the Brahmins and looks at the larger bulk a rather different and duller picture emerges. The brightness of the intellectual scene, such as it was, has prevented historians from looking at the Brahmins as an operational class having not merely cultural attributes — real and fancied — but functional economic and political roles. Indeed, one must inquire why the notion of an elite without economic or political power was possible in the first place, and what this means in reinforcing the diffuse view of power in American society as something more or less balanced or widely distributed. This is not to say that Brahmins did not do other things besides making money, much less that there is any necessary dichotomy between the control of the economy by an elite and its control of culture, but that their ability and freedom to deal with culture and politics depended in the last analysis on their economic importance.

The crucial foundation of business activity in Boston and Massachusetts in the colonial period was the extended family or kinship system, and this system, with rather different personnel, operated after the American Revolution and until at least World War One.[7] The colonial precedent was not consciously imitated,

[5] Richard Hofstadter, *Anti-intellectualism in American Life* (New York, 1963), 177.

[6] Frederic C. Jaher, *Doubters and Dissenters: Cataclysmic Thought in America, 1885 – 1918* (New York, 1964), 142. See also Edward N. Saveth, "Henry Adams: Waning of America's Patriciate," *Commentary,* XXIV (October 1957), 303.

[7] Bernard Bailyn's "Kinship and Trade in Seventeenth Century New England," *Explorations in Entrepreneurial History,* VI (May 1954), 197 – 205, is most important in outlining this phenomenon, and in a sense all I am

but it was found to be naturally relevant to the much more complicated circumstances of industrial enterprise, since it provided a vital source of dependable managerial talent even more necessary as the size and scope of enterprise increased. These extended family groups, for the most part, traced the genesis of their prosperity to the Revolutionary Era and the end of the eighteenth century, when the Cabots, Higginsons, Lowells, and others moved to Boston from the surrounding towns to enlarge, for the first time and in a significant manner, their family fortunes.[8] Intermarriage between well-placed families was an acceptable colonial precedent that was equally sanctioned after the Revolution, and an important means for consolidating and enlarging fortunes, fortunes that were very greatly magnified between the Revolution and the Civil War in a manner that firmly established the financial positions of the major Boston families.

These families cooperated and intermarried easily, gracefully, and for their mutual fortune and friendship. The descendants of the Rev. Francis Higginson by the beginning of this century included such names as Forbes, Cabot, Lee, Lowell, Fiske, Cushing, Jackson, Storrow, Fuller, Channing, Copley, Agassiz, Sargent, Sears, Lawrence, Perkins, Wentworth, and others too numerous to mention, and this relationship was to be of vital importance in the construction of the economic fortunes of the Lee, Higginson & Co. dynasty.[9] Much the same may be said for the other powerful center of Boston economic life, Kidder, Peabody & Co. "The family and social connections of the firm assured to it the best possible clientèle; there was sufficient capital . . . ," Henry Lee Higginson later suggested; "the firm owed in some measure to

---

doing is applying his framework to a later period. Robert K. Lamb, "The Entrepreneur and the Community," in *Men in Business*, 97 – 118, has interesting additional data to corroborate Bailyn. Barry E. Supple's "A Business Elite: German-Jewish Financiers in Nineteenth-Century New York," *Business History Review*, XXXI (Summer 1957), 143 – 78, is unique and valuable in showing the relevance of analyses of family systems and economic development at the end of the 19th century in the case of New York.

[8] Lamb, *Men in Business*, 97 – 98.

[9] Thomas Wentworth Higginson, *Descendants of the Reverend Francis Higginson* (n.p., 1910). See also Cleveland Amory, *The Proper Bostonians* (New York, 1947), 40.

family alliances its well-advised connections with the best financial enterprises of the day."[10] With a family so large and so loyal, and also so well suited to business, it was possible for many to invest widely on the basis of the careful business activities of a relative few, and benevolently to assist the family's extended fortunes. The crucial coordination for this vast undertaking was provided by Lee, Higginson & Co. or Kidder, Peabody & Co.[11] In this manner capital could be raised as well as disbursed, quickly and easily.

The existence of the extended family as the basic structure of Boston-based economic activity determined the mode of recruitment into the numerous organizations controlled by Boston wealth, at least at the highest managerial levels. Boston wealth was commercial and industrial, requiring continuous management and precluding wholesale desertion of business for less mundane pursuits. Brahmins poured into business because it was so easy to do so, as well as quite natural for the sons and grandsons of recent merchant wealth, but also because in certain instances it was easier to bring a hard-pressed relative of modest abilities or fortunes into the business rather than sustain him on handouts. Moreover, in a starkly competitive world it seemed to many Bostonians that the ties of blood and sentiment would guarantee a degree of application, loyalty, and honesty not always assured in unrelated hands. "All through Boston history," a Bostonian once observed, "when a Family loses its financial stability, it has a way of beginning to disappear."[12] To guard against this possibility many wealthy family members established tamper-proof trusts managed by others, less foolhardy and usually related Bostonians. Even if heirs refused to work, the family was protected until some younger man would refurbish the fortune of the clan.[13] The net effect of all these factors was to keep fortunes tied to the extended families.

[10] Bliss Perry, *Life and Letters of Henry Lee Higginson* (Boston, 1921), 272.

[11] See, for example, Edward C. Kirkland, *Charles Francis Adams, Jr., 1835–1915: The Patrician at Bay* (Cambridge, 1965), 66.

[12] Quoted in Amory, *Proper Bostonians*, 39.

[13] *Ibid.*

The senior figure in Boston economic life at the beginning of
this century, Henry Lee Higginson, left Boston and the family
during 1865 – 1868 and consistently lost money in various oil
and cotton ventures. "I was taken in at the beginning of 1868 as
a matter of charity," he later confessed, "to keep me out of the
poorhouse. . . ."[14] Later, when other close relatives were to follow the same cycle, he was to complain but also to pay.[15] John
Murray Forbes preferred employing his indigent Cincinnati
cousin, Charles E. Perkins, whose father was related to the Chan-
nings and Eliots as well, and moving him up the hierarchy of the
Chicago, Burlington and Quincy Railroad.[16] "There is great need
of good trustworthy business men for the management of our
railroads," Forbes wrote the nineteen-year-old Perkins when offering him his first post.[17] When close or direct relatives could
not be found, Forbes preferred hiring the other scions of Boston
elite families. He employed Charles Russell Lowell in 1855 for
the same reason he hired "young Choate" at another time — "he
is nephew or cousin of *the* Choate, and is said to be a fine fellow."[18] Charles Francis Adams, Jr., who had been chosen president of the Union Pacific Railroad by the "Boston group" active
in its affairs since the 1870's, also made it a point to fill vacancies
when possible with "my kids" — young Harvard men.[19] By virtue
of such opportunities Richard Henry Dana in April 1881 could
complain about the Boston elite that ". . . the younger generation have all gone into Western Railroads with all their force,
leaving no room for the humanities."[20]

At the end of the Civil War the wealth of the Brahmins was

[14] Perry, *Henry Lee Higginson*, 271.

[15] Henry Lee Higginson to A. H. Higginson, November 19, 1908, October 11, 1912, Henry Lee Higginson Papers (Baker Library, Harvard Business School), Box XV.

[16] R. G. Overton, "Charles Elliott Perkins," *Business History Review*,
XXXI (Autumn 1957), 304 – 09.

[17] Henry Greenleaf Pearson, *An American Railroad Builder: John Murray
Forbes* (Boston, 1911), 102. Perkins subsequently married Forbes' niece.

[18] *Ibid.*, 101; also 102 – 03. See also Henry Greenleaf Pearson, *Son of New
England: James Jackson Storrow, 1864 – 1926* (Boston, 1932), 100; Perry,
Henry Lee Higginson, 273 – 74, for examples of hiring other Brahmins.

[19] Kirkland, *Charles Francis Adams, Jr.*, 95.

[20] Bliss Perry, *Richard Henry Dana, 1851 – 1931* (Boston, 1933), 118.

almost a century old, but at no point after that time did they lose their entrepreneurial zest or fail to exploit the dynamic opportunities opening up in the wake of the war. Massachusetts in 1869 ranked third nationally in the value of its manufacturing output, and it retained that position until 1909, when it fell to fourth place.[21] The fact that industrial growth and development did not by-pass the state imposed more significant realities on the social elite than alleged groanings over a lost age might imply. For the Boston Brahmins, many of whom were active in railroads and mines far beyond the borders of the state, that allegorical age had ceased to exist for decades. The first national market for copper mine shares was organized on the Boston Stock Exchange in the early 1850's, and was a major reason for the controlling position of the group composed of Agassiz, Quincy Shaw, Henry Lee Higginson, and H. S. Russell in Michigan copper, which, with the Paine-Stanton group, remained Boston-dominated for decades.[22] The Boston Stock Exchange provided the major national market for industrial shares in the 1880's, and Lee, Higginson & Co., Kidder, Peabody & Co., and the latter firm's former New York affiliate, Baring, Magoun & Co., were along with August Belmont the leading American investment bankers operating in the reinvestment of industrial firms in the 1890's.[23] As such they participated in many of the new industrial combinations, dominating some of the more technologically advanced and speculative — industries Schumpeter suggested would be controlled by new wealth and new men. General Electric and American Telephone & Telegraph were Boston-controlled firms at this time, and it was Boston that maintained the outstanding reputation for its willingness to enter new, daring, and hazardous industries. No less a figure than Charles Francis Adams, Jr., organized the Kansas

[21] Simon Kuznets *et al.*, *Population Redistribution and Economic Growth: United States, 1870 – 1950 — Analysis of Economic Change* (Philadelphia, 1960), II, 125.

[22] William B. Gates, Jr., *Michigan Copper and Boston Dollars: An Economic History of the Michigan Copper Mining Industry* (Cambridge, 1951), 32, 44 – 45, 71 – 72.

[23] Thomas R. Navin and Marian V. Sears, "The Rise of a Market for Industrial Securities, 1887 – 1902," *Business History Review*, XXIX (June 1955), 110, 124 – 26.

Stock Yards, and Lee, Higginson assumed the major responsibility for the reorganization and management of General Motors in 1910, the first major intervention by finance capital into the auto industry. By 1913, 75 per cent of Lee, Higginson's business was in public service and industrial bonds.[24] In this manner the Brahmins kept a crucial position in a rapidly developing industrial economy, actively showing important entrepreneurial initiatives at even the most precarious stages of activity. Their interests took them well outside the state and into the railroads and mining camps, where their substantial capital resources and natural abilities found profitable outlets.

III

What manner of men survived for a century and a half the travails and eddies of American economic development, survived and prospered at a time when many more were to fail than to succeed? In part the family structure of the Brahmins was a hedge against failure, since it involved a joint and continuous responsibility that could absorb the failures much more readily. But the qualities of personality associated with the Brahmins in business have significance for their cultural modes and pretensions. Their traits, it may be argued, were well suited for business and capital accumulation, and somewhat less compatible with a culture in depth. The large majority of Brahmins attached no stigma to being in business, which would have been the equivalent of a denial of their ancestors and heritage. The alienated Brahmin who went into letters or the arts was more the exception, but also fully tolerated and appreciated. The Brahmins, for the most part, reflected the larger norms of contemporary society — their society — and in Boston these sons of merchants and industrialists helped shape cultural and economic values. They were businessmen, and with a passion that reveals vital traits and primary goals. There was a Brahmin business style — perhaps not unique to Boston, al-

[24] Harold C. Passer, *The Electrical Manufacturers, 1875 – 1900* (Cambridge, 1953), 56 – 57; N. R. Danielian, *A. T. & T.: The Story of Industrial Conquest* (New York, 1939), 40 – 71; Pearson, *Son of New England*, 100 – 01, 124 – 31; Kirkland, *Charles Francis Adams, Jr.*, Chap. 3.

though no one has looked for it elsewhere — that maximized the chances of success.

Brahmin businessmen worked frightfully hard. Asceticism is perhaps too strong a description, but evidences of it can be found everywhere. "It would of course not be worth while . . . ," James J. Storrow wrote to a young aspiring businessman, "unless you and your wife . . . were prepared to make the definite sacrifice which is involved in accepting a business responsibility and undertaking to succeed."[25] Business was an unremitting commitment, to be taken home, internalized, and permitted to define the guiding lines of one's life. As William Appleton confided in his diary: "I must be busy. I don't know how to stop. . . . I can't help seeing openings for profit, neither can I help availing of them."[26] Hard work and a spartan existence, especially at home and after hours, may be found described in the reverent biographies of Brahmin businessmen authorized by their families.[27] And no one personified these traits more than two of the figures most commonly cited by historians as the antithesis between the Brahmins and business, Charles Francis Adams, Jr., and Henry Lee Higginson.

Higginson is thought of as the sensitive lover of music who wished to sit down at the footsteps of his office every morning and cry before entering.[28] As already mentioned, he was taken into the firm of Lee, Higginson to keep hunger from his door. Higginson is best known for his work in perfecting the Boston Symphony into a first-class musical organization, and for decades he ruled the Symphony with an iron hand that permitted him to fire any member of the group, "if said musician fails to play to the satisfaction of said Higginson."[29] His interest in music, while very great, was less pronounced than his interest in stocks, and his au-

[25] Pearson, *Son of New England*, 120–21.

[26] Quoted in Amory, *Proper Bostonians*, 86.

[27] Arthur S. Pier, *Forbes: Telephone Pioneer* (New York, 1953), 100–01, 181–83, 211; Amory, *Proper Bostonians*, 86–91; Pearson, *Son of New England*, 120–47; and business letters in T. Jefferson Coolidge Papers (Baker Library, Harvard Business School), Vols. 11–12.

[28] Perry, *Henry Lee Higginson*, 267–68 deals with this myth.

[29] According to a contract, see *ibid.*, 308n.; see also his letters in Higginson Papers, Baker Library, Box XV, pertaining to the Symphony.

thorized biographer notes that news of the market soon pushed Liszt out of his letters to his wife.[30] A dependent culture must flatter or tolerate the tastes of its sponsors, and they are sycophantically cultivated by poorer men who encourage the false illusions and self-esteem of their supporters. Higginson developed the Boston Symphony into excellent financial and good technical condition — although he insisted that musicians seeking to form a union be fired — but his taste in music ran to the ninety-minute balanced program, and he soon became the arbiter of Boston's musical taste, an area in which his talents were more limited.[31] His organization of a symphony on business principles resulted in a degree of philistinism, but Higginson's personal code permitted time only for the application of criteria of efficiency. "I believe in toiling terribly, and the only thing that I ask of my body is to give me the power to work and work until I drop. . . . May I repeat that if a man shows himself able to carry a load, he has got to carry it."[32] "For years after we were married," he lectured a relative living beyond his means, "we bought the cheap cuts of meat. . . . By all these little means you can save a good deal of money. . . ."[33] Both privately and publicly he defended the institution of big business against its attackers, noting that "people have forgotten the great benefits which the corporations have brought to the country."[34] In discussing Wall Street he commented that "with a very long knowledge of these men as a whole, I believe them to be an excellent, able, honest set of fellows."[35] As for the acquisition of wealth, Higginson could only aspire to higher goals: "I wish I were inside of Mr. Carnegie's skin; if I were, I would di-

[30] Perry, *Henry Lee Higginson*, 275 ff.

[31] Higginson's musical papers may be found in Higginson Papers, Baker Library, Box XV.

[32] Henry Lee Higginson to W. Cameron Forbes, November 22, 1910 (Houghton Library, Harvard College).

[33] Henry Lee Higginson to A. Henry Higginson, November 19, 1908, Baker Library, Box XV.

[34] Henry Lee Higginson, "Justice to the Corporations," *Atlantic Monthly*, CI (January 1908), 9.

[35] Henry Lee Higginson to Robert H. Fuller, December 23, 1908, Higginson Papers, Baker Library, Box XV.

vide all but $10,000,000 and keep that for my little girl. . . ."[36]

Charles Francis Adams, Jr.'s, paradoxical role is even more interesting because of his brothers Henry and Brooks, who are considered the epitome of the alienated Brahmins, and Charles' own seemingly contradictory utterances on men of wealth and the acquisition of money. There are the usual Adams-like statements full of bitter complaints, attacks on plutocrats or "the average man," and dramatic assertions that "I find myself a stranger in a strange land. . . ."[37] And there is his remarkably sensitive *Autobiography*, the best known passage of which I have already cited.

Despite these acerbic references, Adams was, above all, a Brahmin in business, and he would not have had it otherwise. The life of business suited him quite comfortably, since he loved to make money, borrowed heavily, speculated wildly in the west, and succeeded in making two to three million dollars before his death. He eventually became president of the Union Pacific, but he was forced to resign and found little consolation in that experience. Looking back at his numerous ventures, "One great business success," he wrote, "I did achieve; and it is the only one on which I can fairly plume myself."[38] That was his development of the Kansas City Stock Yards. "I take much pride in its record; and I feel I have a right so to do. *That*, I did."[39] Adams never saw the irony or contradiction between his leadership of a slaughterhouse and his carping complaints about the decline of American values, because he failed to recognize how thoroughly he too had come to reflect them. His final estimate of his life was a confirmation of what he had in fact done. Had he the choice to live it again, Adams remarked in his *Autobiography*, he would not have se-

[36] Henry Lee Higginson to Gardiner M. Lane, July 29, 1908, Higginson Papers, Baker Library, Box XV.

[37] Charles Francis Adams, Jr., to Charles W. Eliot, May 6, 1914, Adams Papers (Massachusetts Historical Society). See also Adams to W. P. Garrison, November 12, 1904, Adams Papers, and Adams to Edward Atkinson, September 24, 1896, Edward Atkinson Papers (Massachusetts Historical Society).

[38] Adams, *Autobiography*, 187. See also Kirkland, *Charles Francis Adams, Jr.*, Chap. III.

[39] Adams, *Autobiography*, 188.

lected the professions nor the military, for in the latter case it now seemed "a little empty." "As to politics, it is a game; art, science, literature — we know how fashions change! . . . What I now find I would really have liked is something quite different. I would like to have accumulated . . . one of those vast fortunes of the present day rising up into the tens and scores of millions — what is vulgarly known as 'money to burn.'" Had he made it, so he claimed, he would not have used it for himself, but for his children and especially for Harvard. "I would like to be the nine-teenth-century John Harvard — the John Harvard-of-the-Money-Bags, if you will."[40] In the last analysis Adams' anti-democratic views were hardly incompatible with the interests of his city and class, and he must be treated as a businessman who rather conveniently assumed that the frailties of the poor absolved the self-serving of the rich.[41] There was, at the end of the century, noth-ing in such a view distinctive to the Brahmins or Boston. And his entire life was testimony to the fact that a cynic who wishes to advance is generally more manipulative and successful than the naive bumbler.

Historians have concentrated on Henry and Brooks Adams to the extent that there is very little more one can say about them, but also in a way that has exaggerated their relative importance in the total Boston scene. They were a minority voice, albeit the most articulate one, and they cast their shadow over the general historical interpretation of the city. The two famous Adams brothers, and such literati as Henry James, were alienated not just by American life and values but also by Boston and their own class — a class that was deeply engrossed in the dominant economic and political events. Yet both brothers were ambivalent, and in a sense their books are really semi-engaged tracts on how their class might survive as well as vivid outlines of the consequences of failure. Though presumably esthetes, Henry and Brooks Adams frequently used economic categories of explanation and economic goals as justification for the militant policies they advocated, poli-

[40] *Ibid.*, 210.

[41] See the outline of his ideas in Kirkland, *Charles Francis Adams, Jr.*, 159 – 60.

cies not merely spartan or regenerative via the spartan life, but also economic in terms of profitability.[42] They were, in their perverse way, strategists for a larger American economic view of the world, preeminently a business view also shared by the more *arriviste* and expansionist followers of Mammon, even though they at times saw these factors as debilitating to culture and aesthetic values. The criterion of success and strength was not aesthetic — the confusing and moving exercise of *Mont-Saint-Michel and Chartres* apart — but economic and strategic in a manner that could be translated into tangible power. Henry's consistently pessimistic, even morbid, tone is really quite extraneous, for it was a quality of personality he had already evidenced in London in the 1860's. He merely felt old before his time, and in any event all three Adams brothers felt oppressed by the shadows of ancestors whose qualities and reputations they could never hope to equal.[43]

There is a self-consciousness in Henry Adams that was partially contrived because his ruminations were public, not private — "he sets himself before himself as the universe," his aunt commented.[44] Merely because he was an Adams he felt he was of general interest. But his condemnation of the society he lived in never really disturbed his friends in power, for he was attacking manners and motives rather than institutions. Henry, at least, could not keep his finger off the pulse of the mainstream of American life, and he moved to Washington to get closer to the seat of power he occasionally felt was also a seat of misery. His friends in power, ranging from Theodore Roosevelt down, were not disturbed or misled by his criticisms, and even Brooks could find a serious hearing, though many regarded him as eccentric indeed.[45] Boston to both men was arid and dull, its society philistine, preoccupied with lesser affairs, and to be avoided. Their attitude toward Bos-

[42] See Thornton Anderson, *Brooks Adams: Constructive Conservative* (Ithaca, 1951), 57 – 58, 75, 152 – 57; Arthur F. Beringause, *Brooks Adams: A Biography* (New York, 1955), 98, 269, 371.

[43] Ernest Samuels, *The Young Henry Adams* (Cambridge, 1948), 122 – 289, makes these points very well indeed.

[44] Quoted in *ibid.*, 297.

[45] Howard K. Beale, *Theodore Roosevelt and the Rise of America to World Power* (New York, 1962), 162 – 66.

ton was not merely a reflection on men beyond satisfaction but on a reality that historians have tended not to explore.

It is possible to hypothesize, of course, that the Brahmins were in business in Boston and elsewhere but were increasingly displaced as a percentage of the total number of Boston big businessmen. Hence the "status revolution" theory of Hofstadter might still be valid. The crucial point to determine for Hofstadter's status revolution thesis is whether the economic elite was synonymous with the status elite; whether the entire status elite was in business or rich is not relevant.

The Boston *Social Register* was first issued in 1890, and included approximately 1800 names. By 1902 it had been enlarged to approximately 4400 names, to include a greater number of children. In 1892 *The Tribune Monthly* of New York published a list of American millionaires and fortunes, including 217 for Boston. Of this number, 120, or 55 percent, were listed in the *Social Register* for 1890. Of the 97 millionaires not listed, many were estates or individuals with family names listed in the *Register* but who could not be directly accounted for or who were excluded for personal reasons.[46] By 1902 Boston had 314 millionaires, according to *New York World Almanac*, and of these 207, or 66 percent, appear in the 1902 *Social Register*. Many of those excluded have family names in the *Register*, but again private circumstances resulted in their exclusion.[47]

In 1902 Boston was home office for 197 industrial corporations, mines, railroads, banks, and utilities listed in *Moody's*, vying with Philadelphia as second largest center for corporations in the nation. Of the highest single officers of each of these companies, 131, or 67 percent, were listed in the *Social Register*. Those not listed in the *Register* tended to head the smaller corporations, though many unlisted names are identical to those of the leading Brahmin

[46] Calculated from *Social Register — Boston, 1890* (New York, 1889), and *The* [New York] *Tribune Monthly*, IV (June 1892), reprinted in Sidney Ratner, ed., *New Light on the History of Great American Fortunes* (New York, 1953).

[47] Calculated from *New York World Almanac, 1902*, reprinted in *New Light on . . . Great American Fortunes*, and *Social Register, Boston, 1902* (New York, 1901).

families.[48] Exclusion, again, was frequently due to personal factors having nothing to do with family origins, but involving such issues as private lives, manners, or the like. Indeed, the boards of directors of these key Boston firms were highly interlocked among the Brahmin families, and show how fully the economic elite in the second or third largest economic center in the United States was in fact also the century-old status or social elite.[49]

IV

Historians have alleged that the estrangement of the older social elite from the main currents of American life at the beginning of this century led, on a political level, to the politics of progressivism and, ultimately, the formation of the Progressive Party of 1912. They have studied the facts in regard to this phenomenon, but, for the most part, their theories fail to correspond to them. The Brahmins too were supposed to have shared in this supposed disillusionment with politics, "dismayed by the increasing materialism of American society, by the growth of political and moral corruption. . . ."[50]

[48] Calculated from *Social Register, 1902*, and *Moody's Manual of Corporation Securities — 1902* (New York, 1902). Even the most exclusive and literary of Boston's clubs, the Saturday Club, was composed of a large number of professionals, mainly business lawyers, businessmen, and politicians, who comprised about one-half of the Club's membership. Those listed as teachers, etc., included men, such as Alexander Agassiz, who made fortunes in business before turning to more intellectual pursuits, and many in this category had substantial inherited wealth. The Club's membership was never more than a small fraction of the Brahmin millionaires. See M. A. DeWolfe Howe, *Later Years of the Saturday Club, 1870 – 1920* (Boston, 1927), *passim*.

[49] Mr. Arthur Viargues has prepared a similar analysis of Philadelphia during this period, showing that by 1902 at least 58 percent of the millionaires were listed in the Philadelphia *Social Register*. Family marriage and economic patterns in Philadelphia were remarkably similar to Boston's, though not quite as extensive. E. Digby Baltzell, *Philadelphia Gentlemen: The Making of a National Upper Class* (Glencoe, Ill., 1958), Chaps. V – VII, provides a wealth of material which shows Philadelphia's evolution differed from Boston's in degree but not in kind, and in fact that the older nineteenth-century status elite moved up the economic ladder after the Civil War to dominate the new and expanding economy.

[50] Saveth, "Henry Adams . . . ," 303.

If the Brahmins were disenchanted by the political direction of
American life there is not much evidence to show their unhappiness was based on disagreements over fundamental considerations, much less that they were cut off from the leading decision-
making circles. Quite the contrary, politics came easily to Boston,
and there was a surfeit of levers for them in Washington and at
home. Both in Massachusetts and in Washington there were no
important differences in the leadership of the Republican, Democratic, or Progressive Parties, and Brahmins could and did support
all three with equanimity.[51] Higginson voted for Wilson in 1912,
as did many of his friends, while others supported Taft or Roosevelt.[52] During the second Cleveland Administration, with former
State Street lawyer Richard Olney in the Attorney General's and
then Secretary of State's offices, the Brahmins were encouraged to
submit their views and proposals, frequently did, and their advice
was followed in crucial instances.[53] Under Roosevelt, whose first
wife had been a Lee, the situation was no different, and Henry
Adams, Lodge, and numerous other Brahmins had continuous
access to the White House. Some Brahmins were excluded and
complained, but frequently only because they supported the
party out of power. But at no time, in fact, were they cut off as a
class from the mainstream of Washington affairs.[54] As Richard
M. Abrams shows in his recent study of Massachusetts politics,
1900 – 1912, the Brahmins for the most part identified with wealth

[51] Richard B. Sherman, "The Status Revolution and Massachusetts Progressive Leadership," in Edward N. Saveth, ed., *American History and the
Social Sciences* (New York, 1964), 200 – 01. Mr. John Rumbarger has
prepared an unpublished study of this problem on a national level.

[52] Henry Lee Higginson to Woodrow Wilson, February 27, 1913, Higginson Papers, Baker Library, Box XV.

[53] Henry James, *Richard Olney and His Public Service* (Boston, 1923),
30; Henry Lee Higginson to Olney, April 19, 1893; C. E. Perkins to Olney,
April 18, 1893; William Endicott, Jr., to Olney, April 23, 1893, in the
Richard Olney Papers (Manuscript Division, Library of Congress), Vol. 5.
In July 1893 Higginson sent Olney a plan for a gold reserve policy that
was subsequently the basis of Administration action. Higginson to Olney,
July 27, 1893, Olney Papers, Vol. 5.

[54] This conclusion is based on evidence presented in this writer's *The
Triumph of Conservatism: A Reinterpretation of American History, 1900 –
1916* (New York, 1963).

and privilege and ". . . committed the traditional social leaders to men of their own class more than to avowed ethical standards."[55] Prior to that time they advanced state-wide reform proposals for conservative goals, pioneering in railroad regulation. After 1900, on a national level, they too shared in the general reform euphoria and lined up with all of the factions advocating measures, unmistakably in the camp of progressivism.

*   *   *

High status is based on power and the social, political, and economic elements that are the components of power. To retain and extend power and status the Boston Brahmins continued in the world of business, where they had made their initial fortunes, and they dominated and channeled the economic life of the region in a way that benefited themselves. Indeed, they were dynamic entrepreneurs and innovators and extended their economic influence and holdings towards the western states. Without economic power the Brahmins would have lost status, and to suggest a dichotomy between status and economic power fails to account for the facts and in no sense does it explain the phenomenon of progressivism and American reform.

The use of such terms as "patrician" or "aristocracy" in connection with the Brahmins, unless precisely defined, can only obfuscate. The Brahmins were a socially cohesive group of extended interrelated and intermarried families engaged primarily in commerce and industry during the period after the Revolution, the notable and much more prominent minority notwithstanding. In relationship to the rest of American society, and in their own eyes, they were an elite of the prime order. But after the Civil War their absolute cultural superiority over other cities may be questioned, ignoring the growth of pretension which should not obscure the fact that had fewer Brahmins gone into business after the Civil War they might have produced more real art, music, and writing. Self-sufficiency in culture after 1870 led to aridity and drove out a good portion of the more promising talent, and subjected Boston to accusations of philistinism from her most famous and gifted lost sons.

[55] Richard M. Abrams, *Conservatism in the Progressive Era: Massachusetts Politics, 1900 – 1912* (Cambridge, 1964), 168.

It is largely the caustic evaluations of the Boston writers and intellectuals that have shaped the American historians' understanding of what was happening to the Brahmins at the end of the last century. The world of ideas has been projected on to the world of economics and politics, with the concomitant assumption of the alienation and displacement of the Brahmins as a class. In the case of Charles Francis Adams, Jr., or Henry Lee Higginson one can see how far random comments varied from functioning institutions. Ideas and utterances are valuable if treated in their appropriate context. In their written form they are more accessible as seeming reflections or interpretations of events than the actions of men of the same class who took wisdom as customarily given, reflected little and wrote less. These men of action became the more important shapers of history. Outside Boston, the writings and speeches of Theodore Roosevelt were less important than the fact that the records of his administration show he accommodated quite comfortably to "good" business. Andrew Carnegie, despite his infatuation with the doctrines of Herbert Spencer, called for government price-fixing of steel; and businessmen in general had little contact with professors who wrote tomes on *laissez faire* or took sides on the social meaning of Darwinism.

If American historians begin cultivating a more naturalistic view of the American political and economic experience, with less reliance on conventional wisdom and more dependence on the facts appropriately leavened by relevant hypotheses, they will probably begin reassessing the vital importance of established power groups in defining and exploiting new political and economic changes. Such an evaluation will have to overcome ideologically conditioned theories of equality of opportunity and simply have to determine who succeeds in politics and economics and how they manage to do so. In the case of Boston the power in hand led to its growth in future decades. The evidence for Philadelphia indicates that the same was true there as well. Assuming that the development of these cities has significance, I should like to suggest that American historians would benefit by looking at competition in American economic history after the Civil War as being, at least in significant part, interurban in character and between more or less cohesive groups that within their own ranks, because of family and marriage ties in some instances, or mutual self-interest in others, followed essentially cooperative norms in their struggle against outsiders. Railroad competition and railroad legislation, implemented or attempted, was frequently a disguise for the conflict between coastal cities for eastbound traffic, or among merchants, Grangers, oilmen, and other groups to equalize their position against competitive coalitions. Railroads themselves were frequently merely the butt of such interurban or regional conflicts.[56] Similarly, the struggle for the control of many giant firms, such as A. T. and T., grew out of rivalries between cooperative alliances of capitalists in Eastern cities. On the legislative front, various urban or regional groups, perhaps broken down by industry within the areas, sought specific forms of legislation during the Progressive Era in order to meet problems posed by other urban or regional groups. References to individual capitalists in American economic history ignore the risks many wished to avoid, and, in the case of Boston, slight the reality.

The national scene aside, the Boston experience is clear. Those with status had money — without economic strength they would have been simple Yankees — and those with money stayed in business in large numbers, effectively dominating it. There was no anti-business party in the post-Civil War period based on opposition to business *from above*, nor was there a serious class basis for such a political position. The Brahmins reflected the dominant norms of the social order, *their* social order, and in Boston helped define them in the period of rapid expansion after the Civil War. Developing the economic modalities appropriate to a new age, and to consolidate their position as the established elite, they brought even greater fresh infusions of wealth into their ranks. Well before Calvin Coolidge told them the obvious truth, the Brahmins knew that the business of America was business.

[56] See the discussion and citations in Kolko, *Railroads and Regulation, 1877–1916* (Princeton, 1965), Chaps. I–II; and David M. Potter, "The Historical Development of Eastern-Southern Freight Rate Relationships," *Law and Contemporary Problems*, XII (Summer 1947), 416–48.

On the Limits of Professional Thought

MAURICE R. STEIN

AN INCREASING NUMBER of sociologists are coming to share the conviction that the range of our discipline must somehow manage to include a broad concern with the problems, patterns, and processes connected with the vast social changes currently shaking all parts of the modern world. Difficulties arise when we try to accomplish this expansion of consciousness and concern through the convenient bureaucratic mechanism of developing new fields of sub-specialization. The game of academic leap-frog which involves inventing fashionable specialties in everything from sociology of poverty to sociology of affluence, from applied sociology to sociology of war and peace, and from sociology of the underdeveloped world to sociology of advanced industrial societies only increases the confusion. Each new specialty develops its own self-contained literature, thereby compounding the problems facing the individual seeking broader perspectives. Even humanistic sociology shows signs of becoming a specialty within the larger fold. It is time that those of us seeking an alternative sociology, whether this be called "humanistic," "critical," or "historical," realize that we have to go beyond criticizing the main drift of the profession and must also refuse to allow ourselves to become a specialty within it.

We should recognize from the start that humanistic sociology is going to be harder to pursue than consensual sociology in many different ways. One of the ways stems from the fact that those of us trying to develop it do so working within conventional aca-

This essay is a revised version of a paper presented to a panel on "Humanistic Sociology" at the 1966 meetings of the American Sociological Association in Florida.

demic settings where there are strong pressures to accept the norms regulating methods of instruction, modes of collegiality, and styles of research and reporting. It is one thing to observe that humanistic sociology demands different methods of teaching, along with different methods of writing, and still another to present actual alternatives. This paper will discuss a few possibilities.

To begin, let me indicate five points at which I think humanistic sociology diverges from consensual sociology:

1. Where the consensual sociologist seeks to segregate his political beliefs, his life history and his emotional hang-ups from his work, the humanistic sociologist tries to explore, expand, and transform these personal dimensions through his work.

2. Where consensual sociology encourages specialization along such lines as methodology, political sociology, applied sociology, etc., humanistic sociology assumes that all sociological work is political, methodological, applied, etc.

3. Where consensual sociology views society as an appropriate object for "value-neutral" investigation, humanistic sociology views society as an historically evolving enterprise that can only be understood through the struggle to liberate human potentialities.

4. Where consensual sociology assumes that life proceeds along predictably stable lines, humanistic sociology tries to be alert to dangerous instabilities and extreme situations.

5. Where consensual sociology concerns itself with other disciplines by ascertaining their systematic logical relationships to the current level of sociological thought, humanistic sociology looks to other fields for help in uncovering and exploring patterns of societal liberation and repression.

These distinctions obviously are oversimplified and require extensive explication. For present purposes, however, they serve as a series of pointers that suggest the contours rather than the details of a humanistic sociology. With these contours in mind, we can raise a few substantive queries.

Recent events on the educational scene have forced some sociologists to contend with the extent to which ordinary academic procedures involve us in the defense of a network of privileges and dominations. The Berkeley student revolt was one such

instance, and it clearly exposed some terms upon which administrative and faculty authority rest. Students are required to subordinate themselves to administrative and faculty needs disguised
as educational programs. The justification for this subordination
and the reward for complying with it are one and the same —
eventual admission to the privileged occupational category of degree holder. Students and some faculty members find themselves
questioning the very occupations to which the degrees provide
access — even sometimes including college teaching. One is not
surprised to find conservative and consensual sociologists upholding institutional authority. The surprising aspect of the situation
is the small number of critical interpretations written from a
humanistic standpoint.

Since the protests against academic authority at Berkeley are
showing signs of being relevant on other campuses, they could
help lay the groundwork for creative conflict throughout colleges
and universities. The problems that arise in such conflicts are central to the development of humanistic sociology, and we must
very quickly develop some kind of investigative framework for
gathering useful information from situations of this kind. As
teachers, we must also begin to ponder the utilities and disutilities
of these situations for the education of students.

One such situation began with the usual combination of protests against the war in Viet Nam, protests against the university's
participation in selective service, and protests against the generally abusive authority structure of the university itself. Many
people on the faculty and from the student body got deeply involved and more than a few were rather profoundly altered by
the experience. From an educative standpoint, students and colleagues alike were able to watch the ways in which the several
intellectual styles represented among the sociology faculty each
led to quite different modes of participation in the ensuing political struggle. One could not help but get a clear picture of the
action-shaping and action-inhibiting effects of even the most abstract sociological styles. At times we debated assertions about the
rank of our institutional structures and patterns of functioning on
a comparative scale that included all American universities. By
drawing up a net balance of functions and dysfunctions in such a

way as to suggest that we were better off than most other places, this kind of comparison stopped any action. At other times we voiced demands for further "reliable" data, presumably to be gathered in the non-existent intervals between action and reaction. Everyone tended to view this political process in terms of his own specialty, and we variously saw ourselves as engaged in fighting against a primal father, or as a conglomerate network of disembodied stages in academic careers, or occasionally as a group of mental patients fighting against a powerful staff.

One outcome of this political activity was an enormously deepened grasp of the innumerable ways in which a bureaucratic environment utilizes codes defining "due process" to keep members of various groups from acting in effective or concerted ways. The entire established system regulating relationships between students, faculty, alumni, trustees, and administrators, which value-neutral, structural-functional sociology of education would take as a "given" object of study, appears during a crisis to function as a network of constraint and control. Under these circumstances, new configurations appear as the several participants invent relationships cutting across status lines which momentarily transform the objective structure and which can permanently transform the participants. A question remains as to whether it is ever possible for the same participants to operate within or accept the old structures. Apparently, the Berkeley campus has never quite returned to the old configuration and perhaps never will.

Dealing with these campus movements may well be one major task which humanist sociologists must face in the years to come. Hopefully, they will continue to generate new educative combinations and potentialities. The students who get most involved in them are likely to be the students who care most about the society and who therefore could become an important source of desirable recruits for the profession of sociology. They are the students who move off the campus to the South, to the Peace Corps, to the slums, and to the bohemias, in an effort to involve themselves in the process of social change. They are also the students who most resent being recruited to a profession. In fact they tend to see those of us who have already been so recruited as having in the process made our peace with affluence and the American establishment. And they tend to be especially suspicious of a profession which claims to offer an opportunity for objective study of society, yet which has so little to say about such major criminal enterprises as the calculated American war against the people of Viet Nam and such dubious enterprises as the sometimes well-intentioned war against the American poor and the inadvertent war against the American environment.

Sociology has in the past been able to situate itself effectively within the main stream of social change in America and in the world. The classical theorists always sought objectivity by starting their theorizing and their research at a point before recent Western history so that they could achieve a more objective perspective on our society by viewing it against the background of earlier systems of social organization. For reasons far too complicated to take up here, thinkers in many different fields during what has come to be known as the period of modernism, the years from 1890 to 1920, were able to get outside the confines of Western styles of thought, to discover or invent a repertory of expressive and investigative forms for dealing with the darker and the brighter potentialities of Western society. In social science, the high spots were undoubtedly Freud's discovery of the unconscious and of a methodology for studying it while altering it, and Weber's discovery of the special role played by the processes of rationalization and bureaucratization in Western history. Objectivity in social science after Freud and Weber, not to mention Marx, could only be the product of careful working through of one's own deepest emotional, national, class, and cultural biases.

The Chicago school, at least during the twenties, offered a program through which sociologists could immerse themselves in the processes of social change while still engaging in significant social research. Robert Park and his immediate associates had an extremely broad-gauged grasp of the world-wide changes that urbanization was bringing about, and the best of them knew deeply that the transition from a predominantly rural to a predominantly urban society entailed important gains and important losses. Park's students were able to benefit from his powerful synthetic probing into urban processes and urban forms to the extent that he provided each of them with sufficient feeling for the totality of urban processes to allow them to study and report upon a particular changing urban area. Each student studied the community which concerned him most, often the community from which he came. Members of the school were thus able to explore significant social problems while simultaneously exploring their own social worlds and contributing to the development of urban sociology.

A new school of humanistic sociology would necessarily have to anchor itself as deeply in the processes of social change that characterize the sixties as did the Park school in the processes of urbanization in the twenties. One suspects that the establishment of such a school is imminent, but that it will take quite different forms from those that humanistic social science assumed during the period of modernism. It would certainly be worth exploring the modes of intellectual, emotional, and practical interaction that distinguished such diverse groups as the Park school, the Frankfort school, the Durkheim circle, the Freudian movement, the Boas circle, and others. There is an enormous amount of secondary material on each of these groups, and the Freudian movement remains an active force to this day.

The school of critical sociology called the Frankfort school, led by Max Horkheimer and represented actively today by Herbert Marcuse, Erich Fromm, and Theodore Adorno among others reacted deeply to the rise of totalitarian movements during the thirties and forties. It represented an effort at synthesizing Hegel, Marx, and Freud, with asides to Nietzsche and Weber, around the problems of advanced industrial society. The school provided a creative matrix for such diverse work as Franz Neumann's analysis of Nazi Germany and Leo Lowenthal's studies in the sociology of literature. Marcuse's recent *One-Dimensional Man* provides the sharpest critique of both protagonists in the Cold War, and his *Eros and Civilization* constitutes one of the most powerful and most radical syntheses of Freud and Marx.

Much can be said about the working of innovating schools of thought in the arts and social science. These schools can be essentially critical of prevailing trends, as in the instance of Frankfort, or deeply ambivalent about them, as in the case of the Chicago school. They can organize around the leading ideas of a single theorist, as did the Freud circle and the Boas group, or they can approximate a company of equals. It is common to find such schools of thought developing independent journals simply because the orthodox journals in the field reject the form and/or the content of their discoveries. Such innovating schools often attract strong-minded persons from diverse backgrounds, with the result that highly individuated intellectual products and styles develop. This often leads eventually to schisms and to conflict. Another outcome is standardization of thinking and training by the second and third generation members of such a school. It is worth noting that innovating schools of this sort usually include among their members science-oriented and art-oriented persons. Such schools will often harmonize and energize persons of quite opposed backgrounds and styles for the period of time when the methods and theories of the school retain their power to liberate deep exploration of emerging realities. After that, their influence both on their members and on the larger society can change drastically.

The problem of innovating schools would seem to be central to the development of humanistic sociology, simply because the encouragement of sociological styles along the lines suggested by the five points listed earlier must inevitably proceed outside of, and in antagonistic relationship to, the ordinary network of roles and training systems that constitute a socially acceptable profession. In this sense, too, if humanistic sociology is somehow to attract, teach, and learn from committed radical students, it can hardly hope to do so by accepting the professional strategies which accept distance from life experience as the price for studying it, and which accept categorization as the central purpose of the research process. Even the proliferation of new politically oriented specialties mentioned earlier can hardly help but impress such students as the pursuit of worthwhile goals by worthless or bureaucratic means.

But the issues are not really this simple. There is at the moment no satisfactory school of humanistic sociology, though there are several distinguished practitioners of humanistic styles both within and outside of the profession. The effort at creating such a school, or at least simulating its existence, by a few would-be followers of C. Wright Mills misses the essence of the latter's contribution. Mills managed to save the anti-bureaucratic side of Weber's theory of bureaucratization from total neutralization by structural-functionalism. He did this because he felt very deeply about the rise of bureaucratic elites, about the rise of mass society, and about the terrifying decline of humane relations between men and between nations in the modern world. This set of concerns allowed him to assemble two good general descriptions of America in the fifties, *White Collar* and *The Power Elite*. It also enabled him to write a brilliant manifesto about the failures of American sociology in the forties and fifties in *The Sociological Imagination*, and several helpful though hardly influential political manifestos like *The Causes of World War Three* and *Listen Yankee*. This body of work offers more inspiration than direction, particularly as we move farther into an epoch of boundless information and boundless technological power. The Fulbright Committee did not have to wait for sociologists to tell them that our war against the people of Viet Nam was a disaster on the way to genocide.

The problems involved in establishing the terms for a humanistic sociology are enormously complicated by the lack of shared experience within the several generations of would-be practitioners of this art. In fields like psychoanalysis and anthropology, there are ways of segregating the practical activities of the trainee from the substantive theories and theories about methods that dominate any current generation of practitioners. And instruction in these practical activities is acknowledged to be of a special character resting upon a controlled but intimate interactive process between supervisor and trainee. In fact, psychoanalytic training even goes so far as to separate the process in which the trainee explores and improves his own modes of psychic functioning, called the "training" analysis, from the process of "supervised" treatment in which the trainee receives guidance in working with patients. One wonders if achieving an "objective" attitude towards society requires any less careful training in grasping one's own cultural, national, class, and even sexual biases. Furthermore, one wonders if these biases can be understood only through self-study and through study of societies, or if such self-understanding and understanding of society must be accompanied by efforts at changing both self and society on multiple levels. Humanistic sociology would do well to opt for the latter. This means that we must evolve modes of supervising and being supervised, in such a way that the fights for academic reform, or the teach-ins, or our community efforts, or our sociological journalism, turn into occasions for mutual teaching and learning.

The heart of our problem lies in the relation to the central processs of bureaucratization which the profession of sociology has accepted. This is a relationship which continually confounds and co-opts would-be humanist sociologists by a comprehensive set of ploys, the proliferation of politically-oriented and politically-labelled sub-specialties being only the most recent. The whole issue probably goes back to the adoption of fragmentary versions of Max Weber's intellectual project by successive generations of American sociologists without any major theoretical or practical recognition that adopting a formally rational model by a social science meant bureaucratizing the practice of that science, unless powerful protections for substantive and substantial (in Mannheim's sense) rationality were simultaneously instituted. Max Weber himself was keenly aware that the powerful gains that formal rationalization permitted could and did involve equally powerful human losses. His American disciples from Talcott Parsons to Robert Merton, and even including many self-conscious rebels against Weber, find themselves serving up categorical distinctions in place of substantive sociological insights despite their best intentions.

One source of many of our difficulties lies in the fact that bureaucratization no longer has even the limitations that Weber saw. We live in an epoch of total bureaucratization in which, to employ Erving Goffman's useful phrase, all institutions tend to turn themselves into total institutions. Jacques Ellul in *The Technological Society*, and even more so in *Propaganda*, shows the processes through which the total environment can become the basis for propaganda. Under these circumstances the familiar distinction between common-sense constructs of action and social-scientific constructs becomes hollow. When the Pentagon has developed languages for assessing "overkill" in the neighborhoods of tens of millions of people, the value-neutral language of sociology and the humanitarian language of common sense both pale into insignificance.

The further development of humanistic sociology, if there is to be any, may well depend upon the extent to which we can teach ourselves and help to teach our students to comprehend and evaluate the devastating changes which accompany technological expansion when it is exploited by selfish, emotionally backward, and intellectually deformed technocratic elites. Our protests must involve persistent refusal to take over the perspectives or the judgments promulgated by these elites. Under some circumstances this may mean defending the most abstract forms of scholarship or of art. Under others it may mean advocating heightened attention to current political processes. In neither case can we afford to allow our choices to be made for us, whether by an academic establishment or by any particular group of student rebels.

To close on a personal note, Herbert Marcuse during his many years at Brandeis helped keep all of us continually aware of the threat posed by the Warfare-Welfare State in its many embodiments. At the same time he never let his awareness of totalitarian terror extinguish his keen sense of humor. We are grateful for having been privileged to share both.

The Limits of Integration

PAUL MATTICK

I

IN AN ADDRESS delivered in Korčula, Yugoslavia, in 1964, Herbert Marcuse raised the question of "whether it is possible to conceive of revolution when there is no vital need for it." Marx, Marcuse related, expected a working-class revolution because, in his view, the laboring masses represented the absolute negation of the bourgeois order. The accumulation of capital destined the workers to increasing social and material misery. They were thus both inclined and driven to oppose and to transform capitalist society. However, if the proletariat is no longer the negation of capitalism, then, according to Marcuse, "it is no longer qualitatively different from any other class and hence no longer capable of creating a qualitatively different society."[1]

Marcuse is fully aware of the social unrest in even the advanced capitalist nations and of actually or potentially revolutionary situations in many underdeveloped countries. However, the movements in advanced nations are movements for "bourgeois rights," as, for instance, the Negro struggles in the United States. And the movements in underdeveloped countries are clearly not proletarian, but national, to overcome foreign oppression and the backwardness of their own conditions. Although the contradictions of capitalism still persist, the Marxian concept of revolution no longer fits the actual situation, for, in Marcuse's view, the capitalist system has succeeded "in channeling antagonisms in such a way that it can manipulate them." Materially as well as ideologi-

[1] H. Marcuse, "Socialism in the Developed Countries," *International Socialist Journal*, II, No. 8, April 1965, p. 150.

374

cally, "the very classes which were once the absolute negation of the capitalist system are now more and more integrated into it."[2]

The meaning and extent of this "integration," Marcuse develops at length in his *One-Dimensional Man*. The integrated man lives in a society without opposition. Although bourgeoisie and proletariat are still its basic classes, their structure and function have been altered in such a way "that they no longer appear to be agents of historical transformation."[3] While the advanced industrial society is "capable of containing qualitative change for the foreseeable future," Marcuse does acknowledge that "forces and tendencies [still] exist which may break this containment and explode the society."[4] In his view, however, the "first tendency is dominant, and whatever preconditions for a reversal may exist are being used to prevent it."[5] This situation may be altered accidentally, "but unless the recognition of what is being done and what is being prevented subverts the consciousness and the behavior of man, not even a catastrophe will bring about the change."[6]

Not only is the working class written off as an agent of historical change but so is its bourgeois opponent. It is as if a "classless" society were emerging within a class society, for the former antagonists are now united in an "overriding interest in the preservation and improvement of the institutional status quo."[7] And this is so, according to Marcuse, because technological development — transcending the capitalist mode of production — tends to create a totalitarian productive apparatus which determines not only the socially needed occupations, skills, and attitudes, but also individual needs and aspirations. It "obliterates the opposition between the private and public existence, between individual and social needs," and it serves "to institute new, more effective, and more pleasant forms of social control and social cohesion."[8] In totalitarian technology, "culture, politics, and the economy merge into an omnipresent system which swallows up or repulses all al-

2 *Ibid.*, p. 140.
3 H. Marcuse, *One-Dimensional Man* (Boston, 1964), p. xiii.
4 *Ibid.*, p. xv.
5 *Ibid.*
6 *Ibid.*
7 *Ibid.*, p. xiii.
8 *Ibid.*, p. xv.

ternatives. The productivity and growth potential of this system stabilize the society and contain technical progress within the framework of domination."[9]

Marcuse recognizes of course that there are large areas where these totalitarian tendencies of control and cohesion do not exist. But he regards this as merely a question of time, as these tendencies assert themselves "by spreading to the less developed and even to the pre-industrial areas of the world, and by creating similarities in the development of capitalism and communism."[10] Because technological rationality tends to become political rationality, Marcuse thinks that the traditional notion of the "neutrality of technology" must be given up, for any political change can "turn into qualitative social change only to the degree to which it would alter the direction of technical progress — that is, develop a new technology."[11]

It is clear that Marcuse is not realistically describing existing conditions but rather observable *tendencies* within these conditions. In his view, it is the unchallenged unfolding of the potentialities of the present system which *seems* to lead into the completely integrated totalitarian society. Preventing this development, Marcuse says, would now require that the oppressed classes "liberate themselves from themselves as well as from their masters."[12] To transcend established conditions presupposes transcendence *within* these conditions, a feat denied one-dimensional man in one-dimensional society. And thus Marcuse concludes that the "critical theory of society possesses no concepts which could bridge the gap between the present and its future; holding no promise and showing no success, it remains negative."[13]

By refusing to accept the apparently unchangeable conditions of a new "barbarism," which arrogantly regards itself as the very height of civilization, Marcuse turns his negativism into effective social criticism, which remains valid even though the general tendencies derived from it may not come to pass, or may not

[9] *Ibid.*, p. xvi.
[10] *Ibid.*
[11] *Ibid.*, p. 227.
[12] *Ibid.*, p. 251.
[13] *Ibid.*, p. 257.

come to pass in the way foreseen by him. Although one may not share his excessive "pessimism" as regards the "foreseeable future," this pessimism is nonetheless warranted in view of existing conditions.

Usually, in the past as well as today, hope for a socialist working-class revolution is given up in the expectation that social problems are solvable by way of reforms within the confines of capitalism. In this view, revolution has become not only highly improbable but entirely unnecessary. The rise of one-dimensional society and one-dimensional man is not only not bewailed but is celebrated as the common achievement of labor and capital to the benefit of all of society. Marcuse differentiates himself from such "critics" of the proletarian revolution by opposing the "final" results of the reformist endeavors. For him, the world is in a bad and hopeless state just because there was not, and apparently will not be, a proletarian revolution, just because Marxism proved no match for the resilience of capitalism and for its capacity not only to absorb the revolutionary potentialities of the working class but to turn them to its own advantage.

In view of the present situation in the advanced capitalist nations, history seems to validate "Marxian" revisionism rather than revolutionary Marxism. The latter was the product of a period of development in which capital accumulation was indeed a period of increasing misery for the laboring population. Around the turn of the century, however, it became clear that in its decisive aspects the Marxian prognosis deviated from the real development; i.e., capitalism did not imply the continuous impoverishment of the working class, and the workers themselves, far from becoming more class-conscious, were increasingly more satisfied with the steady improvement of their conditions within the capitalist system. The war of 1914 revealed that the working class had ceased being a revolutionary force.

The miseries of war and of the prolonged depression in its wake revived to some extent the oppositional inclinations of the working class, and the specter of social revolution stalked the world again. But capitalism once more proved able to side-track the released revolutionary energies and to utilize them in pursuit of its own ends. Practically and ideologically, the Second World

War and its aftermath led to an almost total eclipse of working-class socialism. There is no point in denying this obvious fact. It is true, nonetheless, that the absence of any effective opposition to the capitalist system presupposes the system's ability to improve steadily the living conditions of the laboring population. If it should turn out that this is not a continuous possibility, the present "cohesion" of the capitalist system may well be lost again — as it has been lost in previous crises of long duration.

II

Marcuse bases his pessimism on what appears to him to be capitalism's newly gained ability to solve economic problems by political means. In his view, *laissez-faire* capitalism with its crisis cycle has been successfully "transformed into a regulated profit economy, controlled by the state and the large monopolies, into the system of 'organized capitalism.' "[14] He assumes that this system is able constantly to increase production and productivity, particularly through the instrumentalities of automation, and will thus be able to continue to maintain high living standards for its workers. There exists, Marcuse thinks, actual and potential "abundance," which, though accompanied by "an unprecedented concentration of cultural, military and political power and so much great wealth," satisfies men's material needs sufficiently so as to extinguish their desire for social change and to evoke a "world of identification."

As far as *laissez-faire* capitalism is concerned, Marx's prediction of its decline and eventual demise is obviously still supported by the actual capitalist development. Marcuse, too, insists, that "the economy can only function because of the direct or indirect intervention of the State in vital sectors."[15] He also recognizes that there are "conflicts between the private and state sectors" of the economy, but he does not think "that this is one of the explosive conflicts which could lead to the destruction of capitalism"; particularly not, he says, because these conflicts "are nothing new in the history of capitalism."[16]

[14] H. Marcuse, "Socialism in the Developed Countries," *International Socialist Journal*, II, No. 8, April 1965, p. 140.

[15] *Ibid.*, p. 141.

[16] *Ibid.*, p. 144.

There was always opposition, of course, to government controls as exemplified in *laissez-faire* ideology, yet the present objective conflict between government and business is of a different character because of the relatively faster growth of the government-determined production in the course of the general expansion of capital. The quantitative change points to an undesired, yet inescapable, qualitative change. Private capital must oppose this change with the same determination with which it opposes socialism itself, for an extensive State control of the economy forecasts the end of private enterprise. The objective opposition between state-controlled and private capital production is still clouded and appears as the subjective cooperation of business and government in the nominally market-determined economy. This "cooperation" is possible only because it still subordinates government policies to the specific needs of big business. But the specific needs of big business contradict the general needs of society, and the social conflicts thereby released will turn into conflicts about the role of government in economic affairs, that is, will be political struggles for the control of government in order either to restrict, or to extend, its interventions in the economy. This struggle *transcends* the established conditions and does so *within* these conditions.

It should be clear that the dynamics of capital production are not identical with technological development. It is not production and productivity as such which propel capitalism, but the production of profits as the accumulation of capital. For instance, it is not a physical inability to produce which leads to a decline of production in crisis situations, but the inability to produce profitably. The commodity glut on the market indicates the difference between production and capitalist production. It is, then, not the technical power to produce "abundance" which determines the state of the capitalist economy, but merely the power — or the lack of it — to produce an abundance of profit.

According to Marx, capital accumulation leads necessarily to a decline of profitability relative to the growing mass of capital, and therewith to crises and depressions devastating enough to produce social convulsions and, eventually, the overthrow of the capitalist system. But Marx's "general law of capitalist accumulation," derived as it is from highly abstract considerations of capitalism's structure and dynamics, was not provided with a timetable. The contradictions of capital production could come to a head sooner or later — even much later. Difficulties in the production of capital are, of course, concretely countered by all available means capable of restoring a required profitability, which, if successful, assure the continued existence of capitalism. But a mere increase in production is not a sign of capitalist expansion; it is such only when issuing into capital formation and by doing so in accelerating measure. Although there is an enormous increase in production in times of war, it is accompanied by an excessively low rate of capital formation. Surplus-labor, instead of being capitalized in additional profit-yielding means of production, is utilized in the production of waste and for the destruction of capital already accumulated. Likewise, in times of "peace," production may be increased despite a stagnating or declining rate of capital formation by way of compensatory government-induced production. But this is merely an admission that capitalism would find itself in a depression if it were not for the expanding government-determined sector of the economy.

If the goal of government intervention is the stabilization of the market economy, government-induced production must be non-competitive. If the government were to purchase consumption goods and durables in order to give them away, it would, to the extent of its purchases, reduce the private market demand for these commodities. If it were to produce either of these commodities in government-owned enterprises and offer them for sale, it would increase the difficulties of its private competitors by reducing their shares of a limited market demand. Government purchases, and the production they entail, must fall out of the market system; they must be supplementary to market production. Government is therefore predominantly concerned with goods and services that have no place in the market economy, that is, with public works and expenditures of all descriptions.

The division between private and public production is, of course, not absolute. Political exigencies induce governments to enter the sphere of private market production, for instance, by subsidizing certain commodities and by purchasing surplus products to be utilized in foreign and domestic aid projects. There is some overlapping of private and public business activities in various branches of production as well as in their marketing and financing. Generally, however, one can speak of the division of the economy into a profit-determined private sector and a smaller, nonprofitable, public sector. The private sector must realize its profits through market transactions; the public sector operates independently of the market, even though its existence and its activities affect the private sector's market relations.

The government increases "effective demand" through purchases from private industry, either financed with tax money or by borrowings on the capital market. In so far as it finances its expenditures with tax money, it merely transfers money made in the private sector to the public sector, which may change the character of production to some extent but does not necessarily enlarge it. If the government borrows money in the capital market, it can increase production through its purchases. Capital exists either in "liquid" form, i.e., as money, or in fixed form, that is, as means and materials of production. The money borrowed by government puts productive resources to work. These resources are private property, which, in order to function as *capital*, must be reproduced and enlarged. Depreciation charges and profits gained in the course of government-contracted production — not being realizable on the market — are "realized" out of the money borrowed by the government. But this money, too, is private property — on loan to the government at a certain rate of interest. Production is thus increased, the expense of which piles up as government indebtedness.

To pay off its debts and the interest on them, the government has to use tax money, or make new borrowings. The expense of additional, government-contracted production is thus carried by private capital, even though it is distributed over the whole of society and over a long period of time. In other words, the products which the government "purchases" are not really purchased, but given to the government free, for the government has nothing to give in return but its credit standing, which, in turn, has no other base than the government's taxing-power and its ability to increase the supply of credit-money. We will not enter here into the intricacies of this rather complex process, for, however the credit expansion is brought about and however it is dealt with in the course of an expanding government-induced production, one thing is clear, namely, that the national debt, and the interest on it, cannot be honored save as a reduction of current and future income generated in the private sector of the economy.

If not caused by war, government intervention in the economy finds its reason in the malfunctioning of private capital production. The latter is not profitable enough to assure its self-expansion, which is a precondition for the full use of its productive resources. Profitability cannot be increased by way of nonprofitable production; in so far as capital produces without regard to profitability it does not function as capital. Although its unused productive capacities are put to use by government contracts, "profits" made in this way and "capital accumulated" in this process are mere bookkeeping data relating to the national debt, and not actual profit-yielding new means of production, even where the physical productive apparatus grows with the increase in production. A relatively faster increase in government-induced production than in total social production implies the relative decline of private capital formation. Because government-induced production is itself a sign of a declining rate of capital formation in the traditional sense, it cannot be expected to serve as the vehicle of private capital expansion effective enough to assure conditions of full employment and general prosperity. It rather turns into an obstacle to such expansion, as the demands of government on the economy, and old and new claims on the government, divert an increasing part of the newly produced profit from its capitalization to private account.

Of course, claims on the government, which make up the national debt, can be repudiated, and "profits" made via government-induced production are thus revealed for what they actually are, namely, imaginary profits. But though perhaps unavoidable some day, governments, representing private capital, will postpone this day as long as possible, particularly because the repudiation of debts alone does not guarantee the resumption of a profitable private capital accumulation. Meanwhile, of course, there is a slow but steady depreciation of incomes and debts by way of inflation — a necessary process connected with the expansion of government-induced production by way of deficit-financing.

Notwithstanding the long duration of rather "prosperous" conditions in the industrially advanced countries, there is no ground for the assumption that capital production has overcome its inherent contradictions through State interventions in the economy. The interventions themselves point to the persistency of the crisis of capital production, and the growth of government-determined production is a sure sign of the continuing decay of the private-enterprise economy. To arrest this decay would mean to halt the vast expansion of government-induced production and to restore the self-expansive powers of capital production; in short, it implies a reversal of the general developmental trend of twentieth-century capitalism. As this is highly improbable, the State will be forced to extend its economic inroads into the private sectors of the economy and thus become itself the vehicle for the destruction of the market economy. But, where the State represents private capital, it will do so only with great hesitation and against growing opposition on the part of private capital. This hesitation may be enough to change the conditions of an apparent "prosperity" into conditions of economic crisis.

Capitalism will not turn itself into socialism. But neither can it maintain itself indefinitely as a "mixed economy," wherein government solves the problems of capital production by political means. Government intervention in the capitalist economy is itself restricted by the limitations of capital production. The organization of social production presupposes the expropriation of private capital. It will be just as difficult, however, to make a state-capitalist revolution as it is to make a socialist revolution. But short of the nationalization of productive resources, all state interventions in the market economy — while perhaps raising production to the extent of these interventions — will increase the difficulties of competitive capital formation in the foreseeable future.

III

According to Marx, definite social relations, or production relations, correspond to definite social productive forces released by them and bound to their existence. The capital-labor relationship determines the unfolding of technological development as the accumulation of capital. Only within the frame of capital formation do science and technology expand the capacities of social production by increasing the productivity of labor. Under the social relations of capital production, the given potentialities of socialized production cannot be fully realized, since their realization would destroy relations existing under capitalist production. At a certain point in its development, capitalism becomes a hindrance to a further unfolding of the social forces of production and changes from a progressive into a regressive social system.

Marcuse himself points out that in Marxian theory "the social mode of production, not technics is the basic historical factor."[17] However, he says, "technical progress, technology itself, have become a new system of exploitation and domination," a system which is no longer challenged but willingly, or passively, accepted by all social classes.[18] Although technology is not "the major factor responsible for the situation," technic and technological development, Marcuse explains, "are organized in such a way that the existing system in the highly industrialized capitalist countries is very largely held together by them."[19] In other words, the present technology offers a way out for capitalism and is therefore the most important obstacle to its abolition.

For Marx, too, science and technology are specific to capitalism, but only in the sense that their direction and development find their determination and limitations in capitalist relations of production. Should these relations be abolished, science and technology could take on an unhampered and different course, in accordance with the conscious and rational decisions of fully socialized man. For Marx, it is neither science nor technology which constitutes a system of domination, but it is the domination of labor by capital which — with everything else — turns science and technology into instrumentalities of exploitation and class rule. In Marcuse's view, however, it is not so much capitalism which now determines the state and nature of technology as it is technology which determines the state and nature of capitalism.

Marcuse thinks that "Marx did not foresee technologically ad-

[17] H. Marcuse, *One-Dimensional Man* (Boston, 1964), p. 154.

[18] H. Marcuse, "Socialism in the Developed Countries," *International Socialist Journal*, II, No. 8, April 1965, p. 140.

[19] *Ibid.*, p. 148.

vanced society." Nor did he see "all the things which capitalism could accomplish . . . simply by exploiting its technical break-throughs."[20] Yet, all that capitalism can accomplish in this way, even in Marcuse's view, is its own maintenance by keeping technological progress within the boundaries of class domination. The statement that "Marx did not foresee technologically advanced society" is hardly justifiable in view of Marx's projection of social development toward the "abolition of labor" through the unfolding of the social forces of production, which include science and technology. But it is true that Marx did not believe that much in this direction could be done within the confines of capitalism, which was an additional reason for calling for its abolition.

The utopian "abolition of labor" implies the abolition of capitalism, or of any other successive form of class exploitation. This actually unreachable goal only serves to indicate the general direction which social development must take in order to decrease socially necessary work time (*Arbeitzeit*) in favor of free time. Socialism was, then, conceived as the end of exploitation and the freeing of the social forces of production from their capitalist fetters, so as to assure a maximum of free time. Socialism itself presupposed the socialist revolution. Marcuse thinks it timely, however, to question the continuing validity of the Marxian concept that "the realm of work remains the realm of necessity, whereas the realm of liberty can only develop above and beyond the realm of necessity," because, in his view, "the end of necessary work is in sight; it is not a utopia: it is a real possibility."[21] To be sure Marcuse is careful to make his prognostications in the form of questions, He asks, for instance, "What does it mean when, in mass technological society, work time — socially necessary time — is reduced to a minimum and free time practically becomes full-time?"[22] Although he only raises the question, the question itself seems to imply the possibility of the emergence of such a state of affairs. But, placed in context with capitalism, these are false questions. The technical revolution required to eliminate work time in favor of free time is not compatible with capitalism.

Marcuse himself points out that automation which would turn

[20] *Ibid.*, p. 149.
[21] *Ibid.*, pp. 149, 150.
[22] *Ibid.*, p. 149.

work time into fringe time and free time into full time . . . "cannot be realized within the present system"; it would "mean, plainly, the final catastrophe of the capitalist system."[23] In saying this, Marcuse refutes, at least to some extent, another simultaneously held position, namely, that modern technology "transcends" the capitalist mode of production. But what is new in technology is just this automation, which, if inapplicable in capitalism, means that this mode of production also "transcends" technology, that is, determines the degree of its development. To be sure, there is quite a difference between full automation and partial automation, but why it can only be partial and not full depends again on the mode of production. When automation is seen as the alternative to capitalism and appears nonetheless in capitalism, it should, to that extent, indicate the beginning of the end of capitalism and not its "stabilization" and "integration." Marcuse assumes, however, that capitalism is able to use the new technology, including partial automation, to secure its own existence simply by raising living standards and by an enormous increase in waste production. Sooner or later, however, the system would still be forced to arrest further technical development in the direction of automation, for the number of unemployables would come to exceed that of the employed. Eventually, a small minority would have to provide for the large majority, thus reversing the usual conditions of class society. But where and when to stop this process — since any of its ascending stages brings the dissolution of the capitalist system so much nearer?

Capital, we must here recall, is congealed surplus labor in the form of surplus value, and it feeds and expands on living labor. In so far as technological development is a function of capital formation in value terms, the capital accumulated is the materialization of unpaid work time. The reduction of work time also implies the reduction of unpaid work time, and therewith the reduction of capital formation. To be sure, unpaid work time can be increased at the expense of paid work time, even while total work time is decreased, through the increase of labor productivity in the course of capital expansion. As less work time is needed to produce the commodity-equivalent of the workers' income, more

23 *Ibid.*, p. 142.

of the total work time can take on the form of products appropriated by the capitalists. But the continuous reduction of work time must eventually also reduce unpaid work time and thus stop the process of capital expansion by way of the increasing productivity of labor. Where there is no labor, there can be no surplus labor and, consequently, no accumulation of capital.

Whatever the extent of automatization and computerization, the means of production neither operate nor reproduce themselves. On the quite improbable assumption that their owners, the capitalists, themselves engaged in production, they would thereby cease being capitalists, that is, buyers of labor-power for purposes of exploitation. Assuming, what is more probable, that they succeed in continually reducing the number of productive workers, they would also reduce the unpaid work time relative to the mass of the accumulated capital. Capital-labor relations are value relations, which is to say that the means of production are not that only but are also capital values, and that labor-power is not that only but is the source of value and surplus value. To consummate the capitalist production process, surplus value must have a definite relation to the value of capital, i.e., it must be sufficient to ensure its enlarged reproduction. As value relations are labor-time relations, it should be clear — at least to the Marxist — that a reduction in labor time which would disturb the necessary relationship between surplus value and capital is not compatible with capitalism and will, for that reason, interrupt or end the capitalist production process.

In abstract value terms, a more rapid rise of the capital invested in means of production than that invested in labor-power depresses the rate of profit, which is measured on total capital. Profitability can only be maintained through increasing productivity, through labor-displacing and capital-saving technical innovations. The steady increase in production and productivity through labor-saving devices has the twofold effect of increasing the profitability of capital and reproducing the need for further vast increases in productivity on an ever-narrowing base of capital production. Even if capital-saving devices were to check the growing discrepancy between that capital invested in means of production and that invested in labor-power, and in this manner curb the fall of the rate of profit on total capital, this can only be a temporarily mitigating factor. The consistent displacement of labor must eventually terminate in the destruction of profitability. But neither can capitalism do without the steady displacement of labor, for this is seemingly the only way left open to cope with the growing nonprofitable production within the profit-producing economy. While the displacement of labor is a way out for capitalism, the way itself leads only to a *cul-de-sac*. What Marcuse considers a capitalistic solution to capitalism's difficulties, namely, its new technology, represents, instead, the present and future insoluble contradiction of capital production within the property relations of the market economy.

We will not go into the technical details of why the profit-reducing effect of a declining number of workers cannot perpetually be neutralized, or over-compensated for, by their increasing productivity, and why, for that reason, the tendency of a falling rate of profit must turn into its actual decline at a certain stage of capital expansion. For, in view of the present threat of automation, it is now almost generally discerned that the growing discrepancy between labor and capital must come to a point which would exclude a further progressive capital expansion through labor exploitation.

This growing conviction implies an unconscious acceptance of Marx's theory of accumulation, if only because it is dressed in non-Marxian terms. Instead of deducing the eventual collapse of capitalism from the "productivity of labor," which is only another expression for the accumulation of capital, the inverted "Marxists" deduce it from the "productivity of capital" and its tendency to displace labor. In either case, the system of capital production through labor exploitation comes to an end. Since the growing productivity of labor implies the growing productivity of capital, the end of capitalism by way of automation equates with the end of capitalism for lack of surplus value.

IV

Whereas future events may prove Marcuse right in his pessimism with respect to the chances of a working-class revolution, his "optimism" with regard to capitalism's ability to save itself by technological and political means will most probably be disproved by actual events. At present, of course, Marcuse's assertion can only be answered by a counter-assertion. In view of what has happened since the end of the second world war, it would appear that capitalism has found a way to escape the perils of its class structure and has been able to transform itself into a society freed of effective opposition.

Any particular state of capitalism is transitory. But it is only by considering the general laws of capitalist development that any of its given historical situations reveal its transient nature. The future of capitalism rests on its continuing ability to extract sufficient profits out of social production to ensure its enlarged reproduction. A persistently declining rate of capital expansion indicates, increasingly, the loss of this ability, and this despite a general increase in production through government interventions. However, so long as the increase can still be conciliated with the decrease of private capital formation through the increasing productivity of labor, the "mixed economy" may be experienced not as a temporary possibility but as an actual transformation which resolves the contradictions of capital production.

The question is, then, can capitalism evolve into something other than it is; can the general laws of capitalist development be set aside by technological and political means, which attend to both the profit needs of private capital and the general welfare by the simple expediency of waste production? It is true that this is exactly what has happened. Yet to see this process as a permanent and ever-widening social practice is to assume that capitalism can transform itself into another system in which — to speak in Marxian terms — it is no longer exchange-value but use-value that rules. Such a change would imply a change in property relations based, as they are, on the production and distribution of exchange-value. In other words, it would require a social revolution.

Not so, however, in Marcuse's opinion. The industrially advanced society, he says, is "a static society, despite all its dynamism. Its non-stop expansion, its soaring productivity, its increasing growth produce nothing but more and more of the same, without any qualitative change or any hope of qualitative change."[24] But Marcuse also speaks of a capitalist "metamorphosis" in response

[24] *Ibid.*, p. 141.

to the phenomenon of the cold war, which first provides capitalism with the impetus to "organize" itself and to expand its production. Still, in his view, this "metamorphosis" implies not a
qualitative but only a quantitative change, through "the ever-
increasing tide of goods and the ever-rising standard of living,
which seem ever more desirable," and which provide the masses
with "every reason to integrate themselves into such a society."[25]

However, according to Marcuse, even "the most highly organized capitalism retains the social need for private appropriation
and distribution of profit as the regulator of the economy."[26] If
this is so, "organized capitalism" also retains capitalist value relations, and it becomes necessary for Marcuse to demonstrate that
these relations harmonize with the continuous expansion of production by technological and political means. In this connection,
Marcuse quotes Marx to the effect that "the machine never creates value but merely transfers its own value to the product, while
surplus value remains the result of the exploitation of living labor."[27] Considering automation, however, Marcuse remarks, that
it "seems to alter qualitatively the relation between dead and living labor; it tends toward the point where productivity is determined 'by the machines, and not by the individual output.' "[28]
This also occurred to Marx, who pointed out that social wealth is
not only a value relation but is embodied, in increasing measure,
in a productive apparatus which turns the productivity of labor
into the productivity of capital. "Although the very development
of the modern means of production," Marx wrote, "indicates to
what a large degree the general knowledge of society has become
a direct productive power, which conditions the social life and
determines its transformation," capitalism's particular contribution
to this state of affairs consists of no more "than its use of all the
media of the arts and sciences to increase the surplus labor, because its wealth, in value form, is nothing but the appropriation
of surplus labor time."[29]

[25] *Ibid.*, pp. 142, 143.
[26] *One-Dimensional Man* (Boston, 1964), p. 53.
[27] *Ibid.*, p. 28.
[28] *Ibid.*
[29] K. Marx, *Grundrisse der Kritik der Politischen Oekonomie* (Berlin,
1953), pp. 594, 595.

The diminution of labor as the source and measure of value already takes place under capitalist conditions. Depending on the state of the structure of capital, it may have either a positive or a negative effect upon the accumulation process. Now, when Marcuse says "that even the most highly organized capitalism retains the social need for private appropriation and distribution of profit as the regulator of the economy," he is saying only that the value relations of capital production are here retained and regulate the economy. In other words, the economy is "regulated" by its ability or inability to produce surplus value, and not by its ability or inability merely to produce. The private appropriation and distribution of profit presupposes market relations, and these market relations presuppose value relations. Under these conditions, profit remains surplus value, or surplus labor, even where the relations between "dead" and "living" labor have been reversed.

Marcuse finds that capitalism responds to the challenge of communism by a "spectacular development of all productive forces after the subordination of the private interests in profitability which arrest such development."[30] Moreover, according to Marcuse, it is not only the "challenge of communism" which brings this change about, but also the "technological process and mass production, which shatter the individualistic forms in which progress operated during the liberalistic era."[31] Apart from the fact that these "individualistic forms" were first decisively shattered in technologically backward nations without mass production, were it actually true that these "individualistic forms" are shattered, it could not simultaneously be true that "private appropriation and distribution of profit" is being retained as the "regulator of the economy." And, if the latter be true, it could not be true that "private interests in profitability" have been "subordinated" to the social need of a further "spectacular advance of the productive forces."

One cannot have it both ways; either the economy is left to its "self-regulation" via the value-price relations in a competitive market of individually oriented producers, that is, capitalistically; or it is consciously regulated, more or less successfully, by government decisions considering the national economy as a whole

[30] *One-Dimensional Man* (Boston, 1964), p. 55.
[31] H. Marcuse, *Soviet Marxism* (revised edition, New York, 1961), p. 67.

on the basis of its particular institutional arrangements. A combination of market regulation and planned regulation of the economy can only be a side-by-side affair; it does not really "mix" the economy, but tends, in the course of development, to eliminate one side or the other, unless one of these sides can always be held in a subordinate position. But to hold it there is to limit its effectiveness. Because the expanding government-induced production cannot enhance but can only hem in private capital formation, for its expenses must ultimately be carried by the private sector of the economy, the maintenance of private capital production sets a definite limit to the enlargement of government-induced production. Consequently, the continuous expansion of production must be attained by private production. But this private production is subject to value relations and their market appearances and finds its limits in its own expansion. There are, then, within the capitalist relations of production, limits set to both private production and government-induced production; the limits of the latter are the limits of capital production itself.

V

Capitalism has long ceased to be a socially progressive system of production and has become — notwithstanding all the superficial appearances to the contrary — a regressive and destructive form of social production. It has led to the division of the world into a few highly industrialized countries and a large number of nations unable to lift themselves out of a state of increasing poverty. Yet the destinies of all nations are inextricably intertwined; it is the situation as a whole, the world situation, which finally determines the future of any and all nations. The prospects for even the most prosperous countries must be considered in the light of existing world conditions, and seen in this way they are indeed bleak. The conditions of prosperity form rather small oases in a huge desert of human misery.

No longer able to extract out of their own working populations the quantities of surplus labor that would secure a profitable capital accumulation, the dominating capitalist powers find that the sources of surplus labor in the underdeveloped part of the world are also drying up. Over-accumulation in the developed nations is, in large part, responsible for the lack of accumulation in the underdeveloped. To keep on exploiting the backward areas will slowly destroy their exploitability. But not to exploit them means to reduce even more the already insufficient profitability of capital in the advanced nations. They will thus try to increase rather than to relax their exploitation, if no longer in collaboration with the backward nation's traditional ruling classes, then by way of neo-colonialism, i.e., in collaboration with the new ruling classes that have been tossed up by the anti-colonial movements.

However, the continued economic domination of the less developed nations by Western capital offers no solution for the actual needs of the vast mass of their populations, nor will it solve the basic problems of capital production for Western capitalism. All that it does is to sustain somewhat longer the viability of the disintegrating capitalist world economy, aided by the brutal suppression of all resentment caused by the unrelieved and growing social misery. It is quite safe to predict that, at least in the underdeveloped part of the world, the prevailing misery will lead to ever new rebellions against the dominating foreign powers, as well as against their native collaborators.

It is of course true, as Marcuse says, that the rebellions in the underdeveloped nations are not proletarian movements in the Marxian sense. Even if these national-revolutionary movements should succeed it would merely lead to social conditions such as characterize the capitalist world either in the East or in the West, where socialist revolutions in the Marxian sense seem no longer a possibility. According to Marcuse, "the reality of the laboring classes in advanced industrial society makes the Marxian 'proletariat' a mythological concept; [and] the reality of present-day socialism makes the Marxian idea a dream."[32] There exists, however, no "present-day socialism" which, by its performance, proves the unreality of the Marxian concept of socialism, i.e., the classless society free of economic value relations. Neither does the reality of the laboring classes in advanced industrial society deny the reality of the Marxian concept of the proletariat merely because their living standards have improved and their class con-

[32] *One-Dimensional Man* (Boston, 1964), p. 189.

sciousness has evaporated. As before, society is divided into owners of the means of production and the propertyless working
class, or into controllers of capital and the powerless wage-labor-
ers.

It is only on the assumption that the status quo can be maintained, that all social problems can be resolved within the existing
institutions, that history has come to a stop in the established conditions, that it is possible to deny the proletariat — that is, the vast
majority of the population in the industrially advanced countries
— a rôle in history, which can necessarily only be an oppositional
rôle and thus must find expression in a revived, or newly emerging, revolutionary consciousness. Of course, Marcuse does not
deny further historical development; the factor of automation
alone, he points out, "signals the possibility of a revolution in
capitalism." In his view, however, this is a long way off, for
which reason Marcuse always provides his dismal prognostications with the rider — "in the foreseeable future." But what else is
the "foreseeable future" if not the recognition of some basic
trends which affect and alter existing conditions in a definite direction? The emphasis must then be put not on the possibly
drawn-out persistency of existing conditions, but on the elements
within these conditions which indicate their dissolution.

Marcuse seems to believe that the recent and current conditions of working-class "affluency" in the industrially advanced
nations are here to stay. "There has been," he says, "a split within
the working class itself, turning nearly all the organized working
class into a labour aristocracy," which has brought forth a "new
kind of working class solidarity — solidarity between organized
workers who have a job and a measure of security, as opposed to
those who have no job and no chance of getting one in the foreseeable future either."[33] But this is not a new working-class solidarity but the absence of all solidarity, for, even within the organized sector of the working class, itself a minority, there is no
solidarity but merely, though not always, a mutual agreement to
respect the job monopolies of different unions. Labor unions
simply have become reactionary because the market relations on
which they are based are no longer progressive but regressive so-

[33] H. Marcuse, "Socialism in the Developed Countries," *International
Socialist Journal*, II, No. 8, April 1965, p. 145.

cial relations. This is not a question of "social integration," where the interests of labor and capital coincide, but merely an example of the persistency of obsolete institutions in the decaying market economy.

But this persistency will not assure their present social position in times to come. As capital cannot gain anything from the unemployed, but must sustain them in one fashion or another, it can only gain, if gain it must, from the employed workers. It is very difficult, if not impossible, to undo living standards once reached, without calling forth serious social convulsions. The high living standards in the industrially advanced nations must themselves turn into detriments of capital expansion. For to maintain them under conditions of decreasing profitability implies the continuous extension of nonprofitable production and this, in turn, an increasingly greater need to raise the productivity of labor, which, under present conditions, means the steady growth of unemployment. Unemployment itself becomes an increasing expense, which, in connection with all the other expenses of "affluency," will sooner or later tax to the utmost even the greatest "economic and technical capacities." The "affluency" will not be maintainable unless the nature of society itself is changed, unless the profitability principle is discarded.

This is not to say that "affluency" breeds revolution. It is only to say that no absolute impoverishment is required to produce oppositional sentiments. People need not be reduced to starvation levels before they begin to rebel; they may do so at the first deep inroads into their customary living standards or when access is denied them to what they consider their living standards should be. The better off that people are, the harder they feel any deprivation and the more tenaciously they cling to their accustomed style of life. It is in this sense that a partial loss of the prevailing "affluency" may be enough to destroy the existing consensus.

VI

Marx says somewhere that "the proletariat is revolutionary, or it is nothing." Presently it is nothing and it may well be that it will continue to be nothing. But there is no certainty. Marx also said that "the ruling ideas are the ideas of the ruling classes," which does not prevent the rise of subversive ideas. Obviously, subversive ideas will flourish only under conditions of dissatisfaction. There is not enough dissatisfaction in present-day prosperous society, even if it is a false prosperity. Consequently, there is one-dimensional thought, a society without effective opposition. As nothing else can be expected under such conditions, we have not gone into Marcuse's penetrating critical analysis of the advanced industrial society's ruling ideology. Here we agree with all his observations and are thankful for them. Since Marx, it was to be expected, as Marcuse relates, that the "advancing one-dimensional society alters the relation between the rational and the irrational. Contrasted with the fantastic and insane aspects of its rationality, the realm of the irrational becomes the home of the really rational,"[34] — which is the final outcome of the fetishism of capital and commodity production.

Actually, however, and here Marcuse is himself a witness, non-fetishistic rationality still exists but can, for all practical purposes, be ignored. The opposition that exists cannot become a social force because it represents as yet no material interests strong enough to oppose the material interests represented by the ruling ideology. Where opposition ceases to have material force, it becomes a luxury — the deeper insight of intelligent men who may well despise both society and its victims for defending so obstinately the prevailing irrationality. Yet, the impoverished minority must live within this irrationality and must accept it by necessity, which is then turned into an apparent virtue to make it more palatable. Even where opposition finds political forms, it finds false expressions as, for instance, in the American Negro struggle for civil rights, a meaningless and, even in its meaninglessness, an unrealizable goal. The "outsider" cannot step outside existing conditions — unless he risks all, his very life, by arson and looting.

The sporadic rebellions of despair by small minorities are easily handled by the authorities representing the smug majority, which includes the mass of the working class. Black or white, "the substratum of outcasts and outsiders" can be decimated piecemeal by the very conditions of existence provided for them. But as their number grows — and it is growing — the frequency of their rebel-

[34] *One-Dimensional Man* (Boston, 1964), p. 247.

lious acts will also increase, as will the awareness on the part of many of the smug that perhaps they, too, will soon find themselves on the human refuse heap of capitalism. To judge by the past, the growth of social misery gives power to this misery, and power leads to actions. When Marcuse says with respect to the unemployables that the "economic and technical capabilities of the established societies are sufficiently vast to allow for adjustments and concessions to the underdog, and their armed forces sufficiently trained and equipped to take care of emergency situations,"[35] he correctly describes the existing conditions in the industrially advanced countries. But what is true today is not necessarily true tomorrow and will, in any case, be less so if the trend of capitalist development proceeds as it has in the past.

Of course, the events of the past may not be repeatable; the age of revolutions may well be over and the one-dimensional, stationary, totalitarian society unavoidable. But if we cannot judge by past experiences we cannot judge at all. In that case, everything is possible — even a working-class revolution. This presupposes the continuous existence of the proletariat, which, however, is allegedly already in dissolution, not only with respect to its disappearing class consciousness but in its social functions as well. A distinction is frequently being made between the "classical working class" and the modern working population, of which only the smaller part has productive occupations. But this distinction is artificial, for what differentiates the proletariat from the bourgeoisie is not particular occupations among the former, but their lack of control over their own existence through the lack of control over the means of production. Whatever their occupations, wage-workers are proletarians. Even if more workers are now engaged in nonproductive, so-called service industries, their social position vis-à-vis the capitalists remains unaltered. Due to the concentration of capital and the elimination of the proprietary middle class there are now more "proletarians" than ever before.

The working population may not think, or may not like to think, of itself as being "proletarian" and may, by this reluctance to recognize its social position, contribute to the one-dimensionality of the ruling ideology. However, in order not to lose their

[35] *Ibid.*, p. 257.

utility, all ideologies must in some way relate to factual conditions; if they lose all contact with reality they are on the verge of breaking down. While the well-paid employed worker may not recognize his proletarian status, the unemployed will do so more readily, and the impoverished, treated as an outcast, has no longer any choice.

Capitalism is basically a two-class society, notwithstanding the various status differentiations within each separate class. The ruling class is the decision-making class; the other class is at the mercy of these decisions, which determine the general conditions of society, even though they are formed with a view to the special needs of capital. The ruling class cannot act otherwise than it does; that is, stupidly or intelligently, it will do everything to perpetuate itself as a ruling class. Whatever the decision-makers decide upon has to be actualized in the sphere of production, as the manner of distribution and the patterns of consumption depend on the pattern of production. Without control over the productive process no decisions can be made, no class can rule. The control of production is exercised through the control of the means of production, by ideology and force. But neither property, nor ideology, nor force can produce anything. It is productive labor on which the whole social edifice rests. The productive laborers have more latent power than any other social group. To deny this fact is the main job of bourgeois ideology. It comes to the fore in its economic theories and in the general disparagement of productive labor. However, despite the prevalent notion of the decreasing importance of the industrial working class, more attention is devoted to it than ever before, because, actually, its potential power to control society was never so great as it is now.

The technical-organizational "socialization" of production, i.e., the interdependency of the national production process and the absolute dependency of the whole of the population on an uninterrupted flow of production, provides the working class with almost absolute power over the life and death of society. They could destroy society by simply ceasing to work. While this could not be their intention, being members of the same society, they could nevertheless shake society at its foundations if they were determined to alter its structure. It is for this reason that unions have been adapted to the capitalist establishment to control industrial disputes, that governments, including labor governments, pass anti-strike legislation, and that those most aware of the latent power of industrial action, that is, the totalitarian regimes, outlaw strikes altogether. Because the industrial proletariat, if so inclined, has the power to change society, it is now, as before, the class on which the actual transformation of society depends.

With the record of working-class behavior before us, the workers' indispensability for the actualization of socialism makes socialism even less accessible and apparently no more than a "Marxian dream." Yet, one has only to think of what in all probability is bound to happen without a socialist revolution in order to think of the possibility of a different kind of behavior on the part of the laboring classes. What is bound to happen is in some measure already happening, and the quantitative projection of the present into the foreseeable future points to the utter utopianism of solving social problems by capitalistic means. The phrase "socialism or barbarism" states the only real alternatives.

Ideological conformity depends on conditions of prosperity; it has no staying-power of its own. But, unless all theoretical reasoning is entirely valueless, in so far as it allows for predictability, it points to the demise not only of capitalistic prosperity but to the end of capitalism itself. If class consciousness depends on misery, there can be little doubt that the misery awaiting the world's population will go beyond anything thus far experienced and that it will come to engulf even the privileged minorities in the industrially advanced nations, who still think of themselves as immune to the consequences of their own activities. Because there are no "economic solutions" for the contradictions of capital production, its destructive aspects take on an increasingly more violent character; internally, by more and more waste production; externally, by laying waste territories occupied by people unwilling to submit to the profit requirements of foreign capital which would spell their own doom. While the general misery will increase, the special situations of "affluency" will also dissolve, as the blessings of increasing productivity are dissipated in a slaughterous competition for the diminishing profits of world production. Because it is the working class which will most deeply be affected by a reversal of the fortunes of capital production, or by capitalist excursions into war, it may in all likelihood be the first to break with the one-dimensional ideology of capitalistic rule.

The Society Nobody Wants:
A Look Beyond Marxism and Liberalism

BARRINGTON MOORE, JR.

I

Is IT ABSURD to consider seriously the thesis that a decent society, meaning one without war, poverty, and gross injustice, might be perfectly possible right now? That such a society has been possible throughout recorded history? Practically every educated person might agree at once that the proposition was absurd. Yet their reasons would almost certainly be very different, especially if one were to ask intelligent radicals and intelligent conservatives. That in itself provides a justification for raising the question. To explore it seriously might just possibly turn out to be an instance of what the French call *prêcher le faux pour savoir le vrai*. By regarding it as a possibility one might be able to scrutinize more carefully and critically the usual explanations and make some progress toward understanding the real obstacles both now and in the past. To hold that such a society is possible does not mean after all the same thing as believing that it is at all probable.

Before glancing at some of the reasons usually given to explain why such a state of affairs is out of the question it would be well to clarify further just what is being discussed. I have deliberately chosen the term "decent society" rather than "good society" to avoid some unnecessary disputes. Human beings have rather more difficulty in agreeing upon what they do want than what they do not want. The good society connotes one that has a variety of positive virtues, from satisfying the lower to the higher appetites. Over such questions there can be legitimate and endless differences of opinion. On the other hand, people are much more ready to agree that they would like to escape from pain and suffering, especially from useless and avoidable suffering. As used here, the conception of a decent society has an even more restricted and negative aim than the elimination of useless suffering. It means no more than the elimination of that portion of human misery caused by the working of social institutions. The historically recurring forms of suffering due to such causes can be grouped very roughly under the headings of war, poverty, injustice, and persecution for the holding of unorthodox opinions. Even if it were possible to remove these forms, there would certainly remain all sorts of purely personal unhappiness and indeed tragedy.

Just how much humanity could have accomplished along these lines in the past is of course an enormous and in the end unanswerable question. Nevertheless there are some reasons for thinking that we grossly underestimate what men could have done. There is a tendency to think of past ages as ones in which rich and poor struggled to divide up a supply of goods closely limited by brute scarcity and inadequate techniques. Marxists tell us in effect that a decent society became a realistic possibility only after mankind had passed through the purgatory of the industrial revolution. That is highly doubtful. By the time human societies had accumulated enough technical knowledge to acquire the label civilized, roughly at the point of using a written language, they already possessed the physical bases for establishing societies in which most of their members could have had enough to eat and enough shelter from the elements to prevent outright physical suffering. For some reason or other they did not arrange matters that way. The suspicion remains that a decent society has indeed been a possibility all along.

There are other considerations too. One is philosophical: the notion that a decent society was within the realm of possibility helps to remove unwarranted and unprovable determinism. If we accept determinism and delete from our thinking the gap between performance and potential in specific societies, we have to believe that whatever social arrangements they adopted at a certain point in time were the only possible ones. In the light of what we know about the tremendous range of social institutions at roughly the same level of technology, that opinion seems absurd. There is also a straightforward factual reason. In isolated parts of the world men have at times established fair approximations to a decent society, even without a written language. Though very different from eighteenth-century European conceptions of the life of a noble savage, these societies did not face war as a serious plague, or indeed war was actually unknown; most people had enough to eat and sufficient shelter. Disease became a serious problem only after contact with the whites and resulting demoralization. The grosser forms of oppression were absent. (By no means all societies studied by anthropologists are like that, though a few are.)

If a decent society has been a possibility for at least a very long time, the real problem becomes to explain why humanity did not or perhaps could not want one. For the moment it is enough to take this view as a hint without pressing the point. In any event it seems reasonably clear that by the seventh decade of the twentieth century poverty has ceased to be an objective physical necessity, if such it ever was. Today the problem of poverty is a political one. The technical knowledge and resources exist now to eliminate most physical suffering. This part of the radical argument makes reasonable sense, but with one important proviso that this line of thought sometimes understresses. The problem of population *is* a serious one. A crowded world cannot be a decent world. A rabbit-like multiplication of numbers means not only the dissipation of technical progress; it also puts too much pressure of the wrong kind on technique. There are better things that science can do for us than to think up ways of squeezing more food out of the reluctant earth and simultaneously to design weapons for more efficient annihilation of those who eat the food.

II

Both the radical critique of advanced capitalism and the liberal critique of communism claim to explain why a decent society is impossible now. Radicals assert that the institutions of capitalism are the obstacle; the liberal tradition sees the obstacle in communist theory and practice. Each viewpoint presents a sufficiently accurate if unflattering portrait of its opponent to make the likeness easily recognizable for any observer who has retained some capacity for critical detachment. But as far as I am able to determine, neither one really proves its central thesis that a decent society is inherently incompatible with the institutions of its opponent.

The radicals make by far the more persuasive case. Though their argument comes out of the Marxist tradition, they have to make a clean break with Russian and Chinese versions in order to cope with the facts. In its most tenable form the radical argument accepts and even stresses the point that modern capitalism has largely solved the earlier problems of physical poverty and outright oppression within its own boundaries. Some perhaps even overstress the success of capitalism. But this very success, they urge, now rests upon destruction and the threat of destruction. The real pillars of American society have become war and waste. They take numerous protean forms ranging from outright military expenditures through artificial obsolescence, massive advertising, and stupefying entertainment, on around to space exploration. The revolutionary urge in the backward countries — arising out of a combination of agrarian distress and the need to thrust aside dominant elites with a vested interest in continued stagnation — America opposes with more and more military force. Military budgets are the least controversial items before the American Congress; the pressure is to increase these and cut down on programs of social welfare. Fundamentally, the radicals tell us, the United States does all these things because a constructive and humane use of our tremendous productive powers is incompatible with an economy based on private property and profit. What keeps the wheels of industry turning in our society is still the prospect of a return on capital invested in plants and machinery. Any really serious program directed toward social welfare at home and abroad runs into massive resistance because it interferes with this prospect. Since the painful aspects of this system are mainly exported — at the moment of writing in the form of bombs — and because American productive capacity is big enough to supply enough sops and opiates to keep the mass of the population adequately contented under a rhetoric of liberal anti-communism, there is no effective protest against it.

The liberal critique of communism is less persuasive mainly because it fails to come to grips with the problems of the backward world. Liberals forget the role that revolution has played in the establishment of Western freedoms and underestimate the strong case that can be made for it in backward areas now. But, drawing on conservative notions absorbed into its own heritage, liberalism does draw up an indictment of communist behavior, or of the consequences of revolution, that seems to me just about as formidable as the radical indictment of capitalism. Transferring the means of production to "the people" is no more than a rhetorical phrase that ignores most of the real problems of a decent society. Communist talk about a higher democracy is mainly sham, a cover for terroristic oppression. This terror and oppression exceed by far anything that might conceivably be justified on the grounds of neutralizing or containing the enemies of the revolution, and reach deep into the lives of ordinary citizens. At least such was the case in Stalinist Russia. In China the communists came to power on a wave of real popular support and may for that reason have been somewhat less cruel. Communism inherently lacks any way of achieving responsible authority. Neither their institutions nor their image of society provide any way of making rulers responsible except through pseudo-plebiscites.

Human beings, the liberal argument continues, have always displayed a strong tendency toward selfishness and even cruelty in their relationships with one another. The only way to check these propensities is a set of social arrangements that make the selfishness and cruelty of one organized sector of society work against corresponding tendencies in another sector. It is utopian nonsense to think that these tendencies can be eliminated. The effort to do so can achieve nothing more than concentrating the means of cruelty in the hands of vicious rulers or their competing subordinates.

There are quite a few variations on these two themes of private property and terrorist bureaucracy as the main obstacles to a decent society in the twentieth century. In reminding the reader of the general tenor of these arguments I may have inadvertently omitted some conception that would have made one side or the other appear to be much more convincing. However, conviction on such questions comes much more from predilections than from the power of the argument. If one makes a serious effort to set these predilections aside, one is likely to discover that both the radical and the liberal arguments fail to carry real conviction. They do point to facts that press themselves onto the awareness of all but the most committed thinkers. But the notion of inherent necessity in the way these facts are combined is not a persuasive one.

It is easier to dispose of the liberal argument first. Aside from the way it misconstrues the character of revolutionary drives in the backward countries, there are severe difficulties in its basic assumptions about politics. The notion that pluralism is inherently liberating and centralized power necessarily oppressive simply do not stand up under examination. In fact, liberals with a Keynesian twist to their thinking drop the second point when they advocate specific policies. Competition among elites means very little to those at the bottom of the heap when the elites have very similar objectives and interests, as is the case in the United States today. Likewise it is hard to believe that bureaucracy always has to be oppressive. There are plenty of large bureaucratic organizations in our own country, such as for example the telephone company, that may be very far from as efficient as we would like but that are not necessarily oppressive to their members or toward the rest of society. To make a large bureaucratic organization that produces a very specific service or commodity responsive to human needs may be easier than a more political one. Yet the problem as a whole does not seem to be beyond human ingenuity if large masses of people really wanted to find the answer.

The radical thesis that war and waste are the consequence of modern capitalism and would disappear with the end of capitalism is also impossible to swallow whole, even though westerners who take a stand close to this have gotten rid of the dubious freight inherited from earlier Marxist conceptions. There is good evidence to show that capitalism has displayed imperialist traits all along. So, for that matter, have all sorts of precapitalist societies. Chauvinist nationalism and acceptance of the status quo are not the result of changes in the structure of modern capitalist society to anything like the extent that this thesis holds.

More specifically, in order to make its criticisms stick, the radical argument would have to demonstrate the following points with substantial factual evidence. First, its proponents would have to show that the pressure to create the American military jugger-naut came out of the business community during the close of World War II and the early postwar years, and that furthermore Soviet foreign policy at this juncture did not and could not con-stitute a serious threat to western democracy. Making this point would require demonstration of where the expansionist pressures came from in American industry and their connection with capi-talism, as well as indicating some of the structural reasons for an allegedly cautious and pacific Soviet foreign policy. In the second place, it would be necessary to show that the profits of the big American corporations, or of an influential segment among them, now depend in some significant measure on what they can squeeze out of the backward countries. Along with this point it would be necessary to show that crucial raw materials essential to the workings of the American industrial machine come from eco-nomically backward areas. To my limited knowledge there is nothing in the radical literature that comes anywhere near making a good case along these lines.

To go on raising objections to both the radical and the liberal images of the modern world would be fairly easy, perhaps a little too easy. I do not wish to deny that there is significant truth be-hind the liberal indictment of communism and the radical indict-ment of modern American society. On both sides the indictment makes better sense than the implied defense that each view carries with it. The liberal critique of communism becomes a blatant de-fense of the worst features of American capitalism. On the other side, even those radical criticisms of American society that have shaken free of Moscow and Peking cannot shed the afterbirth of their defense of socialism. The assertions that private property in the one case and bureaucratic terror in the other make a decent society impossible give off a disagreeable odor of comforting self-interest. Both depend very heavily upon the resistance of vested interests as their main explanation for the world's plight. Both concentrate rather myopically upon its present forms. For a mo-ment it might be wise to set these explanations aside. And to re-member that in all ages the decent society has never had much of a constituency.

III

If no one in his right mind really believes that there is any more prospect for a decent society right now than there has been in previous historical epochs, the nagging question remains: why? In various forms the dream is a very old one. What survives of Greek thought is mainly aristocratic and accepts war and slavery in its versions of an ideal society. But popular notions of peace, justice, and enough to eat are at least as old as Christianity. There were even attempts to put peace into practice, that spread like wildfire over large sections of medieval Europe. Why have they always failed? The opposition of powerful entrenched interests in the dominant classes provides a ready answer. But it is probably a superficial one. Human beings show an enormous ingenuity in science, politics, and social life generally, a tremendous capacity to put up with hardship and danger when they really want something. It is difficult to believe that the same expenditure of energy and intelligence would not yield a world without the main institutional evils of poverty, war, and injustice if that is what the masses of the population really wanted. Does the problem therefore come down then *not* to satisfying human wants as they exist, but to the fact that by and large people don't want a decent world?

At this point it is very easy to go off the track into elitist contempt for the masses, to toy with notions of a revolutionary philosopher's dictatorship. This is a strong temptation for radical intellectuals, especially in America. Despite their tremendous value in opening up new lines of understanding, psychoanalytic theories may have a built-in tendency to push thought in this direction because the refusal to seek a decent society does somehow seem irrational. And in a basic sense it *is* irrational. To be sure the venomous fear of liberation found in the authoritarian personality of American society, the commissar mentality in communist countries and many sections of the backward world, and of course in the Nazis and their successors, requires the help of psychoanalytic theory if we are to understand it. So may opposite notions of saving the world through love as in Gandhi. Important as these phenomena are, they may not be the central ones.

There are some reasons for believing that the great mass of the population most of the time in most countries is composed of "good citizens" as defined by their epoch and culture, law-abiding individuals with very little interest in the great political issues of the age, very heavily preoccupied with immediate personal problems. Grudges and frustrations they certainly have. Yet at bottom they also display yearnings for a peaceful world, and definitely one without poverty or gross injustice. Rarely do these yearnings find their way into the historical record. To judge from the way they do come to the surface in occasional moments of revolutionary ferment, they are mainly projections of their immediate circumstances and life situations minus the most obvious harsh features — and not calls for drastic social change. That of course is a crucial limitation. One might then say with epigrammatic shallowness that the reason we have never had a decent world is because there have always been too many decent people in it. This seems to be the message of much modern literary and artistic rebellion. Whether the traditional decencies, especially patriotic loyalties, have become moral obscenities any more than they were in Greek and Roman times may be doubted. That they are obscene now, and that the dangers are vastly greater, is nevertheless clear enough to make it impossible to condemn the rebellion. But confused sentiments remain confusing counsel even if the feelings are understandable and laudable. The epigram remains shallow because it gives no hint why decent people behave the way they do.

Obviously there are historical and other differences in the behavior of decent people. But what we are looking for here is an explanation of a recurring historical phenomenon: the repeated failure of human societies to come anywhere near the type of decent society that was perhaps within their reach at a given stage of development. Competition with other societies provides at least part of the explanation. To some degree or other, every civilized society has found itself in competition with others — a platitude in every sociological textbook. That the mass of the population has gained by this competition is more open to question. Homer puts into the mouth of Thersites the suggestion that this was not the case, as Thersites stands up in the assembly of the Achaians to berate Agamemnon:

Son of Atreus, what thing further do you want, or find fault
with now? Your shelters are filled with bronze, there are
plenty of the choicest women for you within your shelter,
whom we Achaians give to you first of all whenever we
capture some stronghold. Or is it still more gold you will be
wanting, that some son of the Trojans, breakers of horses,
brings as ransom out of Ilion, one that I, or some other
Achaian, capture and bring in? . . . let us go back home in
our ships, and leave this man here by himself in Troy to mull
his prizes of honour that he may find out whether or not we
others are helping him. [*Iliad*, II, 225 – 239; Richmond Latti-
more translation.]

Odysseus, the first military intellectual in the western tradition,
stopped the mouth of Thersites with a blow, amid the applause of
the soldiers in the assembly. Since then, for some three thousand
years Thersites has been the literary byword for what man ought
not to be.

The tale of Thersites can set one to musing even today. Just
possibly it might give us some clues. What makes him and his ilk
and the rest of us fight and do our duty and be "good" citizens?
Even thinkers are good citizens most of the time, though we can
sense how Thersites must have felt. The superior force, authority, and prestige of Agamemnon and his successors (did the
superiority really rest on the control of the forces of production?)
supply only part of the answer. There were enough of us to
smash *that* any time we wanted to, and there are right now. The
moment we stopped being good citizens, went home in our ships,
used our heads a trifle, the whole idiotic show would come to a
stop. . . . Such fantasies are no doubt common enough. But
every "sensible" person knows they are fantasies, that he is too
busy making a living, that the risk is too great.

The apparent and real risk looks like the decisive part of the
explanation. The enemy always looks like and to some extent indeed is a threat to whatever stake Thersites has acquired in the
social order as it actually works. Even for professional and highly
critical thinkers it is often terribly difficult to distinguish reality
and appearance in such threats. Returning to the contemporary
situation for a moment, *if* capitalism were the real obstacle to a

decent society or *if* communism were the obstacle, the ordinary citizen would be obliged to accept the sacrifices involved in the struggle. Because of the stake he has in his society there is always substantial short-term rationality in being the good citizen. That short-term rationality leads to larger results that are totally absurd is obvious enough to require no elaboration.

One aspect of this recurring situation does deserve explicit mention. Most obvious today in disarmament negotiations, though it has much wider implications, this aspect might be called the problem of the first move. The first move toward cooperation and away from fighting always involves the risk that it will not be reciprocated. Therefore the group or individual that makes the move will very likely find itself in a more dangerous position than if it had made an aggressive move. Hence a system of competing units tends to preserve itself. By and large the only way this situation has been overcome is for one group to acquire overwhelming force and subject the others to its control, in short by conquest. And conquerors are not the ones most likely to establish a decent society.

The winners in these struggles also have a vested interest in the existence of their opponents, a reason why conquest is not as a rule complete. The existence of an enemy is necessary to justify the privileges of a ruler. Throughout human history it is not difficult to perceive something resembling a cartel among enemies, with rules governing their relationship to each other. Achilles received Priam courteously in his tent, after killing Priam's son Hector and dragging his body through the dust behind his chariot before the walls of Troy. The constant that makes this cartel work, that prevents wider cooperation from taking place, is the risk felt by the decent citizen. His ordinary common sense, his sensible reluctance to jeopardize what he has gained by behaving himself according to the rules of the game, give the rulers their chance. Suppressing one's fantasies and hopes is one of the oldest and most familiar ways of adapting to reality. Nor is it quite fair to put all the blame for this situation on rulers and ruling classes. To a considerable extent they have been doing the good citizen's bidding in trying to protect and extend his stake in the prevailing order.

The good citizen's reluctance to jeopardize his stake in the prevailing order makes it easier to understand why the demand for a decent society has generally been so feeble. Another aspect becomes clearer with the commonplace observation that there are other people in society besides the good citizens. In any community it only takes one prospective thief to make the law and the policeman, or some equivalent arrangements for repressive control, quite necessary. In a system of independent states it only requires one state with aggressive capabilities to make armies necessary. In both situations there is a powerful temptation to prey on those who behave themselves in a peaceful manner. For these reasons something resembling Gresham's law is always at work in politics. At any given moment there exists a strong temptation to establish a predatory society. And the predatory society enjoys powerful advantages in compelling others to adopt the same behavior. No power drive, death instinct, or other dubious psychological assumption is necessary to perceive why is generally the case. The situation is enough to generate and perpetuate repressive arrangements and aggressive behavior. Meanwhile the pillars of the community, those persons whose privileges depend on the existence of law, order, and repression, can also find in this situation impregnable justifications for the unhappiness they cause others.

Without trying to press these points further we can perhaps see that something in human affairs much more permanent than capitalist imperialism (or even basic features of modern industrial civilization as a whole) must be responsible for the widespread failure to attain a decent society, or even to make much of an effort. Certainly the reasons vary historically. In modern industrial civilization the physical means and technical knowledge available to create such a society are far greater than in the past, while the sense of grievance among the mass of the population, and hence one of the potential leverages for change, is vastly less than was the case over much of Europe and Asia for at least two centuries prior to our own. Nevertheless modern society apparently makes about the same misuse of its far greater resources as did the Romans and the Greeks. For this state of affairs the good citizen of our time may be even more responsible than his ancestors; at least he has had plenty of time to look about and learn.

IV

"How can you expect that outrageously abstract good citizen of yours to act any other way?" an intelligent and nettled radical might exclaim at this point. "Your line of thought amounts to no more than the usual ahistorical pessimism of decaying bourgeois civilization, laced with a touch of snobbish condescension. We at least have an explanation." I would agree that the good citizens of the United States are not at all likely to do much about bringing about a decent society. Many think they have all they want of it anyway. But again to say that this is extraordinarily unlikely does not mean to say that it is really impossible. A good many human institutions good and bad have begun life as apparently futile utopian notions. Hence it does seem worthwhile to speculate further on the prospects for change.

Furthermore, the fact that there is considerable freedom to dissent here in American society increases the suspicion that ordinary good citizens bear a great deal of real responsibility for the absence of any effective demand for a decent society; there are things they *could* do. Partly on that account what I have to say here will be limited to the American situation. Those who suffer from brutal oppression elsewhere know what they want and scarcely need gratuitous advice. Revolutionary movements have certainly betrayed their ideals and spread injustice under the name of freedom. Nevertheless it is high time to break with that mechanical and self-serving rhetoric which expresses a compulsive necessity to balance each criticism of western society with one of revolutionary movements. The violence of those who fight oppression is not to be nicely equated with those who exercise it.

In the United States, then, we do have some room to think and act on behalf of — if not a decent society — at least something a great deal less indecent than what actually exists. What I have in mind might be called a super-New Deal, a situation where the government in conformity with the constitution became an agency to promote the general welfare. Income redistribution is not necessarily the main feature here, though it would certainly be a significant one. The point rather is to conceive of the government as a social instrument that carries out those necessary tasks and provides those social amenities our tremendous productive power makes possible and which single individuals and even groups like corporations cannot provide on their own by pushing their own private advantage. Such a society would not be like capitalism or socialism, or the mixed economy (something we have anyway), as they now exist. To think in terms of capitalism or private property versus socialism actually obliterates many of the key issues. Private property is not a single right over things, but a whole bundle of rights. Social considerations always have to limit the nature of the bundle. In a capitalist society the individual may own his automobile; he can drive it on the highway only with some minimal consideration for others. Thus the real problem comes down to finding, for a whole series of changing situations, the bundle that provides the social results which produce a minimum of futile suffering and a maximum of social benefits. In any half-way decent society it is bound to be necessary to draw on selfish motives to get the necessary jobs done. Working within a framework of government control directed to ends very different from the present one, a substantial remnant of the present capitalist edifice might well be left standing.

That it would take a bitter political struggle to reach such an objective, that there would be very powerful resistance from entrenched vested interests goes without saying. No one can say for sure what might happen to the liberties that do exist in the course of such a conflict. A reactionary counter-movement might suppress them. On the other hand, the risk that they will disappear anyway in the absence of a movement to use and extend them seems even greater. Hence the key problem amounts to the absence of such a movement, or more precisely the fact that it is still a very weak one.

The main factor that prevents many people from even thinking about the possibility of a less indecent society in the United States is of course the state of semi-permanent mobilization against a foreign enemy. Here we return to the present form of the tendency for predatory groups to create and perpetuate a political climate. The only way to break through this vicious circle, at least intellectually, is to ask just who is being predatory and who is gaining and losing from this situation. If it is true, as I suspect it is, that most Americans make at least substantial short-run gains out of their government's policy of being world policeman for counter-revolution, then most of the American population *is* predatory, and there is little hope of accomplishing anything here. Nor, for anyone with some commitment to a decent society, is there any real point to changing camps. The revolutionaries in their efforts to defend themselves are liable to reproduce and indeed intensify the repressive aspects of what they are fighting against.

Though this outcome may be the most likely one, it would amount to mutual defeat, and in a sense, mutual succumbing to mystification in the Marxist sense of this word, i.e. the concealment of real possibilities in the interests of dominant classes. For Americans there is at least a faint possibility of breaking through the mists. In the first place, as every literate person knows, communism has ceased to be a monolithic enemy of the United States. Wherever communists have come to power mainly on their own, they have sooner or later broken away from the control of Moscow. As revolutionary movements of various kinds gain victories (which are never in any case total) in other countries, we can be reasonably sure that local considerations will be sufficiently important to prevent the formation of any unified and massive opposition to the United States. Finally, these revolutionary movements threaten no more than a tiny segment of American property interests. These interests happen at the moment to be highly strategic and influential ones. That is the main difficulty. A different kind of government with a different set of social pressures making it work could take these losses and still make the mass of the American population a great deal better off than it now is, retaining a military posture sufficient to take care of realistic threats. All that is of course pure speculation. We don't have a different kind of government.

Once again the problem comes down to creating somehow, within the context of American society as it now exists, an effective demand for political change. I have no formula. On the other hand, there is now a movement of sorts, actually one whose present dimensions would have astonished any thinker who might have tried to indulge in sociological prophecies only a few years ago. What its future course will be no one can really tell. Nevertheless, the historical record is full of accounts of all sorts of movements that have enjoyed varying degrees of success in changing the basic structure of society. In their different ways they have tried to realize some aspects of the decent society, even if they have always failed to bring off the enterprise as a whole. A few reflections on their experience may suggest some of the conditions of success and failure.

They usually start as tiny and despised minorities, though by no means confined to the lower classes. What gives them their chance sooner or later is a split, sometimes amounting to a political crisis, in the dominant classes. It is very difficult to discern anything very hopeful along these lines in the American scene, partly because anything approaching crisis is likely to be seized upon by reactionary elements as a justification for real repression. There is just a bare possibility that increasing automation might generate a clientele that could be used as effective leverage for desirable changes. All that one can assert with any confidence is that contemporary stability is very likely an illusion.

Looking more closely at the movements themselves one notices that they have to meet a series of contradictory requirements in order to achieve any measure of success. If they are to keep going for any length of time, they have to produce for their supporters a series of tangible benefits. This imperative applies as much to a movement dedicated to peaceful change, such as a conservative labor union, as to revolutionary movements. The Communist Party in China owed a great deal of its success to its ability to take care of the peasants more effectively than its rival, the Kuomintang. In its effort to meet day-to-day grievances, which are usually defined by the standards of the surrounding society, any protest movement runs the risk of merely becoming part of the established order and simply petering out with limited success.

Out of a sort of instinctive awareness of this danger, protest movements try to separate themselves in as many ways as possible from the established order. The early Christians did this, as did later heretic sects in the declining Middle Ages, as well as a host of others, from nineteenth-century revolutionaries and reformers on through movements of cultural rebellion such as dandyism. On balance this withdrawal seems about the only move open to protest in the American scene right now. What it comes down to is boycotting the affluent society. The advantage is that to a considerable extent the boycott can be carried out by individuals and smallish groups and spread without a complicated organizational apparatus. Should it gain momentum in this fashion it could have considerable impact: what might be expected to happen if people simply on their own became un-American enough to refuse to buy consumers' goods? (One possibility might be a crusade that would put the crushing of the Albigensians to shame. There is plenty of vicious hostility to exactly this kind of movement, an hostility that seems to reflect an instinctive awareness of what is at stake.) The implicit goal of such protest movements is to change, sometimes even to destroy, the prevailing bases of legitimacy, to show somehow that what is taken to be just and fair is really unjust and unfair. They seek to withdraw the mandate of heaven. To do that they need not have straightforward economic grievances upon which to focus. Indeed such a focus may limit the movement. In the present situation opposition to war apparently constitutes one point around which such groups tend to grow. So far, however, nothing whatever has really been accomplished by trying to frighten people with the horrors of nuclear warfare. (The limited test ban did not in my estimation come from such a source, but from the Russian desire to stymie the Chinese.) When the real social and political costs of doing something about war come into sight, most people are liable to withdraw or take flight to rhetoric about the United Nations.

Here we encounter the built-in limitations of a protest that takes the form of withdrawal and boycott, its tendency toward romantic escapism. When escape becomes purely a personal matter, or a form of harmless symbolic rebellion like refusing to cut one's hair or wear clean clothes, its effect under contemporary conditions can be one of simply strengthening the prevailing order. Rebellion can be treated as childish idiosyncrasy, and turned to commercial profit as a form of entertainment. Then the dominant groups can congratulate themselves on their broadmindedness without making any significant changes or concessions. If the good citizen is ever going to get a less indecent society, he will have to do more than become willing to let his hair grow and stop buying refrigerators. Indeed he will have to overcome the myth that he can merely plead and reason with his superiors in order to get them to do something they don't want to do. He will have to organize and be organized around specific grievances, and to struggle politically. If that ever happens, some of the very attractive traits in the incipient protest movements, especially their gentleness and idealism, are liable to disappear.

In this fashion the apparently endless dialectic of master and slave may continue to repeat itself. When they have not been crushed and defeated, the victims of a social order generally acquire many of the traits of their enemies from the effort to force through changes, even peaceful ones. The decent society remains a sufficiently remote prospect to enable sober and practical men to put such a catastrophe out of their minds. Only the way in which those people who do try to think about such matters may have changed, or at least begun to change. There is a sense in the air, especially among the young, that Marxism and liberalism have in good measure ceased to provide explanations of the world. Indeed in their official forms these doctrines have become part of what requires explanation. Such ideas are no longer sufficient to tell us why a decent society is impossible: they have become reasons why this society remains out of the question.

PART FOUR

Marcuse as Teacher

WILLIAM LEISS, JOHN DAVID OBER,
AND ERICA SHEROVER

THE ESSAYS IN THIS VOLUME reflect in some measure the impact of
Herbert Marcuse as scholar and writer. In the following pages we
have sought a more elusive goal, namely an assessment of Marcuse
as teacher. Others of his students will object — and rightly so — that
our portrayal is abstract and lifeless, and we can only reply that
the inadequacy is inherent in the blunt instrument of the printed
page. But our essay will, we hope, show what we have learned
from him: Teaching, like every other individual aspect of society,
can only be understood in the context of the general historical situation in which it occurs.

Present American society places the teacher in an ambivalent position. On the one hand, to him is entrusted the compulsory intellectual and occupational training which society requires of its
young and which is relatively independent of outside pressures, at
least on certain advanced levels; on the other hand, society's mandate carries the implicit proviso that "education" is designed for a
certain age group (and can thus be associated with the "irresponsibility" of youth, for example), that the world of the teacher-
intellectual remains outside the "real" world inhabited by adults,
and that consequently the concerns of teaching are limited to the
institutions specifically charged with the function. An illustration
of this ambivalence is the fact that a teacher's right to criticize
governmental policy has often been defended on the grounds of
"academic freedom" — in other words, that freedom of expression
belongs to the teacher as member of an *occupational group*, thus
enabling him to exercise liberties denied to other such groups. On

the other hand, he is reminded that his special privileges properly apply only to the particular area of his professional competence, which is defined by the academic division of labor. The teacher has been relegated to a specific occupational niche within a specific institutional framework, with specified duties and privileges.

In one sense, of course, this makes the job of teaching much easier; indeed, the substantial obstacles to teaching which characterized education in earlier periods have largely disappeared. Hitherto universities had to face problems created by paucity of intellectual resources, scarcity of information, and physical coercion. Today, however, talent is widely recruited and accepted, information is plentiful, no threats of brutal punishment hamper freedom of inquiry, and there has been a vast proliferation of educational facilities. The difficulties of teaching in our own time are much different from those of the past. At present the greatest obstacle to genuine teaching is to be found in a pervading and pervasive cynicism, the dominant intellectual temper of our society.

Cynicism is one of the prime derivatives of that positive thinking which reigns supreme in our time. This way of thinking identifies truth with what exists, focuses on the parts rather than on the whole, disdains any attempt to investigate possible alternatives to the established reality or the means by which these possibilities might be realized, denigrates reason to the level of mere manipulation of facts, and refuses to judge established conditions in the light of already existing possibilities for transcending those conditions. Positive thinking gives rise to the relativization of all value judgments, to agnosticism (in the sense defined by Paul Baran),[1] and to "cool" indifference.

For those who refuse to consider an organization of society radically different from the prevailing one, cynicism is the necessary corollary to the manipulative techniques of positive thinking. Manipulation is one of the crucial links between cynicism and positivism: the "manipulation of variables" (including people) through the invasion of privacy, through advertising, propaganda, and

[1] See "The Commitment of the Intellectual," *Monthly Review*, vol. 16, no. 11 (March, 1965), pp. 1–11.

bold-faced lies.[2] The technique "works" and has become the best means of self-aggrandizement in a society based on the management and control of men and things.[3] Far from being condemned, it is the universally accredited road to domination in the business-government-university hierarchies.

Cynicism has arisen in response to a host of problems ranging from the daily "business deal" and the hiring and firing of professors to the most important issues of life and death in the deployment of military implements and the calculated sacrifice of human life. In the academic business the corporate executives and managers (presidents and deans) who employ the work force (faculty) in order to "handle" the customers (students) share the aims of their industrial counterparts: the prevention of customer malaise, the avoidance of strikes, the satisfaction of stockholders, and the growth of the firm. The academic work force and their customers similarly share, by and large, the attitudes and aims of their non-academic counterparts: they play it cool, they do not "rock the boat," they grind out acceptable reports (books and articles), and so forth.

Cynicism should not be viewed as an isolated and accidental phenomenon. It must be seen as a consequence of and a support for the structure of the larger society, a society in which: a "two-party democracy" is founded on the hidden premise that political convictions are unimportant; an economy is based upon waste and the preparation for atomic annihilation; a nihilistic, mindless hedonism is fostered by a multi-billion-dollar advertising industry necessitated by the overproduction of junk; success through corruption is viewed not with revulsion, but with envy; huge privately owned bureaucracies extol the virtues of rugged (rigged?) consumption. In such a society colleges and universities are gener-

[2] The social scientist, using the latest snooping devices, stands behind his one-way mirror and manipulates his "subjects" (objects) in experiments organized and financed by benevolent military and corporate patrons. And if the "findings" do not confirm the "hypotheses"? He who pays the piper calls the tune.

[3] For a discussion of the relationship between the domination of men and the domination of nature, see the relevant sections of Max Horkheimer's *Eclipse of Reason* and Herbert Marcuse's *One-Dimensional Man*.

ally engaged in producing a new generation of "educated" moral eunuchs, cheerfully and greedily willing to participate in "Machiavellianism for the little man."

In a society where human character is determined predominantly by the cash-nexus and the desire for personal aggrandizement, however, teaching and learning are reduced to a cynical and circular process. The drive of teacher and student alike for successful careers, status, and financial gain results in a denigration of all "knowledge" which does not promote the achievement of those ends. The emphasis placed on the acquisition, accumulation, and marketing of facts results in the limitation of discourse to the acceptable universe of discourse.

To oppose positivism and cynicism, teaching identifies itself with negative thinking.

Negative thinking is first and foremost critical thinking. Negative thinking opposes the self-contentment of common sense which is so ready to embrace the given and to accept the established fact. It cannot stop at the presentation of the facts, but must judge these facts and indicate the objective possibilities for their transcendence; it requires that thought comprehend the historical causes of the present domination in all its empirically observable manifestations.[4] Only critical thought can demonstrate the regressive aspects which are an implicit part of the "progress" and "success" glorified by this society. Any critique which remains within the historical confines of the status quo is unavoidably saddled with the established values of the status quo. Only an analysis which reveals the irrationality of the inner connection between progress in pacification and progress in destruction can provide the possibility for breaking that link.

All of Herbert Marcuse's teaching, both written and oral, embodies negative thinking. Marcuse's teaching recalls the fact that teaching and learning have not always fulfilled the role of protecting and strengthening the existing social relations. Marcuse insists that in its origins and intentions knowledge (in the strictest sense: philosophy) was highly subversive of the established values and institutions. In commenting on Plato's Allegory of the Cave,

---

[4] See the preface (1960) to the Beacon Press edition of *Reason and Revolution* for Marcuse's own exposition.

for example, he points to the role of the philosopher in challeng-ing the beliefs and assumptions of ordinary life and indeed in abolishing the entire structure of established existence. This aboli-tion is not a capricious or arbitrary act, but one which is neces-sary if man is to shape his existence in accordance with his own rational capacities. In this conception, knowledge becomes the in-dispensable guide of political activity: If, as Aristotle thought, the aim of political activity is the securing not merely of life but rather of the good life, then knowledge must be able to show the difference between the two and to demonstrate that only the lat-ter is adequate for man.

The content and method of Marcuse's teaching reflect his be-lief that theory should instruct man in his attempt to establish conditions which would enable him to fulfill his potentialities for a truly human existence. In his lectures and seminars (History of Political Theory, Greek Philosophy, The Warfare State, Liberal-ism, Kant, Hegel, Husserl, Marxism and Communism) Marcuse always tries to show the connections between apparently abstract philosophies and the development of social institutions and politi-cal practice. He is the uncompromising foe of "misplaced con-creteness" and empty abstractions.

In formal lectures and informal discussion his teaching is gen-erously spiced with irony and humor directed at the sacred cows of the Establishment. As he himself remarked with reference to Paul Baran, however, this is a characteristic of those who are truly serious. The individuals who have seen and heard him re-member also the mastery of Socratic method, the fairness and gen-erosity in debate, the sure command of a vast learning, and the unbounded intellectual curiosity. But the essential element of Marcuse's teaching is that knowledge is partisan. Knowledge, in its origin and intention, is *for* life. The current pretensions to "scientific objectivity," intellectual neutrality, and value-free thinking betray the goals of knowledge itself: Knowledge is in-extricably bound up with the attempt to create a free and rational human existence.

Marcuse Bibliography

WILLIAM LEISS, JOHN DAVID OBER,
AND ERICA SHEROVER

April 1, 1967

Chronological Bibliography of Books

1. *Schiller-Bibliographie unter Benutzung der Trämelschen Schiller-Bibliothek.* Berlin: S. Martin Fraenkel, 1925. Pp. 137.

2. *Hegels Ontologie und die Grundlegung einer Theorie der Geschichtlichkeit.* Frankfurt am Main: V. Klostermann Verlag, 1932. Pp. 368.

3. *Reason and Revolution: Hegel and the Rise of Social Theory.* New York: Oxford University Press, 1941. Pp. xii, 431. Second edition with "Supplementary Epilogue," New York: Humanities Press, 1954. Pp. xii, 439. Paperbound edition with new preface, "A Note on Dialectic," Boston: Beacon Press, 1960. Pp. xvi, 431. Translations: Japanese, Hebrew, German, Italian, Serbo-Croatian (Yugoslavia), Polish, Korean. French translation of new preface, "Actualité de la dialectique," *Diogène*, no. 31 (July – Sept., 1960), pp. 89 – 98.

4. *Eros and Civilization: A Philosophical Inquiry into Freud.* Boston: Beacon Press, 1955. Pp. xii, 277. Paperbound edition with new preface, New York: Vintage Books, 1962. Pp. xviii, 256. Second edition with new preface, "Political Preface, 1966," Boston: Beacon Press, 1966. Translations: Japanese, French, German, Spanish (Mexico), Italian, Swedish, Serbo-Croatian (Yugoslavia).

5. *Soviet Marxism: A Critical Analysis.* New York: Columbia University Press, 1958. Pp. 271. Paperbound edition with new preface, New York: Vintage Russian Library, 1961. Pp. xvi, 252. Translations: French, German, Spanish.

6. *One-Dimensional Man: Studies in the Ideology of Advanced Industrial Society*. Boston: Beacon Press, 1964; paperbound edition, 1966. Pp. xvii, 260. Translations forthcoming: French, German, Italian, Spanish (Mexico), Serbo-Croatian (Yugoslavia). French translation of Chapter II, "Dynamismes de la société industrielle," *Annales*, vol. 18, no. 5 (Sept. – Oct., 1963), pp. 906 – 933. Spanish translation of Chapter I, "La Sociedad unidimensional," *Eco: Revista de la Cultura de Occidente* (June, 1965), pp. 199 – 219.

Selected Essays

7. *Kultur und Gesellschaft I*. Frankfurt am Main: Suhrkamp Verlag, 1965. Pp. 179. Republication of entries 26, 30, 31, 32, below.

8. *Kultur und Gesellschaft II*. Frankfurt am Main: Suhrkamp Verlag, 1965. Pp. 182. Republication of entries 23, 36 (German translation and revised), 59, 61 (German translation) below; also essays appearing for the first time: "Das Veralten der Psychoanalyse" (pp. 85 – 106) and "Ethik und Revolution" (pp. 130 – 146). The last essay is available in the original English version in Richard T. De George, editor, *Ethics and Society: Original Essays on Contemporary Moral Problems* (New York: Anchor Books, 1966), pp. 133 – 149.

Books Edited

9. Franz Neumann, *The Democratic and the Authoritarian State*, preface by Herbert Marcuse. Glencoe, Illinois: The Free Press, 1957; paperbound edition, 1964. Pp. x, 303.

Essays, Articles, and Book Reviews

10. "Beiträge zur Phänomenologie des Historischen Materialismus," *Philosophische Hefte*, no. 1 (1928), pp. 45 – 68.
11. "Über konkrete Philosophie," *Archiv für Sozialwissenschaft und Sozialpolitik*, vol. 62 (1929), pp. 111 – 128.
12. "Besprechung von Karl Vorländer: *Karl Marx, sein Leben und sein Werk*," *Die Gesellschaft*, vol. VI (1929), part II, pp. 186 – 189.
13. "Zur Wahrheitsproblematik der soziologischen Methode," *Die Gesellschaft*, vol. VI (1929), part II, pp. 356 – 369.
14. "Zum Problem der Dialektik I," *Die Gesellschaft*, vol. VII (1930), part I, pp. 15 – 30.

15. "Transzendentaler Marxismus?" *Die Gesellschaft,* vol. VII (1930), part II, pp. 304–326.

16. "Besprechung von H. Noack: *Geschichte und System der Philosophie,*" *Philosophische Hefte,* vol. II (1930), pp. 91–96.

17. "Das Problem der geschichtlichen Wirklichkeit: Wilhelm Dilthey," *Die Gesellschaft,* vol. VIII (1931), part I, pp. 350–367.

18. "Zur Kritik der Soziologie," *Die Gesellschaft,* vol. VIII (1931), part II, pp. 270–280.

19. "Zum Problem der Dialektik II," *Die Gesellschaft,* vol. VIII (1931), part II, pp. 541–557.

20. "Zur Auseinandersetzung mit Hans Freyers *Soziologie als Wirklichkeitswissenschaft,*" *Philosophische Hefte,* vol. III, nos. 1/2 (1931), pp. 83–91.

21. "Besprechung von Heinz Heimsoeth: *Die Errungenschaften des deutschen Idealismus,*" *Deutsche Literaturzeitung,* vol. 53, no. 43 (1932), pp. 2024–2029.

22. "Neue Quellen zur Grundlegung des Historischen Materialismus," *Die Gesellschaft,* vol. IX (1932), part II, pp. 136–174. This and item 23 were republished in Japanese translation as *Shoki Marukusu Kenkya* (*A Study of Marx in His Early Days*), (Tokyo: Miraisha, 1961). Pp. iv, 186.

23. "Über die philosophischen Grundlagen des wirtschaftswissenschaftlichen Arbeitsbegriffs," *Archiv für Sozialwissenschaft und Sozialpolitik,* vol. 69 (1933), pp. 257–292.

24. "Philosophie des Scheiterns: Karl Jaspers Werk," *Unterhaltungsblatt der Vossischen Zeitung,* no. 339 (December 14, 1933).

25. "Besprechung von Herbert Wacker: *Das Verhältnis des jungen Hegel zu Kant,*" *Deutsche Literaturzeitung,* vol. 55, no. 14 (1934), pp. 629–630.

26. "Der Kampf gegen den Liberalismus in der totalitären Staatsauffassung," *Zeitschrift für Sozialforschung,* vol. III (1934), pp. 161–195.

27. "Theoretische Entwürfe über Autorität und Familie: Ideengeschichtlicher Teil," *Studien über Autorität und Familie: Forschungsberichte aus dem Institut für Sozialforschung* (Paris: Felix Alcan, 1936), pp. 136–228.

28. "Autorität und Familie in der deutschen Soziologie bis 1933," *ibid.,* pp. 737–752.

29. "Zum Begriff des Wesens," *Zeitschrift für Sozialforschung,* vol. V (1936), pp. 1–39.

30. "Über den affirmativen Charakter der Kultur," *Zeitschrift für Sozialforschung,* vol. VI (1937), pp. 54–94.

31. "Philosophie und kritische Theorie," *Zeitschrift für Sozialforschung*, vol. VI (1937), pp. 631–647.

32. "Zur Kritik des Hedonismus," *Zeitschrift für Sozialforschung*, vol. VII (1938), pp. 55–89.

33. "An Introduction to Hegel's Philosophy," *Studies in Philosophy and Social Science* (the continuation in English of *Zeitschrift für Sozialforschung*), vol. VIII (1940), pp. 394–412.

34. "Some Implications of Modern Technology," *Studies in Philosophy and Social Science*, vol. IX (1941), pp. 414–439.

35. "A Rejoinder to K. Löwith's Review of *Reason and Revolution*," *Journal of Philosophy and Phenomenological Research*, vol. II, no. 4 (June, 1942), pp. 564–565.

36. "Existentialism: Remarks on Jean-Paul Sartre's *L'Être et le néant*," *Journal of Philosophy and Phenomenological Research*, vol. VIII, no. 3 (March, 1948), pp. 309–336. German translation in *Sinn und Form*, vol. II, no. 1 (1950), pp. 50–82.

37. "Lord Acton: *Essays on Freedom and Power*," *American Historical Review*, vol. 54, no. 3 (April, 1949), pp. 557–559.

38. "Review of Georg Lukács' *Goethe und seine Zeit*," *Journal of Philosophy and Phenomenological Research*, vol. IX, no. 1 (September, 1950), pp. 142–144.

39. "Recent Literature on Communism," *World Politics*, vol. VI, no. 4 (July, 1954), pp. 515–525.

40. "Dialectic and Logic Since the War," in Ernest J. Simmons, editor, *Continuity and Change in Russian and Soviet Thought* (Cambridge, Massachusetts: Harvard University Press, 1955), pp. 347–358.

41. "Trieblehre und Freiheit," in *Sociologica: Aufsätze, Max Horkheimer zum 60. Geburtstag gewidmet* ("*Frankfurter Beiträge zur Soziologie*," vol. I [Frankfurt am Main: Europäische Verlagsanstalt, 1955]), pp. 47–66. (Abridged translation of the last chapter of *Eros and Civilization*.)

42. "Eros and Culture," *I. E., The Cambridge Review*, vol. I, no. 3 (Spring, 1955), pp. 107–123.

43. "The Social Implications of Freudian 'Revisionism,'" *Dissent*, vol. II, no. 3 (Summer, 1955), pp. 221–240. Reprinted as the epilogue to *Eros and Civilization* and in *Voices of Dissent*. New York: Grove Press, 1958. German translation in *Psyche*, vol. II (1957), pp. 801–820.

44. "A Reply to Erich Fromm," *Dissent*, vol. III, no. 1 (Winter, 1956), pp. 79–81.

45. "La théorie des instincts et la socialisation," *La Table Ronde*, no. 108 (1956), pp. 97–110.

46. "Theory and Therapy in Freud," *The Nation*, vol. 185 (September 28, 1957), pp. 200–202.

47. "Trieblehre und Freiheit," in *Freud in der Gegenwart: Ein Vortragszyklus der Universitäten Frankfurt und Heidelberg zum hundertsten Geburtstag* ("*Frankfurter Beiträge zur Soziologie*," vol. VI [Frankfurt am Main: Europäische Verlagsanstalt, 1957]), pp. 401–424.

48. "Die Idee des Fortschritts im Lichte der Psychoanalyse," *ibid.*, pp. 425–441.

49. "Preface," to Raya Dunayevskaya's *Marxism and Freedom*. New York: Twayne Publishers, 1958. Pp. 15–20.

50. "Notes on the Problem of Historical Laws," *Partisan Review*, vol. 26 (Winter, 1959), pp. 117–129.

51. "The Ideology of Death," in Herman Feifel, editor, *The Meaning of Death* (New York: McGraw-Hill, 1959), pp. 64–76.

52. "De l'ontologie à la technologie; les tendances de la société industrielle," *Arguments*, vol. IV, no. 18 (1960), pp. 54–59.

53. "Language and Technological Society," *Dissent*, vol. VIII, no. 1 (Winter, 1961), pp. 66–74.

54. "The Problem of Social Change in Technological Society," Lecture presented to a UNESCO Symposium on Social Development. Printed for limited distribution under the auspices of Raymond Aron and Bert Hoselitz. Paris: April 28, 1961. Pp. 139–160.

55. "Idéologie et société industrielle avancée," *Médiations*, no. 5 (Summer, 1962), pp. 57–71.

56. "Emanzipation der Frau in der repressiven Gesellschaft: Ein Gespräch mit Herbert Marcuse und Peter Furth," *Das Argument*, no. 23 (Oct.–Nov., 1962), pp. 2–12.

57. "Zur Stellung des Denkens heute," in *Zeugnisse: Theodor W. Adorno zum 60. Geburtstag* ([Im Auftrag des Instituts für Sozialforschung herausgegeben von Max Horkheimer] Frankfurt am Main: Europäische Verlagsanstalt, 1963), pp. 45–49.

58. "World without Logos," *Bulletin of the Atomic Scientists*, vol. 20 (January, 1964), pp. 25–26.

59. "Industrialisierung und Kapitalismus," in *Max Weber und die Soziologie heute* (Tübingen: J. C. B. Mohr [Paul Siebeck], 1964), pp. 161–180. English translation, "Industrialization and Capitalism," *New Left Review*, no. 30 (March–April, 1965), pp. 3–17.

60. "Perspektiven des Sozialismus in der entwickelten Indus-triegesellschaft," *Praxis*, nos. 2/3 (1964), pp. 260–270. (Address presented at the Conference on Socialist Perspectives in Korčula, Yugoslavia, Summer, 1964. Serbo-Croatian translation, "Perspektive socijalizma u razvijenom industrijskom drustvu," *Smisao i Perspektive Socijalizma*. (Zagreb: Zbornik, 1965), pp. 167–178. English translation, "Socialism in the Developed Countries," *International Socialist Journal*, vol. II, no. 8 (April, 1965), pp. 139–152.

61. "Remarks on a Redefinition of Culture," *Daedalus*, vol. 94, no. 1 (Winter, 1965), pp. 190–207. Reprinted in Gerald Holton, editor, *Science and Culture* (Cambridge, Massachusetts: Houghton Mifflin, 1965), pp. 218–235. Spanish translation in *Revista de Occidente*, no. 30 (Madrid: September, 1965).

62. "A Tribute to Paul A. Baran," *Monthly Review*, vol. 16, no. 11 (March, 1965), pp. 114–115.

63. "Nachwort," to Walter Benjamin's *Zur Kritik der Gewalt und andere Aufsätze* (Frankfurt am Main: Suhrkamp Verlag, 1965), pp. 99–106.

64. "Repressive Tolerance," in Robert P. Wolff, Barrington Moore, Jr., and Herbert Marcuse, *A Critique of Pure Tolerance* (Boston: Beacon Press, 1965), pp. 81–117. German translation: Frankfurt am Main: Suhrkamp Verlag, 1966.

65. "Nachwort," to Karl Marx's *Der 18. Brumaire des Louis Bonaparte* (Frankfurt am Main: Insel-Verlag, 1965), pp. 143–150.

66. "Der Einfluss der deutschen Emigration auf das amerikanische Geistesleben: Philosophie und Soziologie," *Jahrbuch für Amerikastudien*, vol. X (Heidelberg: Carl Winter Universitätsverlag, 1965), pp. 27–33.

67. "Socialist Humanism?" in Erich Fromm, editor, *Socialist Humanism* (New York: Doubleday, 1965), pp. 96–106.

68. "Reply to M. Berman's Review of *One-Dimensional Man*," *Partisan Review*, vol. 32, no. 1 (Winter, 1965), pp. 159–160.

69. "Statement on Vietnam," *Partisan Review*, vol. 32, no. 4 (Fall, 1965), pp. 646–649.

70. "On Science and Phenomenology," in Robert Cohen and Marx W. Wartofsky, editors, *Boston Studies in the Philosophy of Science*, vol. II (New York: The Humanities Press, 1965), pp. 279–291.

71. "Sommes-nous déjà des hommes?" *Partisans*, no. 28 (April, 1966), pp. 21–24.

72. "Vietnam — Analyse eines Exempels," *Neue Kritik* (Frankfurt am Main), no. 36 – 37 (July – August, 1966), pp. 30 – 40.

73. "Zur Geschichte der Dialektik," *Sowjetsystem und Demokratische Gesellschaft* (Freiburg: Herder Verlag, 1966), vol. I, pp. 1192 – 1211.

74. "The Individual in the Great Society," Part I, *Alternatives*, vol. I, no. 1 (March – April, 1966). Part II, *Alternatives*, vol. I, no. 2 (Summer, 1966).

75. "Love Mystified" (Review of N.O. Brown's *Love's Body*), *Commentary*, vol. 43, no. 2 (February, 1967), pp. 71 – 76.

Note: From 1933 to 1938 Herbert Marcuse was a regular book reviewer for the *Zeitschrift für Sozialforschung* and in that capacity he reviewed over one hundred titles on a variety of subjects.

List of Contributors and Editors

E. H. CARR is a Fellow of Trinity College, Cambridge, England, and is the author of *What Is History?* and of *The New Society: A History of Soviet Russia,* which appeared with the titles *The Bolshevik Revolution, The Interregnum,* and *Socialism in One Country.*

STANLEY DIAMOND is Professor of Anthropology, Graduate Faculty, New School for Social Research, New York City, and is the author of "Anaguta Cosmography: The Linguistics and Behavioral Implications," *Anthropological Linguistics,* vol. II (1960) and *The Anaguta—Suburban Primitives* (forthcoming). He has edited *Culture in History: Essays in Honor of Paul Radin.*

M. I. FINLEY is Reader in Ancient Social and Economic History, University of Cambridge, England, and is the author of *Studies in Land and Credit in Ancient Athens, The World of Odysseus,* and *The Ancient Greeks.*

PETER GAY is Professor of History, Columbia University, New York. He has written *The Party of Humanity: Essays in the French Enlightenment; A Loss of Mastery: Puritan Historians in Colonial America;* and *The Enlightenment: An Interpretation,* Vol. I: *The Rise of Modern Paganism.*

LUCIEN GOLDMANN is Directeur d'Études à l'École Pratique des Hautes Études, Paris. He is the author of *Le dieu caché, Recherches dialectiques,* and *Sciences humaines et philosophie.*

MAX HORKHEIMER. is Professor Dr. Emeritus, now living in Frankfurt am Main. He is the co-author with Theodor W. Adorno of *Dialektik der Aufklärung* and author of *Anfänge der bürgerlichen Geschichtsphilosophie* and *Um die Freiheit.*

OTTO KIRCHHEIMER († 1965) was Professor of Government, Columbia University, New York, and the author of *Political Justice* and *Politik und Verfassung.* He was co-author with G. Rusche of *Punishment and Social Structure.*

GABRIEL KOLKO is Associate Professor of History, University of Pennsylvania, Philadelphia, and is the author of *The Triumph of Conservatism, Wealth and Power in America,* and *Railroads and Regulation, 1877–1916.*

LEONARD KRIEGER is University Professor of History, University of Chicago. He has written *The German Idea of Freedom* and *The Politics of Discretion* and is co-author with John Higham and Felix Gilbert of *History*.

WILLIAM LEISS is an Associate in Philosophy, University of California at San Diego, La Jolla.

LEO LOWENTHAL is Professor of Sociology, University of California, Berkeley. He is the author of *Literature, Popular Culture and Society; Literature and the Image of Man;* and *Prophets of Doubt*.

HEINZ LUBASZ is Associate Professor of History, Brandeis University, Waltham, Massachusetts. He has edited *The Development of the Modern State* and *Revolutions in Modern European History*.

PAUL MATTICK is a Marxist writer and former editor of *Living Marxism*, now living in Cambridge, Massachusetts. He is the author of "Marx and Keynes," *Cahiers*, L'Institut de Science Économique Appliquée, Series S, no. 121 (January 1962); "Marxism and the New Physics," *Philosophy of Science*, vol. XXIX, no. 4 (October 1962); and "Dynamics of the Mixed Economy," *Science and Society*, vol. XXVIII, no. 3 (Summer 1964).

ARNO J. MAYER is Professor of History at Princeton University, Princeton, New Jersey, and is the author of *Political Origins of the New Diplomacy 1917–1918* and *The Politics and Diplomacy of Peacemaking 1918–1920* (in press).

HANS MEYERHOFF († 1965) was Professor of Philosophy at the University of California at Los Angeles. He wrote *Time in Literature* and edited *The Philosophy of History in Our Time*.

BARRINGTON MOORE, JR. is Senior Research Fellow, Russian Research Center, Harvard University, Cambridge, Massachusetts. He is the author of *Social Origins of Dictatorship and Democracy: Lord and Peasant in the Making of the Modern World; Terror and Progress: USSR;* and *Soviet Politics: The Dilemma of Power*.

JOHN DAVID OBER is Assistant Professor of History, Connecticut College, New London, Connecticut. He is co-author with Juan E. Corradi of "Pax Americana and Pax Sociologica: Remarks on the Politics of Sociology," in *Catalyst* (Buffalo), no. 2 (Spring 1966).

RICHARD H. POPKIN is Professor and Chairman of the Department of Philosophy, University of California at San Diego, La